T0153548

AGAINST

THE

FASCIST

CREEP

AGAINST THE FASCIST CREEP

ALEXANDER REID ROSS

PRAISE FOR *AGAINST THE FASCIST CREEP*:

"A must-read book for all those looking for a comprehensive overview of the history and space of fascist ideologies and their current transformations." —**Marlene Laruelle, author of** *Russian Eurasianism: An Ideology of Empire*

"Activists, journalists, and researchers who want to understand a surging far right, and how it borrows from the left, should start here." —**Jason Wilson, columnist,** *The Guardian*

"Reid Ross gets to the heart of why it is so difficult to study neo-fascism: Its constant mutations and multiple, sometimes contradictory strands. His book is full of interesting stories about, as he puts it, 'lesser known currents within the fascist movement,' on both sides of the Atlantic. The notion of 'the fascist creep' helps us to understand how fascist ideals migrate from left to right and right to left and how they surreptitiously slip into the heart of the body politic. This book is essential reading for all those seeking to understand and challenge fascism and neofascism." —**Tamir Bar-On, author of** *Where Have All the Fascists Gone?*

"Recent historiographical fashion has tended to portray fascism as a revolutionary form of authoritarian nationalist ideology. However, fascism's attempt to synthesize left and right could produce conservative as well as radical mutations. Alexander Reid Ross's book helps us understand how fascism in the contemporary era is developing in this complex way, and raises vital issues about how it differs from the rising tide of national populism." —**Roger Eatwell, author of** *Fascism: A History*

"This original and sweeping study is crucial reading for scholars and journalists trying to understand the complex and often contradictory relationships among populism, anti-elite demagoguery, scapegoating, conspiracism, and fascism." —**Chip Berlet, co-author of** *Right-Wing Populism in America*

"What Alexander Reid Ross has achieved is remarkable, weaving together a critical historical analysis with a deep understanding and an eye for resistance that can help to inspire a new generation of antifascist organizing." —**Shane Burley, journalist**

"Alexander Reid Ross has written an important study on the contemporary extreme right. Carefully dissecting its antecedents ... he uncovers how a variegated and often factious movement of rightist groups, activists, philosophers, and theoreticians evolved over the past several decades. His book cogently explains how these rightists synthesized seemingly contradictory political orientations, including fascism, socialism, authoritarianism, and libertarianism, to forge an amorphous ideology which animates a number of far right movements in America, Europe, and Russia. Although obscure, their influence persists in the incarnation of the 'Alt Right' movement which has gained new vigor concomitant with the presidential campaign of Donald Trump. *Against the Fascist Creep* is a much-needed addition to the field of political extremism and will be enjoyed by both academics and the general public."
—**George Michael, author of** *Lone Wolf Terror and the Rise of Leaderless Resistance*

"Essential reading for those willing to remain awake to the ways fascist thinking and action continues to raise its ugly head."
—**Joe Lowndes, author of** *From the New Deal to the New Right: Race and Southern Origins of Modern Conservatism*

"This important book is essential reading for every social justice activist, a cautionary story of how any of us can be drawn to aspects of the rhetoric and social world of fascism without recognizing it as such. Now, with the rise of Trump and the Alt-Right in the United States, mirroring similar movements in the United Kingdom and Europe, consciousness of fascist creep is more important than ever. Alexander Reid Ross presents a complex history and reality as a gripping narrative." —**Roxanne Dunbar-Ortiz, author of** *An Indigenous Peoples' History of the United States*

"This book is good for smashing cockroaches and fascism, which may appear more similar after a careful reading." —**Arun Gupta, journalist,** *The Indypendent*

"*Against the Fascist Creep* could not come at a better time. Society is trying to understand the kinds of fascist elements we are seeing in the 21st Century, and this book not only tells a detailed history of fascism around the world, breaking down all its forms to an exact science, it does the most important thing that you will not see much of in other books that cover the subject—it shows the reader how they have been and can be fought." —**Daryle Lamont Jenkins, One People's Project**

Against the Fascist Creep
© 2017 Alexander Reid Ross
This edition © 2017 AK Press (Chico, Oakland, Edinburgh, Baltimore)
ISBN: 978-1-84935-244-4
E-ISBN: 978-1-84935-245-1
Library of Congress Control Number: 2015959318

AK Press	AK Press
370 Ryan Ave. #100	33 Tower St.
Chico, CA 95973	Edinburgh EH6 7BN
USA	Scotland
www.akpress.org	www.akuk.com
akpress@akpress.org	ak@akedin.demon.co.uk

The above addresses would be delighted to provide you with the latest AK Press distribution catalog, which features books, pamphlets, zines, and stylish apparel published and/or distributed by AK Press. Alternatively, visit our websites for the complete catalog, latest news, and secure ordering.

Cover illustration by N.O. Bonzo, www.nobonzo.tumblr.com

Printed in the USA.

Contents

INTRODUCTION

Creeping Coup

In the years before the Nazi invasion, as fascism pulled activists from the ranks of the left, Popular Front leader Léon Blum spoke of a "contagion" gripping France.[1] Some fifty years later, scholar Philippe Burrin would refer to the "fascist drift" that attracted the left to the causes of the right.[2] More recently, warnings of a "creeping fascism" have returned.

If we consider the left's embrace of equality as its defining characteristic, fascism remains decisively on the right.[3] However, fascism also embraces aspects of social and ecological movements usually attributed to the left. The shared ideological space cannot be tidily blamed on co-optation, although many fascists embrace co-optation and "entryism." Instead, fascism emerges as a unique response to the same material conditions. It lies at the extremes of

---

1   See Zeev Sternhell, "Fascist Ideology," in *Fascism: Critical Concepts in Political Science*, eds. Roger Griffin and Matthew Feldman, 5 vols. (Routledge: New York, London, 2004), 1:118.

2   Philippe Burrin, *La Derive Fasciste: Doriot, Déat, Bergery (1933–1945)* (Paris: Le Seuil, 1986).

3   See Norberto Bobbio, *Left and Right: The Significance of a Political Distinction*, trans. Allan Cameron (Chicago: University of Chicago Press, 1996), 60–72.

ideology, courting the public through a rejection of conventional conservatism and a call for the return of a golden era. *Against the Fascist Creep* will focus on those messy crossovers on the margins of left and right, the ways fascism cultivates a movement, and the ways that the left often unwittingly cedes the space for fascism to creep into the mainstream and radical subcultures.[4]

Perhaps the most important strategy of fascism is what scholar Stephen D. Shenfield calls "a gradual or creeping coup, accomplished by means of the steady penetration of state and social structures and the accumulation of military and economic potential."[5] Such an analysis can also be applied to the insinuation of fascism into and out of the US conservative movement by propagandists such as Willis Carto, Jared Taylor, and Richard Spencer.[6] Similarly, the increasing power of the radical right's populist parties in Europe indicates a drift of socialists, liberals, and conservatives toward a counterhegemonic alternative. Many of these parties, like the Brothers of Italy, the French Front National, the Austrian Freedom Party, the Ukrainian Svoboda, the Sweden Democrats, and the Flemish Vlaams Belang have clear roots in the fascist movement. Yet the more power and influence they gain, the less they seem to cling to the hard core of their original orthodoxy, focusing instead on pragmatic policy issues and the complex geopolitical questions pertaining to the European Union and Russia. Concern remains that, on achieving singular power, these parties would revert to fascist positions or at least provide enhanced material support to fascist groups.

---

4   The idea of fascism as an ideology that comes out of the left as well as the right was perhaps first suggested by Zeev Sternhell. Scholar Roger Eatwell further notes that fascism relies on a "spectral-syncretic" quality, joining positions not typically understood as commensurate, such as elements of liberalism and state control. See Zeev Sternhell, *The Birth of Fascist Ideology: From Cultural Rebellion to Political Revolution* (Princeton: Princeton University Press, 1994); Roger Eatwell, "Towards a New Model of Generic Fascism," in Griffin and Feldman, eds., *Fascism*, 1:249.

5   Stephen D. Shenfield, *Russian Fascism: Traditions, Tendencies, Movements* (London: ME Sharpe, 2001), 35 & 180.

6   See George Michael, *Willis Carto and the American Far Right* (Gainsville, FL: University Press of Florida, 2008), 144–56.

The relationship between the fascist movement and the populist radical right, though at times supportive, is fundamentally dynamic, divided, and complex. Openly fascist groups tend to be much smaller, and they tend to argue for a "national revolution" more antiparliamentary than their radical-right counterparts.[7] Hardcore fascism tends to be far more mass-based and revolutionary, radically traditionalist and elitist than most radical-right configurations. Nevertheless, fascist ideology is not always transparent, and left-right crossover along with misleading rhetoric surrounding the State of Israel, Islam, and multiculturalism tends to obscure the extent of racism. This space of relative autonomy between the radical, right-wing populist parties and smaller, dedicated fascist groups is important. It brings a conservative appeal to the radical right, who are also able to attract left-leaning members of the public with social welfare promises. Meanwhile, it enables smaller groups to attract members of the public who desire a more anti-institutional transformation—even if those smaller groups often overlap considerably with larger, radical and conventional right groups through unofficial or mediated channels.

The "fascist creep," as I am using the term in this text, refers to the porous borders between fascism and the radical right, through which fascism is able to "creep" into mainstream discourse. However, the "fascist creep" is also a double-edged term, because it refers more specifically to the crossover space between right and left that engenders fascism in the first place. Hence, fascism creeps in two ways: (1) it draws left-wing notions of solidarity and liberation into ultranationalist, right-wing ideology; and (2), at least in its early stages, fascists often utilize "broad front" strategies, proposing a mass-based, nationalist platform to gain access to mainstream political audiences and key administrative positions. *Against the Fascist Creep* will reveal how these processes of fascism have worked in the past and how they manifest today, as well as ways in which radical movements have organized to stop them in their tracks.

---

7   While it is true that Mussolini and Hitler both turned to parliamentary strategy, they did so explicitly to dismantle liberal parliamentarism, and although Nazi leader Gregor Strasser proposed a "broad front" (*Querfront*) between military, reactionary, neoconservative, and Nazi groups, his strategy was rejected by other Nazi leaders as overly compromised.

So What is Fascism?

Is fascism a kind of attitude, personality, or a manifestation of unconscious drives based on patriarchal repression? Is it simply a mode of political formation present in Italy between 1919 and 1945?[8] Or is it a broader phenomenon—a political ideology with distinct networks that appeared not only in interwar Italy but also in France, Nazi Germany, with the British Union of Fascists, the Spanish Falange, and a myriad of other groups?[9] In the postwar period, early academic descriptions of fascism emerged from the Frankfurt School and a psychoanalytic milieu that identified fascism with a personality type (Theodor Adorno), a "basic emotional attitude of the suppressed man of our authoritarian machine civilization and its mechanistic-mystical conception of life" (Wilhelm Reich), and a reflexive, patriarchal fear of freedom (Erich Fromm).[10]

More recent analysts like George Mosse and Stanley Payne ascribe a checklist with boxes for antiliberal, anticonservative, anti-Marxist, sacralization of politics, leader cult, single party, integral corporatism, media censorship, organic theory of the state, ultranationalism, focus on the youth, and extreme political violence.[11] Following the Cold War and shifts in fascist organizing techniques, a number of scholars moved toward the minimalist "new consensus" refined by Roger Griffin: "the mythic core" of

---

8   A. James Gregor, "Roger Griffin, Social Science, 'Fascism,' and the 'Extreme Right,'" in Roger Griffin, Werner Loh, and Andreas Umland, eds., *Fascism Past and Present, West and East: An International Debate on Concepts and Cases in the Comparative Study of the Extreme Right* (Stuttgart: Ibidem Press, 2006), 115–22.

9   See especially Ernst Nolte, *The Three Faces of Fascism: Action Francaise, Italian Fascism, National Socialism*, trans. Leila Vennewitz (New York: Holt, Rinehart and Winston, 1966); Eugen Weber, *Varieties of Fascism* (Malabar, FL: Robert E. Krieger Publishing Company, 1985).

10   See Theodor Adorno, et al., *The Authoritarian Personality* (New York: Harper, 1950); Wilhelm Reich, *The Mass Psychology of Fascism* (New York: Farrar, Straus and Giroux, 1970), xiii; Erich Fromm, *Escape from Freedom* (New York: Henry Holt and Company, 1969).

11   See Stanley G. Payne, *A History of Fascism, 1914–1945* (Madison: University of Wisconsin Press, 1995).

fascism is "a populist form of palingenetic ultranationalism."[12] That means that fascism is an ideology that draws on old, ancient, and even arcane myths of racial, cultural, ethnic, and national origins to develop a plan for the "new man."

Dissenters from the Marxist camp like David Renton favor an evolution of Leon Trotsky's analysis, viewing fascism as a cross-class alliance between the petite bourgeoisie and the ruling class, which were intent on destroying the vanguard of the proletariat.[13] Post-structuralists like Michel Foucault present fascism, instead, as a product of the accumulation of power and a psychological temptation to be resisted by developing an "art of living."[14] Still other leftist dissidents focus greater attention on the war waged by fascism against modern notions of state and capital, highlighting fascism's character as a revolutionary ideology that poses an intellectual conundrum for the left.[15]

In my opinion, there is no contradiction between palingenetic ultranationalism and a cross-class alliance. Ultranationalism assumes a cross-class "national community." However, fascism's syncretic form of fringe fusion takes place as a result of extreme responses to modern conditions, and it attacks only those members of the left designated as competition for political power. The leading three fascist political figures of the interwar period in France were all former leftists: a former member of the inner committee of the Communist Party, a former anarcho-syndicalist, and the leader of the "neo-socialist" faction of the Socialist Party (then called the French Section of the Workers' International).[16] The movement was

12   Roger Griffin, *The Nature of Fascism* (New York: Routledge, 1994), 26.

13   David Renton, *Fascism: Theory and Practice* (London: Pluto Press, 1999).

14   Michel Foucault, "Preface," in Gilles Deleuze and Felix Guattari, *A Thousand Plateaus* (Minneapolis: University of Minnesota Press, 1983), xii.

15   See Don Hamerquist and J. Sakai, *Confronting Fascism: Discussion Documents for a Militant Movement* (Montreal/Chicago: Kersplebedeb, Chicago Anti-Racist Action, 2002).

16   These would be Jacques Doriot, Georges Valois, and Marcel Déat, respectively. I leave out Charles Maurras and François de La Rocque, not because I disagree that they were fascists, but because there is enough debate over the matter as to render their political leadership somewhat tenuous, comparatively speaking. See Robert Soucy's works, *French Fascism: The*

led by a host of frustrated and powerful leftists joining with sectors of the nationalist radical right to attack liberalism.

Fascism is also mythopoetic insofar as its ideological system does not only seek to create new myths but also to create a kind of mythical reality, or an everyday life that stems from myth rather than fact.[17] Fascists hope to produce a new kind of rationale envisioning a common destiny that can replace modern civilization. The person with authority is the one who can interpret these myths into real-world strategy through a sacralized process that defines and delimits the seen and the unseen, the thinkable and the unthinkable.

That which is most commonly encouraged through fascism is producerism, which augments working-class militancy against the "owner class" by focusing instead on the difference between "parasites" (typically Jews, speculators, technocrats, and immigrants) and the productive workers and elites of the nation. In this way, fascism can be both functionally cross class and ideologically anticlass, desiring a classless society based on a "natural hierarchy" of deserving elites and disciplined workers. By destroying parasites and deploying some variant of racial, national, or ethnocentric socialism, fascists promise to create an ideal state or suprastate—a spiritual entity more than a modern nation-state, closer to the unitary sovereignty of the empire than political systems of messy compromises and divisions of power. This spiritual entity of the future would require the annihilation of the contaminated modern world and a return to the myths of ancestral ties of blood and soil, culture, and language that bind the community together in spite of class antagonisms.[18]

First Wave, 1924–1933 (New Haven, CT: Yale University Press, 1986) and *French Fascism: The Second Wave, 1933–1939* (New Haven, CT: Yale University Press, 1997).

17   This is also observed in Jeffrey M. Bale, "The 'Black' Terrorist International: Neo-Fascist Paramilitary Networks and the 'Strategy of Tension' in Italy, 1968–1974" (PhD diss., University of California–Berkeley, 1994), 9; and Griffin, *The Nature of Fascism*, 30–32.

18   Jeffrey M. Bale, "Fascism and Neo-Fascism: Ideology and 'Groupuscularity,'" in Griffin, Loh, and Umland, eds., *Fascism Past and Present, West and East*, 78.

The other side of the paranoid specter of the parasite or the cancer is the national community as an organic body—whether based on biological race theory or cultural-linguistic ethnocentrism. Fascism relies on the perception of a constituency producing, and produced by, an inherently natural process of hierarchy manifested by warrior elites embedded in the spiritual myths of the nation. In short, fascism is a syncretic form of ultranationalist ideology developed through patriarchal mythopoesis, which seeks the destruction of the modern world and the spiritual palingenesis ("rebirth") of an organic community led by natural elites through the fusion of technological advancement and cultural tradition.

Why Does Fascism Matter Today?

Resentment and revenge are fascism's prime emotions. A whole group identity—the "white working class"—emerged out of the financial crisis of 2008, forged through the crucible of resentment with a clear narrative. Promised under the Reagan administration that abandoning the labor movement would result in fast cash and easy gains, they pegged their hopes to middle-class values and neoliberal politicians throughout the 1990s. This group of people was instead uprooted over the coming decades, most clearly from the "Rust Belt" in the United States. A declassed economic movement that identified with middle-class aspirations in the 1990s and early 2000s now increasingly aligned itself with the "white working class." It sees its downward trajectory as a sign of a greater collapse, the end times, and the annihilation of their country.[19] As their anger builds, unity forms around demagogues catering to the darkest of anxieties and promising the rebirth of former greatness.[20]

---

19   Barbara Ehrenreich, "What Happened to the White Working Class?," *Nation*, December 1, 2015, https://www.thenation.com/article/what-happened-to-the-white-working-class/.

20   In a study of the hyperlinks and keywords shared among networks in Europe and the United States, analysts found a "rising connectivity from 2006 to 2011" to the extent that the white supremacist movement and the neo-Nazi organizations of the United States that were distinct networks in 2006 had consolidated into a single cluster over five years. See

The situation is similar in Europe, where Socialist parties have capitulated to austerity programs. Fascist ideology preys on the resulting anxiety and disillusionment. Fascists insist that a revolution must take place in order to replace the decadence of an unproductive ruling elite with a powerful elite that will return old privileges and advance a "new age" of health, spiritual greatness, and national unity. With the financial collapse, increasing antisystemic leftist protest movements, and the refugee crisis, the radical right and fascism have both expanded manifestly. The radical right's victories in the 2014 European Parliament elections were perhaps the most eye-opening result of such rising stakes, which is in itself the product of decades of efforts from the radical right and fascists to prepare the way for their own success by sowing inflated statistics and prejudice among their populations.

In those elections, the French Front National gained a stunning quarter of the vote; neo-Nazi party Golden Dawn grabbed one in ten votes in Greece; more than one in four Danes voted for the xenophobic Danish People's Party; more than one in ten cast ballots for the Islamophobic Dutch Party for Freedom; the notorious radical-right Austrian Freedom Party gained the vote of one in five citizens; and the virulently anti-Semitic Jobbik found the support of nearly one in nine Hungarian voters. In the United Kingdom, right-wing populist UK Independence Party (UKIP) took first place, beating out both the Labour and Conservative Parties with more than 26 percent of the vote. After the 2015 Paris attacks, the Front National beat its own record, taking in 28 percent of the vote and winning six regions in the first round of the 2015 local elections before mass tactical voting stymied their gains in the second round.[21]

As a result of rising tension linked to Islamist attacks, fascist violence increased drastically—in Germany for instance, attacks

Ralf Wiederer, "Mapping the Right-Wing Extremist Movement on the Internet—Structural Patterns 2006–2011," in *In the Tracks of Breivik: Far Right Networks in Northern and Eastern Europe*, eds. Mats Deland, Michael Minkenberg, and Christin Mays (Berlin: LIT Verlag, 2014), 43.

21   Angelique Chrisafis, "French Elections: Front National Makes No Gains in Final Round," *Guardian*, December 14, 2015, https://www.theguardian.com/world/2015/dec/13/front-national-fails-to-win-control-of-target-regions-amid-tactical-voting.

on refugee homes spiked more than fivefold in 2015.[22] By late February 2016, the number of attacks had already reached 217, on pace to exceed the previous year by around 30 percent.[23] In 2015's national elections, Golden Dawn gained its best results in the Greek general election, Jobbik continued its rise, the Danish People's Party won its highest ever gains, the Swiss People's Party received similarly powerful returns of 30 percent, Slovakia's neo-Nazi People's Party Our Slovakia won 23 percent, and the Sweden Democrats advanced considerably. The year 2016 saw the rise of the right-wing Alternative for Germany party in local elections and a gripping presidential election in Austria, where the FPÖ obtained some 49 percent of the vote for president, narrowly missing the highest ceremonial post in the nation. The UKIP-driven Brexit referendum, laden with xenophobia, passed by a fraction of the British electorate, effectively completing the far-right hijacking of dissent against the EU. In Australia, Pauline Hanson's United Australia Party won three seats in the senate, bringing mainstream credibility to a party that links radical-right politics with street-level fascism. The 2014 European Parliament elections were not a mere flash in the pan. The world is clearly at a turning point.

Islamophobic actions in the United States increased by sixteen times after September 11, 2001, and also tripled after the Paris attacks in 2015.[24] The phenomenon of reaction is often lasting and

---

22   Elizabeth Schumacher, "Report: Five Times More Attacks on Refugee Homes in Germany in 2015," *Deutsche Welle*, January 29, 2016, http://www.dw.com/en/report-five-times-more-attacks-on-refugee-homes-in-germany-in-2015/a-19011109.

23   There were 1,005 reported attacks in 2015, 217 attacks in January and February 2016. See "Die Karte der Schande," *Bild*, February 22, 2016, http://www.bild.de/news/inland/fluechtlingskrise-in-deutschland/die-karte-der-schande-44653590.bild.html.

24   Michelle Mark, "Anti-Muslim Hate Crimes Have Spiked After Every Major Terrorist Attack: After Paris, Muslims Speak Out Against Islamophobia," *International Business Times*, November 18, 2015, http://www.ibtimes.com/anti-muslim-hate-crimes-have-spiked-after-every-major-terrorist-attack-after-paris-2190150; Eric Lichtblau, "Crimes Against Muslim Americans and Mosques Rise Sharply," *New York*

cumulative, as well as spontaneous and decentralized. Islamophobia is also found in schools, where one antihate group noted that a rise in Islamophobic attacks has been registered across the last four years.[25] However, homophobic, xenophobic, anti-Semitic, misogynistic, and Islamophobic acts usually build off one another rather than off external attacks. Each violent act tends to embolden more, larger attacks, causing a surge of irrational anger and a larger creep of society toward angst, despair, and hatred.

In the United States, the Southern Poverty Law Center registered a decline in white nationalist organizations in 2014 but warned that this decline signaled both the underground movement of the Ku Klux Klan and the growth of decentralized, "lone wolf" violence carried out by the same sovereign citizens who have found rallying points at Bundy Ranch, the Sugar Pine Mine, and the Malheur National Wildlife Refuge. The wave of church burnings conducted by a small, white supremacist Asatru cell throughout 2015, along with the massive antimosque movement, indicate a growing militancy amid the increasing polarization of politics. Indeed, the number of Klan groups more than doubled from 72 in 2014 to 190 in 2015, while the number of hate crimes against Muslims increased by 67 percent.[26]

The popularity of the Donald Trump campaign mainstreamed white nationalist organizing and web hubs, which saw Internet traffic increase to record levels. This occurred because Trump's platform derived from white nationalist talking points, such as the elimination of the 14th Amendment and the expulsion of eleven

Times, December 17, 2015, http://www.nytimes.com/2015/12/18/us/politics/crimes-against-muslim-americans-and-mosques-rise-sharply.html.

25 Kristina Rizga, "The Chilling Rise of Islamophobia in Our Schools," *Mother Jones*, January 26, 2016, http://www.motherjones.com/politics/2016/01/bullying-islamophobia-in-american-schools.

26 Mark Potok, "The Year of Hate and Extremism," *Intelligence Report* (online edition), Southern Poverty Law Center's website, February 17, 2016, https://www.splcenter.org/fighting-hate/intelligence-report/2015/year-hate-and-extremism-0; CBS/AP, "FBI: Hate crimes against Muslims up by 67 percent in 2015," CBSnews.org, November 14, 2016, http://www.cbsnews.com/news/fbi-hate-crimes-against-muslims-up-67-percent-2015/.

million immigrants, while Trump himself spread white nationalist images and memes. What was exposed by Trump's campaign, then, was the increasing tolerance for white nationalist ideas among the mainstream, as well as the increasing radicalization of politics in the United States and the influence of fascism.[27]

As one analyst correctly pointed out, the Trump campaign relied on a dispersed "authoritarianism" among the populace and is not just based on a singular leader.[28] This analysis forces us to look not simply at demagogues as the "evil doers," but at the "affective economy" of habits and patterned behaviors.[29] Assessing affective "negativity biases" regarding angst, despair, and hatred, as well as general drift toward authoritarian and reactionary attitudes may lead us to a better understanding of lone-wolf violence delinked from organized groups.[30] Furthermore, it helps expose how emotional responses to alienation, guilt, shame, and frustration guide people toward ideological positions shared between right and left, leading to highly charged actions sparked by convoluted ideological complexes. This was demonstrated by the widespread proliferation of hate crimes after Trump's election in November 2016, during which the Southern Poverty Law

27   Mark Banham, "US White Supremacist Website Stormfront Says Donald Trump is Boosting its Popularity," *International Business Times*, December 28, 2015, http://www.ibtimes.co.uk/us-white-supremacist-website-stormfront-says-donald-trump-boosting-its-popularity-1535119.

28   Doug Gilbert, "U.S. Hard Right Being Bolstered by the Mainstream," Political Research Associates' website, December 23, 2015, http://www.politicalresearch.org/2015/12/23/u-s-hard-right-being-bolstered-by-the-mainstream/.

29   I am borrowing this term from Sara Ahmed, "Affective Economies," *Social Text* 22, no. 2 (Summer 2004): 117–39.

30   Paul Wright, "Neo-Nazi lone-wolf attacks in Europe are more deadly than Isis-inspired terrorist plots," *International Business Times*, March 1, 2016, http://www.ibtimes.co.uk/neo-nazi-lone-wolf-attacks-europe-are-more-deadly-isis-terrorist-plots-1546885. The term "negativity bias" simply connotes a tendency to focus on negative images, sensations, and feelings. See John R. Hibbing, Kevin Smith, and John R. Alford, "Differences in negativity bias underlie variations in political ideology," *Behavioral and Brain Sciences* 37 (2014): 297–350.

Center registered more than 437 acts of harassment in under two weeks—nearly quadrupling the 2015 weekly rate.[31] In this book, we will explore the roots of new fascist syntheses that have attempted to popularize fascist ideas in both the mainstream and the countercultures by stoking this popular animus.

Clarifying Terms and Grammar

Before we proceed, it is important to clarify the terms used in this text, since they provide the basis of the analytical framework—particularly "radical-right," "parafascist," and "protofascist." The *radical right* is generally perceived as a socially conservative milieu that rejects immigrants, religious difference, gender and sexual diversity, and it is, if not openly racist, then racist in deed. It is important not to confuse or conflate the radical right with fascism. They can hybridize and often contain overlap that may bring power to fascists, but fascists typically maintain a more hardcore revolutionary ideology. The radical right is concerned with creating a "closed society," walled off to immigrants and migrants and based around the idea of the nation rooted in territorial claims and family values.[32] Scholar Cas Mudde ascribes three attributes to the radical right: populism, nativism, and authoritarianism.[33] It is important not to underestimate or underplay the violence of the radical right in relation to fascism. The propaganda of the Council of Conservative Citizens, at one time supported by former Republican senator Trent Lott, inspired Dylann Roof to go on a murderous shooting spree in a black church in Charleston, North Carolina, on June 17, 2015. In this way, the semi-legitimacy of the "radical right," and even parafascist "authoritarian conservatives," obscures the direct connection

---

31   Hatewatch Staff, "Update: More Than 400 Incidents of Hateful Harassment and Intimidation Since the Election," *SPLC Hatewatch*, November 15, 2016, http://www.splcenter.org/hatewatch/2016/11/15/update-more-400-incidents-hateful-harassment-and-intimidation-election.

32   See Karl Popper, *The Open Society and Its Enemies,* vol. 1: *The Spell of Plato* (London: George Routledge & Sons, Ltd., 1947).

33   Cas Mudde, *Populist Radical Right Parties in Europe* (Cambridge: Cambridge University Press, 2007).

to white nationalism that can translate to mass and lone-wolf violence carried out by fascists.

The term *parafascist* here connotes a more genuinely authoritarian and conservative ideology than the radical right. Scholars Payne and Griffin identify Francisco Franco, Ioannis Metaxas, and Juan Perón, for instance, as parafascists who embrace some form of corporatism or vertical syndicalism as a model of state-driven economic power, but who typically lack a "mass movement" base that fascists attempt to generate and lead. While Perón's *descamisados* and the cult Franco created around "martyred" fascist leader José Antonio Primo de Rivera did produce the semblance of mass movements, their regimes relied more on the bureaucratization of syndicalism from above and a conservative military establishment than any ultranationalist "revolution from below." For this reason, parafascism has also been called "fascism from above."[34] Participants in the *conservative revolution* can and often do straddle the radical right, parafascism, and fascism. They typically call to mind figures we will discuss in this text, such as Otto Strasser, Carl Schmitt, Martin Heidegger, Julius Evola, Ernst Jünger, Armin Mohler, and others who participated in fascist movements while also criticizing aspects of certain fascist groups. Another term to describe the school of thought that emerged in the interwar period around the ideas of Schmitt, Heidegger, and others is *neoconservative*, which Heideggerian scholar Leo Strauss adapted to liberal auspices and disseminated through the University of Chicago to a host of up-and-coming Republicans who later became associated with the Reagan and Bush administrations.[35]

Although important scholarship recognizes a clear-cut distinction between the radical right, parafascism, and fascism, there

34 Roger Griffin's "Preface," in António Costa Pinto and Aristotle Kallis, eds., *Rethinking Fascism and Dictatorship in Europe* (London: Palgrave MacMillan, 2014), viii–xix.

35 Strauss himself listed fascism with authoritarianism and imperialism as the three essential characteristics of the right in a letter to fellow philosopher Karl Löwith as late as 1933, but he ceased writing in such terms after the discovery of Nazi concentration camps. See Nicholas Xenos, *Cloaked in Virtue: Unveiling Leo Strauss and the Rhetoric of American Foreign Policy* (New York: Routledge, 2008), 21.

also seems to be a growing wave of scholars of fascism who view hybridization as equally important. Constantin Iordachi describes this "new wave" precisely:

> At an analytical level, the differentiation between conservative, authoritarian, radical right-wing and fascist movements and parties is indispensable for comparative work, enabling historians to distinguish between related radical political phenomena and account for similarities and differences within the wider "family of authoritarians" in inter-war Europe. In historical reality, however, these ideal types are never to be found in pure form.… In politics in particular, the fluid nature of ideologies, the dynamics of the political process, and the multiple social-political factors that generally shape the nature and outlook of political regimes generate hybrid outcomes.[36]

As the title of this book implies, much of the development of fascism takes place more as a "process" than an "outcome."[37] This process, or "creep," takes place through the "positive" intermingling of conservatism, parafascism, and hardcore fascist groups, as much as it is a result of the "negative" distinction of fascists identifying themselves in isolation. For instance, it might be important to note that the radical right populist party can act as a container for a heteroclite mixture of ideologies, in particular where it does not necessarily exclude fascist membership and even leadership. It is possible, then, for a radical-right party to become "fascistized" by internal forces over time, leading scholars to contend with the difficult implications of process-oriented analysis.

Fascist Process

The process of "creeping fascism" or fascistization can take place in a political party or group, as with the Nazi Party after Benito

---

36   Constantin Iordachi, "Hybrid Totalitarian Experiments in Romania," in Costa Pinto and Kallis, eds., *Rethinking Fascism and Dictatorship in Europe*, 234.

37   Julie Thorpe, *Pan-Germanism and the Austrofascist State* (New York: Manchester University Press, 2011).

Mussolini's March on Rome, but it can also be seen as a general cultural, social, and political movement from radical-right to para-fascist to fascism. Fascism in Italy went from a pseudo-revolutionary paramilitary force to a compromised parliamentarian coalition with liberals and conservatives, and on to the leading force in a parliamentary system to a dictatorship. From 1928 to 1931, Weimar Germany's government went from Social Democracy to authoritarian conservatism, ending with Adolf Hitler's chancellorship in 1933. While these seizures of power were relatively rapid, they reflect a process by which fascism takes power. Among the most thorough scholars of fascism, Robert O. Paxton elucidates this approach to understanding fascist processes through a stage theory. According to Paxton, fascism passes through five stages:

- A movement-building base dedicated to creating a "new order";
- A process of "rooting in the political system";
- Seizing power;
- Exercising power;
- Either entering a decline period or a period of compromise called "entropy," or a radicalization by hardcore fascist groups who advocate a "second revolution."[38]

In the early stage, fascist groups form through the syncretic allure of a left-to-right alliance. These early formations tend to include xenophobes, traditional conservatives, fundamentalist Christians, and people Cas Mudde refers to as "prodigal sons of the left."[39] The fascist groups often play a relatively minor role within a larger, heterogeneous, populist coalition of different groups. Given credibility and protection by these populist movements, fascist groups can grow their ranks and gain leadership.

In stages one and two, fascist groups "creeping" among radical-right populists maintain a revolutionary, mass-movement stance but lack the cohesion to organize others on a truly

---

38   Robert O. Paxton, "The Five Stages of Fascism," in Griffin and Feldman, eds., *Fascism*, 1:311–12.

39   Mudde, *Populist Radical Right Parties*, 225. I interpret "prodigal sons of the left" to mean those who emerge from the left only to adopt nativist and/or authoritarian positions.

revolutionary level. A unifying fascist leader might come from the outside to unite feuding and disorganized sects, or fascist elements within the radical right may rise to leadership capacity from within. However, in the meantime, during stage two, fascists gaining popularity and prestige increasingly insinuate themselves within institutions of power and authority in order to open the space for expansion. It must be clarified at this point that this is not a book about "protofascist movements"—a term that I am not entirely comfortable with—but about protofascist conditions in which the relationship between radical-right, mainstream, and stage 1 and 2 fascism become increasingly hybridized, allowing fascism an opportunity to wield increasing power within the state itself. Hence, I do not suggest that this or that movement or group (say, the Patriot movement, for instance) will "become fascist," but that it is part of a larger process that facilitates fascism's creep into power.

Creeping Right Along...

The first chapter of this book will uncover the ideological fringes that came together to form fascism in the first place, outlining how the "original fascist creep" took place. The second chapter will describe the quasi-spiritual basis for the "rebirth" of fascism after the war. After the discussion of figures like Julius Evola and Savitri Devi, in Chapter 3, the book moves forward to an analysis of the neofascist formations produced during the so-called Years of Lead as well as the ideological emergence of a new kind of fascist ideology based on the symbolic rebellions of 1968.

Chapter 4 expands the narrative to include the creation of the modern, radical-right populist parties in France and Austria, and the subsequent chapter explores connections between more clearly fascist "Third Position" parties and groupuscules, as well as the fight to stop their advance. Chapter 6 continues the narrative toward an assessment of rising alternative fascist ideologies like national-anarchism, while Chapter 7 elaborates on emerging systems of radical-right and fascist groups and their attempted integration with leftist-driven "new social movements." The next chapter discusses the phenomenon of "autonomous nationalism" in greater depth, followed up with an analysis of the conflictive sites of social protest created by the Tea Party and the Occupy movement. *Against the Fascist Creep* finishes with a contemporary look at emerging configurations of neoreactionary and patriarchal movements, and their crossovers with the left and post-left.

Finally, regarding grammatical issues, I will note for the sake of clarity that I have capitalized Fascism only when referring directly to the interwar Italian variety—both the political party and movement. All other places where fascism is mentioned, the word will appear in lowercase. Also, to clarify, unfortunately the far right has claimed the title of libertarian as its own in the United States. This is not the case elsewhere in the world, but due to context, when I write about libertarians, it should be assumed that I am writing of the far-right variety, not "libertarian socialism." In cases where I do write about the latter, it is typically under the name "anarchism."

Dedications and Disclosures

This book is dedicated to the memory of my grandparents, to their generation of antifascists, and to all those continuing to ensure that the fascist creep is not able to access those levels of power that would bring about the "new age" of intolerance, injustice, and war. I hope the reader will recognize that this text is not an attempt to launch into polemics, as the title might imply, but to engage in serious scholarship and research in order to shed light on a phenomenon that is often elusive and difficult to study for many reasons.

It would be careless to neglect a full disclosure of my partisanship, however. My earliest experience in this kind of scholarship occurred in 2005, when I worked at a human rights publication in Moscow and a close friend was attacked in the streets repeatedly by National Bolshevik squads. After returning to the United States and dedicating myself to global justice work, I participated in the movement against the anti-immigration Arizona SB 1070 and J. T. Ready's Americans First march. Beginning in 2014, I devoted more of my studies to the avant-garde subcultures surrounding fascism and its esoteric side.

Despite, or perhaps because of, my activism, I encourage a great deal of sensitivity when discussing and researching fascism today. For many who have lost family members and spent years in prison, this subject is not something to be undertaken in a cavalier manner. Relationships fall to pieces, lives are put in danger, and trauma can awaken in terrifying ways. Furthermore, allegations of "fascism" make for an excellent broadsword to be wielded at one's enemies, but as such, its blows usually fall upon straw men. Without clear, cogent, and responsible assessment of the meaning and history of fascism, the word is emptied of content.

The concerns over a "Brown Scare" are often thrown around to shield from very real associations, but they can also hold some truth. Like anything with deep social networks, fascism can be incredibly difficult to isolate in one person or groupuscule. As a cultural phenomenon, it can spread through memes, symbols, and catchphrases. Often, people do not even understand the reality behind what they are spreading or have managed to detach themselves from it through the kind of explanations provided by the European New Right, or Nouvelle Droite. At this point, it is imperative to be armed with knowledge but to also recognize a limit to the extent to which one can actually intervene. There are different strategies and tactics for breaking down fascism in different contexts. While some are discussed in this text, more research and discussion must take place. Archives of journals like *Breakthrough*, *Searchlight*, and *Love and Rage* have a tremendous amount of information, some of which is available online at the fantastic Arm the Spirit archive and the Freedom Archives. New resources and publications are also becoming increasingly important.

Acknowledgments

I am deeply grateful first and foremost to my family for supporting me through this endeavor—particularly my mom and my dad, Shay Emmons, and my son Francis. Friends of mine have also helped provide crucial assistance in producing this work. That includes, but is not limited to, Christo Alfred, Kazembe Balagun, Matthew Bristow, Danica Brown, Nick Caleb, Caroline Crow, Kelila Eichstadt, Amye Greene, Arun Gupta, Jordan Karr-Morse, Mike Losier, Paul and Lara Messersmith-Glavin, Hyung Kyu Nam, Stephen Quirke, N. O. Bonzo, Leah Rothschild, and Ahjamu Umi.

Big B, Mic Crenshaw, scott crow, Kieran Knutson, and M. Treloar deserve a great amount of thanks for contributing interviews for this project, as do Leonard Zeskind and Don Hamerquist, as well as Scott Schroder and Elona Trogub. My immense gratitude also extends to Laure Akai, Dmytriy Kovalevich, Rose City Antifa, Mariya Radeva, Sylvére Lotringer, Chris Kraus, Jed Brandt, Aragorn Eloff, Ben Jones, William Gillis, Joshua Stephens, and Stéfanie Noire. Thanks also go out to the Moscow Institute of Science and Art and the Chronicle of Current Events, as well as Aleksey Roschin, Evgeny Ivanov and Fanny Ivanov-Adda, and Katherine Lahti.

I am deeply in debt to people who looked at early drafts and provided crucial feedback; namely, Matthew Lyons, Kevin van Meter, and Kristian Williams. My eternal gratitude goes out to Shane Burley, Peter Staudenmaier, Geran Wales, Jeffrey M. Bale, Luigi Celentano, and Roger Eatwell in particular, who helped considerably in testing, critiquing, and extending the depth of my research in fascism. Lastly, I would like to thank Chip Berlet and Roger Griffin for encouraging me to persevere in my work, as well as the editors who have helped along the way, like those at *It's Going Down*, Josh Frank and Jeffrey St. Clair at CounterPunch. org, Grayson Flory at the *Earth First! Journal*, Sue Udry and Steve Wishnia at the Defending Dissent Newswire, Andy Lee Roth with Project Censored, Adrienne Varkiani with ThinkProgress.org, and of course those indefatigable workers at AK Press, Charles, Zach, Bill, Lorna, and Suzanne.

CHAPTER 1: THE ORIGINAL FASCIST CREEP

The Imperial Origins of Fascism: Colonialism, Conservationism, and Eugenics

The first so-called "national socialist" ever to walk the earth was a Frenchman named Marquis de Morès who spent the 1880s attempting to make a fortune in the cattle industry of the US Badlands. With a sharply pointed mustache that hinted to his status as the most infamous duelist in France, Antoine de Vallombrosa, Marquis de Morès et de Montemaggiore, had a flair for adventure and was moved by the storied Wild West. Thirty miles upstream from his plot lived another adventurer and would-be politician named Theodore Roosevelt, a Progressive who sold his cattle to the Marquis for slaughter, packing, and shipment. The two became friendly and visited each other's houses. They both believed in eugenics, the perseverance of the white race, and the dominion of white civilization over the world. They both hoped to fit the character of the Wild West, gun-slinging cowboys of the rugged interior, but both faced failing businesses and a brutal climate. Their relationship cooled substantially when Morès tried to prop up his failing meatpacking plant by overcharging Roosevelt for his cattle.[1]

---

1   History of this can be found in Hermann Hagedorn, *Roosevelt in the Bad Lands* (Oyster Bay, NY: Roosevelt Memorial Association, 1921).

The Marquis rapidly made himself unpopular in town. As the first rancher to put up barbed wire in the Badlands, the Marquis faced the animosity of local cowboys. When he responded by ambushing three drunken cowboys, fatally shooting one Riley Luffsey, the Marquis found himself in jail. Incarcerated, Morès wrote to Roosevelt, blaming him and challenging him to a duel. Roosevelt responded, "I am not your enemy; if I were you would know it, for I would be an open one."[2] Not long after their falling out came the brutal winter of 1886–1887, after which both the Marquis and Roosevelt abandoned their respective projects. The latter won appointment to the Civil Services Commission after campaigning for Benjamin Harrison in 1888, and just over five years later, won the election for the police commissioner of New York City. The Marquis returned to France in time to participate in the anti-Semitic riots of the Dreyfus Affair, equipping a gang of "butcher boys" from Paris with cowboy hats and boots and rallying them to the chant of *Mort aux Juifs!* ("Death to the Jews!"). It must have been a ghastly sight during a period credited for prefiguring the fascism that would emerge in Italy within a couple decades.

Back in the big cities of the United States, ideas of national socialism flowed through intellectual and political circles—particularly through the publication of articles written by and about Morès's friend Maurice Barrès. Coining the term "national socialism" in 1898 to define an ideology that incorporated the working class into national solidarity, Barrès spread his ideas through political campaigns, French periodicals, and US journals like *Scribners* and the *Atlantic*. His work appeared uncontroversial alongside ecology, the spirit, athletics, and the ever-present reality of business, science, and industry. Indeed, this life of vigorous exercise, adventure, and even mysticism would characterize Roosevelt as he rose through the ranks to become president of the United States. Carried out by conservationist Gifford Pinchot, Roosevelt's philosophy of outdoors recreation intertwined inextricably with his imperialist sense of the supremacy of the white race. The conquest of the West and the Pacific marked a crucial turn in the spread of the white race, the perfection of which became a social responsibility, as well as a

---

2   See Theodore Roosevelt, *Letters*, vol. 1 (Cambridge, MA: Harvard University Press, 1951), 92.

science. Roosevelt wrote to a prominent eugenicist named Charles Davenport that "society has no business to permit degenerates to reproduce their kind. It is really extraordinary that our people refuse to apply to human beings such elementary knowledge as every successful farmer is obliged to apply to his own stock breeding."[3] Whether or not his betters would force the price of his stock down and then sell the steaks dear was, perhaps, a different question for the failed rancher of the Badlands.

Roosevelt's friend and fellow conservationist-cum-eugenicist Madison Grant would write the important book *The Passing of the Great Race* not about the hundred million Natives slaughtered in the centuries-long genocide that paved the way for the "conservationist ethic" of pure, unpeopled wilderness, but rather about the "racial suicide" of the noble classes by their acceptance of immigrants and "sub-species." Addressing his subject with the gravity of scientific objectivity, Grant declared that those seeking "social uplift" do not respond to the realities of "racial limits." Inferior classes reject the principle of heredity, because they have not inherited noble qualities, while the nationalism of the Global South merely represents the revolt of the "servile classes rising up against the master race": "If the valuable elements in the Nordic race mix with inferior strains or die out through race suicide, then the citadel of civilization will fall for mere lack of defenders."[4] In time, Adolf Hitler would write to Grant, commending the author for what he called his "bible."

Later, when Hitler's armies invaded Poland and then Russia, the Führer would impose on his generals to follow a battle strategy gleaned from the pages of Karl May's Wild West stories that thrilled him as a child, along with tales of the Boer Wars.[5] For Hitler, the conquest of Slavic lands represented the same kind of internal colonization as Manifest Destiny. His desire to create *Lebensraum*, derived from a muddled understanding of geopolitical large spaces (*Grossraum*) theory and biological racism, presented the

---

3   Theodore Roosevelt, *Letter to Charles Davenport* (New York, January 3, 1913).

4   Madison Grant, *The Passing of the Great Race: Or, the Racial Basis of European History* (New York: Charles Scribner's Sons, 1922), xxxi.

5   Ian Kershaw, *Hitler, 1889–1936: Hubris* (New York: W.W. Norton & Company, 1999), 15.

Germanic peoples as a colonizing force. Poland and Ukraine were his frontier, Russia his Wild West. As the Waffen-SS systematically exterminated Poles, Slavs, and Jews, German farmers would accompany the push east, effectively colonizing Eastern soil and, in time, transforming the racial and territorial composition into a suitable terrain for the "master race."

The eugenic concerns that motivated Nazis toward the designation of Jews and "inferior races" as "life unworthy of being lived" were nested in the same framework of *homo sacer* used to justify the United States' westward expansion.[6] Representing "bare life," a "sacred man" excluded from the political body who can be killed with impunity, the notion of *homo sacer* comes from esoteric Roman law, but its modern use originated in a Supreme Court judicial decision. Specifically, the 1873 *Modoc Indian Prisoners* opinion formally allowed white settlers to kill those described as "Indians" without being charged of murder.[7] Massacres of villages were the norm during the Indian Wars, as was the wholesale displacement of entire tribes to make way for white settlement. Other European colonial efforts created concentration camps in Cuba and in South Africa, which certainly informed later Nazi versions. The notorious paramilitary Freikorps leaders Paul von Lettow-Vorbeck and Hermann Ehrhardt personified a lineage of German patriotic fighters from the German colonial genocide of the Hereros in what is now called Namibia (a virtual obliteration of an entire ethnic group, as many as 100,000 people) to World War I and on to the paramilitary struggles connected to the Nazis' Brownshirts.[8]

Italian Fascism was perhaps even more directly linked to the colonization of Africa. Fascists insisted that the conquest of Libya would empower the working class, strengthening the nation in ways socialism could only dream of. Ethiopia became the next target for Fascist conquest—a merciless onslaught that included the

---

6   See Giorgio Agamben, *Homo Sacer: Sovereign Power and Bare Life*, trans. Daniel Heller-Roazen (Stanford: Stanford University Press, 1998).

7   Roxanne Dunbar-Ortiz, *An Indigenous Peoples' History of the United States* (Boston: Beacon Press, 2014), 224.

8   In 2002, in an unsettling indication of continuity, US Attorney General John Yoo applied the legal identity of *homo sacer* to Guantánamo detainees citing the 1873 *Modoc Indian Prisoners* opinion as precedent. Ibid.

use of gas against civilians. Hence, historically speaking, fascism is not derogation from imperialism, but a deepening of it—perhaps even a *force majeure*, a consequence of the momentum of centuries of crusades, colonialism, and imperialism through which Europe began to colonize itself.

Ecology and the Organic State

Certain forms of agrarian populism and early environmentalism became crucial milieus for the beginnings of a fascist synthesis. The word "ecology" was coined by Ernst Haeckel, who combined Darwinism and nationalism under the rubric of the supremacy of the "Nordic race": "Civilization and the life of nations are governed by the same laws as prevail throughout nature and organic life," and humanity is only a miniscule part of a huge, interconnected, cosmic web.[9] With a pronounced pessimism about the future of humanity on earth, philosopher Ludwig Klages's essay "Man and Earth" bequeathed the idea of "biocentrism" to the early ecological movement. His theory "anticipated just about all of the themes of the contemporary ecology movement…the accelerating extinction of species, disturbance of global ecosystemic balance, deforestation, destruction of aboriginal peoples and of wild habitats, urban sprawl, and the increasing alienation of people from nature."[10] Much of this destruction, however, was supposedly wrought by Jews through rationalism, urbanization, spiritual oppression, and consumerism.

Biocentrism's sense of interconnectedness suborned human rights to a quasi-mystical natural whole, which fit well with the "race doctrine" of reactionaries like Georges Vacher de Lapouge, who believed that "there are no human rights, any more than there are rights of the armadillo.… The idea of equal rights is fiction. Nothing exists but forces."[11] Such social Darwinist theories of the nation as natural and biological, as well as romantic and antihumanist,

---

9   Ernst Haeckel, quoted in Janet Biehl and Peter Staudenmaier, *Ecofascism* (Oakland: AK Press, 1995), 8. Web edition available at https://theanarchistlibrary.org/library/janet-biehl-and-peter-staudenmaier-ecofascism-lessons-from-the-german-experience.

10   Ibid.

11   Georges Vacher de Lapouge, *L'Aryen son Role Social* (Paris: 1899), 511.

would further inform what became known as the "organic theory of the state," wherein each and every individual forms a cell in the state's body and conformity produces health in body as well as state. It was this idea of the nation as an organic totality that would provide the basic theoretical foundation for Nazism.

Organic statism emerged in the influential writings of Ernst Moritz Arndt, who wrote in *On the Care and Conservation of Forests*, "When one sees nature in a necessary connectedness and interrelationship, then all things are equally important—shrub, worm, plant, human, stone, nothing first or last, but all one single unity."[12] Arndt's student, Wilhelm Heinrich Riehl, brought the nationalism within Arndt's position to a xenophobic pitch: "We must save the forest, not only so that our ovens do not become cold in winter, but also so that the pulse of life of the people continues to beat warm and joyfully, so that Germany remains German."[13] These ultranationalist theories of blood and soil (*Blut und Boden*) also made sense to imperialists like Ernst Blüher, a major influence on the later Freikorps, who adored the "conquerors and organizers" in Africa, identifying nature as a system of predator and prey, strong and weak, masculine and feminine, and who saw culture as founded solely on "male society."[14]

Even today, as we will see, ecology does not stand entirely on the left. Just as when it was established in the nineteenth century, ecology, like *völkisch* ultranationalism, is adopted by idealistic youths of left and right persuasions, and does not manifest any specific national socialist doctrine in itself. Ideas of paganism also spread during the lead-up to the fascist synthesis, as rejections of Judeo-Christian logic spread to new incarnations of Norse mythology and interpretive systems of ancient runes said to hold mythopoetic qualities arising from blood and soil. Of course, the pagan, occult, and spiritualist movements did not produce fascism, but when fused with a völkisch, back-to-the-peasant nationalism, they did help construct the belief that Judeo-Christian ethics had corrupted what was essentially European, which could return through

12   Ibid., 6.
13   Ibid.
14   Klaus Theweleit, *Male Fantasies*, vol. 1: *Women, Floods, Bodies, History*, trans. Stephen Conway (Minneapolis: University of Minnesota, 1987), 27.

the careful production of a new Aryan superman. By the same to-ken, current ecological principles are taken up by fascists who seek to identify migrants as "invasive species."

As the ecological, spiritual, and utopian currents fused through ultranationalism into a dangerous synthesis, pan-German regionalism emerged through the ideology of viciously anti-Semitic Austrian ideologue Georg Ritter von Schönerer, who used student fraternity associations and traditional fencing clubs as the main vehicles for promoting a unification of Austria and Germany under one ethnostate.[15] In the cities, Schönerer's position was embraced by such leading politicians as Karl Lueger, a fierce anti-Semite who would become mayor of Vienna, responsible for conservative, though semi-socialist, policies that modernized the city and served as an early model for Hitler.

Nationalism and Socialism, Collectivism and Individualism

Although fascism is typically identified with collectivism, individualism also historically held an influential role in its germination. In his well-known work, *The Ego and Its Own*, Max Stirner expresses a deeply held racist view of world history in which the white individual acts as the apotheosis of all human evolution. The evolutionary mission of the white man for Stirner must develop through "two Caucasian ages," requiring him to first "work out and work off our innate *negroidity*" and then inner "*Mongoloidity* (Chineseness), which must likewise be terribly made an end of."[16] The transcendence of the individual to the world spirit has only been realized through the evolution of the human history from Asia to Europe, Stirner insists. "No, my good old sir, nothing of equality. We only want to count for what we are worth, and, if you are worth more, you shall count for more right along. We only want to be *worth our price*, and think to show ourselves worth the price that you will pay."[17]

Because he believed that the state issued a kind of equality that levels all distinction to the lowest common denominator,

---

15   Thorpe, *Pan-Germanism*, 19–21, 154.

16   Max Stirner, *The Ego and Its Own*, trans. David Leopold (Cambridge: Cambridge University Press, 1995), 62.

17   Ibid., 241.

Stirner would proclaim, "I do not want the liberty of men, nor their equality; I want only *my* power over them, I want to make them my property, *i.e. material for enjoyment*. And, if I do not succeed in that, well, then I call even the power over life and death, which Church and State reserved to themselves—mine."[18] Stirner's self-liberation would come at the expense of Jews, whose religion he saw as tainted and based on an attempt to haggle and smuggle one's way into heaven.[19]

Although he died in middle age, Stirner became a relatively popular figure among intellectuals of the late-nineteenth century, including the philosopher Friedrich Nietzsche, whose ideas about the "superman" remain controversial to this day. In his later notebooks from 1899, Nietzsche declares that the superman comes about as a countermovement to the increasingly "economical use of men." This countermovement is the expression of a "secretion of luxurious surplus" that "brings to light a stronger species, a higher type."[20] For Nietzsche, democratic society exists in a state of decay, or "passive nihilism"—a bad equality that rejects transcendence, bringing about the need for an accelerated "higher species" composed of the "strong and noble" Napoleon type who transforms passivity into activity.[21]

Such "active nihilism" embodied by the superman would reduce modern society to nothing and build a new world on its ruins, overcoming base legalism with the spirit of action.[22] Yet such a movement cannot proceed without enforcing another tyranny, he would admit.[23] Even the principles of anarchy and complete freedom

---

18   Ibid., 281.

19   Ibid., 285; Stirner likely had no idea that the first rule of the Talmud is to trade fairly. He debases Jews even further, declaring that "they cannot discover spirit, which takes no account whatever of things," Ibid., 23.

20   Friedrich Nietzsche, *Writings from the Late Notebooks*, trans. Kate Sturge, ed. Rudiger Bittner (Cambridge: Cambridge University Press, 2003), 177.

21   Ibid., 150.

22   Friedrich Nietzsche, *On the Genealogy of Morality and Other Writings*, trans. Carol Diethe, ed. Keith Ansell-Pearson (Cambridge: Cambridge University Press, 2007), 33.

23   Friedrich Nietzsche, *Beyond Good and Evil: A Prelude to a Philosophy of the Future*, trans. Judith Norman, ed. Rolf-Peter Horstmann and Judith

become unfree, he insisted, finding their ultimate ends in nihilism as the consequence of "the political and economic way of thinking."[24] Napoleon is, then, the embodiment of two kinds of nihilism, active and passive, the cure and the disease—the superman comes as the result of the lack of a "higher species" in modern society, only to find in alienation a repetition of the same crisis of modernity.

A new political configuration was being born: part individualist, part collectivist; part nationalist, part socialist. The only thing that could hold such disparate ideological positions together was a syncretic, overarching narrative of domination. Effectively, fascism emerged from a mutual enmity against the compromised system of liberal democracy and a final decision to collaborate in its ultimate destruction.

Social Monarchism and the Early Radical Right

Known as the "Nietzsche of France," the Marquis de Mòres's friend Maurice Barrès advocated a quasi-spiritual "cult of myself," which took the shape of the "sentimental Anarchist with a rebel's brain and a voluptuary's nerves."[25] Putting the self forward as "an enemy of the laws," Barrès preached ancestor-worship and faith in *la terre et les morts* (the soil and the dead).[26] He mourned *les deracinés*, the people uprooted by modern life, and hoped for the creation of a new community based on traditional *Amitiés Françaises* (French friendships). Such right-wing "anarchism" became fashionable among a set of nobles of the epoch, like the writer Sibylle Riqueti de Mirabeau (writing under the pen name Gyp), who saw their love of tradition failing as "progress" steamed ahead past the *fin-de-siècle* with great vitality but toward a questionable destiny. Resigning themselves to the perhaps temporary end of monarchy, these reactionaries pursued an occult notion of aristocracy through which their innate nobility would always elevate them above the plebian drives of democracy.

Norman (Cambridge: Cambridge University Press, 2002), 77.

24   Nietzsche, *Writings from the Late Notebooks*, 84.

25   Edward Jewitt Wheller, ed., "Maurice Barrès: The New French Immortal," *Index of Current Literature* XLII (January–June, 1907): 401.

26   Ibid.

Among the most important contributors to the reactionary milieu was the bushy-bearded and bespectacled figure of Édouard Drumont, whose self-published, two-volume work in 1886, *La France juive* (Jewish France), went through more than two hundred editions before its last publication in 1941. Drumont despised both capitalism and Marxism as the workings of Jewish overlords who divorced Europeans from their natural order through a despiritualized materialism advocated first by Adam Smith. As Drumont's tome made the rounds, illustrated editions appeared depicting the leading anti-Semite as a knight fighting off the new Saracens. Anti-Semitism took on the character of a new crusade, where the enemy within "made the press the servant of capital, so that it is unable to speak."[27] By liquidating "Jewish France" and returning to *France profonde*, the spiritual depths of which lay in the souls of forefathers, rural French families would again be able to speak through a mighty and sacred sovereign. However, the sovereign would rule legitimately as a "people's tribune," presiding over an orderly state by fulfilling social needs. Such a state could only come to pass through a socialist revolution against the bourgeois conservative and liberal class. Drumont insisted, *"Ces vaincus de la Bougeoisie seront bientôt à l'avant-garde de l'armée socialiste"* ("The victims of the bourgeoisie will soon be the vanguard of the socialist army").[28] These victims were not mere proletarian slum dwellers, but rather the lower middle class, the small shopkeepers and skilled workers challenged by proletarian advancement and ruined by the early gentrification of imperial city-planning and department stores produced under Emperor Napoleon III's regime.

Drumont's ideas would feed into the radical-right, populist politics of Georges Boulanger, a prominent military figure who played a role in the suppression of the Paris Commune, and then received the blessing of its former right-wing participants and supporters—perhaps most notably the former communard Victor Henri Rochefort and his publication *L'Intransigeant*. The radical right's

---

27   Édouard Drumont, quoted in Michel Winock, *Nationalism, Anti-Semitism, and Fascism in France*, trans. Jane Marie Todd (Stanford: Stanford University Press, 1998), 87.

28   Édouard Drumont, *La fin d'un monde: etude psychologique et social*, ed. Albert Savine (Paris: 1889), 44.

support for a socially responsible monarchy or empire grounded in the national community resonated with Catholic Church doctrine, later made explicit in Pope Pius XI's *Quadragesimo Anno*, which called for the transformation of capitalist production into a new corporatist system that included the input of labor syndicates under the state's patronage (and control).

At this turning point, anti-Semitism stood as the "providential" position of reaction that could destroy ideals of human rights and return Europe to the sovereignty of a futuristic *ancien régime*. So, as establishment anti-Semitic politicians like Lueger and Boulanger proposed ethnocentric social welfare systems for the petite bourgeoisie and the Catholic Church moved to the left to maintain relevance, a popular strain of revolutionary movements and critical liberals edged toward a "new age" led by the "new man" who could recreate old national myths that guided the world toward a future organized by science and nature together.

Left Authoritarianism

The revolutionary tendencies of the nineteenth century grew in tangled patterns out of conflicting interests. From its partial foundations in Jean-Jacques Rousseau's *volonté générale* to Maximilien Robespierre's Cult of the Supreme Being, revolutionary Jacobinism held its own potential for dictatorship, ritualized political religion, and terror.[29] The ensuing development of utopian socialism, most commonly associated with Henri de Saint-Simon, openly professed the need for a kind of natural hierarchy of producers carrying forward the light of scientific management of society, from the Revolution through Napoleon and into the modern era via industrial development and grand projects that would mold France into an "organic nation." Saint-Simonianism came to influence leading economists in power like Adolphe Blanqui and his supervisor, Finance Minister François Guizot, whose slogan was *Enrichissez-vous!* Nevertheless, it also influenced revolutionaries like Adolphe's brother Auguste Blanqui, who forwarded a conspiratorial strategy of insurrectionary communism while maintaining a chauvinist disdain for

---

29   George L. Mosse, *The Fascist Revolution* (Madison: University of Wisconsin Press, 1999), 70.

other nations like Belgium, indicating a path of nationalism that would be taken by some of his followers.[30]

Auguste Blanqui joined and formed secret societies that proliferated and often collaborated throughout Europe during the early-nineteenth century. Another architect of these was Giuseppe Mazzini, an Italian national-liberal who strove to unite Italy under a single republican system.[31] Although the chauvinist tendencies of Blanqui and the nationalism of Mazzini would be rejected by revolutionaries like Pierre-Joseph Proudhon and Mikhail Bakunin, other problems like anti-Semitism would not.[32]

New syntheses that mixed agrarian populism, urban workers' movements, and elite conspiratorialism began to develop among revolutionaries. On the most fundamental level, the grand populist theories of left- and right-wing collectivism, aggregated into nationalism and socialism, met head-on with individualist theories of the vanguard—the conspiratorial elite and the superman. Russian revolutionaries like Pyotr Tkachev and Sergey Nechayev began to fuse Narodnik populism (similar in some respects to the völkisch movement), Blanquism, Bakuninism, and Marxism into a vanguardist doctrine of the seizure of state power through violent acts, including terror and assassination. After Italy's "War of Unification," known as the Risorgimento, revolutionary workers' associations like Bologna's Fascio Operaio emerged, which fused Bakuninism with Mazzini's nationalism.[33]

Three elements would join to create fascism, then: vanguardist revolutionism, the emergent radical right of Lueger

---

30   Georges Sorel's considerations of Blanqui and Proudhon draw some relevant comparisons. See "Materials for a Theory of the Proletariat," in *From Georges Sorel: Essays in Socialism and Philosophy*, ed. John L. Stanley, trans. John and Charlotte Stanley (Oxford: Oxford University Press, 1987), 250–51, and "Critical Essays in Marxism," Ibid., 161.

31   L. M. Findlay, "Introduction," in *The Communist Manifesto*, ed. and trans. L. M. Findlay (Peterborough, ON: Broadview Press, 2004), 22.

32   For this interesting history, see Robert Graham, *We Do Not Fear Anarchy—We Invoke It: The First International and the Origins of the Anarchist Movement* (Oakland: AK Press, 2015).

33   Nunzio Pernicone, *Italian Anarchism, 1864–1892* (Princeton: Princeton University Press, 1993), 43, 67.

and Boulanger, and a more virulent form of reactionary politics aligned with revolution against liberal democracy. Perhaps the earliest iterations of the fusion of revolutionary left and revolutionary right took place in Barrès's journal *La Cocarde*, in print from 1894 to 1895. Among the journal's contributors were revolutionary syndicalists like Eugéne Fournière, Pierre Denis, and Fernand Pelloutier. The intended audience of Barrès's newspaper was the educated and underemployed: "We know to whom we speak," Barrès stated. "To the proletariat of *bacheliers*, to those youths whom society has given a diploma and nothing else, at the risk of turning them into an urban mass of *déclassés*. We know we are in agreement with their reflections and, in any case, with their instinct, clamoring for the resurrection of their native lands where they might be gainfully employed."[34] Barrès's *La Cocarde* appealed to the young "superfluous man," the overeducated college graduate who remained alienated from the economic system despite his credentials and ambition. This new disenfranchised elite, thinking "beyond" the opposition between left and right, would set the stage for a revolt of the intellectuals that found two new voices emerging from revolutionary syndicalism and ultranationalism: Georges Sorel and Charles Maurras.

Left and Right

Linking the "vitalism" of scientist Henri Bergson to the revolutionary violence in the form of the general strike, Sorel connected ancient national myths to workers' solidarity, eventually finding an intellectual ally in Maurras, who had also participated in *La Cocarde*. Sorel wrote that "the defense of French culture is today in the hands of Charles Maurras."[35] A pugnacious anti-Semite and advocate for "national integralism" through his prominent organization Action Française, Maurras developed a syncretic economic plan attuned to monarchist and military leadership, but inclusive

---

34   Maurice Barrès, quoted in Judith Surkis, *Sexing the Citizen: Morality and Masculinity in France, 1870–1920* (Ithaca: Cornell University Press, 2006), 98.

35   Georges Sorel, "Quelques pretentions juives (fin)," *L'Indépendance* 3 (June 1, 1912): 336.

of guilds and trade unions subordinated to a corporate structure
under national rule and aligned with critical liberalism. The inclusion of syndicalism in the interests of a new totalitarian state
unified by national solidarity was enough for Sorel.

This meeting between radical left and right became more pronounced when Sorel's leading disciple Édouard Berth joined with
a cohort of Maurras named Georges Valois. Formerly an anarchist and associate of Pelloutier, Valois shifted toward the social
monarchist tendencies identified with Barrès and Maurras. With
Berth, he founded the Cercle Proudhon, a reading group chaired
by Maurras. This group would continue to recast the Proudhonist
tradition as violently antiparliamentary, as opposed to the nom-
inal reading of Proudhon as a progressive in his early years (and
even during his later, explicitly anarchist stage, as a believer in the
natural progression of the state toward anarchy).[36]

The Cercle Proudhon acknowledged the democratic and anti-
clerical side of Proudhon, avoiding his more egalitarian followers
like Joseph Déjacque, while effectively transforming his revolutionary aspects into what they described as a "counterrevolutionary"
trend in his thought. Their writings included this urgent "Declaration": "Democracy is the greatest error of the past century. If we
want to live, if we want to work, if we want to possess the highest
human guarantees for Production and for Culture, if we want to
conserve the accumulation of moral, intellectual, and material capital of civilization, it is absolutely necessary to destroy the institutions of democracy."[37]

Capitalism breaks down nations, families, societies, and individuals in decadent service to modern life, the Cercle Proudhon

---

36   Maurras and Valois were also inspired by a fusion of critical liberalism
      and reaction. They therefore drew on a syncretic ideological constella-
      tion of Auguste Comte and Frédéric La Play, as well as Louis Gabriel
      Ambroise de Bonald, Joseph de Maistre, and René de la Tour du Pin.
      See Samuel Kalman, *The Extreme Right in Interwar France: The Faisceau
      and the Croix de Feu* (New York: Routledge, 2008), 64–67; also Maurice
      Weyembergh, *Charles Maurras et la Révolution française* (Belgium: Vrin,
      1992), 26–28 and 53–54.

37   Quoted in Charles Maurras, *L'Action française et la religion catholique*
      (Paris: 1913), 166.

insisted. The Cercle's new state would would take on a kind of municipal virtue through the resurgence of a natural citizen whose membership in the alternative ultranationalist community subverted commercialism and consumerism. In the "Declaration" of their side project, *La Cité française*, the circle stated that "one must therefore organize society outside the sphere of democratic ideas; one must organize the classes outside democracy, despite democracy, and against it."[38]

This radical program of extrastate social organizing was joined to an elitist belief in hierarchical order. As disagreements within the left between revolutionary syndicalists and reformist socialists intensified, the reaction persisted in drawing the former away from the latter and toward a possible revolutionary collaboration against liberalism and parliamentarism. By stacking elitism on top of a class analysis, statism could remain in the form of national solidarity and personal excellence. Thus, the fusion (or confusion) of collectivism, individualism, and mutualism allowed the Cercle to reason that syndicalist direct action, and particularly the general strike, could establish a popular system of national unity through stratified classes conscious of their place within an organic state. Sorel increasingly abandoned class as anything but an abstract concept, while the political consolidation of the left against anti-Semitism was increasingly undermined and replaced by a call to left-right revolution against the Republic.[39] While it is debatable as to whether or not Sorel can be considered a protofascist or fascist, he would later express admiration for Mussolini's party, and his intellectual interventions produced an ideal space for the "fascist creep."[40]

In Italy, Sorel was at the same time lauded as an anti-Marxist syndicalist by elitist thinker Vilfredo Pareto and labeled "an eminent

---

38   Quoted in Sternhell, *The Birth of Fascist Ideology*, 84.

39   As early as 1932, foundational thinker of political science Michael Freund could publish *Georges Sorel, Der revolutionäre Konservatismus* (Frankfurt: 1932).

40   "At the present moment, the adventures of Fascism may be the most original social phenomenon in Italy: they seem to me to go far beyond the schemes of politicians." Georges Sorel, "Letter to Benedetto Croce in 1921," quoted in Winock, *Nationalism, Anti-Semitism, and Fascism*, 243.

French Marxist" by influential liberal Benedetto Croce.[41] As Sorel's work pushed away from Marx and parliamentary reformism, he delved into a world of vitalism and myth where only revolution could save civilization from collapse, decadence, and the terminal crisis of intellectual optimism. Between 1907 and 1911, the anarchist newspaper *La demolizione*—edited by an acquaintance of Mussolini's named Ottavio Dinale, as well as Sorel himself—hosted important discussions between Sorelian revolutionary syndicalists and anarchists, and included the writings of influential futurist poet and painter Filippo Tommaso Marinetti.[42] Mussolini would later identify Sorel as "our master," although speculation exists regarding Mussolini's actual adherence to national syndicalism.[43]

Il Duce took on the reputation of a Blanquist or some kind of individualist, and he remained relatively intellectually irrelevant as the synthesis of nationalism and revolutionary syndicalism took place. In his youth, he had translated two works by Russian anarchist Peter Kropotkin into Italian, championed the anarchist Haymarket Martyrs, and defended the reputation of Gaetano Bresci, assassin of King Umberto I in 1900. In a valedictory 1904 article on Kropotkin in the *Socialist Vanguard*, Mussolini would write that after the revolution, "the State—the committee of defense of the interests of the propertied classes—will have no more reason to exist."[44]

---

41   Although some note that Sorel's relevance among revolutionary syndicalists was relatively slight, in the words of scholar Zeev Sternhell, "The importance of a work, however, cannot be judged solely on an absolute plane; one should also take into account its influence and its political function. Sorel's writings represented the conceptual space in which the theoreticians of revolutionary syndicalism evolved." See Sternhell, *The Birth of Fascist Ideology*, 20. The principle contemporary influence of a young Antonio Labriola, Sorel ironically provided perhaps a leading impetus to Italian Marxism.

42   Ibid., 234–35; also Günter Berghaus, *Futurism and Politics: Between Anarchist Rebellion and Fascist Reaction, 1909–1944* (Providence, RI: Berghahn Books, 1996), 60.

43   Richard Drake, *Apostles and Agitators: Italy's Marxist Revolutionary Tradition* (Cambridge, MA: Harvard University Press, 2009), 117; see also Nolte, *The Three Faces of Fascism*, 153–54.

44   Benito Mussolini, "Tutti vi dicono che sono anarchico. Nulla di più falso,"

Believing in the revolution of the workers and the liberation of rural people, Mussolini operated as a radical socialist in Switzerland. He scolded the revolutionary Carlo Tresca for being too moderate when the two were brief roommates, and he also attempted to befriend Leda Rafanelli, all the while maintaining a deep respect for Errico Malatesta.[45] His youthful declarations included such statements as "We acknowledge our heresy. We cannot conceive of a patriotic socialism"[46] and an incitement to clear the way for "the elemental forces of individuals, because another human reality outside of the individual does not exist! Why should Stirner not make a comeback (*tornerebbe d'attualità*)?"[47] As he increased in notoriety, Mussolini would settle for a syncretic fusion of Nietzsche and Marx, which he sometimes associated with anarchism, but mostly with socialism.

Statements like these seem to illustrate Mussolini's egoism in relation to the nationalism, militarism, and syndicalism discussed in increasingly important journals like *La Lupa* and *La Voce*.[48] This growing movement of national syndicalists remained relatively consistent in calling for a devolution of state authority to syndicates,

---

in *Avanguardia Socialista*, April 2, 1904.

45   Philip V. Cannistraro, "Mussolini, Sacco–Vanzetti, and the Anarchists: The Transatlantic Context," *The Review of Italian American Studies*, eds. Frank M. Sorrentino and Jerome Krase (Lanham, MD: Lexington Books, 2000), 110–11; see also Andrea Pakieser, *I Belong Only to Myself: The Life and Writings of Leda Rafanelli* (Oakland: AK Press, 2014); Anatole Dolgoff, *Left of the Left: My Memories of Sam Dolgoff* (Chico: AK Press, 2016), 131.

46   Nolte, *The Three Faces of Fascism*, 152.

47   Benito Mussolini, *Opera Omnia*, 35 vols. (Florence, Italy: La Fenice, 1951–1963), 15:194; also see A. James Gregor, *The Ideology of Fascism: The Rationale of Totalitarianism* (New York: Free Press, 1969), 156. For an analysis of Nietzsche and Stirner, see Stephen B. Whitaker, *The Anarchist-Individualist Origins of Italian Fascism* (Bern: Peter Lang 2002), 86. One should resist the temptation to make too much of Fascism's syndicalist or individualist tendencies.

48   The crucial syndicalists were Arturo Labriola, Robert Michels, and Paolo Orano, while the nationalist voice that predominated was Enrico Corradini. *La Voce* was founded by nationalists Giovanni Papini and raging anti-Semite Giuseppe Prezzolini; see Griffin, *The Nature of Fascism*, 57.

which would be organized according to a meritocracy that some likened to an aristocracy. However, for fear of overthrowing capitalism only to pave the way for something even worse, these deeply compromised syndicalists increasingly maintained that capitalism and market forces would be built upon through a solidarity based on cultural-linguistic nationality rather than class.

One of the most important connections between Sorel and the growing movement of Italian nationalists was Marinetti, with whom he would remain in close contact. Marinetti's followers supported the "destructive gesture of the anarchists," while also establishing a fierce, violent order based on revolutionary ethics that could overcome the boredom and incompetence of everyday bourgeois life. Marinetti's warmongering support for imperialism, his stark misogyny, and his aestheticization of politics were fueled by an energy and dynamism that obscured his lack of theoretical rigor and made him "the point of connection between all the rebels and dissidents who were organizing themselves at that period in order to overthrow the existing order."[49] Thus, fascism arose from the dissident movement of right and left elements fusing aspects of collectivism, individualism, nationalism, and syndicalism into a kind of aestheticized politics of power, elitism, and authority.

The Red Week and Its Fallout

In 1914, Sorel advanced Croce's slogan, "Socialism is dead," after declaring class an abstraction.[50] Later in the year, the prime minister of Italy Giovanni Giolitti enacted reforms that conceded to some moderate reformist demands of left-leaning syndicalists. Syndicalist leaders refused to relinquish their demands, leading to a general strike and a mass insurrection, but the state cracked down and the "Red Week" was suppressed.[51] The outbreak of apparently

---

49   Sternhell, *The Birth of Fascist Ideology*, 236.

50   Georges Sorel, "Materials for a Theory of the Proletariat," 227; see also Sternhell, *The Birth of Fascist Ideology*, 77.

51   Although anarchists like Errico Malatesta sincerely believed in the strike's potential, the syndicalist leaders Alceste de Ambris and Filippo Corridoni seemed more interested in enhancing the strike's "psychological value," escalating the tensions in society in order to build long-term power by

Sorelian violence brought an instant excitement to the revolutionary syndicalist ideal but left many further disillusioned with what was viewed as either premature measures of anarchists or the selling-out of spontaneous revolution by syndicalist leaders. Following the failed revolution, many syndicalists came to believe that the vital struggle of the proletariat should take a mythic national form against materialism.

For national syndicalists breaking away from the Italian Syndicalist Union, the violence of revolution had to be tested in "national war" before it could be used effectively against the bourgeois state. For Mussolini, these movements were advantageous but somewhat beyond his peculiar brand of socialism and its rural focus.[52] At first, Mussolini seemed, as usual, equivocal about whether or not to support the war (or even nationalism). He had risen to the head of leading socialist journal *Avanti!* more through his charismatic personality than his theoretical acumen. In 1914, Italian nationalist Enrico Corradini formed the Fascio Rivoluzionario d'Azione Internazionalista with other syndicalists seeking to enter the war. The "international" was dropped from their name soon after, and Mussolini rose to the head of the ensuing group, Fasci d'Azione Rivoluzionaria, in January 1915 after his expulsion from the Socialist Party. He was, by the end of the year, writing about "Fascism" (in quotations); it remains important to note, however, that "Fascism" described a movement that Mussolini neither started nor perhaps even led. It was more deeply connected to the ideas and actions of intellectuals, nationalists, and syndicalists discussed above.

---

exploiting spontaneous popular revolution. See David D. Roberts, *The Syndicalist Tradition and Italian Fascism* (Manchester: Manchester University Press, 1979), 74.

52   Recognizing the differences between the sharecroppers, day laborers, and landowners, in his early years Mussolini organized campaigns for day laborers, promising sharecroppers that their opportunity would come during the "greatest bloodbath of all"—the revolution. Benito Mussolini, *Opera Omnia*, 5:69; Renzo Felice, *Mussolini*, vol. 1 (Turin: Einaudi, 1965), 56–57; This experience would pay off in 1919 during the Blackshirt campaign in the Po Valley; see Robert O. Paxton, *Anatomy of Fascism* (New York: Vintage Books, 2005), 60–63.

The *Squadristi* Are Born

The cataclysm of World War I transformed the face of Europe. In Italy, Mussolini's Fascists took credit for the victory and Austria's subsequent granting of Southern Tyrol to Italy through the Treaty of Versailles (although they argued it was not enough). A triumphant Mussolini called for a "trenchocracy" made up of veterans to sweep out the technocrats and career politicians in order to make way for a strong state created by the "new man": an antiegoist elitist who represented, nevertheless, the perfect balance between full individual and collective. The true enemy was not necessarily aristocracy anymore, since the trenchocracy could fill their shoes. Instead, the enemy became the "parasitic" rulers and workers who would not fit into the producerist ethos.[53]

A series of factory occupations and strikes brought on the "two red years" (*biennio rosso*) of 1919–1920. By this point, the Sorelian influence had died down, and syndicalists professed a more rationalist model. Mussolini in particular called alternately for workers to model themselves on the French Confédération générale du travail (General Confederation of Labor) and the national councils developed by Kurt Eisner's Bavarian revolution.[54] Amidst the revolutionary tumult, Mussolini joined some hundred other revolutionary syndicalists, futurists, and corporatists in founding the Fasci Italiani di Combattimento (FIC—Italian Fasci of Combat). The FIC got its strength from a loosely knit group of spontaneously formed paramilitary organizations of anticommunist street fighters called the Squadre d'Azione, or the *squadristi*—more widely known as Blackshirts. Their expressed purpose was defending the "national community" (businesses and landowners) from "Bolshevik" worker militancy.

The chief organizer of the squadristi was Roberto Farinacci, who had built up his reputation through the early revolutionary

---

53   Robert Wohl, *The Generation of 1914* (Cambridge, MA: Harvard University Press, 1979), 173.

54   Benito Mussolini, *Opera Omnia*, 8:18; also see Franklin Hugh Adler, *Italian Industrialists from Liberalism to Fascism: The Political Development of the Industrial Bourgeoisie, 1906–1934* (Cambridge: Cambridge University Press, 1995), 132–33; and Roberts, *The Syndicalist Tradition and Italian Fascism*, 76–77.

syndicalist years as a violent anti-Semite. Those who formed *fasci*, or networked political organizations, would also form squadristi, and vice versa, rapidly bringing Fascism a fighting force to attack leftists (and even, to a lesser extent, Catholics and nationalists) in the streets and meeting spaces. The squadristi also developed a broad organizational capacity to absorb disenfranchised members of the public, growing with the help and support of veterans and officers, as well as a "grassroots" orientation through which its members elected their own commanders. Structured in this grassroots way, the squadristi became the bane of existence for leftists and intellectuals who disagreed with Fascism. Villages that supported the left were raided, and revenge attacks became justification for an increasing spiral of vigilantism.

On April 15, 1919, less than a month after the founding of the FIC, a mass rally occurred as part of a one-day general strike. Fascist army veterans attacked workers on their way to the rally, leaving three dead and many times that wounded. The mob, led by Marinetti, then advanced on Mussolini's former journal *Avanti!*, which was ransacked and set ablaze. The group stole the press's sign and brought it to Mussolini's new press, *Il Popolo d'Italia*, where he greeted them from the balcony and delivered a speech.[55]

That September, the ultranationalist adventurer and aesthete Gabriele D'Annunzio stormed into the Croatian city of Fiume with 2,000 irregular troops, claiming it for Italy. Scholar Ernst Nolte claims, "for Italy's younger generation, [D'Annunzio] was Nietzsche and Barrès all rolled into one."[56] Although it was rejected by Italy, D'Annunzio's irredentist, protofascist occupation of Fiume lasted for a year. The radical aesthetic and ideology of D'Annunzio drew in an assortment of revolutionary nationalists, imperialists, and leftists who rebelled against the established leaders of the Socialists, Communists, and Liberals. After he surrendered and returned to Italy, the Fascists lauded D'Annunzio as a hero, and his aesthetics influenced the movement profoundly. He emerged as a possible rival to Mussolini for power in the Fascist movement but decided to submit to the latter's authority.

---

55   Paul O'Brien, *Mussolini in the First World War: The Journalist, the Soldier, the Fascist* (New York: Bloomsbury, 2005), 28.

56   Nolte, *The Three Faces of Fascism*, 149.

The broad, overlapping space that attracted young radicals to D'Annunzio and the squadristi included the rejection of socialism as it existed in party form, faith in individual strength and purpose akin to the "cult of myself," sacralized politics, misogyny, and the nihilist's rejection of the modern in exchange for the radical desire for a "new age." In less than two years, the movement grew from 31 to 834 fasci; from 870 members to nearly 250,000.[57] Among the infamous calling cards of the squadristi were their black uniforms, daggers, black flags—sometimes emblazoned with the skull and crossbones or death's head (*teschio*)—their rallying songs, like "Me Ne Frego" ("I Don't Care"), and Farinacci's torture tactic of choice: forcing subjects to drink castor oil.

While factory occupations raged on, Mussolini declared, "I accept not only workers' control of factories, but also the social, cooperative, management [of industry] … I want industrial production to rise. If the workers could guarantee this rather than the owners, I should be ready to declare that the former have the right to take the latter's place."[58] Mussolini's platitudes included not only workers' self-management but also republicanism, individualism, and anticlericalism. In one exclamation in 1920, Il Duce raved, "Down with the state in all its species and incarnations. The state of yesterday, of today, of tomorrow. The bourgeois state and the socialist. For those of us, the doomed (*morituri*) of individualism, through the darkness of the present and the gloom of tomorrow, all that remains is the by-now-absurd, but ever consoling, religion of anarchy!"[59] Fascism was described, then, in terms approximating a different kind of nation, overcoming anarchy and the left by perfecting them and leading them toward the fulfillment of humanity's spiritual mission. What remained was an elite order of veterans whose confidence and will could lead the country into a new age of national renewal. For these elites, anarchism remained presupposed in a spiritual sense, while the requirements of national unity implied a different political movement beyond the contradictions of anarchism and the state, beyond left and right.

---

57   Alexander J. De Grand, *Italian Fascism: Its Origins and Development* (Lincoln: University of Nebraska Press, 2000), 30.

58   Benito Mussolini, quoted in Weber, *Varieties of Fascism*, 27.

59   Mussolini, *Opera Omnia*, 14:398.

Fascism in Power

Due to the behavior of the squadristi during the "two red years," Mussolini had been unable to gain a credible following in the syndicalist movement. However, in 1921, Edmondo Rossoni left the third largest trade union organization, Unione Italiana del Lavoro, to set up the Confederation of Fascist Trade Unions. In the elections of that year, the Fascists' undeniable power led to their admission into the National Coalition led by the aging liberal Prime Minister Giolitti, who believed he could contain them.[60] Thirty-five Fascist deputies were elected—enough to destroy Giolitti's government from within, leading to a new government led by Ivanoe Bonomi, who brokered a deal between Fascists, Socialists, and syndicalist leaders. Having to contend with regional squadristi leaders, Mussolini dissolved and reconstituted the squadristi into a national militia, putting Farinacci in charge of the consolidation of the squadristi into a top-down organization.[61] Although Jews joined the Fascists in disproportionately high numbers, the movement grew increasingly anti-Semitic under the influences of Farinacci and leading ideologue Giovanni Preziosi.[62] Despite claims that Mussolini's party did not have strongly racist policies in the early years, its founding principles were explicitly imperialist and directed to nationalist chauvinism.

Fascists promised to subsume the revolutionary syndicalism of radical workers under a corporatist system with an overarching leadership council that advocated for a moderately better social wage for the "national community" while repressing autonomous leftist groups and creating an aesthetics of the "new man"—a modern and scientific actor, albeit mythical, powerful, and heroic, fusing politics, society, and economy into a grand, totalitarian project. By 1922, Mussolini's party was allied with trade unions numbering half a million members. Yet for all its *sindacalismo nazionale*, Fascism remained largely a movement of the lower middle

---

60   Emilio Gentile, "Fascism in Power: The Totalitarian Experiment," in Griffin and Feldman, eds., *Fascism*, 4:21.

61   Griffin, *The Nature of Fascism*, 66.

62   Peter Staudenmaier, "Antisemitic Intellectuals in Fascist Italy," in *Comparative Studies for a Global Perspective*, vol. 4, *Intellectual Antisemitism from a Global Perspective* (Würzburg: Königshausen & Neumann, 2016).

classes, for instance lawyers and journalists, backed by a large veterans' movement.

On October 22, 1922, Mussolini's squadristi executed a show of force, occupying numerous government posts in northern and central Italy while some other 30,000 Blackshirts marched on Rome. Though many abandoned the march as heavy rains fell, the demonstration presented the spectacle of public disorder and evoked the threat of civil war. King Victor Emmanuel III subsequently appointed Mussolini as the new prime minister, and Mussolini created a new government that included Liberals, Democrats, Nationalists, and the Catholic populist party, the Popolari—though Fascists rapidly engineered parliamentary legislation like the Acerbo Law that ushered in a broad Fascist majority. The liberals Croce and Pareto endorsed the regime, while the party utilized its new infrastructure to convert southern Italy into a Fascist area.[63] The influx of members into the party created complications, with breakaway factions centralizing their own "original fascism."[64]

Mussolini's party had achieved success but was seriously compromised. After the militia murdered a respected socialist deputy, Giacomo Matteotti, under orders from Mussolini's closest advisors, antifascist sentiment swept Europe, but the left could not advance because of complicated divisions between communists and socialists.[65] The Italian Communist Party's principle theorist, Antonio Gramsci, avoided joining an antifascist bloc of anarchists, liberals, and socialists, hoping that an armed working class would better fend off fascist squadristi without liberal or socialist leadership. Meanwhile, other important liberals and nationalists continued to support the Fascist regime.

In 1924, the Comintern released a statement that the era of capitalism in decay caused all noncommunist politics to become "more or less fascist."[66] This disastrous analysis brushed aside

---

63   Roger Eatwell, *Fascism: A History* (New York: Viking Books, 1996), 62–63.

64   Gentile, "Fascism in Power," 26.

65   Pier Paulo Battistelli and Piero Crociani, *Italian Blackshirt, 1935–1945* (Long Island City: Osprey Publishing, 2010), 5–6.

66   See J. Degras, "Comintern Debates over the Dangers Posed by Fascism," in Griffin and Feldman, eds., *Fascism*, 2:32–34.

fascism's autonomous character and enabled its further creep by polarizing the entire political field. By the end of 1926, the Fascists had moved more deeply toward totalitarian dictatorship, banning political opposition, censoring dissenting press, incorporating a cultural regime in strict conformity to the political line, and enfranchising a population policy based on what deputy Gaetano Zingali called the "famous demographic quintet" of nuptiality, fertility, mortality, emigration, and internal migration.[67] Emigration was curbed, internal migration controlled, and the domestic family encouraged as a part of the cultivation of a new society led by the "new man." Edmondo Rossini's Confederation of Fascist Trade Unions maintained the eleven recognized trade unions in Italy, all deprived of the legal right to strike.

Fascism's relation to crown and altar became increasingly conservative. Victor Emmanuel III remained king, and the institution of the monarchy was subsumed under an increasingly dogmatic Fascism that appealed to universality and eternal principles while suppressing dissent from all sides. Deploying his typically ambiguous rhetoric, Mussolini declared, "The fascist state lays full claim to an ethical character: it is Catholic, but it is fascist; even above all, exclusively, essentially fascist."[68] While many fascists were Catholic, others were atheists, and some were occultists who disliked the compromises of the Lateran Accords, repudiating Mussolini as a demagogue.

Fascism had shocked the world by attaining power in less than five years of formal existence and less than ten years of theoretical existence, yet it was hardly the unified doctrine that Mussolini hoped it would become. It achieved power by exploiting the disillusionment of workers with the leadership of the left and gaining the support of leading liberal and conservative figures like Croce and Giovanni Gentile. In particular, while drawing on disenfranchised members of the working class, Mussolini catered to the fears and anxieties of the lower middle classes and factory owners alike, promising protection from worker agitation while dazzling young intellectuals with thrilling rhetoric of anarchy, revolution,

---

67   Thorpe, *Pan-Germanism*, 213.

68   Mussolini, *Opera Omnia*, 24:89; see also Emilio Gentile, *Contro Cesare: cristianesimo e totalitarismo nell'epoca dei fascismi* (Milan: Giangiacomo Feltrinelli Editore, 2010), 203.

and war. To its young supporters, the legacy of the Risorgimento seemed to resound more with the marching boots of the squadristi than with the hollow echo of liberal politics. For Mussolini's supporters, Fascism offered them the chance of revolution without economic uncertainty, precariousness, and risk, and the ruling classes could hardly disagree. For those in government and behind corporate desks, it seemed wiser to invite the Fascists into the halls of power than suffer full-scale syndicalist revolution, and that is precisely what they did.

Interlude: Demonstration Effect

Groups across the North Atlantic took notice of Fascism's rapid rise and adopted parts of its ideology hoping for similar success. In 1923, the year after Mussolini took power, General Miguel Primo de Rivera overthrew the government of Spain and established a military dictatorship based on an admiration for Mussolini's movement, which he likened to a new spirituality. In the United States, industry saw the Fascists as a viable movement against the rights of labor. That year, the Commander of the American Legion told an audience of legionaries, "If ever needed, the American Legion stands ready to protect our country's institutions and ideals as the *Fascisti* dealt with the destructionists who menaced Italy!… Do not forget that the Fascisti are to Italy what the American Legion is to the United States."[69] The Du Pont fortune helped finance a paramilitary spin-off group from the American Legion called the Black Legion to brutally put down the socialist movement in the United States. With its membership running up to 30,000 people throughout the country, the Black Legion retained ties to the Ku Klux Klan and the American Liberty League, a front group for corporations to lobby for pro-industry goals in the United States and abroad.

Other paramilitary groups like the Austrian Heimwehr began to take fascist form, while new groups sprung up around Europe. In 1925, Sorel's formerly anarchist collaborator Georges Valois initiated the Faisceau des combattants et producteurs in France, proclaiming that "The intellectual father of fascism is Georges Sorel.…

---

69   John Patrick Diggins, *Mussolini and Fascism: The View from America* (Princeton: Princeton University Press, 2015), 206.

We are the inventors, and we were copied in Italy."[70] Two years later, university professor António de Oliveira Salazar took part in a coup d'état that established a military dictatorship in Portugal in 1926. He became the corporatist minister of finance influenced by Italian Fascism and assumed the office of prime minister six years later. Also in 1926, military leader Józef Piłsudski took power in Poland and established a corporatist nationalist state.

To the north, Finnish students spearheaded the Academic Karelia Society to call for a fascist irredentist movement against Soviet political and cultural influence, while Per Engdahl in Sweden launched the Fascist Struggle Organization. Eastern Europe developed significant fascist movements and influences as well, with Hungary's powerful military leader Gyula Gömbös allying himself with Mussolini. In 1927, an anti-Semitic professor launched Romania's notorious Legion of the Archangel Michael, which would grow through the sacralized political violence advocated by its magnetic young leader Corneliu Zelea Codreanu, and which expressed itself through bizarre self-mutilation and blood-drinking rituals as well as political assassinations and ethnic attacks. The English Labour Party politician Oswald Mosley soon moved to fascism, creating the British Union of Fascists in 1932, and the next year General Miguel's son José Antonio Primo de Rivera formed the Falange Española. The most important group that adopted fascism after Mussolini's March on Rome, however, was a small, radical-right populist party in the mostly Catholic, rural region of Bavaria. It was led by an assortment of cranks, conspiracy theorists, anti-Semites, and occultists. Called the German Workers' Party, or Deutsche Arbeiterpartei, it was later renamed as the German National Socialist Workers' Party, or Nationalsozialistische Deutsche Arbeiterpartei (NSDAP), nicknamed the "Nazi Party" by its detractors.

Unlike Italy, World War I ended in total loss for Germany. A naval mutiny turned into a revolutionary movement actuated by the proliferation of workers' councils throughout the country, which overwhelmed the kaiser's political order and forced him to abdicate. Rather than build horizontal systems of power sharing, the Social Democrats parlayed their influence in the council

---

70   Winock, *Nationalism, Anti-Semitism, and Fascism*, 180.

movement into a new republican government. The inchoate government remained weak, with revolutionary challenges from the newly formed Communist Party of Germany (KPD) led by Rosa Luxemburg and Karl Liebknecht, who rejected a parliamentary government in league with bourgeois liberals. The Social Democrats brokered a deal with paramilitary veterans' groups, the most important of which was the Freikorps, to stop the communists and secure governmental legitimacy.

In January 1919, the seasoned Freikorps, their helmets emblazoned with the swastika symbol, were deployed by the new government to put down an eleven-day strike and occupation, known as the Spartacist uprising and led by the KPD. Luxemburg and Liebknecht were arrested, interrogated, and brutally murdered. In Bavaria, workers' councils had solidified into a "Soviet Republic," which in April 1919 began to expropriate food and apartments for homeless people and turn factories over to the workers. On May 3, though, the Social Democrats sent the German army and Freikorps into Bavaria to topple the leftist experiment, prompting an orgy of paramilitary street violence involving some seven hundred summary executions, including those of communist leader Eugen Leviné and anarchist Gustav Landauer.

For the German Freikorps, World War I had not ended. The struggle against communism and democracy was its logical continuation: first to purge Germany of those leftists and Jews who had "stabbed it in the back" by overthrowing the government at the decisive moment, and then to mount the assault against France once again, returning Germany to her former glory. Led by well-trained Prussian army officers from the landed classes, the Freikorps stashed their weapons after the war and maintained "labor communities" where they would work together according to rank and drive away Polish migrant labor.[71] From their rural base, accentuating manly roots in blood and soil, the Freikorps attacked leftists, assassinated leftist leaders, fought the Polish army in border disputes, and maintained an aggressive war against liberal democracy even while supposedly under its command.

A national assembly was called in the wake of brutal counterrevolution, and in the newly created German republic (named after

---

71   Theweleit, *Male Fantasies*, vol. 2, 19.

Weimar, where the constitution was framed and signed) the Social Democrats appeared to dominate the political scene, alongside the "crypto-authoritarian" Catholic Zentrumspartei (Center Party), the Deutschnationale Volkspartei (National People's Party) close to General Paul von Hindenburg, and the Liberal Democrats.[72] In the first decade of the twentieth century, the National Liberal Party, once allied with Bismarck, comprised 47 percent of the Pan-German League, which Nuremberg prosecutor Franz Neumann called "the direct result of Germany's colonial policy and the direct ideological forerunner of the National Socialist party."[73] Without the empire and now divorced from the nationalists, the Liberals seemed purposeless and impotent. The Catholic Center Party, which held a traditional grudge against both the Nationals and the Liberals for religious repression, had little desire to aid their rivals. The German Social Democrats in a coalition government felt weakened in their charge to bring about socialism, and the Communist Party militated against them in elections and the streets. Meanwhile, right-wing nationalists saw the succession of the Social Democrats as an indication of the tacit success of the November Revolution and the Bolshevization of Germany.

The Conservative Revolution

A plethora of war veterans like Hermann Goering, Erich Ludendorff, and Hermann Ehrhardt emerged as national heroes, and a new, fighting sense of German ultranationalism grew around the writings of "conservative revolutionaries" (also called "neoconservatives") like Ernst Jünger. With prose evocative of a modern men's rights activist, Jünger merged his male gaze with both his weapon and the penetration of women: "I plunge my gaze into the eyes of passing women, fleeting and penetrating as a pistol shot, and rejoice when they are forced to smile."[74] In his writings, and the writings of numerous celebrated World War I heroes now participating in the Freikorps, women in general represent oblivion, forgetting, and

---

72   Payne, *A History of Fascism*, 164.

73   Franz Neumann, *Behemoth: The Structure and Practice of National Socialism, 1933–1945* (Chicago: Ivan R Dee, 2009), 206–7.

74   Ernst Jünger, quoted in Theweleit, vol. 2, 38.

abandonment. Proletarian women, in particular, are seen as bestial, communist, dirty, insensitive, and threatening to the men of the Freikorps who inspired the Nazi ethos. Worse still is the presentation of Jews as Salome, Jezebel, and Judith. In these narratives, the threat of rape is ever present for innocent women, although the protagonists torture or kill leftist women without sexual interest.[75]

Jünger's accounts of the war, *The Storms of Steel* and *The Adventurous Heart*, waxed nostalgic about the heroism of the battlefield, the real arena of the "world spirit," while identifying the decline of civilization and something on the horizon—an oblivion, joined with the feminization of Weimar, that had to be overcome. This *Zivilisationskritik* (critique of civilization) became Jünger's trademark, along with a rejection of the Enlightenment in favor of something natural, which he called "deeper Enlightenment." He sought a romanticized "total mobilization" that would capture the spirits and the will of the workers of the nation in a singular industrial effort to bring catastrophe to the modern world and unseat liberal democracy from global power.[76]

"In times of sickness, of defeat, poisons become medicines," he wrote in *The Adventurous Heart*. "All men and things these days are thronging to a magic zero [*magischen nullpunkt*]. So it happens that the flame of new life comes to be; it happens that the flame delivers new life; it happens that you have a part of the flame of being."[77] The nihilist approach to the collapse of Weimar Germany is also a vision of a future resurgence of the real Germany, which Jünger's personal secretary Armin Mohler ascribes to the conservative revolutionary: "The essential core does not decay.... Our hope is placed...in what is left over."[78] This nihilism was echoed throughout the ideology of fascism and sought a total destruction of the present

---

75   Ibid., xi, 68.

76   Elliot Neaman, "Ernst Jünger's Millennium," in Griffin and Feldman, eds., *Fascism*, 3:377.

77   Ernst Jünger, *Das abenteuerliche Herz. Erste Fassung: Aufzeichnungen bei Tag und Nacht*, in *Sämtliche Werke*, vol. 9 (Stuttgart: Klett-Cotta, 1979), 116–17.

78   These lines are quoted in Armin Mohler's text on *The Conservative Revolution in Deutschland*, excerpted in Roger Griffin, ed., *Fascism* (Oxford: Oxford University Press, 1995), 352.

reality, a clearing out of the decadent and parasitic elements that corrupted everything, and a regenerative process that would finally produce something both historic and new—a kind of mythopoetic function of ancestral revival in the present moment.[79] Such a utopian idea was attached to the order of the new day, produced by a new man, represented by Jünger in later novels by the character of the Anarch, a paragon of human excellence based on Stirner's philosophy of the self.

The nihilist egoism popular among conservative revolutionaries spoke to a power vacuum that ostensibly existed within the unrepresented imperial ambitions of the Liberals, the disenfranchised traditionalism of the Catholics, the plebiscitary spirit of populism, and the nationalist return to blood and soil. Numerous reactionary political parties, broadly referred to as the "Patriotic Movement," formed to attempt to fill this gap, often working with conservative revolutionary veterans' groups and nationalist paramilitary outfits based in rural strongholds and carrying out campaigns against leftists and on the Polish border. Among these was the German Workers Party. In 1919, the army sent a failed artist and former army corporal named Adolf Hitler to keep tabs on the party. He would embrace the party as his own, taking a leadership role and changing the name to the German National Socialist Workers' Party. Hitler proposed a totalitarian solution to Germany's woes that Jünger "not only anticipated but also welcomed," according to his admiring biographer Gerhard Loose.[80]

Despite Jünger's triumphal vision, Germany was struck by crisis. The government attempted to dissolve the Freikorps, which responded by marching on Berlin. The putsch attempt was named after a civil servant named Wolfgang Kapp and was joined by Ludendorff, Ehrhardt, and Waldemar Pabst, the man responsible for the killing of Rosa Luxemburg and Karl Liebknecht. After the military refused to act against the putsch, the government fled Berlin and called a general strike, which led to the end of the coup attempt. However, the general strike turned into an armed uprising, and militant workers in the industrial Ruhr region formed a Red Army, putting the government there under worker control.

79   Griffin, *The Nature of Fascism*, 104.
80   Gerhard Loose, *Ernst Jünger* (New York: Twayne Publishers, 1974), 40.

Although they had refused to move against the Kapp putsch, the military joined the Freikorps against the Red Army of the Ruhr, killing and torturing hundreds of people. The leftists fought back bravely, declaring "*No atrocities, no revenge, no punishment; only love for humanity and justice!*" But the uprising of workers' and soldiers' councils ended in bloody oppression.[81]

Ensuing economic destabilization compelled the Weimar government to ask France for a delay in payment of war reparations, but Germany was instead met with a coordinated occupation of the Ruhr by the French and Belgian armies in 1922. The Social Democrats and trade unions responded to the occupation with "passive resistance," and the French authorities expelled 100,000 unionists and state officials, along with their families.[82] The Ruhr crisis and the ensuing political crisis with France created a political opportunity.

Hitler seized on the model of Mussolini's fascism, its populist pageantry, and the showmanship demonstrated in that year's March on Rome. On the eve of November 8, 1923, Hitler proclaimed a "national revolution" at a crowded meeting in a beer hall in Munich, leading General Ludendorff and other paramilitary members of the "Patriotic Movement" in an abortive putsch attempt on the government of Bavaria.[83] Though the sardonically named "Beer Hall Putsch" in Munich failed, his ensuing trial gave Hitler an important public platform to espouse his anti-Semitic beliefs. During his light jail sentence, he dictated his political manifesto, *Mein Kampf,* to his deputy Rudolf Hess.

The Nazi "Left" and the Völkisch Movement

While Hitler served his time in prison, the Nazi Party faced a temporary ban, and Nazi organizer Gregor Strasser joined with

---

81   "Declaration by the Red Ruhr Army, March 20, 1920," in *All Power to the Councils: A Documentary History of the German Revolution, 1918–1920*, ed. Gabriel Kuhn (Oakland: PM Press, 2012), 268. Emphasis in the text.

82   Walter A. McDougall, *France's Rhineland Policy, 1914–1924: The Last Bid for a Balance of Power in Europe* (Princeton: Princeton University Press, 2015), 269–76.

83   See Harold J. Gordon, *Hitler and the Beer Hall Putsch* (Princeton: Princeton University Press, 1972), 57–58.

his brother Otto Strasser and ideologue Artur Dinter to produce a renewed völkisch movement. At the same time, the Communist Party and the Social Democrats recognized at last the threat of fascism controlling the streets through paramilitary force and organized to stop them. The descendants of the Red Army of the Ruhr were the Red Front Fighters' Alliance, or Roter Frontkämpferbundes (RFB). Established in 1924, the year after the Beer Hall Putsch, the RFB provided among the most effective defensive presences against fascist attacks on leftist meetings and marches, as well as an aggressive paramilitary force to break up fascist meetings. The Social Democrats also developed a paramilitary group along similar lines called the Reichsbanner, which grew to around a million members. These antifascist groups would prove difficult obstacles for the maneuvers of the fascist völkisch movement. As in Italy, they shared similar traits with the fascist movement, like ecological considerations, but with Hitler out of the way and with the Nazi Party banned, its ideological solidity faded away. It became easier for other parties to effectively attract people who might otherwise look to the Nazis.

Although the Strasser brothers organized the industrial workers of the north, rather than the agrarian conservatives of the south, their movement advocated neither capitalism nor Marxism, but something else—a society organized "without masters," in a natural hierarchy based on merit and an organic integration of syndicates and corporations bringing the nations of Europe into a new United States of Europe. The imagined "natural hierarchy" took the form of a necessary meritocracy and work ethic, which rejected bureaucratic and administrative "masters" in exchange for solidarity between workers and leaders. Joining ecology and peasant movements to proletarian revolution, the Strassers' work "flew the black flag of the postmedieval Peasants' Wars." Here, they mirrored the 1923 book *Das Dritte Reich* (*The Third Reich*) written by conservative revolutionary Arthur Moeller van den Bruck.[84] In Moeller's book, originally titled *The Third Way*, the insurgent völkisch ideology manifested the same "Third Force" of spiritual authenticity present within the German Protestant tradition, which stood as the

---

84   Kurt Tauber, *Beyond Eagle and Swastika: German Nationalism Since 1945*, vol. 1 (Middletown: Wesleyan University Press, 1967), 109.

solution for the problems of the modern world.[85] Like many other members of the völkisch and "conservative revolutionary" movement that helped foster an amenable environment for the rise of National Socialism, Moeller also called for a Nietzschean superman to unite Germans in a spiritual collective that would overcome political divisions of right and left through a social revolution.

One example of the intellectual milieu in which the left and right could strangely coexist was "National Bolshevism." After the Russian Civil War, "émigrés from the White Army" moved to Germany, forging an ultranationalist sense of anticommunist unity between the countries. Some sought to unite with the Nazis to "liberate" their homeland. At the same time, some of the former top brass in the White Army adopted a semblance of socialism in the belief that state communism would eventually turn toward nationalism. Nikolai Ustryalov, for example, recognized the positive national contributions of the Bolsheviks and hoped that they would abandon internationalism in favor of a strong nationalist political economy—a kind of "national-bolshevism."[86]

In turn, German fascists created the Association for the Study of Russian Planned Economy (ARPLAN), a sort of think tank devoted to understanding the Soviet Five-Year Plan and its possible relevance for Germany. The ARPLAN National Bolshevik group boasted a right-left ideology and network inclusive of communists like Hungarian revolutionary Georg Lukács. It was also joined by Jünger, Ernst Niekisch, and conservative revolutionary Friedrich Hielscher, all of whom envisioned a Eurasian cooperation stretching from Russia's frigid Pacific coast to the windswept beaches of Portugal. To some in the Soviet Union, their commitment to revolution seemed deeper than the revisionist Social Democrats—in spite of a nationalistic fervor that contrasted with the Communist Party's avowed internationalism.[87] The year after Hitler was incarcerated for the Beer Hall Putsch, several top Bolsheviks initiated a movement toward a kind of völkisch fascism that they thought could transcend politics. Nikolai Bukharin told the Twelfth Congress of the Russian Communist Party that the NSDAP had

---

85   Mosse, *The Fascist Revolution*, 8–9.

86   Shenfield, *Russian Fascism*, 35.

87   Eatwell, *Fascism: A History*, 125.

"inherited Bolshevik political culture exactly as Italian Fascism had done."[88] Later that year, on June 20, Karl Radek advised the Comintern Executive Committee to scout out common ground between the rank and file in Communist and Nazi groups.

However, the National Bolsheviks were in the minority. The Comintern officially declared that fascism represented "the old game of the bourgeois left parties, i.e. it appeals to the proletariat for civil peace…by forming trade unions of industrial and agricultural workers, which it then leads into practical collaboration with the employers' organizations."[89] Reeling from their failure to carry out a revolution, the KPD organized to confront the rise of fascism through parliamentary means. Yet Trotsky warned the KPD not to take fascism too seriously and to organize instead against the specter of social democratic collaboration with the bourgeoisie.[90] If Trotsky's stance was understandable given the role of the Freikorps, it mistakenly saw fascism as a servant of the ruling class, rather than a uniquely revolutionary and oppositional collaboration between right and left with an astonishing capacity to exploit conditions of despair, anxiety, and disenfranchisement. It was fascism, not social democracy, that represented a new stage of political crisis for the KPD, anarchists, and social democrats alike. Although Trotsky would later amend his analysis to a more reasonable claim that fascism represented a form of populist, cross-class alliance that served the interests of capital but was not beholden to it, the KPD would continue to attempt to exploit the rise of fascism to their ends against the social democrats, rather than organizing to stifle it. Their equivocal estimation of the Nazi threat, along with the Social Democrats' role in aiding the Freikorps, would sabotage their own militant antifascist campaigns in the streets.

---

88   Nikolai Bukharin, quoted in Payne, *A History of Fascism*, 126.

89   Comintern, quoted in Renton, *Fascism: Theory and Practice*, 56.

90   The KPD's leading theorist until his expulsion from the party, August Thalheimer, went further to identify fascism as a form of right-wing populism based on the "autonomization of the executive power"—a popular dictatorship akin to Bonapartism that should be opposed in its own right. August Thalheimer, "On Fascism," in *Marxists in Face of Fascism*, ed. David Beetham (Manchester: Manchester University Press, 1983), 189.

As ideological splits and confusion over how to deal with fascism emerged, the Nazis attempted to build a mass base through other völkisch, national socialist parties like the National Socialist Pan-German Freedom Movement and the National Socialist Freedom Party. At this point, Gregor Strasser and General Ludendorff were elected to local office, and the former was voted into the Reichstag.[91] Völkisch nationalism became an ideological crossover point between neoconservatives and fascists involving detailed discussions on the intricacies of national policy, corporatism, and national dictatorship. With the refounding of the Nazi Party in 1925, most of the national socialist part of the völkisch movement abandoned the cultural approach and returned to Hitler's political leadership.

Rejoining as a "colleague" rather than a "follower" of Hitler, Strasser firmed up his "socialist" doctrine in a draft program for a projected *Arbeitsgemeinschaft* of the NSDAP (AG), a workers' movement within the Party. The draft relied on a basic völkisch national socialism, proposing a national dictatorship over a hierarchical corporatist state that catered to the petite bourgeoisie over landless farmers and industrial workers.[92] According to the draft's proposals, Jews who immigrated to Germany after 1919 were to be deported, and all who remained were to be deprived of citizenship. For Germans, the party would break up large landholdings to better the share of small farmers and would set up a fascist-corporative state with corporate bosses embedded in guilds and syndicates that remained beholden to "national solidarity." It was similar to the "social monarchism" of Drumont and Barrès or Maurras's "national integralism." The traditional sovereign had been replaced by the figure of the modern dictator, a man of action and the people, but he remained the sovereign nevertheless.

Hitler Regains Control

For his part, Hitler condemned the völkisch movement as a half-measure. After a conference in Bamberg in which he asserted his leadership, the party was brought into line and a Führer cult

---

91   Peter Stachura, *Gregor Strasser and the Rise of Nazism* (New York: Routledge, 2015), 35.

92   Ibid., 47–48.

was implemented. The Strassers maintained popularity, but membership in their urban, working-class areas was small compared to rural areas like Schleswig-Holstein where Hitler's Bavarian pseudo-conservatism found an important radical base. To ease the transition, Hitler brought Gregor Strasser into the position of second in command and escalated the party's propaganda onslaught through massive rituals and ceremonies that built a sense of collective emotional unity. The Nazi Party built an electoral strategy ostensibly to gain power but motivated more by a destructive opposition to the Republic itself. In Strasser's words, "we are pursuing a policy of catastrophe because only catastrophe, that is, the collapse of the liberal system, will clear the way for those new tasks which we National Socialists name...every strike, every governmental crisis, every erosion of state power, every weakening of the System...is good, very good for us, in order to expedite the death of this System."[93]

To defend their meetings and control the streets, Joseph Goebbels and Strasser launched a massive propaganda campaign in support of the brutality of the Sturmabteilung (SA), the party's "Storm Troopers" paramilitary outfit. Organized by World War I veteran Ernst Röhm, who had joined the Nazi Party before Hitler and achieved the status of major power broker within the larger Patriotic Movement, the SA was perhaps the most visible and controversial aspect of the Nazi Party. The Nazis' militancy was aided in no small part by the German army: their newspaper, the *Völkischer Beobachter*, was purchased in part with the financial assistance of the army; key army figures like Ludendorff supported the Nazis; and the army gave the SA arms as volunteer corps. Although the army officially banned Nazis from enlisting and participating in military exercises, the Nazis continued to infiltrate it and played an increasingly important role in the radical-right Patriotic Movement's rallies. Nevertheless, the Nazis remained a relatively fringe, extremist branch of the radical right, with the army's main support firmly behind the traditional conservative Hindenburg.

This changed as the Great Depression swept the world in 1929. NSDAP membership rolls swelled with the new unemployed—now some 40 percent of the population. The SA's working-class rhetoric and camaraderie brought in new recruits, who were also

---

93   Ibid., 76.

attracted by the numerous "Storm Centers," bunkhouses for young men without a home. Providing free room and board, Storm Centers also lent recruits a goal, an ideology inspired by strength, and an outlet for their violent sense of indignation and disenfranchisement. To young militants eager to smash somebody's face or belt out a boisterous song over tall *masskrugs* of lager, Storm Centers became the sites of an ongoing party atmosphere, not unlike neo-Nazi skinhead "rat holes" that would develop fifty years later. Violence against Jews, socialists, and communists deemed responsible for the financial chaos escalated severely as the SA became a hub for a young generation that had not experienced war but looked up to the war veterans of the Patriotic Movement.[94]

Rumors swirled around the SA and their leader Röhm—it was widely known that he was gay and stacked the group's all-male hierarchy with his sexual favorites. Calling himself the *Hochverräter*, or "high traitor," Röhm built up a kind of brutal celebrity that Adorno describes as "characterized, above all, by a penchant for 'tolerated excesses' of all kinds," namely demonstrating masculine toughness.[95] A stocky, confident man scarred by the war (the bridge of his nose had been blasted off), Röhm struck an imposing figure of martial invincibility and power. To maintain this toughness, introspection wasn't allowed, and human concern, if it was permitted at all, was held in utter contempt. The inner horror that such repression and humiliation fostered could only be projected onto out-groups—in particular, women, communists, and other people who "couldn't take it," and therefore could not be tolerated. To be part of the SA, one need only believe that man and truth found their sacred union in Nazism. Little else was needed because, as Hitler put it, "One can die only for an idea which one does not understand."

As the Nazi Party's membership soared, the Social Democrats lost power in the Reichstag, and the new conservative government banned the Communist Party's Roter Frontkämpferbundes. While members of the RFB continued to fight illegally, establishing the Kampfbund Gegen den Faschismus (Fighting-Alliance Against Fascism) the next year, their role in the antifascist struggle

---

94 Otis C. Mitchell, *Hitler's Stormtroopers and the Attack on the German Republic, 1919–1933* (Jefferson, NC: McFarland & Company, 2008), 123–24.
95 Adorno et al., *The Authoritarian Personality*, 763.

dwindled significantly. After the banning of the RFB, the Social Democrats' Reichsbanner continued along with the International-er Sozialistischer Kampfbund (ISK), which had been created by a Jewish philosopher named Leonard Nelson and included dissidents expelled by the KPD and SPD. Although the ISK received the sup-port of intellectuals like Albert Einstein and remained a bold effort, its relative isolation from the broader institutions of the left hindered its broader antifascist goals, and its awkward mix of libertarian and authoritarian ideas ensured its relegation to the margins.[96] Hence, numerous Germans on the heels of the failed Spartacist uprising in 1919 and the Red Army of the Ruhr in 1920 engaged in the strug-gle against fascism following the shock of the Beer Hall Putsch—perhaps enough to produce a viable revolutionary movement. But the conflicts within and between the parties themselves reversed their potential at precisely the moment when the Nazis came to dominate the Patriotic Movement.

Power Struggle

As the financial meltdown persisted, the votes for the Nazi Party jumped from 2.6 to 18.3 percent, but the Communist Party gained votes as well.[97] Seen as radicals who would also work with business, the Nazis could gain ground by winning the allegiance of liberal politicians and the networks they brought with them. One of these was Hjalmar Schacht, who resigned as head of the Reichsbank in 1930 and within the year was meeting with Hitler. He would later be described in the Nazi press as "the man who made the recon-struction of the Wehrmacht [German army] economically possi-ble."[98] Other financial interests—Deutsche Bank, Dresdener Bank, Deutsche Kredit Gesellschaft, and the insurance giant, Allianz—invested in the Nazis, while Heinrich Himmler, Reichsführer of Hitler's personal secret service, the Schutzstaffel (SS), organized a group of peculiar businessmen into the Circle of Friends of the

---

96   Peter G. J. Pulzer, *Jews and the German State: The Political History of a Minority, 1848–1933* (Detroit: Wayne State University, 2003), 320.

97   Renton, *Fascism: Theory and Practice*, 131.

98   *Militaer-Wochenblatt*, January 22, 1937. Quoted in William L. Shirer, *The Rise and Fall of the Third Reich* (New York: Simon and Schuster, 2011), 230.

Economy to promote business support for the Nazi Party. As the Nazis' financial clout grew, so did their sway with the military.

Otto Strasser opposed this corporate advance and was expelled from the party in 1930 for supporting workers' strikes. He created a new group called the Union of Revolutionary National Socialists, also called the Black Front and the Freedom Front, to subvert the Hitlerite faction, but the organization stagnated compared to the successes of the Nazi Party. Although infiltrated and inconsequential in its day, the Black Front would go on to become an important facet of the Nazi mystique for those searching for a redeeming history of Nazism after the war. In the meantime, the KPD altered its position on fascism to be increasingly amenable, viewing a Nazi regime as preferable to the Social Democrats. "First Hitler, Then Us!" became their slogan, and they agreed to collaborate with Hitler's party on certain combined strike efforts and later a vote of no confidence in the government of Franz von Papen. Both the Nazis and the Communists sought an end to Weimar and a revolutionary, new single-party dictatorship based on a mass movement purportedly in the interests of working people. After a dose of Hitler, the KPD believed, the German people would come to their senses. By July 1932, the KPD began to realize their errors and scrambled to create the Antifaschistische Aktion (AFA—Antifascist Action), but it was too little too late.

In the meantime, Gregor Strasser moved to a more moderate position. With Hitler playing the reactionary elites against one another, Strasser's violently anti-Semitic and racist ultranationalism joined with his contradictory economic ideas to place him in league with other reactionary and neoconservative leaders of the day. He began to call for a kind of "broad national front" (*Querfront*) to bring conservatives and reactionaries together in a coalition government under the army led by Kurt von Schleicher.[99] The Hitler cult had a challenge from the "moderates," but it would not last long.

Hitler attained power on the basis of collusion with, and manipulation of, other more established reactionary leaders. A combination of electoral success, parliamentary crises, and palm-greasing brought Hitler to the chancellorship over Germany on January

---

99   Stachura, *Gregor Strasser and the Rise of Nazism*, 10 and 95; Kershaw, *Hitler*, 397.

30, 1933, just over half a year after the creation of AFA, which the Nazis hastened to disband, moving quickly to shut down the Communist Party and shutter the leftist presses. The SA indulged themselves through brutal beatings of prominent politicians and union leaders, and the state police were taken over by an elite squad picked from the SA and Hitler's SS. According to the testimonies of a Prussian official named Hans Bernd Gisevius and the chief of the German General Staff, Franz Halder, at the Nuremberg trials, a plan was hatched by Goebbels and Goering to set the Reichstag ablaze, blame the communists, and issue a state of emergency.[100]

Although the story remains one of the most contested narratives in history, the strategy had an earlier theoretical precedent, at least in juridical form, in the work of Carl Schmitt. A prominent advisor to the Catholic Center Party, Schmitt had secretly worked with former conservative chancellor Franz von Papen as a proxy of the Nazi Party to secure their election in the Reichstag. According to Schmitt's formula, the sovereign exists by suspending the law, putting forward his own arbitrary rule as the condition through which the law can exist. Hence, only in establishing a "state of exception," wherein the law could be "suspended," could a sovereign establish the law as such under his own decision.[101] If the Reichstag fire was not set by the Nazis, it still enabled their creep to totalitarian power, as the outraged German people looked the other way while the Brownshirts smashed all opposition.

A huge state apparatus of oppression was set into motion as the Nazis began arresting, torturing, and incarcerating anarchists and members of the Communist and Social Democratic Parties, including those with seats in the Reichstag. In their last move before dissolving, the National Party and the Catholic Center granted Hitler dictatorial powers through a piece of legislation called the

---

100 The suspicious nature of the case and the trial is brought out by Benjamin Carter Hett in *Burning the Reichstag: An Investigation into the Third Reich's Enduring Mystery* (Oxford: Oxford University Press, 2014), 144–46. However, Hett's account is not without contestation among historians. For instance, see Richard J. Evans, "The Conspiracists," *London Review of Books* 36, no. 9 (May 8, 2014): 3–9.

101 On this subject, see Giorgio Agamben, *State of Exception* (New York: Verso, 2008).

Enabling Act, voted on in one of Berlin's opera houses after the
Reichstag fire. The Nazis hastily eliminated the autonomy of state
governments and placed authority under the central administration.
They then hosted a giant parade, proclaiming the slogan "Honor
work, respect the worker," and occupied the trade union offices the
next day, confiscating their funds and sending their leaders to dis-
mal concentration camps. Many would never again know freedom.

Within a year, stagnation on the labor front led to cries for a
"second revolution" issued from the SA and even Goebbels's propaganda machine. Department stores were raided, consistent with the
Nazi Party's initial pseudo-anticapitalist platform. Along with Jewish businesses, synagogues were ransacked and destroyed, while the
SA's leadership militated for a new popular army from the SA to replace the old martial class of the Reich. Rumors spread that Röhm
was meeting with reactionary politicians Schleicher and Heinrich
Brüning, as well as Gregor Strasser, to create a new cabinet under
a new chancellor.

According to his own account given to the Reichstag, Hitler held a meeting with Röhm that lasted five hours: "I informed
him that I had the impression from countless rumors and numerous declarations of faithful old party members and SA leaders that
conscienceless elements were preparing a national Bolshevist action
that could bring nothing but untold misfortune to Germany."[102] The
Prussian army establishment and Hitler decided that the only way
to retain the certainty of his place would be to dispose of the "second revolution." In the blood purge of June 29–July 2, 1934, also
known as the Röhm Purge and the Night of the Long Knives, the
SS murdered the leaders of the SA, along with former chancellor
Kurt von Schleicher and his wife in their home, Gregor Strasser,
former chancellor Franz von Papen's personal secretary, and scores
of other purported collaborators and accomplices, including Röhm
himself. Hitler thus secured the army's support through a bloodbath, slaughtering both the purported "left faction" and the reactionary opposition. Shortly after Hindenburg's death from old age,
the Reichstag gave Hitler the full powers of the presidency.

The rise of fascism was achieved through intrigue, betrayal,
and deceit. Ultranationalism and the leader cult were the grounds

---

102   Shirer, *The Rise and Fall of the Third Reich*, 193.

for manipulation of gullible opposition on the radical right, while Hitler exploited the weakness of moderates and developed convergences with radical elements of the left. Though the outcome of fascism is an overarching, powerful, and centralized state, its rise is typically attained through paramilitary fighting forces equipped to murder and assassinate, to break strikes and meetings, and to generally disenfranchise the organized left (Socialist parties, Communist parties, large unions and syndicates) from their radical base. Resistance was forced underground, and those who continued to struggle did so however they could—through clandestine publishing, sabotage, assisting the flight of refugees, forming secret syndicates and unions, even adhering to "degenerate" styles and music.

Deceit and Angst

Although fascism is generally typified by its "outcomes," it should instead be seen as a deceptive movement rarely forthright about its destination. People change as power changes them, and one can never know what the promises of one year will lead to in the next. However, as early as 1919, there were clear signs that Hitler fully intended to become a ruthless dictator. His sleight of hand had been to create a large gap between ideology and action, so that the former could attract idealists to the cause, while the latter could dispose of the unfaithful, leaving an apparently limitless horizon of possibilities within the movement. Both Hitler and Mussolini also positioned themselves prominently as people who respected the rules, despite persistently demonstrating their disregard for the law.

Even in the early 1920s, Mussolini characterized his party as one that could cooperate within the parliamentary system, and until 1935, he took a rather light hand in economic interventions, allowing instead a relatively free rein of big corporations. Italian Fascism in power was heavily supported by conservative and liberal elites, and under its rule, taxes on the rich were lowered, wages were cut, infant mortality increased, and food consumption fell. Their original left-wing rhetoric proved ludicrous as they settled into a largely conservative regime based on family, work, and patriotism.[103]

---

103   Emilio Gentile, "The Sacralization of Politics," in Griffin and Feldman, eds., *Fascism*, 3:40.

Meanwhile, from 1934 to 1936, Nazi Germany launched a totalitarian economic plan involving a massive and unwieldy bureaucracy that proved problematic for large industrialists and small businesses alike. Known as *Gleichschaltung*, which means coordination or consolidation, the system brought different sectors of culture and economy under the political control of the growing Nazi bureaucracy. The model involved sweeping financial reforms and increased production to boost the economy out of the Depression, but the key to Gleichschaltung did not simply lie in the ordering of labor and concentration camps in time and space. It actualized a "bringing into line" of the Volk's self-presentation and perception. Labor and recreation regimens toughened up men's bodies and minds for future war, while the imperative of satisfying men and tending to the tasks of motherhood remained a constant pressure on women.[104]

The psychology of fascism, and particularly Nazism, was and remains one of overwhelming angst from which some kind of collective catharsis might liberate the individual. As a release from the psychology of angst, youth-centered groups and programs became extremely important. Young Germans were sent for an extended time into the countryside to work in the fields and learn the proper völkisch philosophy outside of the classroom. A neurotic emphasis on hygiene also became critical, as the physician took the dominant aesthetic role in society. "Degenerate" or "unclean" art was banned and books were burned. Jewish people faced increasing terror at home and in the workplace, while the German Reich offered the working class the promise of cleaner, modernized factories in which to spend their hours. In 1935, the notorious Nuremberg racial laws were passed.

Jews could no longer be citizens of Nazi Germany, they no longer had rights, but the Nazis' popularity continued to rise. As the social programs vaunted the völkisch ideals of the German race, a leader cult developed around Hitler, and the Führer was compared to Martin Luther and even the Messiah sent by God.[105] Yet the Führer's grasp on power remained complicated. He had to contend with

---

104   Kiran Klaus Patel, *Soldiers of Labor: Labor Service in Nazi Germany and New Deal America, 1933–1945*, trans. Thomas Dunlap (Cambridge: Cambridge University Press, 2005), 224.

105   Griffin, *The Nature of Fascism*, 106.

different levels of autonomy maintained by other Nazi leaders, the party apparatus, the old officialdom of Weimar, the different regional and central hierarchies, the SS, and the Wehrmacht.[106]

Disunity

The emergence of fascism in Germany was not immediately embraced by Mussolini, because Hitler's militarism presented serious pragmatic geopolitical, cultural, and political challenges.[107] In 1934, shortly after Hitler took power, Italy brought together fascist and parafascist leaders from all over the world to appreciate a "universal fascism" at a conference in Montreux, Switzerland. It completely failed to unite fascists or even provide a basic platform, and the effects of fascist disunity were present almost immediately. When the Nazis threatened the sovereignty of Austrian fascists by assassinating Prime Minister Engelbert Dollfuss, the Austrofascists drew closer to Mussolini, and the Spanish Falangists supported the Rome-Vienna axis of "Southern Fascism," denouncing the machinations of Berlin.[108]

In Spain, fascist groups competed with one another within the country, alternately identifying themselves with or against fascism depending on the situation, while excommunicating and denouncing other fascist groups as not fascist enough. The leader of the Spanish Falangists, José Antonio Primo de Rivera, rejected the "fascistized right" represented by Calvo Sotelo.[109] Months later,

---

106   M. Rainer Lepsius, "The Model of Charismatic Leadership," in *Charisma and Fascism*, ed. António Costa Pinto, Roger Eatwell, and Stein Ugelvik Larsen (New York: Routledge, 2007), 50.

107   Kershaw, *Hitler*, 551.

108   Falange Española leader José Antonio Primo de Rivera went as far as to insist that "Hitlerism is not Fascism, it is anti-Fascism, the counterfigure of Fascism. Hitlerism is the consequence of democracy, and a turbulent expression of German Romanticism. Conversely, Mussolini is classicism, with his hierarchies, his following, and, above all, reason." Quoted in Stanley G. Payne, *Fascism in Spain: 1923–1977* (Madison: University of Wisconsin Press, 1999), 160.

109   Paul Preston, *The Politics of Revenge: Fascism and the Military in 20th Century Spain* (New York: Routledge, 2005), 24.

the leader of the Spanish National Syndicalists, Ramiro Ledesma Ramos, abandoned an alliance with the Falange (or was expelled), stating that the dissident communist party, Partido Obrero de Unificación Marxista (Marxist Unification Workers' Party), was more fascist than the right wing.[110] The Rome-Berlin axis developed finally in 1936, but even after the Anschluss, the unification of Austria with Germany in 1938, seminal members of the Austrian Nazi Party like Othmar Spann were thrown in concentration camps for diverging from the doctrine of Berlin.[111]

As Italian Fascists set their sights on the South of France, French fascists equivocated in their support, advocating instead a uniquely French form of fascism. Old French national rivalries with Germany were not conducive to positive relations with the Nazis.[112] In Italy, the Italian Fascists Roberto Farinacci and Julius Evola criticized Mussolini's dictatorship for not being fascist enough.[113] As fascism spread throughout Europe, territorial problems increased.

Along with Austrofascism, corporatist regimes were founded in Greece, Hungary, and Romania, while similar movements spread to Japan, South Africa, Argentina, and Brazil. In some ways, fascism's success exposed insuperable problems. Whether it was a pan-German Reich or the vision of a new Roman Empire stretching from the French Riviera to Albania, Greater Romania, the Hungarian "Great Carpathian-Danubian Fatherland," or even Japanese Manchuria, irredentist claims to broader imperial territories acted like bellows to the flame of fascism that was burning wildly out of control. Smaller nations calling for autonomy were engulfed in the grand schemes of inter-European conquest even as fascists declared themselves proponents of organic "national communalism."[114] Such ideological and geographic crises relat-

110   Payne, *Fascism in Spain*, 136–39.

111   Janek Wasserman, *Black Vienna: The Radical Right in the Red City, 1918–1938* (Ithaca: Cornell University Press, 2014), 105.

112   Robert Soucy, *French Fascism: The Second Wave, 1933–1939* (New Haven: Yale University Press, 1995), 244.

113   Andreas Umland, "Classification, Julius Evola and the Nature of Dugin's Ideology," in Griffin, Loh, and Umland, eds., *Fascism Past and Present, West and East*, 486.

114   This term was originally conceived by scholar John Breuilly and articulated

ed to nationalism have always undermined international fascist movements from within, as leftist movements struggle to put out the conflagration from the outside.

Corporations Pick Sides

In 1936, the Spanish Civil War began. Following the election of the Frente Popular (Popular Front), violence between fascists and antifascists came to a head, culminating in General Franco's invasion of Spain from Morocco. First to the defense of the republic were the anarchists, who formed militias and fought against an attempted coup in Barcelona that would have spelled a quick end to the war and their longed-for revolution. The anarchist CNT-FAI (Confederación Nacional del Trabajo–Federación Anarquista Ibérica / National Confederation of Labor–Iberian Anarchist Federation) developed powerful military forces alongside the Socialist and Communist parties, and the world watched as the left struggled valiantly against a looming military power that would have been impossible without significant assistance from anti-Semitic and opportunistic financiers and industrialists.[115] Much is made of George Orwell's criticism of totalitarian regimes and his participation in the fight against Franco, but as late as 1939, he maintained that the British Empire was as bad as the Nazis.[116] Britain and the United States did not support the Spanish Republican cause against Franco. Instead, large corporations sent aid to fuel the nationalists against the workers' movements, while the policy of appeasement proved a miserable failure.

Henry Ford became the leading international figure of the movement toward mass industrialism. Touted as the "Mussolini of Industry" by popular radio commentator H. V. Kaltenborn, Ford was called "the superman" by a Spanish newspaper, and the *Nation*

---

in Thorpe, *Pan-Germanism*, 22.

115   According to leftist scholar Daniel Guérin, heavy industry and big banks investing in fixed capital, machines, and raw materials played a large role in sustaining fascism, rather than see their factories turned over to workers; Daniel Guérin, *Marxism and Big Business* (New York: Pathfinder, 1974); Renton, *Fascism: Theory and Practice*, 81.

116   See Renton, *Fascism: Theory and Practice*, 86.

published an article titled "Henry Ford, Man or Superman?"[117] The image of Ford as the great superman relied on his strange brand of conservatism, patriotism, and traditionalism matched by pugnacious anti-Semitism.

German observers of the assembly line dubbed it "Fordism," and his biography, *My Life and Work*, was a best seller in Berlin.[118] Known for paying his workers above the average wage and pioneering the assembly-line factory model based on rigid order and cleanliness, Ford loathed unions. A company should be united like a country, with class collaboration as the driving motor, he believed. The workers should be treated well but should not have autonomous representation against the bosses. They had their own communities, their own stores, and their own newspaper, the *Dearborn Independent*, in which Ford inveighed from the editorial section against Jewish plots to conquer the world and undermine white, Western civilization. Ford's extreme anti-Semitic ideas were circulated in numerous propaganda pieces against Jews. One such work, *The International Jew*, purportedly held a spot on Hitler's desk.

During the Spanish Civil War, Ford joined US corporations GM, DuPont, Standard Oil, and Texaco to supply the forces of Franco against the Popular Front, which opposed the attempted coup. When German forces swarmed over Austria, the Sudetenland, and Poland from 1938 to 1939, they were transported in Ford- and GM-built vehicles.[119] While the Nazis mopped up in Austria, Ford received the Grand Cross of the Order of the German Eagle. According to a US Senate committee, GM contributed "an integral part of the Nazi war efforts," and "GM's plants in Germany built thousands of bomber and jet fighter propulsion

---

117   Edwin Dakin, "Henry Ford, Man or Superman?," *Nation*, March 26, 1921, 336–41.

118   Reynold M. Wik, *Henry Ford and Grass-Roots America* (Ann Arbor: University of Michigan Press, 1973), 4.

119   Ford and General Motors built "nearly 90 percent of the armored 'mule' 3-ton half-trucks and more than 70 percent of the Reich's medium and heavy-duty trucks…'the backbone of the German Army transportation system.'" US Congress, *The Industrial Reorganization Act: Hearings, Ninety-third Congress, First Session, on S 1167, Part 9* (Washington, DC: US Government Printing Office, 1974), A-22.

systems for the Luftwaffe at the same time that its American plants produced aircraft engines for the U.S. Army Air Corps."[120]

A director of the Morgan bank Guaranty Trust, Grayson Mallet-Prevost Murphy, received the Order of the Crown of Italy from Mussolini for his financial efforts securing loans. Murphy also helped finance the American Legion and was heavily involved in the American Liberty League. In one of the more incredible stories in US history, General Smedley Butler came before Congress to accuse the commander of the American Legion Department of Connecticut, Gerald MacGuire, of presenting checks from Murphy and other Wall Street financiers in exchange for Butler's promise to lead a group like the American Legion in a coup against Franklin Delano Roosevelt. Butler's testimony led to the formation of the House of Representatives' Special Committee on Un-American Activities Authorized to Investigate Nazi Propaganda and Certain Other Propaganda Activities. The committee brought no charges, however, and MacGuire died soon after at the ripe old age of thirty-seven.[121]

Other upper-echelon businessmen in the United States who invested in and aided fascist governments included future heads of the CIA and State Department, the Dulles brothers, Joseph Kennedy (father of JFK), and Prescott Bush (father of George Bush Sr.), as well as news media mogul, William Randolph Hearst, who publicized Hitler's "conquest of the hearts and minds of all classes of Germans."[122] In tandem with the Hearst empire, the National Association of Manufacturers' (NAM) propaganda arm also sang fascism's praises.

---

120   Ibid., A-17, A-142.

121   When the committee published its report, it redacted crucial aspects of the testimony, including insinuations that Du Pont would help provide weapons to the coup through its connections with the American Liberty League. Unfortunately, the two histories of this case do not call Butler's testimony into question and end up sounding like conspiracy theories. See Jules Archer, *The Plot to Seize the White House* (New York: Skyhorse Publishing, 2015) and Glen Yeadon, *The Nazi Hydra in America* (San Diego: Progressive Press, 2008).

122   Quote by William Randolph Hearst, quoted in Clifford Sharp, "How Strong Is Hitler?," *Readers' Digest* 23, no. 137 (1933): 44.

Populist Fascism in the United States

In addition to industrial and financial elites, with their supporters in groups like the American Legion and NAM, a strong populist base of support for fascism also existed in the United States. The Louisiana politician Huey Long drew comparisons to fascism after insisting on redistributing oil profits to his poor white constituency, although he was more of a run-of-the-mill populist. Nevertheless, after Long's assassination at the hands of the son of one of his numerous enemies, his Share the Wealth campaign was taken over by his associate, Gerald L. K. Smith, and brought into a coalition with fellow anti-Semite Father Charles Coughlin, whose radio audience reached some three million people during the height of the Depression. Smith and Coughlin both openly advocated for Nazi policies and against US intervention in World War II after the invasion of Poland in 1939.[123] Another preacher named Reverend Gerald Winrod, nicknamed the "Jayhawk Nazi," managed 100,000 subscriptions to his newspapers the *Defender* and the *Revealer*.[124]

By far the largest right-wing populist movement, the second assemblage of the Klan, organized around the slogan of "100 percent Americanism," attracted millions of members before a rapid decline in the late 1920s. In its wake, a large fascist group called the Silver Shirts emerged, led by a mystical protestant named William Dudley Pelley, who believed in levitation, telepathy, and British Israelism, a bizarre faith that claims English people as the true Israelites and Jews as the spawn of Satan. Anti-Semitic preacher William Bell Riley, the instigator of the modern anti-evolution movement, encouraged his congregation not to "shiver at the sight of a silver shirt."[125]

As Hitler's militarism ramped up, Nazi sympathizers built a mass anti-intervention movement and enlisted aviator Charles

---

123   Chip Berlet and Matthew Lyons, *Right-Wing Populism in America* (New York: The Guilford Press, 2000), 141–46.

124   Jeffrey Kaplan and Leonard Weinberg, *The Emergence of a Euro-American Radical Right* (New Brunswick, NJ: Rutgers University Press, 1998), 33.

125   William Vance Trollinger, *God's Empire: William Bell Riley and Midwestern Fundamentalism* (Madison: University of Wisconsin Press, 1990), 77.

Lindbergh as its spokesperson under the banner of "America First." In 1936, the son of textile magnate William Henry Regnery returned to the US from university in Hitler's Germany and joined the America First Committee. The next year, a different textile magnate named Wickliffe Draper founded the Pioneer Fund to promote eugenics in tandem with Nazi scientists, while encouraging the repatriation of nonwhites from the US. Between Regnery's ensuing Regnery Publishing and Draper's Pioneer Fund, the fabric of 1930s pro-eugenics "race realism" and academic racism would be woven into the later part of the twentieth century.

By the advent of World War II, however, unquestionably the most dominant, explicitly Nazi group in the United States was the German American Bund. In 1937, the *American* estimated the membership of the Bund at 250,000, noting that this included an unknown number of self-styled storm troopers, made up of "the combined remnants of the Ku Klux Klan, Gold Shirts, Silver Shirts, Black Legion, Silver Battalion, Pan-Aryan Alliance, and similar organizations."[126] These storm troopers wore the uniforms of the German SA and contained sections that trained youths in combat exercises at camp sites purchased by the Bund outside of major cities across the country, while their führer, Fritz Kühn, preached about the spiritual "rebirth of the German people."[127]

The Fall of the Reich

Fascism, in this original, global form eventually fell. Yet it did not fall entirely due to external pressures. Even pragmatic policy choices of finance and trade stood in the way of greater fascist unity and led to the beginning of the end of fascism in Europe. The Greek "Third Hellenic Civilization" supported Italy until its leader Ioannis Metaxas realized that arms deals would be better conducted through German industry.[128] Metaxas's favoritism toward Germany contributed to Italian resentment, leading in part to Italy's invasion

---

126   Joseph F. Dinneen, "An American Führer Organizes an Army," *American* 74, no. 2. (1937): 14–15.

127   Ibid., 157.

128   Mogens Pelt, "The 'Fourth of August' Regime in Greece," in Costa Pinto and Kallis, eds., *Rethinking Fascism and Dictatorship in Europe*, 200–14.

of Greece in 1941. When Italy failed to gain the upper hand, the
Nazis had to join the fight, bogging the Third Reich down in an
intermovement war that forestalled Hitler's invasion of the Soviet
Union, which then had to face winter conditions. When the United
States finally entered the war in December, the propaganda machine that had supported fascism retooled its rhetoric around anti-
communism and pushed forward into the war effort. The policies
of Japanese internment, not to mention using the nuclear bomb on
civilian targets, would reveal the extent to which US rejection of
fascism would not rule out employing similar methods.

The disastrous invasion of the Soviet Union and the entrance
of the United States into the war sealed the fate of the Third Reich and the fascist epoch. The German war machine increasingly relied on slave labor to fuel Germany's industrial productivity,
which expanded inexorably as millions perished on the frontlines.
The broad support enjoyed by the Nazi Party in 1940 diminished
apace. Italy was invaded and its southern portion occupied in 1943.
Hitler survived a conspiracy against his life in 1944 that sent the
already paranoid dictator into a grotesque spiral of anxiety. As the
processes that brought about the genocide of six million Jews and
millions of other political dissidents, Slavs, Poles, Roma and Sinti,
LGBQTI people, and disabled people were sped along by bureau-
crats like Adolf Eichmann, the Soviets and Allies converged on
Berlin, and the Reich was officially defeated by May 10, 1945,
at the cost of some twenty-one million military lives and thirty
million civilians.[129]

Fascism, a political ideology that began through the fusion of
left and right, had been an unmitigated disaster. Leftists drawn to
the early flames of fascism either converted or were annihilated—
usually both. Rightists too, like François de La Rocque of the paramilitary Croix de Feu, who flirted with fascism in the 1930s, often
found themselves burned. Even Valois, among the initial producers
of fascism, found himself fighting with the Resistance and perished
in a concentration camp. Conservative authoritarian dictators like
Francisco Franco, António de Oliveira Salazar, and Ion Antonescu
used the violence of fascism for their personal ends but eventually had to suppress fascist groups or risk winding up—like Hitler's

---

129   This estimated number includes China and Japan.

enablers—dead. Following the conflagration, the ruin of Europe, embers still burned among the fascist faithful, who hoped to ignite them anew, this time in purer form, uncorrupted and more elitist, violent, and sacrificial than ever. It is to these embers and their devout guardians, defenders of the "spiritual empire," that we will now turn.

CHAPTER 2: SPIRIT AND SUBCULTURE

Julius Evola and Sacralized Violence

Now that we have unearthed and attempted to reconstruct the rubble of the fascist nightmare, we can gain a better grasp on the workings of fascism and fascist ideology—how it justifies its existence and creeps within the margins of both right and left, seducing both sides with promises of a radical, revolutionary future where the opposing side would no longer exist. However, we have left a major concern untouched: the "occult" aspect of fascism that survived the war—its spiritual-sacred aspect that provided more than a passing curiosity for its leadership. The ideologies of Arthur Rosenberg, Heinrich Himmler, Julius Evola, and numerous other pseudo-intellectuals provided fascism with a kind of mystique that animated the rhetorical framework of right-left syncretism—visions of Nordic gods on earth, mythical Arctic-born superraces, archaic spiritual signs transcending both science and Judeo-Christian ethics, and cosmic spiritual oaths of samurai loyalty.

Perhaps the most influential of these elite spiritualists remaining after the war was Julius Evola. His followers were unique in that they wanted more than populism would offer; they wanted blood, sacrifice, and ultraviolence; they believed in and became a formidable cult of assassins and bombers bent on infiltrating the left and destroying its public reputation by heightening tensions and causing ever-grander spectacles of destruction and terror. According to future head of the fascist Movimento Sociale Italiano (MSI—Italian Social Movement), Giorgio Almirante, Evola could be compared to important leftist intellectuals and theorists: "[He was] our Marcuse, only better."[1] Evola had asserted as early as 1930 in his political review *La Torre*, "We would like a more radical Fascism, more fearless, a really absolute Fascism, made of pure force, impervious to any compromise."[2] Now he hoped to put that potential into action without Mussolini's bungling in the way. This Fascism would renounce the tendency to base political power on a mass movement, emphasizing instead an elite of warrior-aristocrats gaining spiritual power over Europe.

After participating in the Dadaist movement as a young man, Evola attached himself to the traditionalist René Guénon, who preached a spiritual doctrine based on his readings of Arab, Buddhist, and Hindu texts. Guénon denounced the materialism of Judeo-Christian ethics, as well as the warmongering nationalism of his era, preferring instead a return to nature and a sense of inner oneness. Like Hitlerite mystic Savitri Devi, Evola agreed with Guénon that the world had sunk into a dark age, a "Kali Yuga," due to the influence of its Judeo-Christian inheritance and the scientific faith in progress. Evola's spiritual fascism found its first prominent publication in *Ur*, a syncretic mixture of radical syndicalism, anti-Semitism, anticlericalism, and the occult. Following his run with *Ur*, Evola joined Guénon in editing a regular section in *Il Regime Fascista*, the periodical of Farinacci, one of the most vicious and ruthless Blackshirt leaders and a pioneer of Fascist racism in Italy.[3]

As with the occultists of the turn of the twentieth century, Evola looked to the misogynist author Otto Weininger for his theory of gender. For Weininger, women did not exist outside of their recognition by men. Women manifested a kind of "zero" point symbolized by an empty womb. A society dominated by supermen

1   See Julius Evola, "Il mito Marcuse," in *Gli uomini e le rovine* (Rome: Volpe, 1967), 263–69; Roger Griffin, "Revolts Against the Modern World: The Blend of Literary and Historical Fantasy in the Italian New Right," *Literature and History* 11, no.1 (Spring 1985): 101–24.

2   Julius Evola, "Cose a posto e parole chiare," *La Torre*, April 1, 1930.

3   Richard Drake, *The Revolutionary Mystique and Terrorism in Contemporary Italy* (Bloomington: Indian University Press, 1989), 119–20.

could not maintain a strong female identity; instead, women represented the wilderness, the purity of nonmeaning, an inclusiveness, and a passivity. For all that men embody—nobility, violence, order, and hardness—women become the opposite: namely, a soft, spiritual vessel that men fill with meaning.[4]

For Evola, civilization manifested the social repression of the human spirit and particularly the male individual's achievement of greatness. Greater than mass-based civilization, for Evola, was culture, which as he understood it could be carefully curated by elites to channel the energy of the masses toward destruction while leaving the higher echelon of spiritual warriors to play in the ashes. Evola declared himself an ardent reactionary, a counterrevolutionary utterly pessimistic about the concept of human progress. The superman Evola presented was aristocratic and sometimes anarchist. Evola embraced the egoist influence of Stirner through the idea of total freedom of the individual, aspiring to become an "absolute individual" who maintains a connection to the entire universe beyond the body. He agreed with Farinacci's critique of Mussolini as overly moderate and looked down on Mussolini's agreements with the Catholic Church.

According to Evolian racism, the Aryan race is the apogee of virtues like honor, fidelity, and courage. People of color could ascend to Aryanness only through spiritual and cultural practice. Nothing needed to be resisted more, in Evola's opinion, than the notion that Aryans are equal to nonwhites: "We go from the theoretical domain to the practical one, or to 'active racism,' whenever we take a position before the racial components of a given nation, refusing to acknowledge to all of them the same value, the same dignity, and the same right to impart the tone and form to the whole."[5] For Evola, "active racism" meant the defense of Aryan dignity by whatever means. Resenting the notion that he would have to share the same conditions with workers and non-Italians, he wrote, "the so-called improvement of social conditions should be regarded not as good but as evil."[6]

---

4   Kevin Coogan, *Dreamer of the Day: Francis Parker Yockey & the Postwar Fascist International* (New York: Autonomedia), 356–57.

5   Ibid., 257.

6   Julius Evola, *Men Among the Ruins*, trans. Guido Stucco, ed. Michael Moynihan (Rochester, VT: Inner Traditions, 2007), 166–67.

In 1937, the year before the notorious Italian racial laws, Evola wrote to the minister of popular culture that he had been engaged in a ten-year struggle "to give an anti-Semitic orientation to Fascist spirituality."[7] Although he heavily criticized Mussolini's populism, the official Partito Nazionale Fascista (National Fascist Party)'s 1938 racial laws were influenced by Evola's ideology, and his later doctrine on race was applauded by Mussolini himself. The year Evola's mission was accomplished, Farinacci, his cohort for *Il Regime Fascista*, was given a position in the Fascist Grand Council and charged with a ministerial post enforcing the racial laws.

Yet Evola would prefer to remain apart from political activism. "The activist world is also essentially a featureless and plebeian world, ruled by the demon of collectivism," Evola wrote in 1943. "It is not only the scene of triumph of what has been called 'the ideal animal,' but it is also a world…where action, force, strife, and even heroism and sacrifice are seen to become increasingly irrational, devoid of light, 'elemental,' and altogether earthly."[8] Although ultimately unavoidable for the "superman," political activism remained, for Evola, incapable of harnessing spiritual power and bending it to the will. Only a spiritual "doctrine of awakening" could accomplish that.

"As for the doctrines of the 'superman,' they are based on the reinforcement of the vital energies and of the 'I' such as will produce invincibility and superiority to all tragedy, to all misfortune, to all human weakness, a pure force that, though it may be bent, cannot be broken, a will to power that defies men and gods."[9] According to Evola, this Aryan superman first lived in Hyperborea, the Arctic center of human origins. Then Hyperboreans fell from grace, moving slowly southward and losing their icy transcendence. The further south the Hyperborean traveled, the more ape-like he

---

7   Letter from Evola to Dino Alfieri, September 1937, quoted in Dana
     Lloyd Thomas, *Julius Evola e la tentazione razzista* (Brindisi: Giordano,
     2006), 144. Also see Staudenmaier, "Antisemitic Intellectuals in Fascist
     Italy," in *Intellectual Antisemitism from a Global Perspective*, ed. Sarah K.
     Danielsson and Frank Jacob.

8   Julius Evola, *Doctrine of Awakening*, trans. H. E. Musson (Rochester, VT:
     Inner Traditions, 1995), 232.

9   Ibid., 147.

became, marking the history of the world as one of devolution into unthinking, effeminate species with little to no connection to their ancestral homeland in the Arctic. By awakening to the spiritual practices ingrained in the traditions of the Aryan mythos, humanity can reascend to superman status.

After the Allied occupation of Rome in 1943, Evola moved to Vienna, Austria, to work with the SS, where he imagined that an entire universe of superiority could be delivered out of the thin air of ancient texts and esoteric artifacts. While maintaining a sense of superiority over Mussolini's Fascist party, Evola believed that the SS comprised the building blocks for an ideal *Ordenstaat*, or State of Order. Unfortunately for him, the SS work was much blander than he had hoped. Paralyzed from the waist down by a shell while taking a stroll during an Allied bombardment to test his will, Evola returned to Rome disappointed. After the war, however, Evola's call for violence and direct action against NATO would come to paramount influence over the resurgent global fascist movement.

Savitri Devi and the Aryan Myth

Evola's mystical teachings were linked to a growing postwar esoteric fascism that sent its apostles throughout the world. Its high priestess was Savitri Devi. Born in France to a wealthy Greek family, Devi became involved in the spiritual circles of Nazism as a young woman. During the war, she undertook a spiritual and political mission to India to study what she imagined were sacred texts on the origins of the Aryan race. By the late 1930s, Devi had become involved in the Hindu nationalist movement, approving of the idea of *Hindutva* preached by V. K. Savarkar, who notoriously stated that Hindu Indians should treat Muslims like the Nazis treated Jews. Devi claimed to be attracted to Hinduism because it opened her eyes to the relative insignificance of humanity on earth. Due to this insignificance, Devi viewed all "non-Aryan" humanity as parasitic on the vital energies necessary to cultivate the spiritually evolved master race.[10]

---

10   See Nicholas Goodrick-Clarke, *Hitler's Priestess* (New York: New York University, 1998), 44–60.

Like the occult mystics that preceded her, Devi believed fervently in the "new man," for whom violence was nothing less than a spiritual duty. She organized the geographic centers of her belief system around India and Egypt, focusing on the supposedly Aryan pharaoh, Akhenaton, as well as the teachings of Tibetan spiritual leaders who she believed served as intermediaries between modern humanity and the Lemurian root-race identified by spiritualist leader Madame Blavatsky.[11] In her wide-ranging spiritual doctrine, Devi tied together a collection of scriptures in order to find the revealed knowledge of white supremacist power that could regenerate Nazism and return the sacred connection between humanity and their Hyperborean ancestors.

After World War II, Devi's books could only make cryptic reference to her hero, Adolf Hitler, who she claims stood out among other supermen like Jesus Christ, St. Paul, Akhenaton, and Buddha as the greatest "Man against Time" in the short history of humanity.[12] For Devi, Hitler's use of the elite force, the SS, was a deployment of the worldly forces of pain and agony in the service of the universal, spiritual ideal. The SS's death's head (*Totenkopf*) symbolized this usage of worldly violence for the ascendency of the hierarchy of the blood. The rigorous, austere discipline evoked by the SS in their genocidal campaigns marked the perfection of the blood through sacred purity and order.[13]

Like Himmler, who had committed suicide at the end of the war, Devi exalted animals and nature over hundreds of pages documenting the spiritual quality and importance of animal life. To lessen the failings of humanity, Devi encouraged vegetarianism and biocentric ethics not unlike today's deep ecology movement. Embarking on a pilgrimage of Nazi "sacred sites" around Europe, Devi claimed to undergo the ecstasies of a mystic as she conducted solemn rituals at tombs and temples. While propagandizing the return of Nazism from India to Spain, Devi fell in with a tight-knit circle of fascist organizers, and her name was raised along with Evola as one of the preeminent spiritual leaders of neofascism.

---

11   Ibid., 77–75.
12   Ibid., 92–104.
13   Ibid., 117–21.

Francis Parker Yockey and the "World Idea"

Among the most committed followers of Evola to join Otto Strasser, Otto Remer, and Oswald Mosley at a European Social Movement conference in Naples was a Nazi from the United States named Francis Parker Yockey, who sought to link fascists into a network of militants dedicated to the overthrow of US interests in Europe. Likely acting as an agent for the Nazis during the war, Yockey somehow became established as a member of the prosecutor's team at Nuremberg before clashing with his supposed colleagues. Published in 1949, his book *Imperium* would go on to heavily influence fascist thought—in particular, by encouraging a sweeping cultural turn within the fascist milieu. While Remer would delight in its pages, the Buenos Aires-based Nazi publication *Der Weg* heralded *Imperium* as the "bible of the next great European revolution." Evola would also publish his compliments.[14]

Yockey's ideological melding of left and right would set the standard for the remainder of the century. For Yockey, socialism is "the form of an age of political Imperialism, of Authority, of historical philosophy, of superpersonal political imperative." Capitalism belongs to the past, socialism to a future, and "the only distinction between types of Socialism is between efficient and inefficient, weak and strong, timid and bold." Like Mussolini, Yockey believed in a socialism of producers, heroic only when also nationalist.

For Yockey, European nations represent a "spiritual organism" that takes shape through a "World-Idea." They are its essence manifested in cultural form. Such ideas are "living, breathing, pulsating…higher beings" that "utilize human beings for their purposes."[15] These higher spirits are sublimated in race, Yockey believed: "Race, in the objective sense, is the spirituo-biological community of a group…beneath is the strong, primitive beat of the cosmic rhythm in a particular stock; above is the molding, creating, driving Destiny of a High Culture."[16] So race comes to mean, for Yockey, something both biological and spiritual, which

---

14   Coogan, *Dreamer of the Day*, 274.

15   Francis Parker Yockey, *Imperium: The Philosophy of History and Politics* (Sausalito: Noontide Press, 1969), 5.

16   Ibid., 277.

builds "strong character, self-discipline, honor, ambition, renunciation of weakness, striving after perfection, superiority, leadership."[17] Meanwhile, culture becomes the visceral actuation of a transcendent, spiritual organism—its everyday practices and rituals of reproduction, such as art, music, sports, and food, all bent on the perfection of the self and the collective. Beyond nationalism, race fulfills the "World-Idea," which Yockey claimed to understand as tantamount to the history of colonial domination. Yet for him, white culture remained deeply threatened.[18]

His goal remained clear: a kind of national socialist International. "The Internationale of our times appears in a time when the Spirit of the Age has outgrown political nationalism. The Age of Absolute Politics will not tolerate petty-Stateism [sic]," proclaimed Yockey.[19] Like Hitler, Yockey's understanding of "petty-statism" returned to the critique of parliamentary democracy and even provincial forms of monarchy, leading him to seek a higher, spiritual unity in imperium. Like so many fascists, Yockey's quest for a kind of spiritual empire brought an admiration of individualists: "Anarchism, the radical denial of the State, and of all organization whatever, is an idea of genuine political force. It is anti-political in its theory, but by its intensity it is political in the only way that politics can manifest itself, i.e., it can bring men into its service and range them against others as enemies."[20] At once, racial socialism becomes a force of imperialism and authority based on an internationalist, quasi-political theory that views itself as a step beyond the crisis of civilization toward the organic future.

After the publication of *Imperium*, Yockey toured Europe relentlessly with a steamer trunk full of documents and books, broadening the network of postwar fascism. For a time, he worked cordially with Mosley in England, but that ended when Mosley punched him in the face in Hyde Park.[21]

---

17   Ibid., 307.

18   Ibid., 316.

19   Ibid., 201.

20   Ibid., 206.

21   Martin A. Lee, *The Beast Reawakens: Fascism's Resurgence from Hitler's Spymasters to Today's Neo-Nazi Groups and Right-Wing Extremists* (New York: Routledge, 2000), 98.

Yockey traversed the broadening gap between Mosley and Strasser at the time. He personally collaborated with former Strasser's agent and Black Front cofounder, Alfred Franke-Gricksch, who brought him into the circles of the Bruderschaft (Brotherhood), one of the more well-connected fascist networks in postwar Germany. The Bruderschaft sought to take power "through slow and methodical insinuation into governmental and party positions, under cover of such secrecy or camouflage as might be necessary for the success of the operation."[22] Franke-Gricksch would vanish into the Soviet Union after slipping behind the Iron Curtain, but Yockey managed to create an inner circle out of his contacts with the Bruderschaft, which he named the European Liberation Front (ELF).

According to its cofounder, Anthony Gannon, "We knew there was NO chance of a mass movement succeeding in the prevailing political/economic situation at that time, or of the near or midterm future."[23] The ELF instead sought to "take direct action against American bases in England," destabilizing liberal democracy and bringing about a revolution from below based on culture rather than civilization.[24] The ELF's main propaganda document, the "1948 Declaration of London" (actually published in 1949 and written in Belgium), rejected NATO and US involvement in Europe while holding out hope for Russia, where "Western Culture is an instinct, an Idea."[25]

Yockey's Satanic Brood

In the United States, several of Yockey's followers would finance and lead the National Renaissance Party (NRP) toward a pseudo-left fascist position in hopes that Stalinism would ultimately lead the world to fascism. Among the riffraff involved in the formation of the NRP were a New Yorker named James H. Madole and a German-American named Frederick Charles Weiss. The two promoted the NRP by declaring that "what Hitler did in Europe, the

---

22   Coogan, *Dreamer of the Day*, 192.

23   Quoted in Ibid., 175.

24   Nicholas Goodrick-Clarke, *Black Sun* (New York: New York University Press, 2002), 77.

25   Coogan, *Dreamer of the Day*, 177.

National Renaissance Party intends to do in America."[26] Madole practiced a syncretic occultism that combined Madame Blavatsky's theosophist ideas with Aleister Crowley's "magick," developing a bond between Satanism and the fascist occult that scholar Nicholas Goodrick-Clarke notes "anticipated the pagan alliances of neo-Nazis and Satanists in the 1990s."[27]

For some fascists attempting to creep back from oblivion after the war, Satanism appeared to be a viable link to protofascist foundations. Satanism retained a connection to the pagan revival and occult milieu, which included Theosophism, Ariosophism, Crowley's cult (the Ordo Templi Orientis), and the Germanenorden, a secretive, nationalist cult with chapters extant throughout Germany. The latter included a small Bavarian chapter known as the Thule Society, from which many of the high ranking members of the Nazi Party had once emerged. Gazing through the looking glass at the components that comprised a kind of early fascist model, the spiritual element appeared to Madole and others as indispensable.

Madole's syncretic Satanist ideology was repeated by others decades later. One such descendant was the National Socialist Liberation Front (NSLF). With a name derived from Yockey's European Liberation Front, the NSLF had splintered from the National Socialist White People's Party in 1974. Led by a long-haired, pot-smoking Nazi named Joseph Charles Tommasi, the NSLF advocated violence against the "Jewish power structure" and published propaganda including a famous poster of a shadowy, cocked revolver and the line "The future belongs to the few of us still willing to get our hands dirty—Political Terror—it's the only thing they understand."[28] Tommasi's overarching goal was to create chaos and bring down the "System," causing a race war and the eventual "liberation" of the white race.[29] Like leftists, the group advocated armed struggle

---

26   Goodrick-Clarke, *Black Sun*, 74.

27   Ibid., 83.

28   In one perhaps telling coincidence, the famous poster quoted above found its way to Northern Ireland, where it was printed by the Ulster Defense Force in a 1980 manifesto calling for eventual secession of Northern Ireland from the United Kingdom. Ian S. Wood, *Crimes of Loyalty: A History of the UDA* (Edinburgh: University of Edinburgh, 2006), 80.

29   Goodrick-Clarke, *Black Sun*, 18.

from a working-class perspective—the major difference was the anti-Semitic and racist messaging. Also like most leftist groups at the time, Tommasi's Front had little effect and fell apart in short order.

Yet Tommasi's legacy lasted. A ninth-grade dropout and long-time Nazi named James Nolan Mason revived the NSLF to launch a guerrilla war against what he identified as the Zionist Occupation Government. Reviving Tommasi's vintage 1960s national socialist organ, *Siege*, Mason spread the militant message of "armed struggle" against the "System" through bombings, assassinations, and murders of racially mixed couples. Mason became increasingly fascinated with the occult, Satanism, and especially Charles Manson. As we will see, Mason's continuation of Satanist national socialism would go on to influence an important developing subculture within the fascist movement, one that combined disillusionment with Christianity and the notion of a powerful, elitist individual whose cruelty elevates him above the herd and enables him to exploit, conquer, and reign at will.[30]

Asatru and Odinism

Neither the ecstatic violence of Evola, the Indo-Aryan mysticism of Devi, Yockey's Gnostic-like cosmology, nor his partner's Satanic influence would prove necessarily commensurate. In fact, they have contributed to a complex field of images and discourses navigated by fascists in search of proving and testing their individual ideologies. Perhaps no spiritual persuasion has become more important in this field than Odinism.

The most influential person to cobble together a Norse fascism in the United States was Else Christensen, born Else Oscher in the western coast of Denmark in 1913. Christensen participated in the revolutionary undercurrents in her country in the 1930s, which included rowdy clashes between different factions vying for political power, from Trotskyists and Stalinists to national socialists and anarcho-syndicalists. Initially, Christensen aligned herself with the latter, but she soon moved toward the Strasserite faction. She eventually married Aage Alex Christensen of the Danish National Socialist Workers' Party, which maintained a National Bolshevik bent.

---

30   Ian S. Wood, *Crimes of Loyalty*, 80.

After the war, Else Christensen reached out to international white power activists like David Duke and an Odinist named Alexander Rud Mills. Influenced by Mills and Yockey, Christensen asserted that in the unconscious mind of European people resided "the wisdom of our pre-Christian forefathers which we today call Odinism, and which expresses the essence of our folk on the moral and religious plane."[31] With this kind of strangely liminal Odinism of the unconscious, Christensen sought to cover racist ideas with a more acceptable patina in order to disguise their inherent fascism.

Christensen created the Odinist Fellowship in 1969 to teach the "lesson" of Nazi power: that Hitler failed because he quashed the Strasserite faction and joined the right wing. She based her own ideas in part on the work of Ramiro Ledesma Ramos's Spanish organization Juntas de Ofensiva Nacional-Sindicalista (Union of the National Syndicalist Offensive). Christensen opposed "reactionary Francoite authoritarianism" because she believed that Aryan freedom is essentially anarchist and communal in a specifically folkish way. She called on "Aryans" to "retribalize," since a "certain form of socialism is inherent in tribalism." So, Christensen's formulation of Odinism declared that it would honor "the diversity of Nature, including the natural variations of human beings," without relinquishing white supremacism.[32]

Christensen was clear about the tactical strengths of her approach. "You have to go in the back door!" she exclaimed. "Nobody could put a finger on what we said, because we said it in such a way that it couldn't be clamped down at. We still have to do that.... Everybody knows that the Jews rule the whole damned world, so you cannot fight their combined power. You need to watch your step." As scholar Mattias Gardell notes: "Self-sufficient, ecologically sustainable, monoracial tribes would, Christensen suggests, be a practical method for redefining American federalism and for establishing an Odinist union of Aryan republics."[33] One of

---

31   Else Christensen, quoted in Mattias Gardell, *Gods of the Blood: The Pagan Revival and White Separatism* (Durham: Duke University Press, 2003), 171.

32   Ibid.

33   Ibid., 175.

Christensen's principle forms of outreach became a prison ministry, which enabled Odinism to spread throughout the prison population. Yet the Odinist Fellowship was more intent on racial awareness than rituals and practice.[34]

Rivaling the Odinist Fellowship, another heathen named Stephen McNallen created the Asatru Free Assembly in 1976 with a very similar, though distinct and sometimes oppositional, range of ideas. More interested in spirituality than national socialism, McNallen developed the Asatru Free Assembly into a movement focused more clearly on religious rituals, assemblies, and meetings. However, McNallen maintained the "metagenetic" discourse of ethnic Odinism, and even borrowed from Carl Jung's essay "Wotan," in which the latter sees Hitler as the personification of the Wotan/Odin archetype in the German people's collective unconscious.[35] McNallen warns non-Aryans to stay away from Asatru:

> I think they are sadly deceived if they try to take on my ancestors. They need to look to their own ancestral line. For me, joining any ancestral religion is not as simple as deciding you're going to join the Elks Lodge or you're going to join the local bridge club. You're not just joining something that exists right there in that moment in time. What you are really joining is something that includes a whole line of ancestors. The "we" that we see now, is just the tiny tip of the iceberg. But to take on our soul, to take on that which is an intimate part of us, is to take on all of those ancestors as well. I don't think that you can just do that arbitrarily. I can never be an American Indian. I can never be a black man. I don't want to be any of those things. I want to follow my ancestors and my way. Likewise, I would strongly encourage them to do the same.[36]

While clearly advocating Asatru as a racial movement, McNallen also attempted to clear his movement of open Nazis, banning

---

34   George Michael, *Theology of Hate: A History of the World Church of the Creator* (Gainsville: University Press of Florida, 2008), 52.

35   Ibid., 53.

36   Ibid., 273.

uniforms and insignias from their meetings, leading to new splinter groups with more explicitly white supremacist politics.[37]

Yet Gardell argues that the apolitical stance of McNallen's later group, the Asatru Folk Assembly, has "political implications… revolving around a call for decentralization in terms of radical localism, tribal communalism, and Jeffersonian republicanism." These politically ethnonationalist positions highlight the notion that "Body, mind, and spirit were shaped by life in artificial urban environments. At war with himself, alienated man embraced the universal notions of religion and politics that now threaten to destroy the remnants of every organic native culture on the face of the earth."[38]

From the giant nationalist engines of World War II-era fascist states that sought the "total mobilization" of masses of people, fascists returned to what they imagined to be its pure forms, based on innate, mythical, and ancestral elements—both the local rootedness of culture and the transcendence of spirit. What remains consistent through the different, often feuding, ideological systems is a frequent reference to the individual's power over the crowd—a kind of wolf character preying on the unsuspecting sheep who do what society commands. Like the wolf pack, the "tribe" remained a perfect form to carry these ideas—which may be why fascism has emerged prominently in communities organized around avant-garde music niches like neofolk and noise (with its obvious roots in futurism). However, the "warrior aristocrat" of Evola and the Odinist soldier of Christensen would not restrict themselves to music and art; instead, they would leave a trail of blood across the remainder of the twentieth century, from Italy to Argentina to Colorado. It is to this legacy of infiltration and murder that we will turn in the next chapter.

---

37   Goodrick-Clarke, *Black Sun*, 262.

38   Gardell, *Gods of the Blood*, 278–79.

CHAPTER 3:
A BRIEF HISTORY OF FASCIST INTRIGUE

The Politics of Subversion

Following the war, fascist activists including Oswald Mosley, Otto Strasser, and French ideologue Maurice Bardèche attempted to recreate a political movement from the ashes of their ideology. Otto looked to his brother Gregor, murdered in the Röhm purge of 1934, as "a martyr for the idea of a 'German Revolution,'" positioning himself as the rightful alternative to Hitlerism. Nevertheless, both Gregor and Otto Strassers' public statements were characterized by nebulous syncretism against a backdrop of demagoguery. Otto's were as theoretically unimpressive but lacked the same cult following.[1] By the mid-1950s, Strasser had become known for his "Third Position" ideology—an insistence on a common European path of national socialism beyond both capitalism (United States) and communism (Union of Soviet Socialist Republics). In Italy, Mussolini's faithful formed the Movimento Sociale Italiano with many of Strasser's ideas in mind, and the broader movement

---

1   Also, Gregor blamed Otto's brash exit from the party in 1930 for Hitler's eventual triumph. By the early 1930s, Gregor was seen not as a leftist but a moderate in the party, while Otto's claims only underwrote his own lack of political merit in comparison. Stachura, *Gregor Strasser and the Rise of Nazism*, 4–5.

became known as the European Social Movement, with Strasser and Mosley as the two chief influences. However, an important split emerged right away.

The extremists broke with the moderates, believing that violence and explicit racism would bring about a reactionary revolution faster and more effectively than slow integration into the political and economic elites. Led by Stefano Delle Chiaie and an Evolian war veteran named Pino Rauti, their plan was not new despite their name—the Ordine Nuovo, or New Order. Infiltration, provocation, and even framing the left had become the norm for state agencies and extrastate groups. During the late-nineteenth century, Tsarist spies infiltrated the Russian group Narodnaia Volia to turn the Narodnik toward anti-Semitism.[2] During the interwar period, while the Popular Front in France debated supporting the Republicans against Franco in the Spanish Civil War, a group of French military officials formed the Cagoule (hooded cloak), which would conduct terrorist bombings and then blame them on the left to draw the public toward fascist sympathies.[3] During the 1950s, such "dirty tricks" characterized France's Organisation de l'Armée Secrète (OAS—Secret Army Organization), the colonial heir to the Cagoule.

Organized by high-ranking members of the French military who sought to apply the lessons of the country's defeat in Indochina (Vietnam) to the colonial mission in Algeria, the OAS's founding members included former Wehrmacht, SS, and Vichy officials. They studied Maoist guerrilla techniques and leftists strategies in order to develop a "revolutionary war" model that they could apply to the fight against the national liberation movements in the colonies. They also helped engineer the 1958 crisis that brought Charles de Gaulle to power, and they were duly shocked when their heroic figure granted independence to Algeria. In response, they devoted their revolutionary war strategy to sabotaging and attempting to overthrow France's Fifth Republic. Bardèche observed the trends and set the stage for the new era of fascism during the lead-up to a pivotal conference in Venice in 1962:

---

2   Richard Pipes, *The Degaev Affair: Terror and Treason in Tsarist Russia* (New Haven: Yale University Press, 2003), 85–86.

3   Soucy, *French Fascism: The Second Wave*, 47–51.

The single party, the secret police, the public displays of Caesarism, even the presence of a Führer are not necessarily attributes of fascism.... The famous fascist methods are constantly revised and will continue to be revised.... With another name, another face, and with nothing which betrays the projection from the past, with the form of a child we do not recognize and the head of a young Medusa, the Order of Sparta will be reborn.[4]

In attendance at that 1962 conference was perhaps the most important product of the OAS's parafascist-Maoist mixture: a Belgian influenced by Yockey named Jean-François Thiriart.

A communist in high school, Thiriart had changed sides as fascism swept Europe. During World War II, he assisted in locating British and Jewish resistance fighters during the Battle of the Bulge, and he maintained his militancy through the 1950s.[5] In 1960, Thiriart founded a group called Mouvement d'Action Civique (Movement for Civil Action) to resist the liberation of Congo, and later admitted to hiding paramilitary OAS soldiers in his house when they returned to Europe from fighting against the Algerian National Liberation Front. He also published their communiqués in his weekly, *La Nation Européenne*, an organ inspired by Yockey's *Imperium*. However, as decolonization spread, Thiriart's aspiration grew to accentuate the left-wing aspects of fascism and to transform the character of mainstream politics. At the Venice conference, he and others called for a National Party of Europe, demanding increased workers' rights, representation within a new European parliamentary government, the elimination of the United Nations, and decolonization.

The fascist notion of decolonization remained distinct from the Third World decolonization movement, and it seemed to contradict the ideology of the OAS and other pro-colonial and ultranationalist

---

4   Maurice Bardèche, quoted in Tamir Bar-On, "A Critical Response to Roger Griffin's 'Fascism's New Faces,'" in Griffin, Loh, and Umland, eds., *Fascism Past and Present, West and East*, 89. See also Matthew Feldman and Paul Jackson, "Introduction," in *Doublespeak: The Rhetoric of the Far Right Since 1945*, eds. Matthew Feldman and Paul Jackson (Stuttgart: Ibidem-Verlag, 2014), 8.

5   Coogan, *Dreamer of the Day*, 547.

groups from Northern Ireland to Angola to Chile. While fascists attempted to identify their "third way" beyond left and right with the Third World outside of the United States and the Soviet Union, their notion of "European liberation" demanded the expulsion or otherwise liquidation of populations deemed non-European. The strong odor of anti-Semitism and racism continued to emanate from their literature, which emphasized violence against the state, "Zionists," and NATO as a means of achieving the spiritual empire of Europe. Hence, Thiriart's appeal to the left by violently rejecting NATO and embracing Soviet and even Maoist influence retained only a short-term promise of liberation from capital with a long-term plan of genocide. This support for decolonization was, more or less, a disingenuous ruse to cater to possible left-wing recruits.

Upon his return from the Venice conference, Thiriart was arrested by the Belgian police for passport fraud. Undaunted, after leaving jail, he founded an organization called Jeune Europe (Young Europe), likely named after a Nazi group that, in turn, had relied on the prestige of Mazzini's Young Italy and Karl Schapper's Young Germany—two revolutionary groups predating the International. Thiriart's Jeune Europe set up schools throughout Europe to train a young vanguard in ideology and physical combat.[6] They trained with members of the Evolian terrorist group Ordine Nuovo and the OAS, extending their network into the "groupuscular" neofascist underground.[7]

Thiriart even renounced fascism from time to time, calling himself a national communist. Continuing to support neo-Nazi terrorism into the 1960s and 1970s, Thiriart called for a single European empire, inclusive of the Soviet Union. He supported Muammar al-Qaddafi's ideas of nationalist direct democracy and Fidel Castro's revolutionary strategies. In general, the Nazi-Maoist ideology remained grounded in the "guerilla war" tactics of the OAS. Thiriart also advocated entering leftist groups and encouraging division. By intriguing within the Communist Party of Belgium, Thiriart

6   Ibid., 254.

7   See Jeffrey M. Bale, "Right-Wing Terrorists and the Extraparliamentary Left in Post-World War 2 Europe: Collusion or Manipulation?," *Lobster Magazine* 18 (October 1989): 14, available at 8bitmode.com/rogerdog/lobster/lobster18.pdf.

managed to create a split, drawing followers of "National Communism" to his own Nazi-Maoist party, the Parti Communautaire Européen (an outgrowth of Jeune Europe).[8] Thiriart's success in his pursuits was relatively small, and his influence remained restricted to fascist circles; however, that network of fascist groups and leaders would gain momentum through the 1970s during what was called the *anni di piombo*, or the Years of Lead.

The Years of Lead

In 1966, a CIA front group called Aginter Press was set up by a former OAS officer named Yves Guérin-Sérac to bring fascists the credibility of press passes while providing material support to pro-colonial forces and gathering intelligence on and undermining left-wing groups. The next year, in Greece, ultranationalist military forces linked to a network of paramilitaries involved in terrorist attacks used political instability largely blamed on the left to stage a military coup d'état.[9] In 1968, amid that year's global social tumult, the US-backed military government in Greece quietly invited some fifty Italian neofascists to tour their coup government. The tour apparently involved meeting officials and discussing strategies and tactics.

Having already discussed the terms along with leading members of the secret services, military, and judiciary at a three-day conference in Rome three years prior, these Italian fascists would carry back to Italy a so-called strategy of tension that would be waged over the course of fifteen years of bombings, assassinations, and vicious attacks staged by fascists operating either through infiltrated or completely phony left-wing groups in order to create chaos and draw the public toward the right wing and a "state of order."[10] Although Ordine Nuovo and other groups had carried out

8   Coogan, *Dreamer of the Day*, 542.

9   Stuart Christie, *Stefano Delle Chiaie: Portrait of a Black Terrorist* (London: Anarchy/Refract, 1984), 21; Bale, "The 'Black' Terrorist International," 238.

10   Stuart Christie, *General Franco Made Me a "Terrorist": The Christie File: Part 2, 1964–1967* (Hastings: ChristieBooks, 2003), 244–45. While some claim that Evola was a kind of a spiritual anarchist—and he did hold

other attacks throughout the 1960s, the largest catalyst for what became known as the Years of Lead took place on December 12, 1969, when a huge explosion ripped through Milan's Piazza Fontana. Killing sixteen and injuring eighty-eight, the blast was accompanied by three other explosions in Rome targeting banks and institutions, like the Altare della Patria. The coordinated attacks took place on the same day that the Council of Europe expelled Greece. Going off a tip that an organization involved was formed by anarchists, police arrested 150 anarchists in the wave of repression that followed.

Five days after the bombing, one of the members of the Italian fascist delegation to Greece, Stefano Serpieri, who was also a member of the Italian secret services, reported to the head of the counterintelligence bureau that "Mario Merlino was the author of the bombing at the [Rome] Altare della Patria [Tomb of the Unknown Soldier], and he had received his instructions from the fascist leader Stefano Delle Chiaie who, in turn, had received his from Yves Guérin-Sérac, director of the Aginter Press agency in Lisbon."[11] Merlino claimed to have converted to anarchism after going to Greece, bringing an anarchist signature to the media's reports on the bombings.

Magistrates traced evidence to the "revolutionary traditionalist" Franco Freda, as well as Ordine Nuovo cofounders Rauti and Delle Chiaie. Another fascist named Giovanni Ventura was found to have a stash of American, Soviet, French, German, and Romanian intelligence documents. Complicating matters, Ventura claimed to be a leftist infiltrating Freda's operation. The problem was not that Ventura or Freda were leftists or rightists posing as leftists, but that their syncretic ideology spanned both while rejecting the organized base of either. When it came to such fascist action, the left's crisis was how to clearly define left-wing ideology, strategy, and tactics in contradistinction to not just fascism but to the qualities that have always linked fascism to some strains of the left: namely, elitism,

---

Stirner in high regard—after World War II, he believed that "civilization" had been brought to Italy and that it would be impossible to bring about an "age of culture" without first ridding the country of NATO occupation and communism.

11   Christie, *Stefano Delle Chiaie*, 29.

illiberalism (that is, rejection of certain ideals *as* liberal, rather than on their own merits, or lack thereof as the case may be), and authoritarianism. Without addressing and critiquing these fundamental qualities, including their implications on strategic aggression and a readiness to sacrifice civilians, the left was all the more prone to creeping fascism slipping in and out of its manifolds.

Ten fascists, including Freda, Ventura, and Rauti, were arrested and charged with a number of bombings, but when the court released them on bail, Freda and Ventura fled to Franco's Spain.[12] Remaining behind was one of Freda's colleagues, Claudio Mutti, who subscribed to the "national communist" ideas of Thiriart. Mutti would help edit the Italian edition of Thiriart's *La Nation Européenne* journal and would maintain an esoteric fascist current linked to a growing ideological movement called the "European New Right," also known as the Nouvelle Droite.[13]

To Blur the Left and Right

Orienting oneself during this time would have been far more difficult than understanding the dynamics of what took place with the privilege of a historical lens; however, even that is far from easy. This is largely because the conflation and confusion of right- and left-wing groups was a deliberate tactic by fascists to delegitimize the left. To be sure, asserting the need to decolonize Europe from NATO and the United States seems like a viable left-wing position even today. Even a kind of third-world nationalism for Europeans also seemed to Maoists like an appropriate stage of collective unity that would achieve eventual internationalism through a chain of national revolutions throughout Europe. Hence, fascists like Rauti and Delle Chiaie could swim in the sea of left-wing thought, joining with different groups and then tearing them apart or using them for the ends of attacking their mutual enemies while discrediting communism rather than fascism in the process.

---

12   Ibid., 31.

13   Giovanni Savino, "From Evola to Dugin: The Neo-Eurasianist Connection in Italy," in *Eurasianism and the European Far Right: Reshaping the Europe-Russia Relationship*, ed. Marlene Laruelle (Boulder: Lexington Books, 2015), 104–10.

Other purportedly "converted" fascists formed leftist groups like the Movimento Studentesco, Avanguardia Operaia, Grupo Primavera, XXII Ottobre, and an entire network of distribution companies and organizations connected to Freda and Ventura. The presses that once churned out Hitler now switched to Che Guevara but were run by the same people. Merlino infiltrated and disintegrated the Circolo Bakunin, and members of Ordine Nuovo and Delle Chiaie's Avanguardia Nazionale infiltrated the Maoist group Partito Comunista d'Italia (Marxista-Leninista), causing dissent until being exposed. Another group, Organizzazione Lotta di Popolo, melded Cuban, Chinese, and Arab nationalism with Italian Fascism in their propaganda, which drew the ridicule of a media eager to point out the similarities between right- and left-wing terrorism.[14] In a report after a conference where these strategies and tactics were explicitly articulated, an Aginter Press agent noted, "The introduction of provocateur elements into the circles of the revolutionary left is merely a reflection of the wish to push this unstable situation to the breaking point and create a climate of chaos.… Pro-Chinese circles, characterized by their own impatience and zeal, are [especially] suitable for infiltration."[15]

The situation was, to say the least, chaotic. When a Stirnerist individualist with a circle-A tattoo on his arm named Gianfranco Bertoli threw an explosive at a memorial ceremony in a Milan police station, he yelled, "Viva Pinelli, viva l'anarchia!" in an apparent reference to Giuseppe Pinelli, an anarchist arrested in the aftermath of the Piazza Fontana bombing who died mysteriously under police custody. Nevertheless, stories started emerging that he had not thrown the explosive into the station but tossed it on the sidewalk to do maximum damage to pedestrians, killing four and wounding forty. He was also found to have spent time traveling not only in anarchist networks but also with and among well-known fascists connected to international terror networks.[16] Whether Bertoli was another example of the creeping spaces of

---

14   Luciano Lanza, *Secrets and Bombs: Piazza Fontana 1969*, trans. Paul Sharkey (Hastings: ChristieBooks, 2002).

15   Quoted in Bale, "Right-Wing Terrorists and the Extraparliamentary Left in Post-World War 2 Europe," 15.

16   Bale, "The 'Black' Terrorist International," 513–28.

the marginal left-right crossover, or was in actual fact a state infil-
trator is difficult to know.

Despite the amateurish way it was sometimes carried out, with
many agents walking an intentionally blurry line between right and
left, there certainly was a campaign being conducted through networks within the Italian government to give training and support
to fascist terrorist cells with the intention of undermining the left
and polarizing the Italian public, forging it into a force that could
be wielded by a right-wing government looking for an excuse to
crack down.[17] In some cases, these networks united—as with an
abortive coup attempt plotted for December 8, 1970, the year after
the Piazza Fontana bombing. Led by fascist military figure Junio
Valerio Borghese and his group the Fronte Nazionale, the plot involved Avanguardia Nazionale and Ordine Nuovo, along with loyal
members of the national police, in an attempt to occupy government buildings and "arrest" then-president Giuseppe Saragat. It
was called off at the last minute thanks to a mysterious phone call.

These networks operated under the codename "Gladio," the
name for an ancient Roman gladiatorial sword.[18] They included the
foot soldiers of Ordine Nuovo, Avanguardia Nazionale, and Thiriart's
Jeune Europe groups, all of which maintained distinct networks and
ideologies with a large amount of geographical and personnel overlap.
Their arms tended to come from troves of weapons stashes throughout the country supplied by members within the military and political
establishment, many of whom had served under Mussolini and were
recruited by the United States's Office of Strategic Services (OSS) after the war to maintain vigilance against a possible Soviet invasion or
a "Fifth Column" takeover by the Italian Communist Party. When
postwar intelligence transferred from the OSS to the new Central

---

17   Bale, "Right-Wing Terrorists and the Extraparliamentary Left," 6.

18   Senato della Repubblica, *Commissione parlamentare d'inchiesta sul ter-
      rorismo in Italia e sulle cause della mancata individuazione dei responsabili
      delle stragi: Il terrorismo, le stragi ed il contesto storico-politico—Proposta di
      relazione* (Rome: 1995), 294–95; Senato della Repubblica, *Commissione
      parlamentare d'inchiesta sul terrorismo in Italia e sulle cause della mancata
      individuazione dei reponsabili delle stragi: Stragi e terrorismo in Italia dal
      dopoguerra al 1974—Relazione del Gruppo Democratici di Sinistra l'Ulivio*
      (Rome: June 2000), 95.

Intelligence Agency (CIA), the latter inherited the Gladio networks. Some 350 deaths resulted from their deployment—mostly innocent civilians, but also numerous targeted assassinations.

Extensive coordination existed between Gladio in Italy, Aginter Press in Portugal, and two Spanish organizations: the Paladin Group, founded in 1970 by former SS colonel Otto Skorzeny, and the fascist Círculo Español de Amigos de Europa (CEDADE—Spanish Circle of Friends in Europe), whose agents were trained by Franco's regime.[19] Through these operations, fascist agents could maintain connections throughout the world, scheming alongside anti-left movements from Angola and Mozambique to Argentina and Bolivia. Operatives like Delle Chiaie went back and forth to Latin America, building important networks between Europeans and those state security and paramilitary operations under the coordination of the CIA's Operation Condor.[20] Groups like the right-wing Peronist Alianza Anticomunista Argentina (Argentine Anticommunist Alliance), led by an esoteric fascist named José López Rega, could plug into a network that included Nazi war criminals like Klaus Barbie, Otto Skorzeny, and Johann von Leers. In Chile and Bolivia, coups were orchestrated with the help of fascists under a relatively consistent pattern: first, a wave of crime, disruptions, and terror attacks perpetrated by previously unknown or nonexistent groups purporting to be leftists, followed by a strong militarized reaction in the name of maintaining order, and the ensuing enfranchisement of neoliberal economics.[21]

19 See Anton Shekhovtsov, "Alexander Dugin and the West European New Right, 1989–1994," in Laruelle, ed., *Eurasianism and the European Far Right*, 40.

20 Anna Cento Bull, "Self-Narratives of the *anni di piombo*: Testimonies of the Political Exiles," *Imagining Terrorism: The Rhetoric and Representation of Political Violence in Italy 1969–2009*, ed. Pierpaolo Antonello and Alan O'Leary (London: Modern Humanities Research Association and Maney Publishing, 2009), 188; Regine Igel, *Andreotti: Politik zwischen Geheimdienst und Mafia* (Munich: Herbig Verlag, 1997), 232–33; Bale, "Right-Wing Terrorists and the Extraparliamentary Left," 11.

21 Bale, "The 'Black' Terrorist International," 379; Jorge Magasich-Airola, *Los que dijeron "No": historia del movimiento de los marinos antigolpistas de*

While the Operation Condor regimes in Latin America re-sembled Franco's authoritarian conservative government in Spain, the links to fascism did not coalesce into outwardly facing fascist movements. Instead, scholar Guillermo O'Donnell more accurately frames them as "bureaucratic-authoritarian" regimes that constrict the understanding of *lo popolo* to organs directly administered by state authorities.[22] Their connections to fascism were strategic, diplomatic, and in some ways spiritual, involving the bizarre occult beliefs of Evola and Devi. The Condor networks developing in the 1970s and 1980s were also tied to other operations in Central America, requiring extensive connections in the United States and abroad. Not only did Delle Chiaie cultivate links to the ARENA party in Honduras and paramilitaries in Guatemala, but the Contras in Nicaragua were also connected to a private intelligence complex based in the United States that included Willis Carto's fascist network, as well as the John Birch Society and its Roy Cohn-led Western Goals Foundation, and perhaps the most extensive and well-connected anti-left network of this era, the World Anti-Communist League, headed by Roger Pearson, one of Carto's long-term friends and fascist collaborators.

The Nouvelle Droite

Pearson and Carto had already begun to develop a new ideological movement embedded alongside these acts of concrete subversion to undermine the left and replace it with a supposed left-right hybrid, which in their case took the shape of a strange mixture of "national communist" and Evolian trends. In 1965, the pair invited a young man going by the name of Fabrice Laroche to guest edit their periodical, *Western Destinies*. An OAS supporter and member of the circles around the protofascist group Europe-Action, Laroche's real name was Alain de Benoist. His ideas at the time were published in the books *Courage Is Their Homeland*

1973, vol. 1 (Santiago: LOM, 2008), 341.

22   Guillermo O'Donnell, "Tensions in the Bureaucratic-Authoritarian State and the Question of Democracy," in *The New Authoritarianism in Latin America*, ed. David Collier et al. (Princeton: Princeton University Press, 1979), 305.

and *Rhodesia: Land of the Faithful Lions* in 1967.[23] Though originally characterized by pro-colonial celebrations of early European
warrior societies united by honor and loyalty, Benoist's ideology
transformed through the paradigm-shifting events of 1968 into
a syncretic new formulation organized under the banner of the
"Nouvelle Droite."[24]

In 1969, Benoist helped create the Groupement de recherche
et d'études pour la civilisation européenne (GRECE—Research
and Study Group for European Civilization), which produced
a "neo-Gramscian" analysis of social conditions and attempted to gather together a populist bloc based on antiliberalism and
anti-Marxism without necessarily condemning socialism. Instead,
GRECE drew a distinction between "organic" socialist nationalism, on the one hand, and "decadent" internationalism, on the
other. As scholar Tamir Bar-On puts it, "The other right-wing,
revolutionary children born in the wake of the May 1968 events
were simply trying to outduel their leftist opponents on their own
cultural terrain."[25] They looked to the protofascist roots of national
socialism to synthesize the ideas of Proudhon and Sorel, Nietzsche
and Barrès, and Maurras, Schmitt, and Evola, in an attempt to
recapture what they saw as the unity between left and right that
had prefigured twentieth-century fascism and to "demonstrate how
even left-wing revolutionaries ... could be utilized in order to delegitimize liberal democracy."[26]

Benoist's work fit into a larger framework of radical-right
and fascist action and thought, as explained by Guérin-Sérac of
Aginter Press:

> Our number consisted of two types of men:
>   (1) Officers who have come to us from the fighting in In-
> do-China and Algeria, and some who even enlisted with us after
> the battle for Korea;

23   Christopher Flood, "The Cultural Struggle of the Extreme Right," in
      Griffin and Feldman, eds., *Fascism*, 5:167.
24   Tamir Bar-On, *Where Have All the Fascists Gone?* (New York: Routledge,
      2007), 28.
25   Ibid., 48.
26   Ibid., 180.

(2) Intellectuals who, during this same period turned their attention to the study of the techniques of Marxist subversion.… Having formed study groups, they have shared experiences in an attempt to dissect the techniques of Marxist subversion and to lay the foundations of a counter-technique.[27]

For his part, Benoist supported the paramilitary OAS and met with Pino Rauti while in hiding following an attack. From their intellectual ivory tower, Benoist and the Nouvelle Droite encouraged the fascist movement in a kind of return to the source, and their works investigating and co-opting left-wing theories have been disseminated broadly as a facet of a broader fascist discussion.[28] Benoist's attempts to resuscitate the reputation of nineteenth-century racist thought formed part of a foundation for the revival of fascism, not in the sense of historical memory, but in the sense of its cultural origins and roots. Upgrading Evolian cultural politics with Gramscian rhetoric, the Nouvelle Droite focused its energy on "grey eminences" within the intellectual sphere, gathering a kind of cultural influence that could direct political policy without risking unpopular associations with specific politicians.[29] The effort came at an extremely portentous time.

In 1977, the Italian left-wing Red Brigades pulled off a daring kidnapping of former prime minister Aldo Moro in broad daylight in Rome, later executing him and leaving his body in a car parked between the headquarters of an important trade union and that of the Communist Party. The founder of the Red Brigades, Renato Curcio, had found his way to Marxism through a stint with the Italian section of Thiriart's Jeune Europe, Giovane Nazione. From this group, later renamed Giovane Europa, Curcio likely moved to the bona fide left wing via the Catholic left.[30] However, Curcio was

27   Yves Guérin-Sérac, quoted in Christie, *Stefano Delle Chiaie*, 15.
28   For more on these connections, see Guillaume Origoni, "Pino Rauti: une figure de l'extrême droite italienne," *Fragments sur les Temps Présents*, May 31, 2013, available at https://tempspresents.com/2013/05/31/pino-rauti-extreme-droite-italienne-guillaume-origoni/.
29   Bar-On, *Where Have All the Fascists Gone?*, 90.
30   See Stephen A. Atkins, *Encyclopedia of Modern Worldwide Extremists and Extremist Groups* (Westport, CT: Greenwood Publishing Group, 2004), 70.

in prison at the time of Moro's kidnapping, partly because the Red Brigades had been so thoroughly infiltrated.[31] Despite the questionable circumstances surrounding the assassination of Moro, the Italian police seized on the opportunity to arrest major intellectuals and activists of the growing Autonomia Operaia movement, including a bookish university professor named Antonio Negri.

While Negri languished in prison, accused of masterminding all of European terrorism, the Italian translation of Benoist's *Vu de droite* (*View from the Right*) was published, denouncing egalitarianism as the cardinal enemy of humanity: "The enemy as I see it is not 'the Left' or 'communism' or even 'subversion' but the egalitarian ideology, whose formulations, religious or lay, metaphysical or pseudo-scientific, have never ceased to flourish for two thousand years, and in which 'the ideas of 1789' are nothing but a stage, and of which the current subversion and communism are the inevitable outcome."[32] The Nouvelle Droite stood against "equality" and in favor of "difference" and "diversity." To "equalize" is to force all people into one common group, taking away their "right to difference," Benoist claims. Cementing his reputation as the "Gramsci of the right," Benoist promoted a cultural struggle to gain hegemony, seeing metapolitics, the lived attitudes behind political associations, as the ultimate form of influence. The "hot summer" of 1979 saw the peak of the Nouvelle Droite's popularity as leftist intellectuals and activists throughout Italy remained in hiding or in jail.

Generally, Benoist's success was symptomatic of a broader post-'68 movement seeking to decontextualize right-left ideological opposition through catchphrases that manufacture artificial unity. "What is the greatest threat today?" Benoist asked in 1980. "It is the progressive disappearance of diversity from the world. The leveling-down of people, the reduction of all cultures to a world civilization made

---

31   Frederic Spotts and Theodor Wieser, *Italy: A Difficult Democracy; A Survey of Italian Politics* (Cambridge: Cambridge University Press, 1986), 179–80.

32   See Jonathan Marcus, *The National Front and French Politics: The Resistible Rise of Jean-Marie Le Pen* (New York: New York University Press, 1995), 24; Richard Wolin, *The Seduction of Unreason: The Intellectual Romance with Fascism from Nietzsche to Postmodernism* (Princeton, NJ: Princeton University Press, 2009), 261.

up of what is the most common."[33] A new man is coming, Benoist predicted, and this movement beyond the crisis of humanity would occur through a kind of "positive nihilism." Humans would "build on a site which has been completely cleared and leveled.… If a new right is to be brought into being we have to start from scratch."[34] Beginning from the annihilation of multiculturalism and returning to the rootedness of a sacred European tradition, with all its inegalitarian implications, it will restore diversity by reproducing original, authentic cultural integrity, rather than its liberal copy.

This authenticity resonates within a potential pan-European "spiritual empire" that would transcend national identity by federating into regional structures in order to protect cultural differences from the eroding qualities of globalism, antiracism, and multiculturalism: "We have the right to be for Black Power, but on the condition of simultaneously being in favor of White Power, Yellow Power and Red Power," Benoist declared.[35] A few years later, in the early 1980s, he insisted, "The truth is that people must preserve and cultivate their differences.… Immigration merits condemnation because it strikes a blow at the identity of the host culture as well as the immigrant's identity."[36]

As opposed to integrationist culture, which even today the Nouvelle Droite identifies as colonial, "rooted" cultures tied to their traditional practices and identities are to be preserved and internally homogenized, uniting in common though differentiated struggle against US imperialism. Central to the claims of the Nouvelle Droite is the premise that white "identity," not multicultural capitalism, stands for individuality and power, while the latter manifests a kind of obedience to a group norm imposed by egalitarianism. Benoist's most quoted line is likely his insistence that it would be better to wear a "Red Army helmet" than to "think about spending the rest of our lives eating hamburgers in the Brooklyn area."[37] Hence, cultural identity could refer

---

33   Alain de Benoist, "Regenerating History," in *Fascism*, ed. Roger Griffin (Oxford: Oxford University Press, 1995), 346.

34   Ibid., 348.

35   Alain de Benoist, quoted in Ibid., 169–70.

36   Ibid., 127.

37   See Jean-Yves Camus, "A Long-Lasting Friendship: Alexander Dugin

to implicit nationalism that perpetuated hostility to immigrants while embracing even Soviet Communism if necessary, as a way to save Europe from the United States's tasteless culture of homogenizing integration.[38]

When it emerged, the Nouvelle Droite did not actively set up its own political apparatuses, but it did draw on the same antagonisms in society that fueled leftist critique—particularly the sense that authenticity was dissolving into one superficial, pseudo-multicultural simulation of reality. If the Nouvelle Droite blamed racism and capitalism for the failure of liberal multiculturalism, it advocated for a system of global apartheid as the only solution, because forced integration in Europe would be racist against whites. Thus, to this day, the Nouvelle Droite rejects assimilation, insisting that diversity is the rule, while identifying that "diversity" with fragmented ethnicities envisioned as homogenous cultural units existing in a larger pluralist system—a heterogeneous system of homogenous parts.[39] In particular, Benoist's conception of "globalism" as the forwarding of a centuries-old practice of forced integration into a singular "lowest common denominator" culture, now brought about through displacement and consumerism, hit home with many seeking an escape from modern life. Seeing US imperialism as an extension of the Judeo-Christian form of hegemony, Benoist insists upon the return to pagan roots and ancestral knowledge.

To forward its metapolitical hegemony, the Nouvelle Droite continues to use methods for dissemination such as think tanks and cultural commentary, molded to appear as banal (and elite) as possible. Pierre Krebs, a German progenitor of the Nouvelle Droite, explains the metapolitical approach: "We are not interested in political factions but in attitudes to life. Commentators will carry on writing irrelevant articles categorizing us under 'New Right' but also under 'left-wing.' Such terms are pathetic and leave us cold, for

---

and the French Radical Right," in Laruelle, ed., *Eurasianism and the European Far Right*, 85.

38   For an interesting summary of the difference between identification and integration, see Griffin, *The Nature of Fascism*, 188.

39   Tamir Bar-On, "Intellectual Right-Wing Extremism," in *The Extreme Right in Europe: Current Trends and Perspectives*, ed. Uwe Backes and Patrick Moreau (Oakville: Vandenboeck & Ruprecht, 2011), 346–47.

neither the right nor the left are our concern. It is only basic attitudes to life which people have that interest us."[40]

The way Krebs problematizes the label of the Nouvelle Droite by placing it in scare quotes is indicative of a general trend in Nouvelle Droite circles to obscure its actual ideological position in attempts to turn more deeply into an unidentifiable cultural trend that is harmonized with an almost intuitive influence in everyday life. Yet the Nouvelle Droite's connections to fascists like Bardèche are impossible to miss, as when Benoist's journal *Eléments* published advertisements for Bardèche's explicitly fascist journal, *Défense de l'Occident*. During the height of the Years of Lead, Nouvelle Droite offices in places like Brussels boasted a collection of periodicals including Rauti's fascist weekly *Linea* alongside Nouvelle Droite ideologue Marco Tarchi's *Diorama Letterario*.

Hobbit Camp and Browning the Ecology Movement

A former MSI member, Tarchi organized academic conferences in Italy to discuss how the Nouvelle Droite might address modern problems through cultural and metapolitical means. According to the former Nouvelle Droite ideologue Robert Steuckers, Tarchi owed "his genuine way of working to the political activist Pino Rauti."[41] In 1978, Tarchi penned an extensively researched essay on fascism drawing on critical academic analyses of the subject before finally familiarizing it as "festive…communal, disinterested." In fascism, "Ritual arose as a mediator between the realm of values and the indistinct mass of citizens, and what it forged was a community which was simultaneously sacred and profane."[42] Tarchi's understanding of fascism contradicts the history of the

---

40   Pierre Krebs, "The Metapolitical Rebirth of Europe," in Griffin, ed., *Fascism*, 349.

41   See Robert Steuckers, "Answers to the questions of Pavel Pulaev about my modest biography, my experiences in the French New Right Circus, etc.," *Le blog de Robert Steuckers*, February 2014, http://robertsteuckers .blogspot.com/2014/02/answers-to-questions-of-pavel-tulaev.html.

42   Marco Tarchi, "Between Festival and Revolution," in *International Fascism: Theories, Causes, and the New Consensus*, ed. Roger Griffin (New York: Oxford University Press, 1998), 273.

German war machine and centralized state structures, which he claims undermined the pure concept. Far from authoritarian, Tarchi claims, fascism represents something deeply natural, "the choice of the qualitative and organic community...transcending the level of historical contingencies to find articulation in the realm of cultural expression in ... the myth of the 'community of destiny.'"[43]

To build his "festive" revolution, Tarchi initiated a Hobbit Camp in 1977 and again in 1981. The Hobbit Camp formed a convergence point for leftists and rightists to join in a celebration of ecological attitudes and communality presented as a release of the tension of the Years of Lead. Like Benoist, Tarchi played off the leftist ideas of Guy Debord and the Situationist critique of everyday life, attempting to reorder left and right oppositions and urging young people into a festival atmosphere highlighting both the authentic and the mythical. In this version of the Nouvelle Droite, fascism manifested community over society through an immersion in rituals that brought a collective sense of identity.[44]

Like Evola and Yockey, the antiliberal Nouvelle Droite, which continues to this day, hopes for a future scenario based in the traditions of the past, where warriors and intellectuals dominate social organization in a "natural" or "organic" way. To them, the leveling of such cultures manifests a deep betrayal of racial differences, requiring "a head-on clash both with a pseudo-antiracism which denies differences and with a dangerous racism which is nothing less than the rejection of the Other, the rejection of diversity."[45] Since,

---

43   Marco Tarchi, quoted in Bar-On, *Where Have All the Fascists Gone?*, 277.

44   See Marco Tarchi, *Dal MSI ad An: organizzazione e strategie* (Bologna: Società editrice il Mulino, 1997), 68; *La rivoluzione impossibile: dai Campi Hobbit alla nuova destra* (Florence: Vallecchi, 2010); Michele Angella, *La nuova destra: oltre il neofascismo fino alle "nuove sintesi"* (Florence: Fersu, 2000), 76; and Nicolai Hannig and Massimiliano Livi, "Nach der Revolte: 1968 als Ausgangspunkt eines bewegten Jahrzehnts in Italien und Deutschland," in *Die 1970er Jahre als schwares Jahrzehnt: Politisierung und Mobilisierung swischen christlicher Demokratie und extremer Rechter*, ed. Massimiliano Livi, Daniel Schmidt, and Michael Sturm (New York: Campus Verlag, 2010), 38n21.

45   Alain de Benoist, quoted in Bar-On, *Where Have All the Fascists Gone?*, 25.

according to this logic, racism is the rejection of whiteness, white culture, and white power, for Benoist, the Nouvelle Droite could characterize its foes as "racist" for criticizing whites who are simply trying to defend their traditions. Thus, while rehashing existing leftist theories, the Nouvelle Droite also has provided an important outlet for the narrative of white victimhood associated with "reverse racism," "white genocide," and the "colonial" invasion of Europe by immigrants and refugees.

If this ideology sounds incredibly familiar, that is because it is relatively easy to locate in a continuum that stretches from the early metapolitics of blood and soil to those right-to-left movements that took shape after 1968 leading up to the present day. One embodiment of that continuum, for instance, was August Haußleiter, cofounder of the Green Party of Germany. A former member of the fascist Sozialistische Reichspartei (SPR—Socialist Reich Party) before it was banned, Haußleiter made a political comeback in the 1960s by turning to student-led ecology and antinuclear movements in an attempt to recruit young people into a red-brown alliance. In 1980, he was elected chairman of the Greens, but stepped down after leftists exposed his Nazi past. Throughout the 1980s, broad efforts took place to weed out "national revolutionaries" who entered the Green Party, which led to another group called the Ökologisch-Demokratische Partei (ÖDP—Democratic Ecology Party). Formed in 1982 and led by Herbert Gruhl, the ÖDP was noted for pervasive Holocaust denial, rejection of the notion of social justice, and support for the "natural ecology of the Volk." Through these formulations, biodiversity was seen as intuitively ingrained into the genetic fiber of European society, presenting immigrants as a kind of "invasive species."[46]

We have now almost come full circle from the emergence of protofascism to its intentional redeployment in the late 1970s. The point of the Nouvelle Droite and Gladio networks had been laid out fifty years earlier, on May 4, 1923, when the rising leader of the Nazi Party Adolf Hitler declared, "Our task is to create the sword that [the Leader] will need when he is there. Our task is to give the dictator, when he comes, a people ready for him!"[47]

---

46   Lee, *The Beast Reawakens*, 217–18.

47   Eberhard Jäckel and Axel Kuhn, eds., *Hitler: Sämtliche Aufzeichnungen,*

Gladio and the Nouvelle Droite both functioned to serve this purpose. While Gladio networks engaged in a terror campaign to draw people away from the left, the Nouvelle Droite commandeered the chief points of the left for their own usage. For the Nouvelle Droite, antiracism meant white power, and diversity could be seen as a rejection of equality. Neither group operated openly as political organizations, choosing instead to recreate the conditions for fascism by spreading angst and extending their influence over the cultural sphere. While their work was effective to some extent, a missing ingredient in the fascist movement's resurgence would emerge as a powerful force through the 1980s and into the 1990s. Although often at odds with fascists and "national revolutionaries," the radical right has effectively enabled the greater growth of the fascist movement and helped mainstream their talking points. It is to this volatile relationship between fascism and the radical right that we will turn in the next chapter.

1905–1924 (Stuttgart: Deutsche Verlags-Anstalt, 1980), 923–24. See Kershaw, *Hitler*, 183–85, for context.

CHAPTER 4: THE RADICAL RIGHT

Radical Right Populism in the United States

The radical right is becoming perhaps the most important and influential political actor in the North Atlantic today. Able to summon large constituencies of both left and right to plebiscitary initiatives like Brexit, the radical right significantly affects the actions of the mainstream conservative, liberal, and socialist parties. It is often noted that the radical right is not in fact fascist but relies instead on a kind of conservative, ethnocentric populism to draw together a broad constituency of people fed up with the status quo. Yet what is less discussed is the root and source of the populist radical right, as well as its continued connections to fascism. By excavating these sources, we can obtain a better picture of how the creep from fascism to radical right and vice versa occurs.

After the war, fascist networks in the United States retained their Americanism while taking full advantage of the Red Scare. Senator Joseph McCarthy, who worked with high-ranking members of the neo-Nazi SRP (Sozialistische Reichspartei) to derail the Malmedy war crimes trial in 1948, was set to deliver a speech—written by Francis Parker Yockey—at an event organized by the successor of the German American Bund, the German-American Voters Alliance. He abandoned the plan due to popular outcry.[1] McCarthyist

---

1 Coogan, *Dreamer of the Day*, 238–40.

"Americanism with its sleeves rolled up" was embraced by the American Legion, Regnery Publishing, and NAM, top members of which spun off to create the John Birch Society—an optimal space for fascist ideas to creep under the radar of conspiracy theory and anti-Semitic code.[2] Perhaps the most unifying figure on the radical-right-to-fascist political spectrum, however, was Willis Carto.

Early in life, Carto developed a profound appreciation for homegrown fascist ideologues like Lawrence Dennis who had called for a fascist top-down takeover of the United States by corporate "out-elites"—corporate and financial heavyweights resentful over Roosevelt's New Deal. Although Dennis renounced his fascist position after the war, Carto was more brazen, hoping to work with a growing international network of fascists and conservatives to create a broad front against communism and a virulent anti-Semitism veiled as "anti-Zionism." Under the auspices of a journal called *Right*, Carto sought to unite the disparate branches of the right—the States's Rights and Citizens' Council movements, Christian Identity pastors, cultural traditionalists, conspiracy theorists, Norse reconstructionists, and anti-interventionists.

Among these groups, perhaps Christian Identity would prove the most directly fascist. Christian Identity pastors believed in British Israelism—the notion that Eve had been impregnated both by Adam and the serpent, with the first "seed" becoming the genetic line of the English and the latter becoming that of Jews. Thus, it was the English, and not the Jews, who inherited the Tribe of Israel. The chief acolyte of Christian Identity was a charismatic California preacher and state leader of Gerald L. K. Smith's fascist Christian Nationalist Crusade named Wesley A. Swift. Asserting a violently

---

2   For more on the John Birch Society, see Michael, *Willis Carto and the American Far Right*; Eric Foner and John A. Garraty, *The Reader's Companion to American History* (Boston: Houghton Mifflin, 1991), 597; Rachel Tabachnick, "The John Birch Society's Anti-Civil Rights Campaign of the 1960s, and its Relevance Today," Political Research Associates' website, January 21, 2014, http://www.politicalresearch.org/2014/01/21/the-john-birch-societys -anti-civil-rights-campaign-of-the-1960s-and-its-relevance-today/ #sthash.2CfgLij8.dpbs; Elinor Langer, *A Hundred Little Hitlers: The Death of a Black Man, the Trial of a White Racist, and the Rise of the Neo-Nazi Movement in America* (New York: Picador, 2003), 114–15.

anti-Semitic and anticommunist message, Christian Identity's ability to integrate fascism into Christianity would make it one of the most essential nodes of Carto's emerging network. For his own part, however, Carto remained a convinced Yockeyist.

When police arrested Yockey in possession of a number of forged passports and documents in 1960, Carto visited him in jail. Two weeks later, Yockey died in what was ruled a suicide. Through Carto's publishing houses, institutes, and periodicals, *Imperium* and Yockeyist ideas found their way to the US radical right in theory and in practice.

While launching attacks against the political establishment, *Right* attempted to revitalize interest in the understory of fascist ideology and its contradictory combination of populism and natural aristocracy. Rehashing Madison Grant's *The Passing of the Great Race* among other sociobiological tracts, *Right* espoused theories about the supposed Khazar origins of Ashkenazi Jewry and the "Caucasoid" lineage of the Egyptian civilization. One of its leading contributors, Roger Pearson, was a fascist who ran a British group called the Northern League, which argued against racial intermixing and in favor of the return to nationalist culture against supposed degradation.[3] *Right* foregrounded demographics in many of its articles, suggesting that the civil rights era was part of the gradual decline of the white race. Like Yockey, Carto saw culture as a living organism with a life cycle and insisted that the United States was in a period of decline. Only the ever-popular awakening of a Nietzschean "superman" could rescue the country.[4]

In terms of international politics, *Right* took on awkward alliances to collectively oppose Zionism. For instance, the journal supported Puerto Rican independence and rejected the statehood of Alaska and Hawaii.[5] When they looked to the civil rights movement, scholar George Michael notes, both Carto and *Right* espoused "an apartheid type of fascism in which the world should consist of racially separate nation states."[6] Mirroring the Klan's efforts to work with the Nation of Islam, Carto sought to bring white

---

3   Michael, *Willis Carto and the American Far Right*, 33–34.

4   Ibid., 39–40.

5   Ibid., 34–35.

6   Ibid., 52.

nationalists together with black nationalists and attempted to unite black and white against the "common enemy" of "Zionism—the poisoner of all people."[7] American Nazi Party leader George Lincoln Rockwell also wrote for *Right*, but so did more "credible" conservatives who opposed the black freedom struggle.[8] Publicly, Carto never veered far from a populist political program set into place by the umbrella group Liberty Lobby, which he founded in 1958 to pull together conservatives in an attempt to transform US politics. With this ideological framework, Carto worked to fascistize the US conservative movement while maintaining the traditional "Gone with the Wind"-style southern nostalgia of the Klan along with corporatism and agrarian populism.

The Origin of the Modern Patriot Movement

After campaigning for radical-right populist George Wallace in his 1968 presidential bid, Carto created a split in Wallace's American Independent Party, supporting a "coalition of various state parties registered under the labels of the American Independent Party, Conservative Party, and Constitutional Party."[9] It was here that the seeds of the modern Patriot movement would germinate. Constitutional Party leader William Potter Gale had fought a guerrilla war in the Philippines while serving in the US Army. An associate of Wesley Swift, Gale created his own paramilitary group called the US Rangers in 1959. He authored a textbook, *The Road Back*, replete with instructions for pipe bombs, sabotage, and tactical warfare.[10] The Rangers inspired a larger group founded by his friend Robert DePugh and known as the Minutemen, an extremely

---

7   Ibid., 54.

8   Rockwell himself was similarly determined to discuss possible alliances with the Nation of Islam against multicultural liberal democracy. See Manning Marable, *Black Leadership* (New York: Columbia University Press, 1998), 173–74.

9   Michael, *Willis Carto and the American Far Right*, 101.

10   David Neiwert, *In God's Country: The Patriot Movement and the Pacific Northwest* (Washington: Washington State University, 1999), 23; Kevin Flynn and Gary Gerhardt, *The Silent Brotherhood: Inside America's Racist Underground* (New York: Free Press, 1989), 49–50.

anticommunist group that organized themselves in a manner similar to many Marxist-Leninist groups.[11] Tied to Christian Identity, the John Birch Society, and the Klan, the Minutemen kept a kill list of some 1,500 people associated with what they called the "Communist hidden government."[12]

The year after the Wallace split, Gale joined with a retired dry cleaner and Henry L. Beach, former Oregon state liaison for the interwar fascist group the Silver Legion of America, or Silver Shirts. Together they created Posse Comitatus in Portland, Oregon, in 1969.[13] Informed by the fascist tradition's take on the settler-colonial myth of the pioneer posses of the nineteenth century, Posse Comitatus followers were instructed to set up local communities accountable and responsible only to themselves and not to the federal government. Withdrawing from taxes and federal bureaucracies, Posse Comitatus identified the county sheriff as the executor of the "supreme law of the land." As Posse Comitatus grew, a movement of antigovernment protesters calling themselves "sovereign citizens" emerged. Rapidly growing to more than a hundred thousand followers, sovereign citizens spread with or without organized groups, linked by conspiracy theories and tactics of sabotaging the federal government (and their enemies) through fraudulent lawsuits, tax schemes, liens, and checks. One of their early initiatives was the creation of small, local militias inspired by the Rangers and the Minutemen.

Posse Comitatus's stronghold in the Northwest grew through Christian Identity and Klan networks. Eventually generating an intense following through the congregation of Richard Butler, who had been introduced to both Christian Identity and Swift by Gale. With his faithful and heavily armed flock, Butler built a compound in Hayden Lake, Idaho. Called Aryan Nations, Butler's new group had a home base for zealous fascism built on a territorial claim for a "white homeland" in the Northwest United States. He called his claim, along with the violent means by which he hoped to obtain it, the "Northwest Imperative." As a 1970s resurgence of the Ku Klux Klan developed through the leadership of the charismatic and

---

11   Michael, *Willis Carto and the American Far Right*, 109.

12   Neiwert, *In God's Country*, 53.

13   Ibid., 52.

youthful David Duke, new intersections took place between the older, patriotic, Christian Klansmen and the younger, more flashy and revolutionary fascist movement.

A new direction seemed to appear for US white supremacists virtually overnight. A devoted Nazi from the age of thirteen, Duke made it his mission to revivify the tarnished image of the Klan, creating the Knights of the Ku Klux Klan and establishing himself as its leader. Wearing a smug smile and a sleek suit, Duke's bravado and charm would seduce media and audiences across the United States. He used to joke, "We're going to make sure all the Jews are equal—equally dead," and astonishingly his audiences would laugh.[14] Duke's real skill was in mainstreaming racism by exploiting the sense of alienation and discontent felt by the white working class. His new Klan took off, establishing the seedbed for a new generation of white supremacists to emerge from the fusion of the Nazi and Klan movements. In 1979, a local branch of a rival Klan, Virgil Griffin's confusingly named "Invisible Empire, the Knights of the Ku Klux Klan," forged an alliance with American Nazi Party members in North Carolina and opened fire on a group of protesters from the Workers Viewpoint Organization (later called the Communist Workers Party) in Greensboro, killing five.[15] Duke resigned from the Knights of the Klan amid a scandal over the selling of a membership list and pseudonymously writing a sex manual for women called *Finders Keepers* and self-defense guides for African Americans written under the pseudonym Mohammed X, although he cited the increased violence as his reason for going more mainstream.[16] Although Duke's legacy was significantly tarnished, he built up his reputation as a "respectable racist" through the National Association for the Advancement of White People, which argued that white rights were not equally protected under the law due to the rise of anti-white racism. With a radical-right platform of economic populism, environmental appeals, and racism cloaked in the

---

14   David Duke, quoted in Langer, *A Hundred Little Hitlers*, 132.

15   Along with notorious Nazi organizers, the Klan(s) were joined by two informants who had warned police of the massacre in advance. See Elizabeth Wheaton, *Codename Greenkil: The 1979 Greensboro Killings* (Athens: University of Georgia Press, 2009), 45–46.

16   Langer, *A Hundred Little Hitlers*, 141.

language of equality, Duke stunned the US in 1989 by winning election to a seat in the Louisiana House of Representatives.

Leaderless Resistance Finds Its First Victims

As opposed to the European Social Movement and neofascist networks, which drew on the esoteric spiritualism of Evola in a general rejection of the conservative right, US fascism viewed the right as its breeding ground. However, the fascist movement did not refuse to learn from leftist movements. Just as the John Birch Society and the Minutemen based their structures on oddly Marxist-Leninist configurations, a new intervention into the strategies and tactics of fascism called for "leaderless resistance." This generally meant armed cells composed of five to seven people, linked to a larger structure of militant cells ideologically based in the Northwest Imperative and intent on committing acts of terror against interracial couples, Jews, communists, and the federal government. The goal was to create a cascading political disruption that would bring about the catastrophe of liberal democracy and the rebirth of the white "natural citizen."

As the Klan's resurgence faltered, Texas Klan leader Louis Beam began to promote this new ideology of "leaderless resistance." When the farm crisis of the 1980s set in, Carto and his network attempted to capitalize on the financial dysfunction by spreading anti-Semitic ideas among rural people, along with the idea of leaderless resistance that gained traction in Posse Comitatus. On February 13, 1983, tax resister Gordon Kahl was pulled over with his son and wife and refused to be served, engaging instead in a firefight that cost the lives of two marshals. Kahl sped away in a patrol car but was tracked down to a bunker in Lawrence County, Arkansas, where he was shot dead by law enforcement after delivering a fatal wound to a local sheriff.[17]

To avenge Kahl's death, one of Beam's disciples, Aryan Nations member Robert Mathews, took the lessons of leaderless resistance into his cold heart and organized a militant white nationalist group.

17   Leonard Zeskind, *Blood and Politics: The History of the White Nationalist Movement from the Margins to the Mainstream* (New York: Farrar, Straus & Giroux, 2009), 75–77.

Also informed by neo-Nazi William Pierce's novel *The Turner Diaries*, Mathews's group took the name "The Order" (named after a fictional group in Pierce's novel that sparks a race war through racially motivated murder, terrorist strikes, and political assassinations), but in more secretive circles became known as the Brüders Schweigen (Silent Brotherhood). Although deeply imbedded in the Christian Identity myth, members of the Order also organized around an especially racist form of Odinism.

The Order committed bank robberies, armored car heists, and counterfeiting operations, hoping to generate enough strength to assassinate a kill list that included some of the most central names in the conspiracy theory pantheon. With the millions of dollars they were able to steal from armored cars and banks, the Order established networks of safe houses throughout the United States, while also allegedly bestowing hundreds of thousands onto white power organizations around the country.[18]

They murdered a Denver talk radio host named Alan Berg, known for debating right-wing callers, and then the Order came crashing down in 1984, when an informant put federal investigators on their trail. An FBI siege against Mathews ended in his fiery death. The rest of the ring was arrested and imprisoned, with member David Lane becoming among the most important white supremacist movement prisoners in the world (his "14 Words"—"We must secure the existence of our people and a future for white children"—have gained the authority of a Bible verse for neo-Nazis).[19] In the ensuing backlash, federal authorities rounded up neo-Nazi and Christian Identity leaders Robert Miles, Richard Girnt Butler, and Louis Beam, putting them on trial in Fort Smith, Arkansas, for sedition. The trial also implicated leaders like Frazier Glenn Miller Jr., who had been present at Greensboro, National Alliance leader William Pierce, and Tom Metzger, who will be discussed at length in the next chapter. Nevertheless, only Miles, Butler, and Beam were charged, and the jury eventually acquitted them.[20]

---

18   Neiwert, *In God's Country*, 58.
19   Ibid., 57–59; also Zeskind, *Blood and Politics*, 96–106. On the motivations
       and ideas of members, see Mattias Gardell, *Gods of the Blood*, 191–204.
20   See Zeskind, *Blood and Politics*, 141–71, for a thorough telling of this
       bizarre trial.

The Modern Militia Movement

While the Order's short existence from 1983 to 1984 was unsuccessful at igniting a race war, it did inspire ensuing white supremacist violence. Back in mountain country, Patriot movement pioneers David and John Trochmann hoped to generate local support for sovereign citizens' communities. Soon, David and his friend, a supporter of the Aryan Nations named Randy Weaver, came under the microscope of the FBI, which opened an investigation of possible gunrunning. When Weaver refused to cooperate with proceedings, US marshals attempted to stake out a safe place around the premises of his rural home in Ruby Ridge, Idaho, to arrest him. However, the Weavers' dog spotted agents snooping outside of the house, and his sons gave chase. Marshals shot the family dog. Weaver's adopted son opened fire, killing a marshal, and a ten-day standoff ensued. During the standoff, a sniper's bullet missed one of the young men, hitting Weaver's wife in the head as she held her infant daughter. Marshals also shot and killed Weaver's son, Sammy.

"Just as Mathews was the heir to Gordon Kahl," journalist David Neiwert writes, "so were Randy and Vicky Weaver perceived as the descendants of Mathews' The Order."[21] As a crowd of fascists gathered outside the house to support the Weavers, a famous veteran and right-wing icon named Bo Gritz emerged to negotiate a peace. The most highly decorated Green Beret of the Vietnam War, Gritz made a name for himself after the war by returning in search of missing prisoners of war. Gritz's adventures in Vietnam, though unsuccessful, purportedly provided fodder for a very successful Hollywood industry of postwar adventure movies and TV shows set in Vietnam and elsewhere, including *Rambo* and *The A-Team*. Yet Gritz was also a fellow traveler of David Duke and a leading member of Willis Carto's attempt at a radical right party, the Populist Party. Somehow, Gritz brokered a truce between the Weavers and law enforcement, ending the standoff. He celebrated afterwards by returning to the gathering of skinheads and white supremacists declaring, "Mr. Weaver wanted me to pass this along to those of you out here" and stiffening his arm outward in a Nazi salute.[22]

---

21   Neiwert, *In God's Country*, 238.

22   Ibid., 66.

Gritz was a symbol of veterans for whom, like the Freikorps, the war had not ended. Vietnam had been lost due to the protesting hippies and corrupt political class who sold out Middle America. The right had to defeat the enemy at home—the feds and the hippies—to put America to rights, reversing the changes of the civil rights movement and returning the United States to its former glory. If it were not for the fact that the Patriot movement had its start in fascist networks, it would be easier to place them, like the interwar Patriotic Movement, in a conservative revolutionary milieu. Nevertheless, even with its fascist roots, it becomes necessary to analyze the Patriots in light of their present form, rather than simply their genealogy. Hence, the Patriot movement can be placed in the hybridized, process-oriented category of the fascist creep, because it was created by fascists out of the broader settler-colonial orientation for the purposes of advancing fascism, despite being ostensibly autonomous from it.

This strategy would be clarified just two months after the standoff at Ruby Ridge, when Christian Identity pastor Pete Peters held a gathering of Patriots at a ranch in Estes Park, Colorado, bringing Beam together with Tom Metzger, John Trochmann, and Larry Pratt, one of Pat Buchanan's operatives. Together, these organizers and ideologues agreed that a militia movement was necessary to foreground leaderless resistance against the encroaching federal government. The militia movement would grow as a populist front, intertwined with the fascist movement, but separated by a clear John Birch Society-like ideological buffer to better organize in the general population. Galvanizing around issues of "property rights" and against conspiracies hatched by the New World Order and the Zionist Occupation Government, a range of literature was distributed by the growing militia movement warning against an apocalyptic scenario in which the UN's environmentalist blue helmets overrun the United States and depopulate the West, commissioning the Crips and Bloods to do house-to-house searches to take away citizens' firearms and cart gun owners off to FEMA camps. The militias found their early support base not in overt neo-Nazi organizations, but in the Wise Use movement, founded during the 1980s and based on the fusion of ranchers, loggers, local law enforcement, and Posse Comitatus members.[23]

---

23   Zeskind, *Blood and Politics*, 310–19; Stephen E. Atkins, *Encyclopedia of*

Property Rights

The Patriot movement's strong focus on capitalism as "private property rights" has found a solid base in the United States's libertarian movement, which developed a free market economic platform through the "anarchist-capitalist" ideology of Murray Rothbard. Typically seen as far right, the ideological platform of libertarianism came to be most effectively spread through the efforts of the Cato Institute, founded by Rothbard and Charles Koch in the early 1970s, and through Citizens for a Sound Economy (the forerunner of FreedomWorks and Americans for Prosperity), which launched in 1984 with Ron Paul as its first chairman. However, the movement has deeper roots in a merger of leftist and right-wing ideas that took place in the 1960s.

After his articles faced rejection by the *National Review* for their anti-interventionist line toward Vietnam during the early 1960s, Rothbard joined a small clique of historians in the new left who argued that the "New Deal" had not succeeded in saving the United States from the Great Depression.[24] Attempting to bring political poles together, Rothbard created the journal *Left & Right*, arguing that conservatism manifested "a dying remnant of the *ancien régime* of the pre-industrial era, and, as such, it *has* no future." Against the "confused, middle-of-the-road movement" of socialism, libertarianism projected "Liberal *ends* by the use of Conservative *means*" (a slogan strikingly similar to the parafascist Österreichische Aktion's "Stand with the Right, think with the Left").[25] Rothbard actively sought out left-wing allies like William Appleman Williams, a professor disenchanted with the old left but vehemently opposed to imperialism. Nevertheless, Rothbard's favorite historian was Harry Elmer Barnes, arguably the most important leader of the movement to deny the Holocaust. In his obituary for Barnes, published in the

---

Right-Wing Extremism in Modern American History (Santa Barbara: ABC-CLIO, 2011), 221–24; David Helvarg, *The War Against the Greens: The "Wise Use" Movement, the New Right, and the Browning of America* (Boulder: Johnson Books, 2004), 278–79.

24   John Payne, "Rothbard's Time on the Left," *Journal of Libertarian Studies* 19, no. 1 (Winter 2005): 10–11.

25   Ibid., 13. See also, Wasserman, *Black Vienna*, 132.

final issue of *Left & Right* in 1968, Rothbard proclaimed, "All persons leave an irreplaceable gap when they die; but this gap is truly enormous in the case of Harry Barnes, for in so many ways he was the last of the Romans."[26]

Rothbard extolled the Students for a Democratic Society (SDS) and Che Guevara for their anti-imperialism, while blaming the right wing for rejecting the revolutionary spirit.[27] When the SDS split in 1969, Rothbard stated that the sectarian hardening of Marxist positions that resulted would lead to the eventual failure of the movement. In particular, Rothbard argued adamantly against women's liberation as a priority for social movements and saw the split as an opportunity for new libertarian groups to take the lead. In the same year, Rothbard brought disenchanted former members of both the SDS and the right-wing group Young Americans for Freedom together for a libertarian conference intended to be the major point of origin for the modern libertarian movement.[28] Yet the conference was undermined when a former speechwriter for Barry Goldwater and contributor to Carto's *Right* named Karl Hess took the podium dressed in a guerilla uniform adorned with an Industrial Workers of the World pin and exhorted attendees to leave the conference the next day and join a peace march.[29]

With his attempt at rallying a left-right movement a complete failure, Rothbard attached himself to the so-called Austrian School of economics, which revolved around the writings of Friedrich Hayek and Ludwig von Mises. Hayek had been influenced by Othmar Spann, the corporatist theorist of the interwar Austrian Nazi Party, before moving to Mises's liberal economics.[30] The Austrian School diverged from Spannian corporatism, insofar as they advocated the primacy of free markets and individual transactions rather than "universalist" economic planning. Together

---

26   Murray N. Rothbard, "Harry Elmer Barnes, RIP," *Left & Right* 4, no. 1 (1968): 3, available at lewrockwell.com/1970/01/murray-n-rothbard/remembering-harry-elmer-barnes/.

27   Payne, "Rothbard's Time on the Left," 15.

28   Ibid., 19.

29   Ibid., 20.

30   See Wasserman, *Black Vienna*, 81; Alan Ebenstein, *Hayek's Journey: The Mind of Friedrich Hayek* (New York: Palgrave McMillan, 2003), 40.

with Milton Friedman, these new capitalist luminaries gravitated toward the University of Chicago, joining with the conservative right in an attempt to iron out free-market policies that would deregulate industry and finance and bring greater powers to business to squash unions and environmentalists. The result, including the Koch-funded magazine *Reason*, which enthusiastically defended apartheid in South Africa and paved the way for Silicon Valley libertarianism, provided the crucial underpinnings of a functioning economic and political discourse tentatively operating under the moniker of "neoliberalism."[31]

Wise Use

The powerful combination of free market "property rights" ideals, law enforcement, and civil society formed the backdrop of the industry-funded Wise Use movement, which hosted events, held rallies, and encouraged visceral hatred of environmental activists. Wise Use apostle Chuck Cushman would pass out militia flyers while on tour and help consolidate the efforts of property rights and county rights movements backed largely by Posse Comitatus. According to David Helvarg's important work *The War Against the Greens*, "in the West militias used Wise Use groups as their primary recruiting ground, arguing for military resistance to the government and its 'preservationist' backers, and formation of three- to six-man 'Autonomous Leadership Units' that look and act suspiciously like terrorist cells."[32] Harassment of environmentalists often followed Wise Use rallies, including well poisonings, dead animals, and swastika paintings. Harsh words about tar and feathering or killing environmentalists sometimes led to real acts of violence, including rape.[33] Among the talking points of Wise Use was "property rights" against illegal government "takings." Due to environmental protections for wetlands

---

31   Mark Ames, "Homophobia, Racism and the Kochs: The Tech-Libertarian 'Reboot' Conference is a Cesspool," Pando.com, September, 18, 2014, https://pando.com/2014/07/18/homophobia-racism-and-the-kochs-san-franciscos-tech-libertarian-reboot-conference-is-a-cesspool/.

32   Helvarg, *The War Against the Greens*, 273–75.

33   Ibid., 218–223.

restoration, Wise Use activists insisted, the government could just take away people's land through immanent domain.[34]

In Bellingham, Washington, one of the key Wise Use organizers shared a speaking event with Bill Hinkle, a longtime member of Carto's Liberty Lobby and an activist for the Populist Party, which was running David Duke for president of the United States in a campaign managed by Ralph Forbes, former western commander of Rockwell's American Nazi Party. In the early 1990s, Hinkle joined other Patriot movement and Wise Use activists in embracing the *Ultimatum Resolution*, a prolix text calling for the dissolution of the Union and urging citizens to separate "ourselves, one by one, according to state boundaries," warning that "the bloody history of mankind is getting close to being repeated in America.... If [the Ultimate Resolution is unsuccessful], bloodshed and anarchy in the streets of America appear to be inevitable."[35] Another key member of Wise Use and the Populist Party in the Pacific Northwest, Kim Badynski, came to Washington under the auspices of the Northwest Imperative, joined in Aryan Nations programming, and rose to become the Grand Wizard of the Washington chapter of Duke's Knights of the Klan.[36]

Taking a page from Duke's rhetoric, the industry-supported Wise Use movement galvanized violent, anti-left mobilizations by bringing together fascists and those increasingly and intimately intertwined with them. "In trying to organize among unemployed loggers, resource workers, small independent business people, and frustrated middle managers, they have even incorporated a thinly veiled 'anti-capitalist' message," Helvarg observed. "They use class resentment as a cudgel by portraying environmentalists as wealthy elitists, part of a 'green establishment' with links to transnational corporations, the Rockefellers, and the United Nations."[37]

The nationalist hatred of immigrants is also baked into Wise Use, which promotes a network of anti-immigration and "population

---

34   US Senate, *The Militia Movement in the United States*, ed. Arlen Specter (Washington, DC: US Government Printing Office, 1997), 17–18.

35   Gyeorgos Ceres Hatonn, *No Thornless Roses* (Las Vegas: Phoenix Source Publishers, 1993), 102.

36   Zeskind, *Blood and Politics*, 298.

37   Helvarg, *The War Against the Greens*, 84.

control" groups linked to a white nationalist lobbyist named John Tanton. The so-called Tanton Network receives money from foundations like the Pioneer Fund, which since its founding in 1937 has maintained a mission of proving a connection between race and intelligence. The Tanton Network then spreads these funds around to organizations that will carry its message through to policy makers and the public, usually via distillations of talking points developed by racist academics like Arthur Jensen and Richard Lynn, who also received Pioneer Fund money. It is also a large funder of anti-immigrant groups like Californians for Population Stabilization, and Tanton has received awards for his "conservation" efforts from corporations like Chevron, who commended him for ensuring "wise use of land and water in the Petoskey area."

Tanton's own persuasions are influenced by old 1920s, Nazi-originated quota systems. In particular, Tanton "practically worships" John Bond Trevor, one of the architects of the Immigration Act of 1924, whose group, the American Coalition of Patriotic Societies, was indicted on sedition charges in 1942 for the promotion of fascism.[38] The Tanton Network advocates a European majority in the United States, insisting that the "Latin onslaught" of immigration to the country be resisted on political, social, and ecological grounds. Tanton serves as editor of a journal published through his Social Contract Press, which focuses on perceived "anti-European" prejudices tacit within the ideology of "multiculturalists." The Social Contract Press also published a translation of Jean Raspail's racist, anti-immigration French book *The Camp of the Saints*. Canadian authorities banned Tanton's own book, *The Immigration Invasion*, as hate literature.

A new web of semi-legitimized fascism had emerged by the 1990s through Duke's resurgence of the Klan and election to political office, along with the birth of Wise Use and the modern Patriot movement out of Posse Comitatus, with its direct links to the Silver Shirts, the Minutemen, Christian Identity, Aryan Nations, and Willis Carto's fascistized conservative network. The militia movement that would develop out of this formulation was able to maintain a veneer of plausible deniability in its relationship to fascism,

---

38   "John Tanton," Southern Poverty Law Center's website, https://www
      .splcenter.org/fighting-hate/extremist-files/individual/john-tanton.

as well as a horizontal structure that affected a vague "social move-ment" attitude. Hence, Patriot groups span a gamut of ideologies, from radical-right populism to protofascism, making its presence felt in political causes like Pat Buchanan's 1992 and 2000 presiden-tial campaigns, the 2009 Tea Party, and Donald Trump's successful 2016 presidential bid.

Perhaps the direct target of the Wise Use movement was a new ecological group called Earth First! (EF!). Formed in 1979 by frustrated conservationists, EF! rejected the ideals of social justice, seeking instead a grassroots movement dedicated specifi-cally to defending wilderness against logging, mining, and cattle grazing. EF! came to include thousands of activists agitating for direct action against extractive industries and promoting tactics of sabotage and nonviolent disobedience to further their aims. Yet EF! also advocated controversial opinions tied to white suprema-cist, anti-immigration, and depopulation claims mixed in with the "deep ecology" of Norwegian philosopher Arne Næss and copi-ous references to pagan and Asatru beliefs.[39] As EF! changed from within, adopting more left-leaning social justice values after facing heavy criticism from the left, cofounder Dave Foreman abandoned the movement to form the Rewilding Institute, ironically taking money from the Weeden Foundation, which is linked to the Tan-ton Network and its larger Wise Use network.[40] Although EF! is today a movement committed to anti-oppression, white national-ism remains a significant problem that conservationists tend to ig-nore, again exposing how the fringes of combative movements like the Patriot and militant environmental movements can cross over in a murky, marginal area of hybridization and fascist creep.

Le Pen's Front National

As decolonization increasingly became the new normal, the populist radical right's rhetoric shifted toward anti-immigration, represented

---

39   See Martha Frances Lee, *Earth First! Environmental Apocalypse* (Syra-cuse: Syracuse University Press), 101–104, 107.

40   "Funders of the Anti-Immigrant Movement," Anti-Defamation League's website, January 27, 2014, http://www.adl.org/civil-rights/immigration/c/funders-of-the-anti-immigrant.html.

by the popularity of the book from France that Tanton selected to publish, Raspail's *The Camp of the Saints*, which had made a significant impact across the Atlantic since its publication in 1973. Among the most disgustingly lurid novels of macabre violence published in the twentieth century, *The Camp of the Saints* evokes comparisons to interwar literature of Freikorps and conservative revolutionaries, as well as Pierce's *The Turner Diaries*. Raspail concentrates on themes of shit, slime, and dirt, and describes in detail the brutal rape and gory violence that transpires as fictional immigrants annihilate European-descended populations in the former colonies and invade Europe. The novel's success marked a shift in radical-right rhetoric that carried over Madison Grant's fear of the decline of the "great white race" into the modern era. It was an ecstatic and nightmarish vision of a new global race war from South Africa to France to Alabama. One of its loudest mouthpieces was Jean-Marie Le Pen.

While he did not openly advocate the Nouvelle Droite's ideology, Le Pen's philosophy issued from guttural European ultranationalism and maintained a "conservative revolutionary" nostalgia for Vichy France. Aside from supporting the OAS along with Thiriart, Le Pen also boasted of his friendship with Léon Degrelle, the Belgian Rexist (social monarchist) leader who served loyally under fascist occupation and who Hitler thought of as an ideal son. Le Pen had served as a paratrooper in Algeria, facing allegations of torture, and in France he served as a deputy to the populist radical right party of Pierre Poujade.[41] As Poujadism drifted into memory, Le Pen opened a publishing house and began to peddle old fascist memorabilia and speeches from the Nazi era. Le Pen's public support for the OAS and Nazi collaborators, along with his barely disguised anti-Semitism, was matched by his ability to organize with conservatives in support of a violent mass movement, which made him a force to be reckoned with in French politics. While the Nouvelle Droite led efforts to detour the left into the right through a fascist twist, Le Pen would take a more direct route into right-wing politics.

In 1964, French neofascists formed a fighting force called Occident out of the Fédération des Étudiants Nationalistes, the parent group of Benoist's Nouvelle Droite in the 1960s. Rejecting

---

41   As documented in Pierre Vidal-Naquet's landmark *Torture: Cancer of Democracy* (London: Penguin Books, 1963), 92.

the movement toward Third World liberation, Occident called
for legitimacy for the far right against Marxism. The same year
as Le Pen managed the presidential campaign of a Vichy figure
named Jean-Louis Tixier-Vignancour, "Algerie Française" activist
Mark Frederiksen formed the Fédération d'Action Nationale et
Européene (FANE—Federation of National and European Action) alongside the Action Française leader François Duprat's
Groupes Nationalistes Révolutionnaires (Revolutionary Nationalist Groups), both of which were connected to Occident. After the
French government banned Occident in 1968, several organizers
within its circles—including Duprat and a militant student group
called Groupe Union Défense, also known as the "Black Rats"
(Benoist's former group)—created a new, separate group called Or-
dre Nouveau (ON—New Order). With Catholic integralists and
other ultranationalists, ON launched a new political party in 1972,
three years after its inauguration, called the Front National (FN).

The disparate sects joined under the original credo, *La droite
sociale, populaire et nationale* (The social right, popular and national), which obviously tied together the words "national" and "social."
According to ON's weekly paper, the Front was created "to break
out of the political ghetto." Toward these ends, it modeled the party
after Italy's fascist Movimento Sociale Italiano, even appropriating
its symbol of the tricolor flame.[42] Le Pen promised to "bring together the *fasces* of our national forces so that the voice of France is heard
once more, strong and free."[43]

As Le Pen's leadership failed to garner votes at the ballot box,
some core fascists mutinied. Le Pen proved an unmovable object,
however, with the unwavering support of "national revolutionary"
Duprat at his side. Le Pen's apartment was bombed, and in 1978,
Duprat was assassinated with a car bomb. In the coming years, new
leaders like Jean-Pierre Stirbois would play down the "national revolutionary" angle, supporting instead a "solidarist" ideology that
worked better with the rhetoric of the Nouvelle Droite. Nothing
could shake Le Pen's grasp on power, and his narrative was clear:
"France for the French, Algeria for the Algerians."[44]

---

42   See Marcus, *The National Front and French Politics*, 18–19.

43   Jean-Marie Le Pen, quoted in Renton, *Fascism: Theory and Practice*, 13.

44   Eatwell, *Fascism: A History*, 317–18.

Xenophobia was rampant in France at the beginning of the 1980s. Even the French Communist Party led a campaign against immigrants. At one point, the Communist mayor of Vitry led party sympathizers in bulldozing an immigrant workers' hostel.[45] In 1980, the Front failed to even obtain enough signatures to run for election, but the next year, the Socialist Party won the presidential elections, sparking a strong radicalization of the right.

Though he saw parliament as a necessary means of taking power, Le Pen championed the regimes of Franco and Augusto Pinochet. For Le Pen, France requires a "true French revolution" to set the country and its people to rights against the "unjust equalities" that cause a decline in birth rate and invasion from abroad.[46] As for abortion, Le Pen railed against "official anti-French genocide"—a plan by leftists to destroy the ethnic stock of France. Drawing a comparison between the social and the human organism, the leader of the Front proclaimed, "Killing the child is Killing France." For "survival," Le Pen called for a population policy that would restore virile, fertile, and manly French *identité* against the ethnic invaders.[47] As for homosexuality, although Le Pen has openly claimed that it should not be a "privileged status," in other places he has made it clear that socialist-inspired homosexuality would be "the end of the world."[48]

As the Front grew in stature, it attracted an increasing number of people from the Nouvelle Droite. Despite his attempts at tact, Le Pen could not restrain himself from his usual anti-Semitic commentary, calling the Holocaust a "detail" in the history of World War II and referring to Jewish minister Michel Durafour as "*Monsier Darafour-crématoire.*"[49] When AIDS (called SIDA in France) started to spread in France, Le Pen described the victims as *sidaïque*—a reminder of the Vichy term *judaïque* or "judaic." Le Pen's popularity waned. With the death of its major tactician

---

45   Marcus, *The National Front and French Politics*, 78.

46   Ibid., 102.

47   Peter Davies, *The National Front in France: Ideology, Discourse, and Power* (New York: Routledge, 2001), 131.

48   Ibid., 132.

49   Peter Fysh and Jim Wolfreys, *The Politics of Racism in France* (New York: Palgrave-McMillan, 2003), 142.

and strategist, Stirbois, and the important splits between Nouvelle Droite-inspired ideas of free trade and "national preference" (protectionism and corporatism), the Front began to slip in the standings. However, the Front would gain new wings through the 1990s as it advanced corporatism and ultranationalism through the aid of Nouvelle Droite theorists like Bruno Mégret, with his "Third Way" economic ideology, and Pierre Vial, whose "Land and People" ideas returned to völkisch Nazism.[50]

Austrian Freedom Party

Le Pen's Front National was not the only radical-right populist party developed out of a fascist organization's attempts to emerge from the "fascist ghetto." During the creation and maturation of the FN, mainstream Austrian politics continued to grapple with the inevitable dilemmas of a country that saw itself as a victim of the Nazis rather than a willing participant. For roughly ten years after the war, Austria remained divided among the four Allied powers, and during that time the Sozialdemokratische Partei Österreichs (SPÖ—Social Democratic Party of Austria) plotted to emerge victorious through the developing postwar electoral system of the Second Republic. To engineer their success, the SPÖ created a new group called Verband der Unabhangigen (VdU—Association of Independents)—basically a "third force" container for 688,000 former Nazi Party members, which the socialists hoped would split the right-wing vote.[51] For the VdU, fascist policy in Austria had been buried in the past; the new "real fascism" came in the form of totalitarian dictatorship implanted by the Soviet Union, the days of interwar Social Democracy, and the modern formulation of the Second Republic. These former-Nazi "antifascists" equated de-nazification with fascism, advocating an insular, closed society instead of one open and vulnerable to the

50   Kevin Passmore, *Fascism: A Very Short Introduction* (Oxford: Oxford University Press, 2002), 100.

51   Walter Manoschek, "FPÖ, ÖVP, and Austria's Nazi Past," in *The Haider Phenomenon in Austria*, ed. Ruth Wodak and Anton Pelinka (London: Transaction Publishers, 2002), 5. Also, see Andrei S. Markovits, "Austrian Exceptionalism," in Ibid., 108.

CHAPTER 4: THE RADICAL RIGHT

intrigues of the great powers.[52] When Austria became sovereign, the VdU transformed into the Freiheitliche Partei Österreichs (FPÖ—Austrian Freedom Party), led by former agricultural minister of the Austrian Nazi Party, Anton Reinthaller. It was lost to many observers that the Social Democrats had effectively created a fascist party out of pure opportunism.

During the decade of Social Democrat Bruno Kreisky's reign, beginning in the early 1970s, the role of Austria in the Holocaust and the admission of former Nazis into state offices remained an unpopular subject not to be discussed in polite company. The loss of an absolute majority in 1983 led to Kreisky's fall and the rise of a new governing coalition of the FPÖ under a more liberal leadership. The FPÖ's inclusion in government raised very little controversy abroad. That changed in 1985, when the FPÖ's defense minister, the son of a Nazi Party member, shook hands with Walter Reder, an SS war criminal freshly released from an Italian jail. The defense minister, Friedhelm Frischenschlager, apologized but excused himself with the assertion that he had only committed a "humanitarian" act by welcoming home a prisoner of war.[53] The Social Democrats closed ranks with the political establishment, refusing to condemn Frischenschlager and in the process legitimizing the growing reaction from the right. Yet the FPÖ liberal-leaning leadership's cautious support for Frischenschlager disappointed the rank and file, who rallied instead behind a young, charismatic, former youth leader shooting up through the ranks of the FPÖ.[54]

Noted for his trendy outfits, pop culture branding, and 1980s yuppie style, Jörg Haider, protested Frischenschlager's apology. Exploiting the moment to try to redeem Nazi war criminals, Haider called Reder "a soldier who had done his duty for the Fatherland."[55] Like Frischenschlager, Haider was not old enough to have been a Nazi Party member, but his parents were Nazis living on "Aryanized" Jewish property. He emerged from the protofascist

---

52 Manoschek, "FPÖ, ÖVP, and Austria's Nazi Past," 6.

53 Markovits, "Austrian Exceptionalism," 156.

54 David Art, *The Politics of the Nazi Past in Germany and Austria* (Cambridge: Cambridge University Press, 2006), 178–79.

55 Hella Pick, *Guilty Victims: Austria from the Holocaust to Haider* (New York: I.B. Tauris, 2000), 157.

pan-German ideology espoused in the traditional student groups and fencing clubs of Austria and Germany. Perforce, his right-turn politics evoked those of the bygone era of the völkisch National Socialist Pan-German Freedom Movement and the National Socialist Freedom Party that had prepared the way for the refounding of the NSDAP in 1925. Haider and the FPÖ inner circle described the "national" idea of multicultural Austria as a "miscarriage," advocating a return to the Volk instead. To accomplish this maneuver, they rallied around a *Führerpartei* structure, which downplayed the old pan-Germanism and ultranationalist militancy in an attempt to pass the charisma of the leader off as a model of the "authentic Austrian." In 1986, Haider became the leader of the FPÖ to the jeers of the political establishment. The European Parliament later labeled him the "yuppie fascist."

Haider's xenophobic rants against Eastern European immigrants marked his populist bent against the established political parties and functionaries. At the same time, his appeal to Austria's past led to embarrassing moments, such as his characterization of the Waffen-SS as champions in "a struggle for freedom and democracy."[56] Like other reactionary populists, Haider cultivated an image of the edgy playboy to overcome the appearance of conventional political compromise, on the one hand, and the stodgy fascist old guard, on the other. Haider's "casual dress" appealed to the common man in what scholar Andre Gingrich sees as the combined registers of "mainstream celebrity" and "nonconformist rebel." These two integrated forms developed into a kind of yuppie entourage known as the *Haider Buberlpartie*, which dazzled the nightclubs of Austria in the late 1980s with fancy cars and early-model cell phones, distributing propaganda like postcards and showing up the representatives of other political parties who lacked the same chic flair.[57] Of course, the FPÖ was not all glam; like the Front National, the FPÖ generated political advantage in the streets by cultivating popularity among some groups within state law enforcement and veterans groups.

It would not be Haider's postmodern opportunism and charlatanism that would shake the Second Republic to its core in 1986,

---

56   Ibid., 184.

57   Andre Gingrich, "A Man for All Seasons," in Wodak and Pelinka, eds., *The Haider Phenomenon in Austria*, 77.

however. Controversy struck harder than ever that year, when national icon Kurt Waldheim, of the conservative Austrian People's Party, was exposed for lying about his Nazi past during his run for the presidency of Austria, the highest office in the nation. Waldheim's glittering career included a two-term stint as the secretary general of the UN, and his campaign slogan was "the Austrian the world trusts." Although he had insisted that, during the war, he had "not seen a single SS person" and "was against the Nazis," journalists uncovered the truth that he had been a member of the Nazi Students' League and an SA riding club and that he was possibly a war criminal whose unit had been responsible for the deaths of thousands of Jews in Yugoslavia. Scandal abroad led to a strengthening of the core support for Waldheim in Austria as a domestic matter, and he took home just over half of the vote for president in the second round of the elections. The Social Democratic prime minister, Fred Sinowatz, resigned immediately, as the election of Waldheim cast an even darker shadow on the coalition government with the FPÖ, which had doubled its previous number of votes.

President Waldheim found international support only from the Arab world, the Soviet Union, and the Catholic Church, while the United States put the former UN secretary general on the watch list, banning him entry as a possible war criminal. In Austria, Haider gained popularity by rejecting any introspection about Austria's Nazi past, continuing to insist that the elections were an Austrian affair. It did not matter what European liberals and leftists would think.

In 1987, the year the United States banned Waldheim, a crisis known as the Historians' Quarrel (*Historikerstreit*) broke, and Ernst Nolte, a former student of Nazi philosopher Martin Heidegger and among the most prominent historians of fascism, was criticized for a slide toward Holocaust denial and relativism. Nolte was one among an increasing number of revisionist historians questioning the severity of the Holocaust, whether by calling its very existence into question or by placing it alongside other genocides, undermining its quality as a unique example of depravity in human history. As historians around the world challenged the legacy of the Holocaust, Austrian nationalists doubled down on their support of Waldheim against international opinion, while, in France, the Front garnered its highest election results in its fifteen-year history. Many sensed a direct challenge to the embattled legacy of European democracy on the horizon. Through this pressurized political terrain at the end of the Cold War, a renascent fascist movement would emerge.

CHAPTER 5: THE THIRD POSITION

Between Radical Right and Nazi: The National Front

A few years before Le Pen's Front National came England's National Front (NF), founded in 1967 as an effort to mainstream numerous competing fascist sects through a unified political party based on an anti-immigrant platform that advocated social welfare. The NF emerged from the impetus of Arthur K. Chesterton, a former leader of Mosley's interwar British Union of Fascists. Chesterton had founded and led the League of Empire Loyalists, an extremist right-wing political interest group created to generate support for imperialism in the United Kingdom's Conservative Party. The League gained the support of young fascists John Tyndall and Colin Jordan, who formed the World Union of National Socialists in 1962 along with George Lincoln Rockwell and Savitri Devi. After participating in the first incarnation of the British National Party, established in 1960 by the National Labour Party and the White Defence League (both spin-offs of the League of Empire Loyalists), Jordan and Tyndall founded the more militant National Socialist Movement. After a spat over a lover and disputes over strategy and tactics, Jordan and Tyndall went their separate ways. The former created a more militant and explicitly fascist group called the British Movement, and the latter followed up a call from Chesterton to help create a populist right-wing party that would take a hard line on immigration. The result was the NF.

By the time Tyndall had taken the reins of the NF in 1977, British industry was sagging heavily. A member of the Conservative Shadow Cabinet, Enoch Powell, delivered a speech cautioning the British public against "rivers of blood" resulting from immigration, increasing the tensions between right and left. The anger and anxiety of working-class youth against both the Labour Party and the moderates in the Conservative Party found expression in an aggressive, raw rock music known as Oi! Played largely by skinheads, Oi! generally had a more macho character than most of the emerging punk scene. Oi! bands expressed a range of political positions, but as time passed some of these groups generally garnered a reputation for being racist and leaning toward the right. This was certainly true of the band Skrewdriver, whose more outwardly violent lyrics gained a following of boisterous toughs that was racist but not overtly fascist—at least at first. It was here that the NF sought to find supporters who could defend their marches and politicians from violent counterprotesters.

The NF and Jordan's British Movement began to build security teams from the skinhead subculture, bringing together the aggressive styles of working-class bands with a nationalist message: "England is for the English." Like the German storm troopers, fascist skinheads spent their time guzzling beer, pursuing sexual adventures, and beating up immigrants and nonwhites. One skinhead leader, Nicky Crane, became the new face of the British Movement's involvement with the increasingly fascist section of the skinhead scene.[1] Crane maintained a close relationship with the NF-affiliated Skrewdriver singer, Ian Stuart Donaldson, working on art and even lyrics for Skrewdriver albums and becoming a security fixture at their shows.

Although the NF felt the wind in their sails on the streets, their electoral advance was forestalled by the election of Margaret Thatcher, who "stole" important issues like anti-immigration and pulled the Conservatives further to the right. In 1980, after their political embarrassment at the polls, a split developed within the NF between the mainstream faction and a more openly fascist

---

1   For more on Crane, Donaldson, and the NF see Jon Kelly, "Nicky Crane: The secret double life of a gay neo-Nazi," *BBC News Magazine*, December 6, 2013, http://www.bbc.com/news/magazine-25142557.

group linked to the Nouvelle Droite and the skinhead scene. Led by organizer Patrick Harrington, the apostates insisted on taking the NF in a more explicitly violent direction in tune with the Strasserist Third Position.

The Harrington group had also fallen under the influence of Italian émigré Roberto Fiore, who was in exile from Italy under suspicion of participating in the bombing of Bologna's train station along with his group Terza Posizione—the bloodiest act of the Years of Lead. Upon entering the United Kingdom, Fiore found safe haven in the central London apartment of Nouvelle Droite ideologue Michael Walker. With Walker, Fiore linked up with Nouvelle Droite circles, and his spiritual adherence to Evola's doctrine filled in lingering questions for the Harrington group—particularly on the notion of the "political soldier." Along with Nick Griffin and Derek Holland, Harrington formally broke with Tyndall's leadership, forming the Official National Front and engaging more deeply in a movement to win the faith of alienated youth by courting the music scene. Although the skinhead aspects of the fascist movement worked with white working-class elements, skinheads also remained unpopular with intellectual types and were easily identified with fascism by opposition movements. Another parallel movement would form of aesthetes who agreed with skinheads on ideology, but recoiled from their vulgarity.

The New Avant-Garde

Beginning in 1978, punk bands and political organizers responded to the skinhead violence by creating the Rock Against Racism (RAR) movement. The acts associated with RAR tended to be anarchist, but there were some important exceptions. One prominent band in this radical, antiracist punk scene was Crisis, whose first EPs had a driving urgency backed by the Trotskyist ideology of the Socialist Workers Party and Tariq Ali's International Marxist Group, to which band mates Tony Wakeford and Douglas Pearce belonged, respectively. Guitarist Wakeford and bassist Pearce found replacemnts for the band's vocalist and drummer, and the next year dissolved the band to form a new experimental group called Death in June. By this point, they were disillusioned with the left and began to play shows featuring Nazi aesthetics and symbols, developing a genre called "neofolk" that mixed ancestral roots, fascist themes, and coded references to Evola and Strasserism.

A gay man, Death in June's frontman Douglas Pearce (also called Douglas P) was profoundly turned off by the staunch homophobia of skinheads and much of the white power scene. As his politics drifted toward the Third Position, Pearce became increasingly interested in Röhm, the SA, and what he saw as the complicated shades of grey between the conventional left and the Nazi's purported left-wing, such as it was. He spoke in interviews of how he and Wakeford came across "National Bolshevism, which is closely connected with the *Sturmabteilung* [SA] hierarchy." He explained, "People like Gregor Strasser and Ernst Röhm who were later known as 'second revolutionaries' attracted our attention."[2] Without any mention of the attacks on Jews and assassinations of leftists carried out by the SA, Pearce's message almost sounded compassionate and politically correct. In a 1985 interview with *Sounds* magazine, Pearce divulged his thoughts on the Strasserist position, recalling the Blood Purge of June 30, 1934:

> Our interest doesn't come from killing all opposition, as it's been interpreted, but from identification with our understanding of the leftist elements of the SA which were purged, or murdered by the SS. That day is extremely important in human history.... They were planning execution or overthrow of Hitler, so he wouldn't be around. We'd be living in a completely different world, I should imagine.... It's fascinating that a few people held the destiny of the world and mankind in their hands for those few hours and let it slip, and it could've gone either way.[3]

The "understanding of the leftist elements of the SA" appears to be more like admiration, as Pearce contemplates a brighter Nazi future that was cut down by the Hitlerist faction. Really, Strasser

2   Quoted in Robert Forbes, *Misery and Purity: A History and Personal Interpretation of Death In June* (Amersham: Jara Press, 1995), 15.

3   Douglas Pearce, quoted in *Midwest Unrest*, "Death in June: a Nazi band?," Libcom.org, November 19, 2006, https://libcom.org/library/death-in-june-a-nazi-band. Original quote from an interview in *Sounds* magazine in 1985.

was a staunch anti-Semitic reactionary who sought a kind of national front with neoconservatives under military rule—neither he nor the brutal paramilitary Röhm were leftists. Such admiration for the SA also appears in the Death in June album, *Brown Book*, which features a rendition of the Horst Wessel song, as well as an SS-style death's head on the cover.

In response to the RAR movement, members of the Strasserist splinter group of the NF created Rock Against Communism. Festivals featuring fascist skinhead bands and neofolk groups began to take shape in 1985 on land provided by Griffin's parents. The next year, Harrington and Holland opened a nightclub called the White Noise Club to host an increasing number of shows.[4] It was not long before former Death in June member Wakeford would enter into a formal relationship with the NF's Strasserist wing, forming his own neofolk band, Above the Ruins, which contributed a song to a benefit album for the NF. Aside from being embraced by and embracing the Official NF, the publication of Above the Ruins's cassette release was tracked back to Walker, whose magazine the *Scorpion* also printed a positive review of the band's latest record in 1985.[5] With its syncretic configuration of political ideology, Third Positionism took root in the skinhead and neofolk subcultures as a kind of palingenetic ultranationalism that, with a pessimistic and nihilist sense of modern life, looked toward a revolutionary new age born of traditional culture that could thrive amid the collapse of liberal multiculturalism.

New Alignments

The transformation of the leftist punk band Crisis into Third Positionist neofolk band Death in June during the early 1980s was part of a broader transformation occurring toward National Bolshevism, the Third Position of Otto Strasser, and the idea of the

---

4   See Nigel Copsey and John E. Richardson, *Cultures of Post-War British Fascism* (New York: Routledge, 2015), 145.

5   James Cavanagh, "Piss Poor Poet Found in the Dustbin of History," *Who Makes the Nazis*, March 3, 2011, http://www.whomakesthenazis .com/2011/03/piss-poor-poet-found-in-dustbin-of.html; "Illiberal Rock," *Scorpion* 8 (Spring 1985): 35.

"national revolutionary" movement. Many of these discoveries, according to Pearce, were made in Berlin, where a thriving neo-Nazi scene was developing along with the skinhead movement and Third Positionist politics. That this was happening in Berlin should be no surprise. Postwar administrations of the ruling Christlich-Demokratische Union (Christian Democratic Union) had recuperated unrepentant Nazis into the fold of politics and society. German remilitarization had taken place under the leadership of former Nazis. Hitler's chief of general staff of the army, Adolf Heusinger, served as the first inspector general of the West German army from 1957 until 1961, at which point he took over as chairman of the NATO Military Committee. By 1976, 214 of 217 army generals were veterans of the Third Reich. By the time Pearce was making his "discoveries," official veterans' events of the German army sometimes featured "Heil Hitler!" salutes and memorials to Third Reich casualties, and reports pointed to the bountiful sub rosa trafficking of SS songbooks, Nazi hate rock, and other banned Nazi memorabilia.[6]

The army was not the only sector of society marred by prominent appearances of neo-Nazism in Germany. In the early 1980s, Otto Remer's protégé, Michael Kühnen, forged a new political path by entering the Freiheitliche Deutsche Arbeiterpartei (FAP—Free German Workers' Party) and turning it toward vicious fascist skinhead campaigns against guest workers and refugees. While the party remained small, according to polls, some 79 percent of Germans agreed with its stance against too many foreigners.[7] The FAP sought to build its membership base by moving away from Remer's obvious Hitlerism toward Strasser's Third Position. Meanwhile, the Third Position movement got a push from the pamphlet *Farewell to Hitlerism*, which marked a crucial fascist appeal in favor of the East, rather than NATO.

To make matters more confusing, Horst Mahler, cofounder of the Marxist-Leninist Red Army Faction, began to shift toward fascism through Maoism and then the Greens. He, however, did not mind referencing Hitler. In a 1982 interview with post-structuralist Sylvère Lotringer, Mahler explained his position:

6   Lee, *The Beast Reawakens*, 286–87.
7   Ibid., 200.

Why did Hitler gain the support of Germans, with their particular intellectual tradition? It seems that Hitler relied on something in everybody's mind which was ignored by both Marxists
and liberals.... In the ecology issue, for example, some of the
terms used are in contradiction with standard Marxist or socialist schemata. For example, a form of conservative romanticism
is now embraced by "soil ideology"—their mystical attachment
to the ground, the cyclical sowing, nurturing, reaping. They also
hang on to conservative standards of family life. However, I'm
not ready to repudiate or denounce these ideas simply because
Hitler also relied on them. We are mistaken if we think that we
can stamp every problem of political orientation with "Left" and
"Right." It doesn't work anymore.[8]

Mahler was indeed on his way to a fascist ideology, which
brought a new question to the minds of leftists. How could such
a stalwart member of the left switch to fascism? Was the Red
Army Faction's strategy of heightening tensions in society in order
to expose the German state as fascist commensurate with fascist
terrorism?

As leftists continued to mull over these questions, other
neo-Nazis in Germany, like the founder of the Federal Criminal
Police Office (Bundeskriminalamt), Odfried Hepp, assisted national liberation movement groups like the Palestine Liberation
Organization and the Fractions Armées Révolutionnaires Liba-
naises, which was, in turn, linked to the militant left-wing French
group Action Directe.[9] Also, in Italy during this period, Thiriart's
disciple Claudio Mutti converted to Islam, marking the trend toward "anti-Zionist" solidarity. In the United States, another bizarre
left-right groupuscule would soon emerge calling itself the Aryan
Republican Army and basing its strategies and tactics on the guerrilla ideas generally perceived as leftist.

The FAP experienced setbacks when the state brought new
charges against Kühnen. He moved to France in 1984 to seek asylum

---

8   Horst Mahler, "Look Back on Terror," in *The German Issue*, ed. Sylvère
     Lotringer (Los Angeles: Semiotext(e), 2009), 105.

9   See Bale, "Right-Wing Terrorists and the Extraparliamentary Left,"
     n199.

with members of the neofascist group FANE.[10] The FANE had just
split off from Le Pen's Front National to create a new third-position
political party called the French and European Nationalist Party
(Parti Nationaliste Française et Européen), which immediately began associating itself with skinheads and radical-right parties across
borders like the Vlaams Blok in Belgium and the National Front in
England. This new party also linked up with CEDADE in Spain
to maintain militant networks throughout Europe.

Durruti, Autonomy, and the National Bolsheviks

Increasingly, fascist groups took on independent positions that were
outside the auspices of their recent collaboration with the secret services of various governments.[11] In the late 1970s, after the death
of Franco and the transformation of the Spanish state, CEDADE
split, leading to the 1983 creation of Bases Autónomas (Autonomous Bases), an early "grassroots network" claiming to identify
with the anarchism of Buenaventura Durruti, despite aiming their
violent attacks against anarchist and communist groups. It seemed
that a burgeoning movement for "armed spontaneism" was taking
shape. A number of groups, including Terza Posizione and the
Swiss Third Way, began to form a loose network—the March 12
Group—that Thiriart dubbed "the International of mailboxes."[12]
    Also joining the March 12 Group was a new faction emerg-
ing in France from a collection of smaller French neofascist groupuscules. An alphabet soup of groups came together to form the
Mouvement Nationaliste Révolutionnarie (MNR—Nationalist
Revolutionary Movement), which within months was joined by
the "Black Rats" and others in a new formation called Troisième
Voie (TV—Third Way). Like the MNR, TV called for a "Europe
independent of the blocs," against right and left, which was to
be brought about through a second French revolution. This revolution would secure an end to unskilled immigration through a

10   Lee, *The Beast Reawakens*, 201; Lee McGowan, *The Radical Right in Ger-
      many: 1870 to the Present* (New York: Routledge, 2014), 185.
11   Bale, "The 'Black' Terrorist International," 557–58.
12   Nicolas Lebourg, "Arriba Eurasia?" in Laruelle, ed., *Eurasianism and the
      European Far Right*, 128.

decentralized state strengthened by taxes on capital and the expropriation of multinational corporations.[13]

Led by fascist Jean-Gilles Malliarakis and Nouvelle Droite ideologue and fascist organizer Christian Bouchet, TV insisted that it had become "the only national revolutionary movement in France," and it pushed an agenda against "Yankee Imperialism" and in favor of "organic democracy."[14] For security, TV formed the Jeunesses nationalistes révolutionnaires, an openly violent, organized, and militant fascist skinhead group. Drawing from a synthesis of thinkers such as Proudhon, Niekisch, Blanqui, and Ledesma, TV also produced satellite groups for workers and students, as well as "bootboys." Bouchet led the leftmost faction Les Tercéristes Radicaux (Radical Third-Positionits), which advocated "a 'Trotskyist' strategy whereby TV would enter the 'bourgeois' Front National as an organized faction, obtain positions on the party's national council, and thence begin subverting and transforming it from within."[15] This form of "entryism" would be shunned by the larger TV organization, which only numbered a few hundred militants. In response, Bouchet formed a new groupuscule called Nouvelle Résistance (NR—New Resistance), declaring "active support to all anti-system resistances abroad" and to what scholar Jeffrey M. Bale calls "the utilization of a complex infiltration/entryism strategy *vis-à-vis* other political, social and cultural groups."[16] Through its radical strategies, Third Position ideology, and international orientation, NR would become a major contributor to the March 12 Group.

---

13   Jeffrey M. Bale, "'National Revolutionary' Groupuscules," in Griffin and Feldman, eds., *Fascism*, 5:273.

14   Ibid., 274.

15   Ibid., 275. According to Bale, this stance was controversial due to the resentment of many "national revolutionaries" of career politicians, whom they deemed "whores." "Entryism" is gleaned from Trotsky's attempts to alter the French Section of the Workers' International (Section Française de l'Internationale Ouvrière) from within during the emergence of neo-socialism in the 1930s by Léon Blum's chief competitor, Marcel Déat, later of the Rassemblement National Populaire (National Popular Rally) party.

16   Ibid., 277.

NR sought to "enter" the Front National under false pretenses, while the Front set its own sights on forging alliances with other European radical-right parties in order to create a force in the European Parliament. Its first ally, the Italian fascist Movimento Sociale Italiano, proved problematic in forging a strong coalition, so the Front turned to another populist party in Germany called the Die Republikaner (REP—The Republicans). Experiencing a fast rise in popularity at the same time, the REP was led by former Waffen-SS member Franz Schönhuber. Demanding the liquidation of trade unions and the welfare state, Schönhuber likened the suffering of the victims of Nazis to the suffering of Germany after the war. In the words of historian Martin A. Lee, "Schönhuber eschewed terminology that could be pegged as neo-Nazi, fashioning the Republikaner into a radical, right-wing populist party that purported to advocate for the interests of the little guy."[17] The REP identified Hitler as a criminal and insisted that an original leader would have to take power whose "enciphered similarities will be evident to the experts."[18] Die Republikaner's position was more mainstream than the neo-Nazi Nationaldemokratische Partei Deutschland (NPD—National Democratic Party of Germany), but it soon became a victim of its own success. With votes sagging, Schönhuber attempted to broker a coalition with a more openly fascist party. After his party voted to remove him, he would eventually cast his lot with the NPD. In retrospect, it would appear that Schönhuber may have indeed "entered" Die Republikaner party to transform its initially center-right ideology into a radical-right and parafascist one. On the other hand, his reign may have also been symptomatic of the radical turn that the populist right took during the 1980s. Under Schönhuber, it became difficult to distinguish the Republikaners from the fascists, but the same was true of the Front National, which had developed a relatively open relationship with fascists among the Nouvelle Droite, MNR, TV, and NR, as well as the Jeunesses nationalistes révolutionnaires.

In some cases, like that of the Movimento Sociale Italiano, the populist radical right openly identified with fascist ideology during this period, while in other cases the populist radical right would

---

17   Ibid., 232.

18   Ibid., 233.

use skinhead and fascist groups as stewards for marches and rallies. Pivotal to this new phenomenon was Skrewdriver's leader Ian Stuart Donaldson, who, with fellow neo-Nazi skinhead Nicky Crane, set up his own promotional organization for neo-Nazi music, Blood and Honour, taking over Rock Against Communism and developing networks throughout Europe and the United States.[19]

Large antifascist and antiracist movements coalesced to combat the expanding power of the National Front, Front National, Die Republikaner, FAP, and other groups. In France, fascist skinheads were met with violence in the streets by antiracist street gangs like the Red Warriors. When the group SOS Racisme formed under the aegis of the Socialist Party to hold mass demonstrations and disrupt the Front National, they helped the Red Warriors, who used vans given to them for wheatpasting to increase the capacity of their flying squads raiding Nazi hangouts. Another antifascist group supported by SOS Racisme, the Black Dragons grew to upwards of 1,000 members, most of them black.[20] Meanwhile in the United Kingdom, Rock Against Racism was joined by the Anti-Nazi League (ANL), which assembled rowdy mass demonstrations against the National Front that often ended in three-way violence between police, fascists, and antifascists. Later, Red Action emerged, focused more directly on violent opposition to fascists.[21]

In Germany, a new group was formed, drawing on the name and legacy of one of the militant left-wing interwar groups, Antifaschistische Aktion (AFA). AFA developed in a social climate influenced by the Autonomen Bewegung, or Autonomous Movement. Like Autonomia in Italy, the Autonomen grew out of disillusionment with the official left and an urgency of social needs.

19 Betty A. Dobratz and Stephanie L. Shanks-Meile, *The White Separatist Movement in the United States: "White Power! White Pride!"* (Baltimore: Johns Hopkins University Press, 2000), 64.

20 "ANTIFA—Chasseurs de skins," directed by Marc-Aurèle Uecchione (Resistance Films, 2008), http://www.youtube.com/watch?v=EfDbTg-b6uyc; Aude Konan, "Black Dragons: The Black Punk Gang Who Fought Racism and Skinheads in 1980s France," *okayafrica*, August 10, 2016, http://www.okayafrica.com/featured/black-punk-black-dragons-france/.

21 See Dave Renton, *When We Touched the Sky: The Anti-Nazi League, 1977–1981* (Cheltenham: New Clarion Press, 2006).

Becoming leading figures in rent strikes, antinuclear direct action, peace demonstrations, and feminist organizing, the Autonomen established a strong reputation as a horizontally organized movement in the 1980s and early 1990s. Their horizontalism and anarchist proclivities did not lack organization. They built extensive networks of squatted social centers to share resources like information, housing, food, clothing, and entertainment. Stylistically, the Autonomen became famous for their black clothing, hoods, and masks, which enabled them to avoid the surveillance of the police and fascist groups—a trend not limited to Germany.[22] The ANL in England and SOS Racisme in France drew on socialist and liberal support, while fascist skinheads often appreciated the help of sympathetic members of the police. But the groupings of antifascists that began to assemble under the name Anti-Fascist Action in the United Kingdom took a more independent, hard-left stance against the far right. The pattern would repeat itself in other countries, and from this emerging international network, nicknamed Antifa, a larger, global antifascist movement would take shape.

Skinheads in the United States

The fascist skinhead scene in the United States emerged in the early 1980s as a largely unaligned movement. While US skinheads—like Skrewdriver in England—came off as apolitical at first, the movement hardened, as did its racist message. Soon enough, white nationalist leaders across the country sought to unite the movement as a political and social force under their control. Perhaps the most effective of these organizers was Tom Metzger.

A former Knights of the Klan leader, Metzger wanted to become the lynchpin that united the existing fascist and far-right networks with the new wave of disorganized fascist violence. Having been a part of the Barry Goldwater and George Wallace campaigns, as well as the John Birch Society and Christian Identity, Metzger was extremely well connected to the old guard of the fascist elite in the United States. He had helped Duke win his state House seat in Louisiana, and he then ran for congressional representative in

---

22   For more on the Autonomen see George Katsiaficas, *The Subversion of Politics* (Oakland: AK Press, 2006).

California on the Democratic ticket. After winning the Democratic primary, Metzger was trounced in the general election and decided to move "beyond" electoral politics, establishing the White Aryan Resistance (WAR) in 1983 as a Strasserist organization dedicated to instigating a race war and white revolution.[23] As Metzger worked to harness the violent power of racist skinheads, he developed a populist politics pitted against multinational corporations.

Metzger hosted a public-access television show that he called *Race and Reason* (named after the Carleton Putnam book that inspired a young David Duke). His platform brought him the power of supporting certain leaders and ignoring others, giving young organizers a limelight they wouldn't forget and lifting other older leaders out of obscurity. It would become an important position that influenced Metzger to push his already populist politics further to the "left." Through his son, John, WAR became involved in high schools and colleges across the United States. Developing some of Duke's techniques, John Metzger's method included organizing the White Student Union and the Aryan Youth Movement, which would disseminate aggressively racist propaganda via paperboy techniques, locker-stuffings, and event organizing.[24] The teenager would soon begin making the rounds of TV shows, from *Sally Jessie Raphael* and *Geraldo* to *Larry King Live*, joined by other youths committed to the racist cause.

John, along with a teenage recruit named Dave Mazzella and a few other skinheads, was asked to appear on the *Oprah Winfrey Show*. Before the show collapsed into a slew of racial epithets, Tom, who was in the audience, would deliver the populist line "[It isn't the blacks who are the problem], it's the creeps on Wall Street and Washington of our own race."[25] This point illuminates a greater populist sentiment that WAR attempted to forward: capitalism was holding the white race back, and (at least publicly) revolutionary white separatism was the only answer. Metzger's attempt to creep over to issues "owned" by the left, such as anti-Wall Street rhetoric,

---

23   See Mark S. Hamm, *American Skinheads: The Criminology and Control of Hate Crime* (Westport: Greenwood Publishing Group, 1993), 42–46.

24   Dobratz and Shanks-Meile, *The White Separatist Movement in the United States*, 67–69.

25   Langer, *A Hundred Little Hitlers*, 189.

would bring some valuable allies—for instance, a Trotskyist who took over as the editor of WAR's newspaper. However, the most successful endeavor thus far, and the one that Metzger would increasingly push, was entryism among apolitical skinheads.

Mazzella became one of Metzger's chief "lieutenants." A Klan member who would grow close to both John and Tom, he acted as an apostle of WAR. He could travel in his van from city to city making contacts and deepening "racial consciousness" by uniting dislocated skinhead crews under WAR. Metzger would train Mazzella in the proper "bashing" techniques, first provoking fights with black men, then taking out a baseball bat, beating them up, and claiming self-defense. Mazzella's correspondence with Louis Beam, Grand Dragon of the Texas Knights of the Klan and author of the essay "Leaderless Resistance," also helped develop his understanding of skinhead crews, not as backward tribal structures but rather as a nonhierarchical and decentralized, militant force, which could be directed to certain issues and strategic positions through media networks built by concert tours, newspapers, and informal advertising.[26] While the skinheads "did their part," Metzger summoned people with long hair or short, Christian or Odinist, Western or Soviet, to involve themselves in the project of "overthrowing the totally corrupt capitalist system that is strangling all life among all people on this planet and… building a radical, futuristic, truly revolutionary new order of white people. Any non-Jewish white man who shares this objective and is committed to the cause is welcome. The revolution is on! Smash the system! Build the movement!"[27]

Metzger would repeat the line originally spoken by Mazzella: "Skinheads are our front-line warriors."[28] Just as the Official National Front had openly supported the political soldier line, Metzger took a Third Positionist line in favor of skinhead violence

---

26   Ibid., 177.

27   Ibid., 183.

28   Dave Mazzella's full quote is "Skinheads are our front-line warriors. They roam the streets and do what's necessary to protect the race." Found in "Extremist Admits Gang's Racial Attack," *Los Angeles Times*, June 30, 1987, http://articles.latimes.com/1987-07-30/news/mn-409_1_supremacist -gang.

with a statement that would fatefully connect his organization with murder.

The Chicago Strategy

One of the earliest notorious appearances of a dangerous new form of violence in the United States took place in Chicago, where a fascist skinhead group called Romantic Violence joined with the Klan to create a significant disruption for leftist organizers and communities of color. Metzger had been to the Midwest, planning meetings with Klan leader Thomas Robb and other white supremacists to forge a new cooperative alliance dubbed "the Chicago strategy" by antiracist organizers who opposed it.[29] Groups like the John Brown Anti-Klan Committee joined in the Coalition to Stamp Out Racist Graffiti to confront the new tactics. In September 1985, the Coalition called a protest against fascists in Aetna Plaza, and sixty antiracists showed up, only to be beaten back by a combination of skinheads, Nazis, and Klan members. I interviewed M. Treloar who was present at the time:

> [Protesters] surrounded the racists—there were only about fifteen of them, but they came prepared with shields made of wood with razor blades imbedded in them, and other stuff, and they actually kind of knew how to fight. The Nazis and Romantic Violence and the Klan attacked, and actually dispersed the crowd, because they basically didn't know how to fight and weren't organized to fight. They then ran for their cars...and those of us standing around were like, "Okay, they've gone to their cars. They're getting stuff out of their trunks. Oh shit." That was exactly the scenario that happened in Greensboro.[30]

Police intervened to break up the fascist rally, but not soon enough to spare the antifascists painful embarrassment. The Prairie Fire Organizing Committee's journal *Breakthrough* called the incident, "a turning point in understanding what confronting the Klan in

---

29   "Chicago: Confronting the Racist Right," *Breakthrough* XI, no. 1 (Winter/Spring 1987): 8–10.

30   Interview with author, November 15, 2015.

Chicago would mean. Throughout the winter and early spring, as the fascists continued their campaign, the anti-racist movement intensified its efforts to become a meaningful political force."[31]

In Minneapolis, a fascist skinhead group calling itself the White Knights assembled, but before it could align with other white nationalists into a larger force, an antiracist skinhead crew called the Baldies became aware of its presence. As street fights rapidly escalated into pitched battles, the White Knights were driven out of Minneapolis, and the prominent Twin Cities racist skinhead band Bound for Glory was excluded from all local music venues through the vigilant work of antiracists. To confront a growing threat in other cities like Cincinnati, Detroit, Milwaukee, Indianapolis, and Lansing, antiracist skinhead groups formed an umbrella organization called Anti-Racist Action (ARA) in 1988, coordinating the fight against fascism through a network based on anarchist principles of mutual aid, later, integrating feminism as well.

Cofounder of the Baldies and ARA, Michael Crenshaw, recalls the tendency of the skinhead movement to produce politically ambiguous scenes where playing Skrewdriver albums was tolerated, even among antiracists. Yet the ability to branch out to other cities enabled a more solid sense of belonging for like-minded leftists: "What was so important about the '80s when we started to reach out to other cities outside of Minneapolis was building other relationships, and seeing that there were other black skinheads, that there were other Latino skinheads."[32] Referring to the Oi! music scene, ARA cofounder Kieran Knutson told me that it was a forum for the expression of a general milieu: "It's populist music, it's easy to see why people could go in a couple different directions from it."[33] The antiracist skinheads came from the same culture as the fascist skinheads and developed along similar lines, Knutson told me: "Like the left-wing radicals of the punk scene [were] a semi-spontaneous, organic reaction to conditions, so was the fascist initial push."[34] By engaging in long-standing campaigns, however, ARA expanded beyond the skinhead and punk milieu to

31   "Chicago: Confronting the Racist Right," 12.

32   Interview with Mic Crenshaw, August 31, 2015.

33   Interview with Kieran Knutson, August 6, 2015.

34   Ibid.

embrace new strategies and tactics, while including members of the militant left who added to the theoretical texture of the network. Members of ARA absorbed the lessons of the Autonomen and other international leftist struggles from zines like *Wind Chill Factor*, by Chicago's Balaklava Autonomist Collective, and journals like Toronto-based *Arm the Spirit*, which circulated along with punk music at concerts and events. Fleshing out the discussions on theory, the Los Angeles ARA chapter started a journal called *Turning the Tide*, edited by a former member of the John Brown Anti-Klan Collective.

Zündel, Creativity, and the Rise and Fall of Resistance Records

As ARA was taking shape, tensions were growing between antiracists and Nazi skinheads throughout North America, for instance in Toronto where the Nazis initially named themselves after the National Front.[35] The fascists grew increasingly organized and violent—particularly against the Tamil population, and changed their name to the Heritage Front.[36] At the same time, ARA groups organized and developed a community defense strategy to confront the skinheads, exposing the fascist leader Ernst Zündel, a true believer in Hyperborean supremacy who also believed that Hitler remained alive in underwater enclaves of Antarctica developing UFOs to aid white America in reconquering the world.[37] Although it would seem as though Zündel's insane beliefs would prevent him from being a threat, his publishing enterprise provided a huge amount of Holocaust denial literature disseminated illegally in Canada, Germany, and elsewhere in the world. In particular, his pamphlet *Did Six Million Really Die?* became a global hit among white nationalists.

---

35   Interview with Toronto ARA cofounder Big B, November 12, 2015.

36   "Anti-Fascism in Toronto" and "Interview with a Member of Anti-Racist Action," *Arm the Spirit*, no. 16 (Fall 1993): 3–11.

37   Troves of Zündel's propaganda were discovered in the home searches conducted in 1981 after the Munich bombing. See Deborah E. Lipstadt, *Denying the Holocaust: The Growing Assault on Truth and Memory* (New York: The Free Press, 1993), 157–63 for more on Zündel.

On trial in Canada for propagandizing Holocaust denial, Zündel brought in Fred A. Leuchter as a witness, an electrical engineer employed by prisons in the United States to modernize their means of execution. Leuchter had visited the death camps at Auschwitz and Birkenau to surreptitiously chisel out pieces of wall in an attempt to disprove the existence of gas chambers based on the content of poison gas in his samples. When the tests came back negative, he published a report through the Aryan Nations. However, the lab that he used to test the walls insisted that they had not understood the reasoning behind the request and had performed the wrong tests for the samples.[38] Zündel was convicted, and Leuchter disgraced. Meanwhile, ARA organized efforts to expose fascists and throw off police, for instance by publicly announcing a demonstration near a known fascist's residence and then hurrying the gathered protesters onto public transportation for an action at a different, undefended site. Through this kind of creativity and tenacity, ARA brought defeat to the fascists in Toronto.[39]

Yet the Nazi skinhead movement of Canada also made an international impact through the white power religious organization Church of the Creator, founded by Ben Klassen, which would inspire the devotion of a young, skinhead apostle in Canada named George Burdi. In a scene riven by splits between Christians and Odinists, the almost atheistic religion and white power ideology of Klassen's creation provided another crucial layer. Klassen favored a sacralized form of political fascism, denouncing Christianity as a Jewish contrivance while embracing parts of Odinism for what he viewed as Aryan traits of strength and violence. The white race has forfeited too much of its power to multiracialism, he claimed—especially through Christianity's "suicidal" intention to "turn the other cheek," act "meekly," and embrace poverty.[40] Denying any evidence that the stories of the Bible actually took place, Klassen conceived of Judaism as "a racial religion," and advanced "Creativity" as a new set of beliefs to combat Jewish people as the critical enemy of the Aryan people.

38   See *Mr. Death: The Rise and Fall of Fred A. Leuchter, Jr.*, directed by Errol Morris (Lions Gate Films, 1999).

39   Interview with Toronto ARA cofounder Big B, November 12, 2015.

40   Michael, *Theology of Hate*, 25.

Although Klassen admired Hitler, he believed that the Führer had not understood philosophy. While Klassen insisted that a racial war was already in progress, he also believed that apocalyptic violence could be avoided if the white race withdrew all philanthropic support for other races, allowing them instead to "wither on the vine," as "nature would take its course." In order to struggle against the "grave danger of extinction," nothing short of total geographic separation between whites and nonwhites was necessary, Klassen preached, and it was the destiny of whites to obtain the most desirable territories by hook or by crook.[41] In truth, Creativity was launched as more of a political instigation to race war than a religion, using the latter status to both gain adherents from and undermine other religions. Practitioners of Creativity have occasionally found intersections with Odinism, organizing events together like concerts, but Klassen believed that Odinism manifested a less appealing palingenetic renewal than Ancient Greek or Roman religions. He also reprimanded Stephen McNallen, of the Asatru Folk Assembly, for rejecting Hitlerism, although he maintained an amicable correspondence with Christensen.

In 1992, Klassen sold most of his land to William Pierce. This was in anticipation of losing a pending lawsuit filed by the Southern Poverty Law Center on behalf of the family of a black man murdered by a Church of the Creator "reverend." Klassen killed himself the next year and the Church temporarily imploded, but not before it had reached George Burdi, who would help ensure its survival. As a teenager helping Zündel package and mail out his Holocaust denial literature throughout the world, Burdi learned the skills of distribution and met with some of the leading figures of fascism, such as Holocaust denier David Irving. By the age of twenty-one, he was leader of the Canadian branch of the Church of the Creator. When Zündel sent Burdi a Skrewdriver tape to review, Burdi became enraptured and formulated a new place for himself within the white power movement: "Here I was, in a movement that surrounded me with middle-aged and elderly men, and suddenly I heard this voice—this amazing, soulful, mighty voice—that was from a young man, like myself."

The profound effect that Nazi skinhead music had on Burdi drove him to form his own band in 1989, RAHOWA, an acronym

---

41   Ibid., 31–32.

for Racial Holy War (and one of the Church's central tenets). Burdi's strident rhetoric endorsing violence and hatred, suffused with his Creativity doctrine, made him a powerful organizer. He moved to Detroit to found a new office (close enough to Canada to maintain a tax evasion racket) with another Creativity devotee named Mark Wilson. The two of them launched Resistance Records, among the most successful distributors of white supremacist and fascist music in the world, selling some 60,000–100,000 records, tapes, and CDs in just under three years.[42]

Wilson had been first in line to become Pontifex Maximus of the Creativity movement before Klassen pulled the plug. A skinhead from Milwaukee, he was an early member of the Northern Hammerskins, a chapter of the Dallas-based Hammerskin Nation formed in the late 1980s, which spread quickly throughout the United States. By the time the Hammerskins had formulated an organized, chapter-and-membership-based network, the leaders of US neofascism began to take notice and to vie for power over the new group. Particularly important among these attempts to gain hegemony over the skinheads were efforts launched by Willis Carto, Christian Identity pastor Pete Peters, and National Alliance leader William Pierce. Skinheads revered Beam and Pierce in particular, seeing them as the driving force behind lone-wolf leaderless resistance.[43] Nevertheless, Metzger would loom largest in the world of skinhead organizing at the end of the Cold War.

Portland: PUSH Comes to Shove

In Portland, Oregon, a largely white city originally established in the mid-1800s with the help of racial exclusion laws, one of the strongest fascist skinhead forces emerged, supported by a developing, nationwide fascist network. The early years of the skinhead movement in Portland were marked by a more discrete racism. Symbols of overt fascism were downplayed in favor of those of World War I: the Iron Cross, a skull with a sword through it, a skull wearing an Imperial WWI helmet and a German flag. Their adaptation of WWI symbols highlighted the fact that their organizers

---

42   Ibid., 110–11.
43   Zeskind, *Blood and Politics*, 208.

consciously sought to obscure their own fascism while building a protofascist movement based on the same principles as the interwar Patriotic Movement in Germany. This was generally how the early racist skinheads established themselves in the punk scene as a kind of ambiguous subcultural niche within the larger scene of street punks, squatters, and drug addicts.

However populist, the scene in Portland incorporated heavy elements of fascism under the surface. One of the earliest groups, Portland United Skinheads (PUSH), was led by the Mulligan brothers, Hank and Eugene, who were veterans of the original National Front scene in the United Kingdom and adroit manipulators of young and impressionable minds.[44] PUSH promoted the chaotic culture of drug abuse, crime, and squatting prominent in Portland, and they added to it a strange celebration of German nationalism, which they could pass off as either ironic, an appreciation for militant aesthetics, a respect for tradition and culture, or a longing for a homeland over and against the US government. Elinor Langer describes their "apolitical" composition as "anarcho-protofascist"— the preparing of a seedbed for fascist authoritarianism through a permissive and/or clueless subculture of parties, illegalism, and a cult of violence.[45]

When the skinhead scene made its way to Portland in 1985, it found a rough-and-ready base of angry, working-class white males with plenty of violent tendencies. The most prominent bands in the Portland white pride scene at that time were, importantly, punk bands with ambiguous messages. Taking full advantage of both the political ambivalence of their audience and the plasticity of the punk genre, Poison Idea and Lockjaw would layer their music with contradictions, such that they could be labeled as anti-Nazi or Nazi depending on the observer. Skinheads became notorious for

---

44   Langer, *A Hundred Little Hitlers*, 46.

45   Ibid. For more on the aesthetics of hate and fascism, see Nancy S. Love, "Playing with Hate: White Power Music and the Undoing of Democracy," in *Doing Democracy: Activist Art and Cultural Politics*, ed. Nancy S. Love and Mark Mattern (Albany: SUNY Press, 2013), 216. On the hidden role of women and decentralized membership in skinhead groups, see Kathleen Blee, *Inside Organized Racism: Women in the Hate Movement* (Berkeley: University of California Press, 2002), 4–6.

picking random fights, slashing people they didn't like in mosh pits, and in March 1986, a crew murdered a random man outside of a club apparently without cause.[46]

Langer's comments here are significant: "When the skinheads entered a club en masse on a particular night, they were not merely blindly asserting power: they were acting out a political agenda involving who was playing and who was coming that, at least in their own opinion, was a matter of right against left." These actions helped cement the reputation of Portland skinheads as a violent force that could intimidate venues, take over spaces, and break up left-wing benefits. Their ultimate goal was to take over the Portland music scene as its leaders and transform it into a propaganda outfit for white supremacism.[47]

When Lockjaw disbanded in 1987, its former members went on to form a new band called Machine with a lowlife named Ken "Death" Mieske. Mieske had just been featured in avant-garde director Gus Van Sant's short film about the Portland underworld, *Ken Death Gets Out of Jail*, right after his release from jail on burglary charges. As a homeless youth, Mieske was taken in by Portland's bohemian subculture, but while in jail, he had met a relative of Richard Butler, and after that he began signing his journal entries "Sieg Heil" and started communicating with racist skinheads on the outside. Now that he was out, he joined the skinhead crew East Side White Pride with Steven Strasser, Nick Heise, and Kyle Brewster. The crew's structure was a "practically anarchic" model of leaderless resistance and brotherhood.[48]

The next few months did not pass without event. A Singaporean man, Hock-Seng Chin, and his wife were assaulted by three skinheads, resulting in a prime-time Town Hall discussion, broadcast over KATU, featuring racist skinheads on a panel with an African American state senator. With the help of longtime national socialist Rick Cooper, the white supremacists organized outreach for the event and attempted to present a cogent and coherent platform to the general public, underlined by the Northwest Imperative: "The only total solution to racial problems is total geographic

---

46   Langer, *A Hundred Little Hitlers*, 51.

47   Ibid.

48   Ibid., 83.

separation."[49] The skinhead identity and its connection to Cooper's hardline fascist ideology was crystalizing as a clear, practical hegemonic position; the skinheads acted as the horizontal network of shock troops, serving a more developed Nazi hierarchy to intimidate people of color out of the Pacific Northwest and open more "living space."

Cooper had been involved with the National Socialist White People's Party since the late 1960s, and he intended to form a separatist compound called Wolfstadt, which would fly the swastika over the Columbia River. Connected to skinhead networks in England and to fascist organizations throughout the United States, Cooper could pass the latest issue of Donaldson's *Blood and Honour* publication on to the appropriate groups; he could find people to help WAR organize and promote a Skrewdriver tour of the United States; and he could facilitate the first, and then a second, Town Hall debate with KATU with the hopes of gaining "sympathy and eventual support from people watching Town Hall in the comfort of their homes."[50] The benefits of the alliance between Cooper's current sect of Nazism, the National Socialist Vanguard, and the skinhead crews outweighed the mutual mistrust. It also revealed a cross generational evolution of patronage, as well as a hierarchy in which Metzger maintained power.

Cooper's connection to WAR would be crucial in determining the future of the fascist creep in the United States. Attempting to organize skinheads throughout the country into a consolidated group of "WARskins," Metzger dispatched Mazzella to Portland to work closely with East Side White Pride. In a recorded phone conversation with Metzger broadcast over the WAR telephone message board, Cooper declared that skinheads came to Portland "to take advantage of the job situation and also to work in a relatively fertile area in that white people in this area are basically sympathetic to white racial causes." Metzger responded, "It all sounds great, Rick, sounds like a lot of action, and, unofficially, the fights and attacks against the race-mixers and some of the race-traitors and the racial scum has been picking up because of the new warriors moving into the area, but I'm sure there will be more on that later. When it

49   Ibid., 57.
50   Ibid., 88–89.

comes out it will be all at once."[51] This statement turned out to be prophetic, but Metzger had no clue that it would also mean his own imminent ruin.

In two weeks, East Side White Pride would murder an Ethiopian immigrant named Mulugeta Seraw, with Ken "Death" Mieske swinging the bat. The news would make headlines across the country, and Metzger's operation and involvement would take center stage— his public insistence that his "warriors" had increased the violence would prove his undoing. Mazzella would testify against Metzger and Mieske in a class action lawsuit brought by the family of Seraw and the Southern Poverty Law Center. The 1989 case against Metzger bankrupted WAR and broke Metzger financially, but the skinhead wars were just heating up. Throughout the early- to mid-1990s, violent exchanges between ARA, skinhead crews of Skinheads Against Racial Prejudice (SHARP) and Red and Anarchist Skin Heads (RASH), and fascist skinhead groups like Volksfront, which claimed Portland as their new turf, grew increasingly intense. Adopting the "traditional skinhead" fashion, SHARPs emerged during the early 1980s to confront the rising threat of racism. By the early 1990s, SHARP chapters had developed throughout the US, with the New York chapter developing a new group known as RASH that would more firmly promote left-wing politics among the populist milieu of antiracist skinheads. According to Treloar, groups representing both existed to defeat the rise of fascist skinheads in Portland. At the same time, a new antifascist group emerged. The Coalition for Human Dignity incorporated a broadening diversity of tactics, including armed community defense and the outing of fascist skinheads at their apartments and jobs to remove basic necessities and push them out of Portland. Both Burdi and Mazzella would later renounce their racist views, advocating openness and tolerance for all.

Pagan Noise

Metzger was also interested in the parallel track of avant-garde Nazism forwarded by the British scene. In the winter of 1987, Mazzella took San Francisco-based Bob Heick to Metzger's home in

---

51   Quoted in Maurice Dees and Steve Fiffer, *Hate on Trial* (New York: Villard Books, 1993), 235.

Fallbrook, California, and the two became close allies. Heick was a failed musician who had bought a copy machine in 1986 and began to disseminate white power propaganda, like Tommasi's old National Socialist Liberation Front flyer about political terror.[52] He had founded the American Front (AF) in the mid-1980s as a loose organization based on the English National Front. When Heick got in touch with Metzger, his opportunities expanded. On May Day, 1988, WAR joined the AF for a "White Workers Day"-themed march through the streets of San Francisco. Later that year came the Manson-Family-style celebration of the murder of Sharon Tate on 8/8/88 (8 represents the eighth letter of the alphabet; hence, 88 or HH—Heil Hitler), held by the AF, Anton LaVey's Church of Satan, goth band Radio Werewolf, and noise musician Boyd Rice.

Heick would famously pose for photos with Rice the next year in an issue of a rock fanzine called *Sassy Magazine*. Both personalities wore AF uniforms and brandished opened blades. The journalist writing the article repeatedly noted Heick and Rice's humor and charisma, describing them as pleasant people. Recalling the episode, Rice seemed smug: "The article is mostly centered around Bob, because I kept steering it, bringing in [Charles] Manson, and all these other things.… Bob was saying, 'Admit it! This is the most fun you've had in a year!' [The interviewer] said, 'Well, yeah.'"[53] Rice was already deeply involved in the fascist elements of the avant-garde by this point. Forming the Abraxas Foundation, which he later described as "a fascist think-tank," Rice took as his symbol an "anti-equality" sign and presented a doctrine of individualism, authority, and misanthropy.[54] He became heavily involved with LaVey's Church of Satan and pioneered the modern fascist creep through his experimental industrial/noise music and forays into Satanist and British Israelism.

Rice saw James Nolan Mason, the leader of the revived 1980s National Socialist Liberation Front, as a heroic figure. Like Mason, Rice was also obsessed with Charles Manson, with whom he became pen pals. The murderous cult leader instructed Rice to "co-opt

---

52   Hamm, *American Skinheads*, 41.
53   Interview with Cindy Stiles, *Tangents*, 1997, available at http://www.boydrice.com/interviews/tangents.html.
54   Gardell, *Gods of the Blood*, 296.

the skinhead movement," and Rice promised his "good friend" Heick that Manson's vision of race war, "Helter Skelter," would fit in perfectly with the Nazi creed.[55] Metzger would later bring Rice on *Race and Reason* for an interview in which the musician presented himself as obviously and unapologetically fascist.[56]

LaVey's Satanism and fascism certainly seemed made for one another. Among LaVey's teachings was the admonition that, "If you are going to create a god in your own image, why not create that god as yourself. Any man is a god if he chooses to recognize himself as one."[57] This cult of the self proclaims, "Blessed are the strong, for they shall possess the earth. Cursed are the weak for they shall inherit the yoke."[58] The strong and victorious are heroic, for LaVey, and Odinism, he declared, "is a heroic and admirable form of Satanism." Hence, Odinist paganism would take root in the white supremacist movement through avenues like the Nouvelle Droite, the Order, and the Abraxas Foundation, and Satanic groups like the Order of Nine Angles and the Black Order. Inspired by Spengler and Yockey, these groups embrace the notion of spiritual warriors while worshiping the Heathen gods of the great catastrophe, Rangarök. These gods include Loki, the trickster; Fenrir, the wolf of chaos; Surt, the giant of fire; Garm, the hellhound; and the forces of the apocalypse, from which a new renaissance will emerge.[59] For members of the Abraxas Foundation, Hitler was "an occultist trying to bring about a pagan revival," and the Nazis were a pagan group seeking to restore the rights of blood and soil.[60]

---

55   According to Rice, his affiliation with the AF existed only through his close friendship with Heick. Though he insists he was never a member of the AF, membership was never a basis of affiliation with the group, anyway. Denying that his personal friendship with Heick—then leader of the militant racist skinhead group—and his usage of fascist symbology adds up to being a racist, Rice declares that he is not a "Jew-hater."

56   An edited version of this interview is available at "Tom Metzger Interviews Underground Musician, Boyd Rice," YouTube, April 8, 2011, https://www.youtube.com/watch?v=tO6L3hrMdi0.

57   Anton LaVey, quoted in Gardell, *Gods of the Blood*, 288.

58   Ibid., 289.

59   Ibid., 295.

60   Ibid., 298.

As Rice's star rose in the fascist scene, he took on a protégé, a young skinhead named Michael Moynihan, who later created his own band, Blood Axis. Deploying the *Kruckenkreuz* as its main symbol (also used by Austrofascists), Blood Axis released its first tracks in 1989, which included a speech by Oswald Mosley set to dramatic organ music. Described by Gardell as a "heathen anarcho-fascist," Moynihan welcomed the increasing fascist turn in Satanism, declaring that "heroic fascism" in its pure form would serve as an antidote to our "victim culture."[61] Another Satanic group known as the White Order of Thule agreed, explicitly citing an interest in entryism: "White youth are far more likely to read the Satanic Bible than *Mein Kampf*, so the Aryan revolutionary should pragmatically seek to guide the heretics in a radical direction."[62] By 1992, Moynihan had started his own publishing company, Storm Books, through which he published *Siege: The Collected Writings of James Mason*, which the Nouvelle Droite publication the *Scorpion* heralded as giving "insight" into the mind of "a relatively sophisticated and isolated pragmatist."[63]

Moynihan further pursued his interests in the occult, collaborating with New Age publishing house Inner Traditions in the publication of Julius Evola's *Men Among the Ruins*, the pivotal text of Italian postwar fascism. Later, Moynihan would move to the Pacific Northwest and join Feral House as an editor. Though not explicitly fascist, and publishing books on a range of "extreme" beliefs and behaviors, Feral House was founded and run by a journalist named Adam Parfrey, who also collaborated with Rice on an album, and whose prior publishing house, Amok Press, published Goebbels's novel, *Michael*. Continuing the work of Amok with Feral House, Parfrey has published a plethora of books related to Charles Manson, secret societies, and the occult, along with Satanist tracts, the green anarchist musings of John Zerzan, "post-left" screeds by Bob Black, and Moynihan's own books. In 2015, Feral House published a book on the white nationalist skinhead movement coauthored by notorious and unrepentant neo-Nazi agitator Eddie Stampton.

---

61   Ibid., 318.

62   Ibid., 319.

63   George Ritzer, "Siege Mentality," *Scorpion* 18 (circa 1996).

Among the most important of Moynihan's works is a highly-praised book on the black metal music scene published in 1998. Titled *Lords of Chaos: The Bloody Rise of the Satanic Metal Underground* and coauthored by Didrik Søderlind, this book describes in intimate detail the lives, actions, and thoughts of key players in the Scandinavian black metal scene, including pagan white supremacist Varg Vikernes, who has been outspoken in his disdain for immigrants and support for white pride. Varg was convicted in 1993 of murdering rival band member Øystein Aarseth (also known as Euronymous) and torching four ancient churches that stood on former pagan holy ground. According to Moynihan, Varg (whose name means "Wolf" in Norwegian) becomes his avatar, the Scandinavian figure of the wolf and criminal—particularly associated with the mythical wolf Fenrir.[64] Generally describing black metal sympathetically as a curiosity, Moynihan and Søderlind's text helps gloss over the ethical implications of the violent ultranationalism involved, presenting the same combinations of Satanism and Odinism developed in Abraxas with the subcultural allure of a musical genre.

National-Anarchism: Fraud and Fury

The black metal scene, noise, and neofolk all contained nonfascist elements, which core fascist musicians relied on and exploited to gain followers and avoid stigma. Generally speaking, this growing cultural milieu also generated subcultural currents that remained at best ambivalent in their treatment of fascism. As the 1990s continued, what had been a cultural void filled almost exclusively by hate rock was growing and becoming increasingly subtle, marked by festivals not unlike Tarchi's Hobbit Camp rather than skinhead barroom brawling and Sieg Heiling. In the words of scholar Raphael Schlembach,

> In the late 1990s and early 2000s the repertoire of fascist bands diversified markedly. In part, youth culture accepted a return to more traditional German folk music, while on the other hand

---

64   Michael Moynihan and Didrik Søderlind, *Lords of Chaos: The Bloody Rise of the Satanic Metal Underground* (Los Angeles: Feral House, 2003), 213.

American influences of heavy metal bands created a new fascist metal genre, the NS-Black-Metal. This diversification not only allowed for new styles and genres to emerge, but also for the acceptance of a non-commercial DIY music scene and a more skeptical view of personality cult and stardom. Here this shift was already characterized by the appropriation and reinterpretation of music and lyrics associated with left-wing anti-establishment bands and labels.[65]

One of Moynihan's European collaborators was Christian Bouchet, the creator of Troisième Voie and Nouvelle Résistance. Nouvelle Résistance boasted a collection of music distribution enterprises, like Rouge et Noir, and magazines, such as *Raven's Chat*, *Requiem Gothique*, and *Napalm Rock*, which calls Varg Vikernes a "proud Viking warrior."[66] In the early 1990s, *Requiem Gothique* joined English tendencies initially laid out in the short-lived paper *Black Ram* in developing a milieu alternately called national-anarchism, anarcho-nationalism, and national libertarianism. In the words of *Black Ram*, "the pseudo-'nationalism' of the 'nation-State'—which anarchists unequivocally oppose...must be distinguished from the nationalism of the people (Volk) which in its more consistent expressions is a legitimate rejection of both foreign domination and internal authoritarianism, i.e. the State."[67] Soon the idea of national-anarchism came to be applied to an ideological tendency under the leadership of former National Front member, Troy Southgate.[68]

Joining the hierarchy of the Official National Front during the 1980s, Southgate identified with the Strasserist tendency at its apogee. After an eighteen-month sentence for assault in 1988, Southgate returned to find the Official National Front in the midst of another split. In 1989, Harrington created the Third Way think tank, while the faction led by Roberto Fiore and Nick Griffin

---

65   Raphael Schlembach, "The 'Autonomous Nationalists': New Developments and Contradictions in the German Neo-Nazi Movement," *Interface: A Journal for and about Social Movements* 5, no. 2 (November 2013): 302.

66   Bale, "'National Revolutionary' Groupuscules," 282.

67   As quoted in Nathan "Exile" Block's Tumblr account, *LoyaltyIsMightier ThanFire.tumblr.com*, June 6 (year not given).

68   Lebourg, "Arriba Eurasia?," 133.

founded a Catholic organization called International Third Position.ʹ After remaining for a few uncomfortable years in the latter group, Southgate set out on his own, launching the short-lived English Nationalist Movement and generating a new synthesis that incorporated "revolutionary nationalists" like Strasser, Codreanu, and Degrelle, along with utopian socialists such as William Morris and Robert Owen. The ensuing ideology stood in contrast to what Southgate viewed as the increasingly Mussolini-friendly tendencies of the International Third Position and the overly conformist tendency of the NF.

Southgate believed that the British Isles could join the other Third World nations in a global community of strictly defined racial Volk. This ethnopluralist racial position sought to reclaim the British Isles for whites only. Southgate's "revolutionary nationalists" would rule by the kind of direct democracy outlined in Qaddafi's *Green Books*. Based on family, clan, and national heritage, Southgate's ideal Britain could be achieved only through a revolutionary movement that drew together right and left trends against the state. In 1993, Southgate created the Liaison Committee for Revolutionary Nationalism as a hub for Nouvelle Résistance, the American Front, the National Liberation Front of Canada, and a New Zealand group called National Destiny.[69] As Southgate navigated the fascist scene, he became increasingly drawn to a branch of the left-to-right ecology movement cofounded by a British intellectual named Richard Hunt.

Hunt's UK-based journal, *Green Anarchist*, advocated positions that were just as problematic as, if not worse than, its US counterparts. Hunt's "beyond right and left" political ideology generated particular hostility from the left. A supporter of village-level anarchism on a bioregional basis that operated outside of present contexts of nation-states and consumer societies, Hunt argued that racism was natural to people but unhelpful in the context of anticapitalist movements. While Hunt supported blood-and-soil-style bioregional movements, he incorporated nationalist histories

---

69   An excellent history of Southgate's résumé can be found in Graham D. Macklin, "Co-opting the Counter Culture: Troy Southgate and the National Revolutionary Faction," *Patterns of Prejudice* 39, no. 3 (September 2005): 301–26.

and "ethnopluralism" in keeping with Benoist's ideals of diversity. When Hunt backed the United Kingdom's involvement in the Persian Gulf War based on patriotic sentiment, he was pushed out of *Green Anarchist* and formed a new journal entitled *Alternative Green*, which more explicitly advocated for a decentralized bioregionalism with traditionalist and nationalist tendencies, seeing the potential of national and cultural rebirth after the collapse of industrial civilization.

Southgate would increasingly attempt to produce a palatable fascism through the national-anarchist tendency by publishing books on the splits in the NF, the thought of Jünger and Strasser, and the ideology of traditionalism. In keeping with Jünger's idea of the Anarch, Southgate's "third-position anarchism" continues to see the individual locked in a Darwinian struggle against multicultural society and advocates becoming a political soldier through a "leaderless resistance" strategy. Like Benoist and other Nouvelle Droite theorists, Southgate openly touts the thought of Yockey and Evola, as well as the Nazis' "green" theorist Walter Darré. This theoretical transformation of fascist ideology represented a larger adjustment to the changing terms of nationalist struggle. Just as Thiriart helped reshape fascism to include vague attributes of national liberation struggles even while fighting against them, Southgate was part of a larger movement, which included Bouchet and rising subcultural genres. This transition would play an integral role in situating the fascist movement after the fall of the Berlin Wall and the ensuing renegotiation of the Third Position in what was becoming more of a one-sided struggle against neoliberalism.

CHAPTER 6: NATIONAL BOLSHEVIKS

The Wall Comes Tumbling Down

As the Soviet Union dissolved and skinhead violence increased, a number of German neofascist and far-right groups faced bans, including Kühnen's FAP. This led many on the far right to consider the advantages of "autonomous structures" without membership. A scattered network of regional groups coordinated by charismatic leaders seemed appropriate to organize a revolution against the rising specter of "globalism."[1] In 1988, the first whispers emerged through *Die Neue Front*: "A specter is haunting the West...the Autonomous National Socialists."[2] These were neo-Nazis in black masks wreaking havoc on antifascists by using their own tactics against them.

German Chancellor Helmut Kohl had largely ignored fascist sentiment in the army and violence in the street while flirting with fascist rhetoric in public. For Christmas, he once gave a speechwriter a book by British Holocaust denier David Irving, and his personal chaplain once declared, "The Jews and the Poles are the

---

1   Jan Schedler, "'Modernisierte Antimoderne': Entwicklung des organisierten Neonazismus 1990–2010," in *Autonome Nationalisten: Neonazismus in Bewegung*, ed. Jan Schedler and Alexander Häusler (Weisbaden: VS Verlag, 2011), 16.

2   Ibid., 20.

biggest exploiters of the German people."[3] It was a chilling coincidence that the wall between East and West Berlin came down on November 9—known as the holiest of Nazi holidays, the day of the Beer Hall Putsch and Kristallnacht—in 1989, signaling the end of an era and the birth of a new one.

After the fall of the Berlin Wall, historian Leonard Zeskind explains, "Old-fashioned racial nationalism swept across Germany like a whirlwind from hell."[4] In East Germany, the fall of the Berlin Wall was followed by mobs of skinheads thronging the streets, brutalizing and terrorizing the Asian population in particular, who had found shelter under the aegis of socialist cosmopolitanism. Holocaust denial spread over the country, and the ruling party absorbed the ultra right's platform of canceling asylum and deporting refugees.

For the right, a new generation was born. Among the constituents of the neo-Nazi NPD, Schönhuber's Republikaner party, and throughout the radical right grew the new "generation of 1989," a group that saw itself as young, dynamic, and opposed to the old generation of 1968. Organizing around the ideological framework of the Nouvelle Droite, the new school of thought embraced green ideas to the point of, with Hans Jonas, calling for a powerful hierarchy that eschewed hedonism in favor of heritage, tradition, and honor. The post-structuralist writings of Georges Bataille, Michel Foucault, and Jean-François Lyotard mingled with right-wing elitism and the critique of consumerism to forge a new balance between authoritarianism and an imagined, liberating future.[5] In this atmosphere, Oklahoma White Knights of the Klan leader Dennis Mahon took a tour of reunified Germany, ending with a cross burning in a forest outside of Berlin. Pierce, of *The Turner Diaries* infamy, also travelled to Germany frequently, hosted by the NPD. On one occasion, he told an NPD crowd, "It is essential—not just helpful, but necessary—for genuine nationalist groups everywhere to increase their degree of collaboration across borders."[6]

3   Lee, *The Beast Reawakens*, 259 & 270.

4   Zeskind, *Blood and Politics*, 225.

5   Neaman, "Ernst Jünger's Millennium," 3:380–81.

6   Heidi Beirich, "Hate Across Waters," in *Right-Wing Populism in Europe*, eds., Ruth Wodak, Majid KhosraviNik, and Brigitte Mral (London:

The Precipice of Catastrophe

As the Soviet Union's influence waned during the 1980s, Chancellor Kohl advanced an anti-immigrant platform to contend with the growing strength of the populist radical right, such as the Deutsche Volksunion (German People's Union), which was described by US Army intelligence as "a neo-Nazi political party."[7] In 1991, a surge of Nazi skinhead violence erupted in the industrial city of Hoyerswerda, where over a hundred skinheads assaulted a guest worker hostel, beating several immigrants, and marched in the streets for days, flying Third Reich flags and chanting *Auslander raus!* (meaning "Foreigners Out!" and close to the Nazi-era *Juden raus!*, or "Jews Out!"). Violence touched off throughout Germany, with the resulting number of violent racist incidents exceeding the previous year's ten times over.

The violence was driven by new neo-Nazi groups called "Freie Kameradschaft" (Free Comrades), "Freie Kräfte" (Free Forces), "Freie Netzwerke" (Free Networks), and "Freie Nationalisten" (Free Nationalists).[8] Identifying with a broader "national resistance," which was more difficult for the state to monitor and suppress than political parties, these groups still maintained ties to the radical-right parties while also experimenting with their own forms of neo-Nazi violence. Mobilizing in groups of between ten and thirty militants, the Freie Kameradschaft quickly generated a web of some 150 regional and supra-regional groups throughout Germany, engaging in hardline nationalist political struggle through marches, acts of violence, and vandalism—with little appearance of the sort of organized and coordinated efforts one would expect from political parties.[9]

Rather than demonstrate support for the guest workers and immigrants, Kohl declared that the violence occurred because of too many immigrants and declared a state of emergency against

Bloomsbury, 2013), 94.

7   See Lee, *The Beast Reawakens*, 271.

8   Schedler, "'Modernisierte Antimoderne': Entwicklung des organisierten Neonazismus," 21.

9   Britta Schellenberg, "Developments within Germany's Radical Right: Discourses, Attitudes and Actors," in Wodak et al., eds., *Right-Wing Populism in Europe*, 152.

the invasion of refugees. Neo-Nazis and sympathizers attempted to stack the ranks of the German police, standing back and encouraging others to stand back as people were assaulted, buildings set ablaze, and property destroyed.[10] Similarly, the judicial system, inherited largely from the Nazi-era courts, gave slaps on the wrists for those accused of crimes like murder. The legal code was altered so that, in the case of immigration questionnaires—to give one example—the size of an immigrant's nose appeared as an item along with eye color, hair, and weight. German hospitals even began to demand that blood from foreigners not be used in the treatment of patients.[11]

With authorities looking the other way, the violence only increased. In August 1992, neo-Nazis attacked a refugee center for Roma in Rostock to the cheers of thousands of locals. Police did nothing, and the Nazis moved to a hostel for guest workers, setting it ablaze with Molotov cocktails. The pogrom lasted for a week before antifascists were finally able to converge in support of immigrants. Police attacked the protesters rather than the fascists. While 1991 was a landmark year for violence, 1992 saw fire-bombings increase by 33 percent. According to a national survey conducted by the Institute for Applied Social Sciences, more than half of Germans believed in the slogan "Germany for the Germans."[12]

According to Hamburg's State Office for the Protection of the Constitution, one of the German state's intelligence offices, some 80 percent of hate crime suspects in 1992 were "neither active in right-wing extremist organizations, had any contact with these organizations, nor could even be classified as skinheads." Right-wing violence was instead "based in loose subcultural networks rather than organized parties," and it was generally "unplanned and undertaken after the consumption of large amounts of alcohol," with no leaders.[13]

---

10   Ibid., 266.

11   Ibid., 270–71.

12   See Michael Schmidt, *The New Reich: Violent Extremism in Unified Germany and Beyond* (Hutchinson, 1993), 10 & 156.

13   George Steinmetz, "Fordism and the (Im)Moral Economy of Right-Wing Violence in Contemporary Germany," in *Research on Democracy and Society, Volume 2: Political Culture and Political Structure; Theoretical and Empirical Studies*, ed. Frederick D. Weil and Mary Gautier (Greenwich, CT: JAI Press, Inc., 1994), 281.

Finally, in the fall of that year, the Social Democrats capitulated to Chancellor Kohl's demands and cut off the political refugee program.

Autonomen and Anti-antifas

In 1989, according to scholar George Katsiaficas, an alliance of antifas emerged to coordinate Germany's Antifascist Action. Protests against neo-Nazi mobilizations and police support brought together thousands in "black blocs." It was this vibrant movement, as well as ecology struggles like the United Kingdom's antiroads movement and animal liberation, that proponents of the new trend toward "left-wing fascism" attempted to "enter" or co-opt. At one point, German neo-Nazis approached antifas to offer a deal to form a joint alliance against the police, but they were rejected out of hand.[14] Failing entry into some kind of coalition, the Nazis attempted a new approach. In 1992, former member of the FAP and associate of Kühnen, Christian Worch, developed a new strain of Freie Kameradschaft attuned to a co-optation of the Autonomen's style. One of its anti-antifascist tactics was to publicly reveal the addresses and names of antifascists. "I have simply adopted and adapted the networks of leftist autonomen," Worch boasted.[15]

This trend was embraced by the March 12 Group, which developed into a new "Brown International" based on National Bolshevik geopolitics in 1991. The group called itself the European Liberation Front (ELF), after Yockey's group of the same name in the 1950s. Within two years, they would have a European secretariat and would have organized themselves under a "nondogmatic Evolism," including a rejection of the "System" and "the globalization of McDonald's." With Thiriart, Southgate, Bouchet, and others, the ELF could coordinate strategies across nations—for instance, an effort to infiltrate environmental parties in Spain, France, Germany, Poland, and Italy.[16]

As Southgate and others on the neofascist "left" broadened the scope of Strasserism and National Bolshevism to include

---

14   Katsiaficas, *The Subversion of Politics*, 231–33.

15   Schedler, "'Modernisierte Antimoderne': Entwicklung des organisierten Neonazismus," 20.

16   Lebourg, "Arriba Eurasia?," 130.

national-anarchism, "national resistance," and "left nationalism," a general exchange of ideas facilitated in no small part by the ELF was taking place between Europe and the newly emerging Russian Federation. Scandal shook the world of letters, as the post-'68 satirical publication *L'Idiot International*, once supported by Jean-Paul Sartre, invited Benoist and Russian fascist Eduard Limonov to participate in the editorial board and write columns. In 1992, traveling to Russia on behalf of a revived ELF to meet with political leaders, Jean-François Thiriart had an important effect on the ideological direction of post-Soviet politics. Robert Steuckers and Benoist also played a direct and ongoing role in reorganizing the political spectrum of Russian politics by providing Russian neofascists with access to networks within Europe and by traveling to Moscow to assist in strategy and planning.

Duginism, Such as It Is...

The dual ideologies of Stalinism and fascism are merged and preserved most notoriously in the philosophy of Alexander Dugin, a follower of the spiritual ideas of Evola and the geopolitics of Karl Haushofer, Rudolf Hess's teacher. National Bolshevism had remained an important current in Soviet thought through the Joseph Stalin and Nikita Khrushchev eras, and grew to prominence under Leonid Brezhnev. In the 1980s, it joined with ultranationalist trends evoking the Black Hundreds (Chernosotentsy), who had carried out pogroms against Jews in Ukraine during the latter part of the nineteenth century. These currents converged in groups like Pamyat, an influential ultranationalist organization whose name translates as "memory." During the breakup of the Soviet Union, Dugin joined the Pamyat movement and sat briefly on its central council. However, he found Pamyat too modern for his tastes and moved on to pursue traditionalism in other milieux. He toured Western Europe and developed personal relationships with Nouvelle Droite figures like Thiriart, Benoist, and Steuckers. Through the influence of Steuckers, a fellow traveler with the Front Nouveau de Belgique (New Belgian Front) and the Vlaams Blok (Flemish Bloc), Dugin first encountered geopolitical theory.[17]

---

17   Shekhovtsov, "Alexander Dugin and the West European New Right,

Dugin's dream was a strange mix of the spiritual and the geo-political. He laid out his ideas in a book titled *The Foundations of Geopolitics*, in which he grapples with the extant theories of a Eurasian manifest destiny and the unification of Europe along a Paris–Berlin–Moscow axis.[18] Dugin considers Eurasia a palingenetic territorial imperative, through which the Russian spirit might soar with the advancement of the purity of its soul. Eurasianism must confront "Atlanticism" in a metaphysical combat between the alchemical elements of water and fire. Magical spells become necessary to subdue the Atlanticists through the National Bolshevik completion of "the dialectical triad 'The Third Rome—The Third Reich—The Third International'" marked by "the cause of Atsefal, headless bearer of the cross, the hammer and sickle, and the sun crowned by the eternal swastika."[19] Dugin's philosophy grew to envelope "Chaos magick" and the interconnection of virtually all beliefs and ideas. His bizarre postmodernism combines pseudo-intellectual references to the usual panoply of "great thinkers" in the fascist pantheon—Heidegger, Evola, Nietzsche, Jünger, and Schmitt with contemporaries such as Benoist, Steuckers, and even select leftists like Frankfurt School intellectual Herbert Marcuse and "green anarchist" John Zerzan to add to the syncretism.[20]

Dugin's writings throughout the 1990s pointed to National Bolshevism as the ideal of the conservative revolution, through which militants would need to muster vital energies to assail the culturally degrading forces of Jewry and cosmopolitanism. In a 1997 article called "Fascism—Borderless and Red," Dugin extolled the "genuine, true, radically revolutionary and consistent, fascist fascism" emerging in Russia after the fall of the Soviet Union.[21] For

---

1989–1994," 36–37.

18   Shenfield, *Russian Fascism*, 94.

19   Ibid., 196.

20   Anton Shekhovtsov, "The Palingenetic Thrust of Russian Neo-Eurasianism: Ideas of Rebirth in Alexandr Dugin's Worldview," *Totalitarian Movements and Political Religions* 9, no. 4 (2008): 491–506; Александрп Дугин: «Настоящий посмодерн»!, Арктогея, http://arcto.ru/article/922, 2003.

21   Alexander Dugin, "Fascism—Borderless and Red" [1997], trans. Andreas Umland, May 30, 2009, https://www.linkedin.com/pulse/syrizas-moscow-connection-fascism-borderless-red-dugin-umland.

him, fascism had become the natural third principle after the failure of liberalism and communism. In terms of influence, he was able to join the editorial board of *Zavtra*, a journal known for its red-brown alliances, and make high-level friends among intellectual and political circles.[22] Yet Dugin did not merely set out to advocate fascism, but rather to orchestrate the fascist creep. In the words of scholar Marlene Laruelle, "Dugin has gone further. He has invested himself in revamping the tradition of the German Conservative Revolution in order to foster fascism's reintegration into the realm of the 'politically correct' by rebuilding its intellectual genealogy."[23] His mission, like the Nouvelle Droite to which he is connected, is to give fascism "a people ready for it."

According to the analysis of scholar Markus Mathyl, the Dugin-inspired Natsional-bol'-shevistskaia partiia (NBP—National Bolshevik Party), along with Dugin's key group, Arctogaia, operated on three levels: the institutional, the political, and the subcultural.[24] Institutionally, their international affinity with the Nouvelle Droite has been well known, as Dugin's geopolitical Eurasianist ideas of a "multi-polar" world draw heavily from the ideology of ethnopluralism. Dugin has lectured extensively at the Military Academy of the General Staff of the Armed Forces of Russia, and received a prestigious appointment to Moscow State University for several years. His geopolitical works continue to find a relatively wide audience outside of academia. Nevertheless, Benoist was gradually turned off by the Eurasianist bellicosity toward "Atlanticism," and the relationship between the Nouvelle Droite and Russia's political scene grew somewhat tenuous. This is not true of Bouchet's "national revolutionary" ideology and Thiriart's national communism, which have been more broadly commensurate with Dugin's ideology.[25]

22   Shenfield, *Russian Fascism*, 192–93.

23   Marlene Laruelle, "Dangerous Liaisons: Eurasianism, the European Far Right, and Putin's Russia," in Laruelle, ed., *Eurasianism and the European Far Right*, 10.

24   Markus Mathyl, "The National-Bolshevik Party and Arctogaia," in Griffin and Feldman, eds., *Fascism*, 5:192.

25   Camus, "A Long-Lasting Friendship," 81–82.

The Communist Party from Red to Brown

In one of his more important early moves in the political realm, Dugin helped write the platform for the newly formed Kommunisticheskaya partiya Rossiiskoi Federatsii (KPRF—Communist Party of the Russian Federation), led by Gennady Zyuganov. An old-school Communist apparatchik whose résumé stretched back to the Khrushchev era, Zyuganov rose to become one of the top-level authorities of his native Oryol Oblast before becoming one of the chief functionaries in that region. As the Soviet Union crumbled, Zyuganov launched incisive critiques against Boris Yeltsin and Mikhail Gorbachev for their capitulation to liberalism, leading the hardline communists into an alliance with Russian nationalists known as "national-patriotic alliance." He also collaborated with Thiriart and Benoist, meeting with them on their travels to Russia for roundtable discussions and strategy sessions on the possible formulation of a "Euro-Eurasian military partnership."[26]

Zyuganov's populist perspective delineated between "good, patriotic Bolsheviks" like Vladimir Lenin and Stalin on one side and "bad, cosmopolitan communists" like Trotsky and Gorbachev on the other.[27] The cosmopolitans inevitably caused the decline of Russian life through the injection of capitalism, which, to Zyuganov's mind, is controlled by Jews.[28] Yeltsin's dangerous habits and the increase of sex work, gambling, and the reckless pursuit of profit—all emerged from the invasion of foreign capitalism, threatening the values of the fatherland. In the 1996 election, Zyuganov won 32 percent of the electorate, only three percentage points behind Yeltsin (in that election, the candidate defined as "moderate" openly supported a Pinochet-like military regime). Although he has never come closer to taking the presidency, Zyuganov worked extremely hard to maintain political relevance, particularly as a leading member of the opposition to Yeltsin, and part of that work has been not

---

26   Ibid. Also see Savino, "From Evola to Dugin," 107; Shenfield, *Russian Fascism*, 192; and Lee, *The Beast Reawakens*, 320.

27   Thomas Parland, *The Extreme Nationalist Threat in Russia: The Growing Influence of Western Rightist Ideas* (New York: Routledge, 2005), 83; Mathyl, "The National-Bolshevik Party and Arctogaia," 5:190.

28   Parland, *The Extreme Nationalist Threat in Russia*, 84.

only the retention and celebration of old Communist Party militants who uphold anti-Semitic and anti-immigrant views but also
full collaboration with fascists. Zyuganov's home province of Oryol
became dominated by the KPRF, which entered into an open partnership with the violent neofascist Russkoe natsional'noe edinstvo
(RNE—Russian National Unity) involving mob-style hits, public demonstrations featuring "Death to the Jews!" chants, and the
proclamation of a "red-brown" alliance.[29]

In 1998, a KPRF official named Albert Makashov generated controversy when he stated that the "Zhidy" (an ethnic epithet
against Jews) caused the ruble crisis. He apologized later, explain-
ing that he meant to use the word "Zionists." The next year, he
called for the expulsion of all Jews and was visited by an admiring
David Duke, whose book *The Ultimate Supremacism: My Awakening
on the Jewish Question*, about "Jewish supremacism," boasted an introduction by Yeltsin's former press secretary and could be found in
the lobby of the Duma.[30] Makashov would later clarify his politics
to a Cossack rally: "So, the word 'anti-Semite' is illegal, et cetera, et
cetera. Yet everything done for the good of the people is legal. The
people are always right. We will remain anti-Semites, and we must
triumph."[31] This form of anti-Semitism remains bizarre and twisted
in its attempts to become modern, catchy, and edgy, and to appeal
to the traditionalism and nostalgia of cultural revivalist movements
like the post-Soviet Cossack societies.

Some of Zyuganov's most telling alliances have been with
the "more or less national socialist" party, the Natsional'no-
respublikanskaia partiia Rossii (National Republican Party of
Russia), as well as the Soiuz venedov, a fascist group based in St.
Petersburg that "promotes the worship of pagan gods of the Slavic
pantheon" while translating and disseminating German Nazi propaganda in Russia.[32] Other propaganda officials who have teamed

29   Shenfield, *Russian Fascism*, 153–54.

30   Beirich, "Hate Across Waters," 94–95.

31   Celestine Bohlen, "Russia's Stubborn Strains of Anti-Semitism," *New
      York Times*, March 2, 1999, https://partners.nytimes.com/library/world/
      europe/030299russia-fascism.html.

32   See Hilary Pilkington, Elena Omel'chenko, and Al'bina Garifzianova,
      Russia's Skinheads: Exploring and Rethinking Subcultural Lives (New York:

up with Zyuganov include the ultra-right communist nationalist, Alexander Prokhanov, whose popular newspaper *Zavtra* supported the KPRF until 2005 when it transferred support to the Rodina (Motherland) party.

Limonov's Sour Grapes

One of the creepiest fascists in Europe has been Eduard Savenko, who more often uses the surname Limonov. He was the son of a Russian secret police (the People's Commissariat for Internal Affairs) officer in the city of Dzerzhinsk, which was named after the first head of the Soviet secret police, Felix Dzerzhinsky. Young Eduard bounced around the underbelly of Russia during his adolescence, committing general acts of vagrancy, robbery, and poetry until leaving the country with his Jewish wife in 1974. While in New York City, Limonov came under the influence of punk subculture and lived like a character out of a William S. Burroughs novel.

As a revolutionary, Limonov loved to inhabit the underworld of houseless people, junkies, and sex workers in New York City, but he also longed for a hardened ideology involving armed class war and true national pride. As a novelist, he used themes of homosexuality and drug use to produce a kind of decadent milieu, through which a semi-coherent revolutionary creed could be propagated. As a dilettante, Limonov made his way into the discomania circles of Studio 54's owner, Steve Rubell. Yet "Eddie darling," as he is called in some circles, was drawn more to the asceticism of the left and the Socialist Workers Party.

In a biographical piece in the Italian daily *Il Fatto Quotidiano*, Limonov's link to Stirner's egoism is clarified: "Good Limonov comes to terms with what was said by Max Stirner—that is, the idea that no sacred cause and no system or ideology are so large that they will never be overtaken by personal interests."[33] Limonov's avant-garde, punk disaffection easily took an increasingly right-wing

---

Routledge, 2010).

33   Achille Salleti, "Limonov, la biografia avventurosa di un oppositore di Putin," *Il Fatto Quotidiano*, January 22, 2014, http://www.ilfattoquotidiano .it/2013/01/22/limonov-biografia-avventurosa-di-oppositore-di-putin /477223.

turn through relationships made with the Nouvelle Droite during the 1980s and early 1990s, culminating, as mentioned, in a stint as an editor of the left-to-right satirical journal *L'Idiot International.*

These connections to the European fascist movement made Limonov instantly useful for the career of populist, radical-right buffoon Vladimir Zhirinovsky. The two entered into a partnership in 1991 once Limonov finally moved back to Russia, ending his long exile. It might have been Limonov who made Zhirinovsky into an international force the next year by introducing him to Le Pen.[34] As a result of that meeting, Zhirinovsky's Liberal'no-demokraticheskaya partiya Rossii (LDPR—Liberal Democratic Party of Russia) received technical support from the Front National.[35] Later that year, Zhirinovsky took some 25 percent of the electoral vote for president of Russia. Zhirinovsky brought Limonov into his shadow cabinet as the intelligence department head, and Limonov joined with Dugin to form a new group called the National Bolshevik Front, adopting Eurasianism as their collective destiny.

After information came out about Zhirinovsky's Jewish heritage, Limonov distanced himself with a brutal attack entitled *Limonov against Zhirinovsky.* In this book, he describes his break with Zhirinovsky as that of a "real Russian" disgusted by a Jewish intriguer. "A Jew masquerading as a Russian nationalist is sickness," Limonov wrote.[36] Some speculated that he had engineered the synchronized revelation of the information of Zhirinovsky's Jewish ancestry and the publication of his denunciation to gain independent political power. However, his break with Zhirinovsky runs deeper, and, he claims, involves his dissatisfaction with the LDPR's subordinate relationship to corporate special interests.

---

34   Anton Shekhovtsov, "Vladimir Zhirinovsky's Contacts with the European Far Right in the Yeltsin Era," *Anton Shekhovtsov's Blog,* October 28, 2014, http://anton-shekhovtsov.blogspot.com/2014/10/vladimir-zhirinovskys-contacts-with.html.

35   Zhirinovsky's advocacy for an International Center of Right-Wing Parties received only verbal support at the time, but the project of a "conservative revolution" umbrella organization in Russia has largely fallen to Zhirinovsky's opposition: Rodina. Ibid.

36   Eduard Limonov, quoted in Shenfield, *Russian Fascism,* 95.

Considering Zhirinovsky a political opportunist ready to sell the LDPR to whoever pays him, Limonov renamed his National Bolshevik front the NBP, or National Bolshevik *party*, seeking to challenge the Russian radical right at the polls. Around this time, Limonov's novels were published in Russia, and the lurid depictions of bisexual life led to a conflagration of hatred and denunciation from the right wing. Limonov persevered, though, releasing tract after tract of violent, hate-filled screeds, insisting that women secretly yearn to be raped and beaten, and that Russians secretly desire fascism.

As If National Bolshevism Had Politics...

Perhaps what makes Limonov such an important figure is his ability to maneuver between the radical right's chauvinist leaders, foot soldiers of extreme fascism, and artsy liberals who eat up his bohemian flair like *pelmeni* with a side of *smetana*. He attached himself to the Nouvelle Droite until their obscure intellectualism bored him enough to seek out vulgar populists. Once he had his fill of the populist claptrap, he soaked in the limelight of the art world, absorbing the questionable praise with the same relish as Boyd Rice and other edgy fascists. His relationship with the ELF and Dugin helped cultivate the next phase in his chameleonic existence: his own bizarre quasi-political party.

Giving vent to his ideas in novels, the platform of the NBP, and published articles in English-language newspapers like *eXile*, Limonov has a considerable following in Russia among those who aspire to world domination, sex, drugs, and revolution. For many, he represents the subcultural side of the Russian Federation—what makes it both strong and decadent at the same time. Avant-gardists like Sergei Kuryokhin have teamed up with Limonov's NBP, and the party's biweekly *Limonka* "decisively influenced the emergence and growth of the Russian skinhead movement in the mid-1990s by propagating a fascist style and corresponding dress code."[37]

To many, he represents both the counterpart and the manifestation of the Novi Ruski (New Russia) style of Russian chauvinism.

---

37   Mathyl, "The National-Bolshevik Party and Arctogaia," 5:193.

Limonov insists that he does not care enough to hate other racial groups or religions, but the position of the NBP would require an ethnic Russian to serve as president. His followers reconcile their own fantasy of supreme egoism with the portrait of the Stalin as someone who led Russia to the heights of patriarchal grandeur, over and against the self-pity, repression, and denial of modern liberalism. Hence, Limonov is not at all reluctant to identify with fascists like Hitler, Goebbels, and Goering in the same breath as he hails Nestor Makhno, Mikhail Bakunin, and Lenin. His self-identity is that of a decadent on the cutting edge of avant-garde exploration, reaching the new heights of both dignity and crapulence at the limit of understanding, where good is bad and bad is good and "only paradox is true."[38]

Feeding off the milieu of anarchic decadence, Limonov stands at the head, but not as the embodiment, of the NBP. With "an incinerating hatred of the anti-human system of the triad of liberalism/democracy/capitalism," the NBP advocates "a traditionalist hierarchical society, based on the ideals of spiritual manliness, and social and ethnic justice" combined with "modernism, the up-to-date, and the avant-garde." As such, it represents the palingenetic idea, expressed through the vehicle of an authoritarian party based on social justice in accordance with ethnocentric patriarchy. Limonov's adoration of Stalin derives from his appearance as a historical "great man"—"the Bolshevik Caesar of our country in its best period."[39]

For the NBP, the "rebirth" of National Bolshevik "great men" could produce a new, glorious "Greater Russia" or Eurasian state through an "economic dictatorship" that would weed out the weak and nationalize all industries while allowing small businesses to flourish under private or collective ownership. Like most of the ultra right, the NBP preaches a strict anti-IMF doctrine, insisting on price controls for basic necessities and the opening of abandoned or empty houses to veterans and large families. In terms of culture, the NBP declares that it must "grow like a wild tree. We do not intend to cut it down. Complete freedom. 'Do what you will' will be your sole law."[40]

---

38   Shenfield, *Russian Fascism*, 210.

39   Eduard Limonov, quoted in Lee, *The Beast Reawakens*, 312.

40   Shenfield, *Russian Fascism*, 213.

As scholar Stephen Shenfield points out, however, a tension remains between their condemnation of the "cosmopolitan intelligentsia," on one hand, and their glorification of the liberated, heroic artist, on the other. As to the maintenance of order, the NBP insists upon a transposition of the role of the "sheriff" onto the Russian police system, empowering a local law enforcement official with control over the local police, the implication being that the sheriff would be privileged over regional political jurisdiction and legislative regulations (à la Posse Comitatus).

Limonov's articles seek a "third way" of personal achievement and egoism, which could overcome the obstacles of capitalism and oligarchic clientelism to found a great nation of glorious revolutionaries uninhibited by any form of repression. The common ground between the macho playboy culture of Russian capitalism and National Bolshevik egoism is the sense of fast-and-loose freedom backed up with brute force and intense misogyny, which sees women as sex objects in the office, the household, and the nightclub. To feel their own inner greatness and meld with the nostalgia of the downtrodden for the Soviet era, men like Limonov must rescue a sense of Stalin as a "great man" under whom Russians felt strong, stable, and productive.

A New Dawn in the Balkans

With Soviet influence all but demolished, Yugoslavia broke into combative states, and fascists were split by region on whether to support the austere socialism of pan-Serbian nationalist Slobodan Miloševic or the NATO favorite, Franjo Tudjman, whose regime gave free rein to Croatian reincarnations of the Nazi-era fascist organization Ustaši. More than two hundred German neo-Nazis went to Croatia to join the Croatian forces, along with French, British, Austrian, Spanish, and Portuguese fascists.[41] A number of these neo-Nazis had earlier joined Michael Kühnen in his so-called international brigade expedition to support Baghdad during the "anti-Zionist" Persian Gulf War. The fighters linked up with the Hrvatska Obrambeni Savez (Croatian Defense Association), which looked to a new national socialist state in greater Croatia

---

41   Lee, *The Beast Reawakens*, 297.

that harkened back to the days of Ante Pavelić, the fascist dictator who oversaw the massacre of hundreds of thousands of Jews,
Serbs, and Gypsies. Although he had not made the trip to Baghdad, one of the neofascists who joined the rally to Croatia's side
was Douglas Pearce, from the band Death in June, who claims to
have volunteered at an army hospital that served both Serb and
Croat casualties of the war but also insists that he would have
fought alongside his fellow nationalists in the militia if it had been
deemed necessary.[42]

The regime of Tudjman for which they fought reignited the
old patriotic legacy of the Ustaši forces installed with Nazi support during the war to liquidate the Serbs from Croatia. Tudjman's
government returned the old symbols of fascism to the country's
public events, established the old fascist war criminals as heroic
freedom fighters, and set about reimagining a new economic order.
The Ustaši-era currency was implemented, the Square of the Victims of Fascism was renamed the Square of Croatian Heroes, and
the regime formally rehabilitated Nazi collaborators.[43] A Holocaust
denier, Tudjman had spent twenty years in the Croatian army and
spent much of the 1960s as a political figure within the League
of Communists. However, his views on Croatian history led to a
two-year sentence at the hands of the Tito government for counterrevolutionary activity, and he increasingly committed himself to
anticommunist activity as Milosević rose to power in neighboring
Serbia. As Western fascism backed Croatian nationalism, Germany
sent $320 million worth of weaponry, including tanks, missiles, and
MiG jets to bolster Tudjman's bid for national unity against Serbia.
NATO supported Croatia with raids and stood back as the Croa-
tians bombed UN posts in 1995.[44]

Plenty of fascists came to Milošević's aid as well, or at least to
enjoy the purifying fires of genocidal war. Milošević's expansionary
desires for a Greater Serbia attracted Russian and Greek fascists

---

42   See Midwest Unrest, "Death in June: A Nazi band?," Libcom.org, Nov-
      ember 19, 2006, https://libcom.org/library/death-in-june-a-nazi-band.
      Original quote from an interview in *Sounds* magazine in 1985.
43   Stephen E. Atkins, *Holocaust Denial as an International Movement* (West-
      port, CT: Praeger, 2009), 139–40; Lee, *The Beast Reawakens*, 301.
44   Ibid., 299–300.

and whetted the appetite of none other than Limonov, who ventured to Serbia to take part in the violence. Although he denies actively participating in the fighting, there is one YouTube video of him machine-gunning a Bosnian city from a safe distance away.[45] He exclaimed that the "Serbian tactics" of war criminal Radovan Karadžić made for "the fresh air of war."[46] Along with support from the NBP, the Serbian side also appreciated the support of what was then a little-known, cultish Greek group called Chrysí Avgí, or Golden Dawn.

Golden Dawn had emerged as a political organization in the mid-1980s, after ultranationalist activist Nikolaos Michaloliakos transformed his esoteric fascist magazine *Chrysí Avgí* into the bedrock of a new movement. Landing in jail with high-level ultranationalists imprisoned after the overthrow of the military government in the mid-1970s, Michaloliakos made connections that allowed him to rise to greater prominence. His magazine attempted to rekindle a kind of national socialist movement in Greece identified also with their own peculiar version of what they called "anarchism," but it would largely remain unrecognizable to most anarchists:

> We are pagans…because we are Greeks, because it is impossible for us to accept other values than those that stem from the miracle of the Greek Spirit.… We are Nazi if this term does not annoy you (it does annoy us), because in the miracle of the 1933 German Revolution, we saw the Strength that will rescue mankind from the Jewish rot.… We are anarchists because we are uncompromising and fanatics…and we will be until the moment that the Dawn of the National-Socialist Power will dominate.… We are extremists because we learned to love and hate without measure, deeply and eternally.[47]

---

45   Balkani, "Russian Writer Shooting at Sarajevo," YouTube, March 9, 2010, https://www.youtube.com/watch?v=tH_v6aL1D84.

46   Shenfield, *Russian Fascism*, 84–85.

47   Unsigned article from *Chrysí Avgí*, quoted in Sofia Tipaldou, "The Dawning of Europe and Eurasia?," in Laruelle, ed., *Eurasianism and the European Far Right*, 195.

During the 1980s, Golden Dawn established connections with CEDADE, penning an introduction to the New European Order's neofascist "Barcelona Declaration," which calls for a eugenics-produced "Europe of white people" threatened in the "biological perfection which is [its] destiny" by "useless bio-psychic parasites" such as "subhuman Jews." In the 1990s, Golden Dawn expanded its contacts to include Le Pen and the Afrikaner Weerstandsbeweging (Afrikaner Resistance Movement) in South Africa. In 1994, Golden Dawn continued to establish connections with European neofascists aligned with the FANE-created Parti Nationaliste Française et Européen (French and European Nationalist Party).[48] During the major conflicts in the Balkans, Golden Dawn members helped organize a group to fight for the Republika Srpska (Bosnian Serb Republic) against Muslim Bosnians. Known as the Greek Volunteer Guard, this corps sought to support Eastern Orthodox Christianity and fought with war criminal Ratko Mladić during the Srebrenica massacre, which cost the lives of some 8,000 Bosniak men and boys and caused the displacement of between 25,000 and 30,000 elderly, women, and children. Ruled an act of genocide, the bombardment of Srebrenica ended with the Greek Volunteer Guard hoisting the Greek flag over the town at the urging of Mladić himself, according to scholar Takis Michas.[49]

The Post-Soviet Right Turn in Eastern Europe: Made in America

A general movement toward fascism was not restricted to the conflict in former Yugoslavia, and it was in many places aided by the post–World War II fascist diaspora connected to Washington, DC. Led by one of the intellectual fathers of the US new right, Paul Weyrich, the Committee for the Survival of a Free Congress (later the Free Congress Foundation) built strong networks in Eastern Europe, facilitated in no small part by Laszlo Pasztor, a member of the Nazi-aligned organization Nyilaskeresztes Párt (Arrow Cross Party) in Hungary, where he spent time in jail for collaboration with

---

48   Ibid., 200–201.

49   Takis Michas, *Unholy Alliance* (College Station, TX: Texas A&M University Press, 2002), 22.

the fascist regime. Weyrich's Heritage Foundation brought fascist Roger Pearson on the editorial board of its publication, and Pearson also served as head of the World Anti-Communist League, which was officially renamed the World League of Freedom and Democracy in 1991. The League, along with Weyrich's Free Congress Foundation and the National Republican Heritage Groups Council helped bring together a wide-ranging network for "liberation" from Soviet control inclusive of fascist émigrés and cranks like Radi Slavoff from Bulgaria's Natsionalen front (National Front); Method Balco and Josef Mikus, veterans of the Slovakian fascist Jozef Tiso's regime; a former SS Cossack Division officer named Nicolas Nazarenko, who maintained correspondence with Willis Carto's *Spotlight* journal; and Florian Galdau of the Romanian Garda de Fier, or Iron Guard.[50]

In Romania, after Nicolae Ceaușescu's "National Communist" regime fell, a new post-Soviet rehabilitation of interwar authoritarian conservative leader Marshal Ion Antonescu began on the parliamentary level. Antonescu had been a part of the power-sharing coalition government with the Iron Guard, rendering him at best a pragmatic conservative militarist allied with some of the most vicious fascists of the 1940s. The top Romanian weekly, *Romania Mare*, denied the Holocaust and published lines like, "Who is an anti-Semite? Someone who hates Jews more than necessary." Furthermore, a Holocaust denier named Paul Everac took the directorship of state television.[51]

The Magyar Igazság és Élet Pártja (MIÉP—Hungarian Justice and Life Party) emerged in Hungary as a kind of "third way," splitting off from the ruling Magyar Demokrata Fórum (Hungarian Democratic Forum) after the publication of a "quasi-Nazi document." Openly anti-Semitic, biological-nativists, MIÉP gave voice to a militantly racist sector of the Hungarian population, while the mainstream Democratic Forum, which played a large role in the Velvet Revolution of 1989 against Soviet influence "was not

50   Russ Bellant, *Old Nazis, the New Right, and the Republican Party* (Boston: South End Press, 1991), 6–16.

51   Quoted in Paul Hockenos, *Free to Hate: The Rise of the Right in Post-Communist Eastern Europe* (New York: Routledge, 1994), 188; see also Lee, *The Beast Reawakens*, 301–2.

extreme right wing" but "was open in that direction."[52] In Bulgaria, the fascist Bulgarian National Front, also backed by the National Republican Heritage Groups Council, threw its support behind the Sayuz na Demokratichnite Sili (Union of Democratic Forces), which participated in a joint government with the ruling Balgarska Sotsialisticheska Partiya (Socialist Party) after the elections of 1990. Like German unification after the fall of the Berlin Wall, the process of "liberation" from the Soviet yoke was marred by a creeping fascism that significantly influenced mainstream political parties and paved the way for future fascist and ultranationalist gains.

The tragic genocide in the Balkans and the Russia's ruble crisis in 1998—along with the political anxiety it caused—showed the world that Eastern European liberation from Soviet hegemony would not be straightforward. The Balkans war increased militancy on the fascist front in Europe while further entrenching a sense of antagonism against neoliberal governance. With the influence of the Nouvelle Droite and the opening of a renewed militant front against globalization and neoliberalism, new radical groupuscules began to emerge taking on the traits and characteristics of leftist groups while bonded to the overall party structure of the radical right. In Russia, these forces were further fueled by hatred of the Chechens, which drove Prime Minister Vladimir Putin into the national limelight and brought him the accolades of numerous fascist groups.

In September 1999, a series of apartment bombings shattered residential blocks in three cities around Russia. Chechen terrorists were immediately blamed for the attacks, although three FSB (secret police) agents were apprehended after local police followed evidence related to one bomb that had been located and defused.[53] Putin rattled the sabers of war, galvanizing a winning campaign for president in the 2000 elections. He also is said to have cleared potential opposition by holding a backdoor meeting with one of

---

52   László Karsai, "The Radical Right in Hungary," in *The Radical Right in Central and Eastern Europe Since 1989*, ed. Sabrina P. Ramet (University Park, PA: Penn State Press, 1999), 134.

53   See John B. Dunlop, *The Moscow Bombings of September 1999: Examinations of Russian Terrorist Attacks at the Onset of Vladimir Putin's Rule* (Stuttgart: Ibidem, 2012).

the officers of the RNE, which under the leadership of Aleksandr Barkashov had amassed independent electoral power. The ensuing palace coup that deposed Barkashov reduced the party to a shadow of its former self, opening more votes to Putin's Yedinstvo (Unity) party.[54]

Upon Putin's election, far-right leader Aleksandr Ivanov-Sukharevsky lauded him as a "hyper-link between Marxism and Russism" in the Narodnaya natsionalnaya partiya (People's National Party) newspaper. In the same issue, the poet Nina Kartoshova raised the White Army call, "We need a Russian Orthodox Hitler!"[55] By 2001, while Limonov was being arrested for illegal arms trading and attempting to foment revolt in Northern Kazakhstan, Dugin enjoyed rising influence with Putin's new regime, which brought Moscow increasing hegemony in Eastern Europe through "soft power" business investments and partnerships with populist parties both right and left.[56]

---

54   Shenfield, *Russian Fascism*, 264.

55   Nina Kartoshova, quoted in Vladimir Pribylovsky, "The Attitude of National Patriots Towards Vladimir Putin in the Aftermath of March 26, 2000," Panorama.ru, 2000, http://www.panorama.ru/works/patr/bp/10eng .html.

56   Laruelle, "Dangerous Liaisons," 16.

CHAPTER 7:
FASCISTS OF THE THIRD MILENNIUM

Realigning Political Imperatives

The fall of the Berlin Wall and the problematic "liberation" of Eastern Europe changed the face of global politics. The antifascist struggle transformed with it. The apparent victory of neoliberalism had brought on a new wave of fascist resentment, which found greater overlap with the populist right and left. People who lost out in post-Fordist economies of neoliberalism were becoming increasingly sympathetic to fascism and the radical right. Rather than opposing and forging a path between the now nonexistent Soviet Union and NATO, fascists saw themselves as fighting on only one front. While scholars increasingly situated fascism and the "ultra right" in the milieu of autonomous struggle that some scholars have compared to the antinuke or environmental movements rather than traditional political parties, fascists gained increasing prominence in the populist radical right. The reconfiguration of global politics brought about a renewed involvement in antiliberal social movements by fascists working both in autonomous groupuscules and larger political parties. Many have argued that the defining qualities of fascism are a revolutionary, single-party dictatorship with a strong and organized paramilitary presence, yet the experience of the 1990s would show far more complex underpinnings.

Although intervention in Eastern Europe mostly took the form of US neoliberal hegemony, which was based on collusion with neofascist and far-right groups, the neoliberal approach was not without domestic dissent in the United States. The paleoconservatives in the US Congress, like Jimmy Duncan and Walter Beaman Jones, argued forcefully against neoliberal policies, free trade, and the World Trade Organization (WTO). Similarly, the Libertarian Party rejected NAFTA-style free trade policies and globalization's erosion of national imperatives, arguing instead for community-focused, decentralized governance stripped of federal social programs. In France, as well, the Front National protested the General Agreement on Trade and Tariffs, seeing it as a challenge to French national sovereignty. Broadly, the radical right increasingly warned against the organization of the European Union, which was being encouraged by much of Europe's political establishment, particularly Italian Prime Minister Giulio Andreotti.

On October 24, 1990, Andreotti publicly admitted to the Chamber of Deputies the existence of fascist networks operating under the auspices of Operation Gladio. Seen as the anchor of establishment politics, Il Divo Julio—a pun on Divine Julius, an epithet for Julius Caesar—had served in top levels of the Italian government since the late 1950s and was prime minister twice during the Years of Lead in the 1970s. On the heels of the revelations of the Gladio networks came a massive corruption scandal. This one-two punch severely undermined the ruling Democrazia Cristiana (Christian Democracy) party, as authorities launched a large-scale investigation. Prominent television magnate Silvio Berlusconi would play a tremendous role in the public vetting and stoking of the corruption story, framing it as *Tangentopoli*, or Bribe City. Andreotti finally resigned in 1992.

In spite of the revelations of fascists linked to the state security services just three years prior, the fascist Movimento Sociale Italiano's leaders Gianfranco Fini and Alessandra Mussolini (granddaughter of the infamous fascist leader) seized upon the accusations of fraud and corruption aimed at the mainstream parties, garnering close to 50 percent of the electorate in the 1993 elections. Although the two of them narrowly lost their elections in Rome and Naples, respectively, in the southern provinces of Latina, Chieti, Benevento, and Caltanissetta, the MSI prevailed. In the words of scholar

Antonio Carioti, "It was the voters who promoted the Flame [the MSI] to the role of protagonist in the Italian government."[1]

Fini, the relatively youthful new leader of the MSI, capitalized on the staggering gains by creating a new organization called the Alleanza Nazionale (AN—National Alliance) and developing a more mainstream-friendly style. Rauti, cofounder of Ordine Nuovo, had rejoined the MSI during the Years of Lead and was not happy with this rebranding. Attempting to rekindle the MSI's openly fascist spirit through a new group called Fiamma Tricolore (Tricolor Flame), Rauti created an outreach arm called Forza Nuova (New Force), putting Roberto Fiore, formerly of the Official National Front and Terza Posizione, in charge of the new organization. Forza Nuova would make itself known by putting up posters and holding annual celebrations on events like the anniversary of Mussolini's birthday, and Fiamma Tricolore would become, in the words of Antonio Carioti, "a magnet for skinheads and neo-Nazis."[2]

Meanwhile, Fini led the new AN into a coalition with Berlusconi, who had forged a populist political party under the soccer slogan, "Forza Italia!" The gains were staggering, as the AN became the third most powerful party in the country, polling at 13.5 percent. In certain districts, the AN polled even higher than Forza Italia, bringing Italy into a new kind of regional politics between Berlusconi and the AN. Now calling the AN "post-fascist," Fini insisted that he remained "faithful to the roots of the MSI" and "committed to preserving the era of Mussolini."[3] The implication was that the AN could not be considered nonfascist, for it had evolved beyond fascism to a new ideological platform (similar to the way postmodern discourse surpassed modernism). The AN was making a similar transition to that facilitated by Carto's publications in the United States and the Front National's *Identité*

---

1   Antonio Carioti, "From the Ghetto to the Palazzo Chigi: The Ascent of National Alliance," in Griffin and Feldman, eds., *Fascism*, 4:92.

2   Martin A. Lee, "An Overview of Far Right Politics in Europe," *Intelligence Report* (online edition), Southern Poverty Law Center, August 28, 2001, https://www.splcenter.org/fighting-hate/intelligence-report/2001/overview-far-right-politics-europe.

3   Gianfranco Fini, quoted in Carioti, "From the Ghetto to Palazzo Chigi," 4:92.

in France, maneuvering a spectrum of white nationalist and fascist perspectives into conservative discourse through carefully crafted messaging and public relations strategies. With the postmodern critique of ideology prevailing after the Cold War, the radical right began supporting what Tony Blair called a "Third Way" between socialism and capitalism. The right had not shifted toward the center; the center had shifted right.

Berlusconi's coalition soon grew to encompass another regional force in the north, the Lega Nord, or Northern League. Started in the early 1980s by Umberto Bossi, a former Marxist-Leninist who lost faith in the Soviet Union, the Lega Nord was and remains directed toward the regional autonomy of northern Italy. In the late 1990s, Bossi grew disappointed with the stagnation of the party's electoral gains and moved further toward secessionism for a place he defined as the "Padania" region, guided by traditionalism, nationalism, and anti-immigration. The new Lega Nord held annual ceremonies where people would dress in medieval garb and perform a kind of spiritual rite of rebirth, bringing the water of the Po springs to the Venice lagoon.[4] While the structure of the AN attempted to smuggle its fascist background into the moderate policies of mainstream parties, the Lega Nord swung to the ethnocentric right, insisting that *Padani* maintained better, stronger economic livelihoods than those of the rest of Italy. Particularly worse off were the "extra Europeans," who they claimed cause the demographic deterioration of Padania.[5]

Under Berlusconi's "post-political" leadership, the Italian populist radical right was set to enjoy greater political success than it had since the fall of Mussolini's government in 1943. While in power, however, the AN worked in subtle ways, increasing their control over the economy by maneuvering to install new leaders over the Banca d'Italia, Italy's central bank. The relationship between the

---

4   Leonardo Goi, "Lega Nord's last temptation: anti-politics in the time of Grillo," *openDemocracy*, March 28, 2013, https://www.opendemocracy.net/leonardo-goi/lega-nords-last-temptation-anti-politics-in-time-of-grillo.

5   Benito Giordano, "The Politics of the Northern League and Italy's Changing Attitude Towards Europe," in *The EU and Territorial Politics Within Member States: Conflict or Co-Operation*, ed. Angela K. Bourne (Boston: Brill, 2004), 214–15.

AN and Berlusconi remained one of both affinity and compromise: the former needed the latter to ward off marginalization, making the AN one of Berlusconi's most reliable allies.[6] Nevertheless, soon after the huge victory, the Lega Nord declared that its side of the coalition had been betrayed by the AN and Forza Italia. On January 17, 1995, Berlusconi was forced to resign amid scandal and allegations of his own corruption. In place of Forza Italia emerged a new leftist Popular Front, but it too fell to pieces, allowing for the resurgence of Berlusconi's Freedom Alliance at the beginning of the new century.

The "Yuppie Fascist" Gets Austria in Hot Water

Following the collapse of the Soviet Union, Austria lost its preferred status as a neutral country, providing a buffer between the East and West. Trade unions began to echo the xenophobic rhetoric of the FPÖ. Haider's party carved out new terrain by feeding anti-immigrant attitudes toward refugees from the Balkans and anxiety over European integration into the European Union. The Waldheim affair led to an official transformation of state discourse. Austria could no longer be viewed as an innocent victim of Adolf Hitler; instead, it was starting to look like a junior partner in the Holocaust. The FPÖ remained the only party refusing to accept the new narrative, and they cast themselves as the intransigent party of the right—the "real Austria" that lay beneath the neoliberal changes that were uprooting the country's independence.

The FPÖ's political hierarchy remained rooted in the kind of nostalgia and relativism of their younger days when they were the VdU. Haider famously complimented the Nazis stating, "In the Third Reich, they had respectable employment politics to keep people occupied, not even the government in Vienna can do that." (He did not mention that the Nazis engaged in a massive system of slavery.)[7] When he won the title of party chairman for Lower Austria, Ernest Windholz thanked his electorate with the Nazi oath, "Our honor is our loyalty." Another leading FPÖ official,

---

6   Carioti, "From the Ghetto to Palazzo Chigi," 4:105.

7   Ruth Wodak, "Discourse and Politics," in Wodak and Pelinka, eds., *The Haider Phenomenon in Austria*, 40.

Reinhart Gaugg, invented an acronym for "Nazi": "New, attractive, single-minded, and ingenious."[8] Even in the face of such provocation, as Austria's Social Democrat coalition government privatized national industries, and as EU integration reduced tariffs, support for the radical right only increased.

Haider's rhetoric comparing 140,000 unemployed to 180,000 immigrants matched Le Pen's similar xenophobic slogan "One million unemployed is one million immigrants too many." Both were riffs off the old Austrian Nazi posters of "500,000 Unemployed—400,000 Jews." Similarly, as the Soviet breakdown triggered a wave of immigration, the FPÖ's theorist Andreas Mölzer deployed a Nazi term, *Umvolkung*, to warn against a coming "ethnic inversion." Another Nazi slogan the party used was *Stop der Überfremdung*, or "stop the foreign invasion."[9] From 1989 to 1992, the "immigrant problem" went from a nonissue to the second most important ranking on a pre-election survey.[10] In 1991, 49 percent of poll respondents answered "absolutely not" when asked about accepting asylum seekers. In 1993, the FPÖ pushed harder with the "Austria First" referendum, advocating a twelve-point program that included freezing immigration, increasing law enforcement, eliminating fast-track citizenship, and stepping up deportations.[11]

In 1997, the FPÖ declared, "We reject multicultural experiments because they expressly lead to and result in societal conflicts." Multiculturalism was to blame for violence, not fascist street gangs. Rather than multiculturalism, the FPÖ adhered to a notion of *Volksgruppen*, including "Germans, Croats, Roma, Slovaks, Slovenes, Czechs and Hungarians"—all of whom required their own autochthonous homelands. The FPÖ declared the Germans as the major Volksgruppe in Austria, while declaring their responsibility to protect German minorities in other homelands. By insisting on the rights of German minorities to not integrate and to exist apart from the Volksgruppen of the Czech Republic and Hungary, for instance, the FPÖ set up a kind of renewed pan-German ideology aligned with the slogan, "We are not

8 Manoschek, "FPÖ, ÖVP, and Austria's Nazi Past," Ibid., 8.
9 Bunzl, "Who the Hell is Jörg Haider," Ibid., 63–64.
10 Gärtner, "The FPÖ, Foreigners, and Racism," Ibid., 19–20.
11 Ibid., 24.

against foreigners, we're for the indigenous population."[12] Each Volksgruppe is different for the FPÖ, though certainly unequal. For instance, Haider once referred to black people as "especially aggressive."[13] This ideological position falls very close to the ethnopluralism of the Nouvelle Droite. Like Benoist, Haider supposedly studied Gramsci, believing that, "He who has a dominant influence on people will gain power."[14]

In 1999, Haider would reach his apogee, with his party attaining 27 percent of the vote for the Austrian parliamentary elections and entering into a coalition government of the right. Austria was soon stung by sanctions from the EU, which saw the FPÖ's rise as anathema to its own goals. Austrians were excluded from intergovernmental ambassadorial meetings, and the EU refused to place offices on Austrian territory. The sanctions got Haider to step down from his role as party leader, but he remained a crucial figure in the party as governor of Carinthia. The jury is out on the true nature of Haider's ideological beliefs. He may have simply been an opportunist exploiting the history of Austrian military failure and its relationship to the country's historic failure to come together as a Volk. Either way, though, the FPÖ's approach to both Austria's past and the specter of fascism at the time would only invite more violent measures to close society against immigration, religious and sexual difference, artistic expression, and other cultural and social complexity.

Social Movements at a Crossroads

The victories of the populist radical right throughout the 1990s came in no small part as a protest vote against neoliberalism. Their success rode the coattails of a broad-based left movement that reached its peak in the dynamic protests against the WTO conference in Seattle in November 1999. Leaders from around the world converged for the conference, as did radical strategies and tactics developed from forest occupations to urban disruptions. Activists

---

12 Ibid., 26–27.

13 Wodak, "Discourse and Politics," 35–36.

14 This idea in itself is remarkably similar to the "national communalism" of the old pan-Germanist conception of the Sudeten Germans in Bohemia. See Gingrich, "A Man for All Seasons," 85.

locked themselves together in intersections around the conference center and held a carnival in the street, effectively shutting down the entire area. In the ensuing police riot, the conference was cancelled and the left claimed victory, moving on to other summits in other cities to maintain the momentum.

Less widely observed was the fact that fascists and the radical right also celebrated that victory and observed the tactics of the left with a keen eye. The World Church of the Creator's new Pontifex Maximus, Matthew Hale, declared,

> What happened in Seattle is a precursor for the future—when White people in droves protest the actions of world Jewry not by "writing to congressmen," "voting," or other nonsense like that, but by taking to the streets and throwing a monkey wrench into the gears of the enemy's machine.… It is from the likes of the White people who protested the WTO (and who in some cases, went to jail for illegal actions) that our World Church of the Creator must look for converts—not the stale "right wing" which has failed miserably to put even one dent in the armor of the Jewish monster. Did the right wing hinder the WTO?… No, it was the left wing, by and large, which stymied the WTO to the point where their meeting was practically worthless, and we should concentrate on these zealots, not the "meet, eat, and retreat" crowd of the right wing who are so worried about "offending" the enemy that all too often, they are a nice Trojan Horse for the enemy's designs.[15]

Mimicking their attempts in the 1970s to enter, undermine, and exploit the radical left, white supremacist and fascist groups were able to, in a sense, join forces with the antiglobalization movement, often by temporarily abandoning explicit race politics to participate in large-scale antisystem protests. Even old-school Louis Beam joined the movement, prophesizing "millions in this country of every political persuasion confronting the police state on streets throughout America."[16] The libertarian movement joined in as well,

---

15   Matthew Hale, quoted in Hamerquist and Sakai, *Confronting Fascism*, 35–37.

16   Ibid., 38.

which only gave more attention to figures like Alex Jones warning about the "prison planet" constructed by New World Order officials at the UN who plotted to kidnap patriots and intern them in make-shift FEMA concentration camps.

Some on the left noticed the subtle contradictions at work. Former Sojourner Truth Organization member Don Hamerquist cautioned his left-wing audience: "Many third position fascists explicitly aim to recruit from the ranks of the left.... Indeed, elements of third position politics are hard to distinguish from common positions on the left, even from positions held in some of the groups that are closest to us."[17] The two problems could not necessarily be understood together—on the one hand, fascists aligned with Troy Southgate and Christian Bouchet hoped to infiltrate the left, while on the other hand, fascist groups became increasingly difficult to discern from leftist groups on some levels. What complicated events in Europe was that these latter elements were not aligning themselves with parties or even larger groups but saw themselves as "Free Nationalists" or "Free Comrades" able to float into and out of single-issue protests.

Anarchism and Fascism

From 1998 to 2001, the number of Freie Kameradschaft groups in Germany nearly doubled, from 80 to 150. The neo-Nazi Sven Skoda recalls, "We were once again free from organizational structures and decided to continue by virtue of necessity."[18] Most of these groups were guilty of daily brutality and harassment of immigrants, queer people, and anyone who did not fit their ideological niche; however, some would prove far more dangerous. One Freie Kameradschaft group spawned a cell called the Nationalsozialistischer Untergrund (NSU—National Socialist Underground), responsible for a murder spree across Germany including two bombings and fifteen bank robberies. During the six years of killings, which cost the lives of nine immigrants and one policewoman, police at one point claimed that a Turkish drug ring

---

17   Ibid.

18   Sven Skoda, quoted in Schedler, "'Modernisierte Antimoderne': Entwicklung des organisierten Neonazismus," 21.

was responsible, thereby criminalizing the victims and bringing disrepute upon their families. Finally, after an armed robbery, police tracked down two NSU members in a camper. The two shot themselves after setting their camper ablaze, and a third member turned herself in after setting the trio's apartment on fire.

It was later revealed that the police investigation into the cell had been tampered with by the Federal Office for the Protection of the Constitution, Germany's intelligence service agency, leading to the resignation of that agency's president, Heinz Fromm, as well as state-level resignations of the presidents of the agency's Thuringia and Saxony offices. Scandal increased as the public was told about the wages received by fascist informants connected to the NSU, which meant the intelligence agency had been effectively supporting fascists and sustaining their efforts. The agency knew much more about the killings through their network of informants and not only refused to act but hampered the police investigation. To wit, their informants were sometimes known within fascist circles and likely operated as double-agents.[19]

Was the fascist movement becoming increasingly decentralized, or was there a deeper structure at play? While the networks of Freie Kameradschaft seemed disorientingly disorganized, the investigation into the NSU has exposed deeper roots linked to counterintelligence within state agencies. The appearance of autonomy, mobility, and spontaneity helped fascists incite violence against immigrants and others while maintaining the appearance of a horizontal network attractive to young antiauthoritarians.

More of this tendency can be seen in the development of national-anarchism through the efforts of Southgate and Bouchet in the United Kingdom. Supposedly converting to anarchism through a growing relationship with Hunt from the *Alternative Green* journal, Southgate merged his Liaison Committee for Revolutionary Nationalism with the ELF in 1997. The next year, he plunged headlong into the occult with his new group, the National Revolutionary

---

19   The most extensive material available on this ongoing scandal can be found in Stefan Aust and Dirk Laabs, *Heimatschutz: Der Staat und die Morderie des NSU* (Munich: Pantheon Publishing, 2014). Also see the Netflix original series *NSU: German History X*, directed by Züli Aladag, Florian Cossen, and Christian Schwochow (2016).

Faction (NRF). Southgate enjoyed a status of "anarchist heretic," bringing together Evola's spiritualist racism and a rejection of the abstractly defined nation-state in favor of a Jungian racial psyche. His new ideological formation touted paganism, Nouvelle-Droite ethnopluralism, and "blood and soil" ecology, all of which were in full display at the Anarchist Heretics Fair he organized in 2000.[20] From Southgate's pedigree within the fascist movement to his merger with the ELF, it is clear that he is a member of an implicit, if not public, hierarchy involving the networks he has helped create since the late 1980s. Yet, a veneer of anarchist utopianism helps to soften ultranationalist politics and their insinuations of "natural hierarchy," order, and discipline.

The scheme worked, attracting prominent members of the Green Party and Green Socialist Network, leading to internal inquiries and some degree of scandal before dedicated green anarchists joined antifascists in shutting down several other attempted gatherings. Southgate still encourages entryism as an "exciting" prospect for "attempting to take over, from within, the organization which you have targeted and then recruiting it in the service of our own agenda. If such an organization has influence within the community or even power over it, we will find ourselves in a position of great strength."[21] This strategy would define the NRF's attempts to insinuate itself within the antiglobalization, ecology, animal rights, and anarchist movements.

So in both the cases of the expansion of the Frei Kameradschaft and the development of the national-anarchist tendency, fascists appeared to develop horizontal ideology and models of networking. However, these models were shown to be functional, taking the pressure off parties and intellectual leaders while optimizing street-level organizing and violence. They were not indicative of a horizontalization of fascist ideology in general, which continued and continues to maintain intrinsically hierarchical power centers coordinated by ideologues within broader networks.

---

20   Macklin, "Co-Opting the Counterculture," 315–16.
21   Troy Southgate, "The Case for National-Anarchist Entryism," National-Anarchist.net, September 18, 2010, http://www.national-anarchist.net/2010/09/case-for-national-anarchist-entryism-by.html.

Ideological Shift

Groups began to adapt to new strategies and tactics all over the
world after September 11, 2001, leading to disorienting results. Unlike the Oklahoma City bombing, fascists around the world commended the attackers, sympathizing with their struggle against the
Zionist Occupation Government and wishing them well. While
the events of September 11 ratcheted up Islamophobic sentiment
across the North Atlantic, white supremacist groups continued to
agitate against global trade and the "New World Order."

A faction of Heick's American Front, the Satanic skinhead
group from San Francisco, changed its name to New Resistance to
match its trans-Atlantic allies under Bouchet at the ELF. The new
leader of the American Front proclaimed:

> I am far from a White supremacist. To me a White suprema-
> cist is a reactionary of the worst kind. He focuses his energies
> on symptoms rather than the disease itself. The disease is the
> System—International Capitalism—NOT those who are as ex-
> ploited, often as badly or worse, as White workers are by it. Yes,
> We actually see more in common, ideologically, with groups like
> Nation of Islam, the New Black Panther Party or Aztlan than
> with the reactionaries like the Hollywood-style Nazis or the
> Klan. In the past we've worked with Nation of Islam and single
> issue Organizations like Earth First! and the Animal Libera-
> tion Front when the opportunity arose. I'm sure the future holds
> more common actions and Revolutionary coordination between
> our "Front" and others of like mind.[22]

While the American Front boasted of working with Earth
First! and the ALF, they and their European Liberation Front
partners increasingly embraced the philosophy of what Dugin
started calling the "fourth political theory." According to Dugin's
"Fourth Position," fascism could be relegated to interwar Europe as a historically failed doctrine. Today's "actionists" must
strive beyond the realm of fascism while resolving to learn its
lessons, remaining "conservative revolutionaries" or "national

---

22   Quoted in Hamerquist and Sakai, *Confronting Fascism*, 42.

revolutionaries" toward the cause of ultranationalist values and against multicultural "globalism."[23]

Similar to Fini's "post-fascism," Dugin's fourth political theory brings with it the mystique of a totalizing spiritual idea that transcends all worldly attempts to define it. Nevertheless, at its core, it is unquestionably palingenetic ultranationalism. In addition to Griffin's definition, Dugin also fits Umberto Eco's evaluation of syncretic "Ur-Fascism"—the mythical understanding that all things return to one underlying spiritual essence, "a *fuzzy* totalitarianism, a collage of different philosophical ideas, a beehive of contradictions" involving traditionalism, irrationalism, identitarianism, elitism, belief in life as struggle, and the characterization of the enemy as at once both powerful and inferior.[24]

Antiglobalization and Autonomy

In Italy, the antiglobalization movement reached a high point between 2001 and 2004, with huge protests taking place in Naples in March 2001 and in Genoa four months later. During this period, Thiriart's former acolyte Claudio Mutti activated his network with former young militant Carlo Terracciano, attempting to create a red-brown alliance within the movement. By dismissing left and right polarization, the two worked to criticize Berlusconi for "Atlanticism" while also attacking the cosmopolitanism, "utopian internationalism," and "mondialism" that polluted the movement.

In 2003, Mutti and Terracciano entered the Campo Antimperialista to rally support around halting the Iraq War. When its members found out about the involvement of fascists, the Campo

---

23   Perhaps nobody has done more than Bouchet to propel Dugin into the neofascist international spotlight. Bouchet's publishing company Éditions Avatar has published Dugin's work for the West, and he maintains a kind of Duginist website dedicated to "resistance to the new world order" called Voxnr.com on which Dugin has a regular column. Marlene Laruelle, "Russia's Radical Right and its Western European Connections: Ideological Borrowings and Personal Interactions," in Deland et al., eds., *In the Tracks of Breivik*, 95.

24   Umberto Eco, "Ur-Fascism," *New York Review of Books*, June 22, 1995, http://www.nybooks.com/articles/1995/06/22/ur-fascism.

was effectively abandoned. Although the fascist creep failed to gain control of the antiglobalization movement, it did cause organizers to adjust their ideological positions. Rather than maintain an antiglobalization movement that in some ways appeared to be against "globalism," migrant rights, and racial integration, movement organizers advanced the rhetoric of "alter-globalization" or "counterglobalization," intimating a sense of internationalism and inclusivity. On the other side, a harder-edged anti-imperialist movement began to emerge in which Duginists would gain greater hegemony.

After their adventure in the Campo Antimperialista, the two decided to create a think tank based on Dugin's ideas, and established a journal called *Eurasia*. The journal managed to stay afloat with the participation of high-level Italian academics and political figures, maintaining hegemony by publishing "young students and scholars in political science or economics, who welcome the opportunity to have an article published by a journal with an editorial board comprised of international experts, but with no understanding of the journal's underlying doctrines."[25]

During this trans-European attempt to "to stand with the Right and think with the Left," Strasserists and "Free Comrades" began to soften their language toward the State of Israel.[26] Christian Worch, one of the ideologues of "Free Comrades," declared that "the Jews are one people, so they have a God-given or natural legal right to their own state." He also states that the dissolution of Israel would lead to a refugee crisis in Germany, and that Israel has nuclear weapons trained on European cities as blackmail for military defense. While remaining critical of the State of Israel's policies on a pragmatic level, Worch insists that he is "against anti-Zionism" and also rejects "pro-Israel" politics.

Behind his words is a tacit anti-Semitism, but his conciliatory expressions about "one people" deserving "their own state" is central to the rationale of ethnopluralism in its Third World differentialist phase. Recalling the same course of thought that brought Benoist to vote for the Communist Party in 1984, Worch claims, "Marxism and Socialism do not always make a pair of shoes, but they certainly

---

25   Savino, "From Evola to Dugin," 108–9.

26   Wasserman, *Black Vienna*, 132.

can."[27] Similar efforts at rapprochement between right and left over issues of globalism were enacted by the National Front, FPÖ, Vlaams Belang, and other radical-right populist parties, which also softened anti-Zionist rhetoric while increasing opposition to NATO and American values of consumerism.

In 2001, Bill White, an organizer and propagandist with ambiguous politics, described the perspective of the antiglobalization protester as "a broad blend of left-wing socialism and far-right nationalist and libertarian views" that "has been slowly infiltrating both extremes of the political spectrum, particularly in the anti-globalist movement, and has been leading to a new synthesis of doctrine—'beyond left and right'—that is coalescing around a number of tendencies—national-anarchism, social nationalism, national bolshevism—that some are calling the fastest growing ideological movement on the fringe." Claiming to adhere to both Maoist and Trotskyist ideas, White enthusiastically supported this fusion of left and right, although many leftists saw it as more of a transfusion of reds from the left to the right. "The extreme Old Leftists of the anti-globalist movement call conferences to attack these ideas, and…the self-righteous defenders of neo-liberalism try to force these doctrines' square peg into their round hole of 'hate' and 'fascism,'" White declared.[28] Although White would join the National Socialist Movement just five years after penning those words, his outrage over accusations of "'hate' and 'fascism'" almost seem sincere.

Social Nationalism in Poland

At this point, it became important for the left to clarify its own ideas in order to take a combative distance from the entryists. The problem was not that the critiques of multiculturalism, consumerism, and the opposition between left and right were all becoming "branded" by

---

27   Christian Worch, "SvD-Gespräch mit Christian Worch über 'Die Rechte,' nationalen Sozialismus und Israel," *Sache des Volkes* (blog), November 3, 2014, https://sachedesvolkes.wordpress.com/2014/11/03/sdv-gesprach-mit-christian-worch-uber-die-rechte-nationalen-sozialismus-und-israel/.

28   Bill White, "Anti-Globalist Resistance Beyond Right and Left," in Griffin and Feldman, eds., *Fascism*, 5:365.

fascists, but rather that some populist elements within social movements refused to address why and how their ideas contrasted from those of fascists, if they did at all. Among the so-called old left attempting to draw lines in the sand against the Nouvelle Droite and entryist tactics, White singled out a Polish anarcho-syndicalist named Laure Akai, who called for an "anti-Nationalist-Anarchist, Anti-Synthesis conference" in 2002. I interviewed Akai in 2015, and she told me about a noticeable increase in entryist tactics in the Polish left. New groups forming today include Social Piłsudskiists, who maintain the legacy of Józef Piłsudsky, the interwar authoritarian ruler of Poland. Among the early syncretic fascists to approach Akai was a radical named Jaroslaw Tomasewicz who wrote for both anarchist and fascist publications at the time very openly, and eventually published a booklet called "The Children of Sorel and Piłsudski," attempting to unite the syndicalist and nationalist strands in Poland's left- and right-wing tradition.

The booklet made the rounds at protests and gatherings; "anarchists were distributing it," Akai told me, "and Workers Initiative [an anarcho-syndicalist union] put it on their website." One of Tomasewicz's associates, Remigiusz Okraska, moved to the right, and published a magazine called *Obywatel*, with start-up money from unspecified funds. *Obywatel* published fascist articles, but they were exposed after publishing a piece by someone with a little more name recognition: Horst Mahler, the former member of the Red Army Faction who had switched teams and began working for fascist causes.

According to Akai, "foreign people didn't recognize the Polish fascists so much, but some Germans saw the Mahler article. Then there was an international scandal, because also on the editorial board of the magazine were people from Attac." A large, trans-European protectionist and antiglobalization group, Attac's international leaders became concerned that their Polish associates were too right wing for comfort. "Many anarchists defended [*Obywatel*] and talked about crazy antifascists," Akai told me. Social Piłsudskiism has since incorporated a more anarchist bent, drawing on theories of cooperatism produced by anarcho-syndicalist Edward Abramowski, as well as ultranationalism. Hence, they believe in the spread of joint-owned cooperatives with the ultimate aim of unifying the nation in a kind of national socialist solidarity. In this way,

Social Piłsudskiists maintain a proximity to the Zadruga Movement, an interwar, völkisch, blood-and-soil movement organized loosely around cooperatism and harkening back to paganism.[29]

Another Zadruga-like group in Poland is Niklot, which had also become known in the 2000s through attempts to infiltrate and influence the left. Originating in the late 1990s as a neo-pagan group with Zadruga ideology, Niklot is known to trace its influences to Evola and the Nouvelle Droite. Joining in protests with the Self-Defense (Samoobrona) party, Niklot also participated in National Bolshevik-led gatherings like the European Environmental, Peace, and Alternative Movements conference. Meeting with Dugin in 2004 and 2005, Niklot's leader Mateusz Piskorski joined an increasing trend among neofascists to act as official election monitors in Eastern Europe, from Belarus and Ukraine to Russia, to ensure that the political process favored the candidates they supported.[30] Piskorski later established the European Center for Geopolitical Analysis, which has enabled greater networking and communications among Eastern European Eurasianists.

As for Bill White, after a few years he became entangled in the trial of Matthew Hale, of the World Church of the Creator. Hale had spoken approvingly to an undercover informant about the assassination of a judge, who was later killed by another hitman for different reasons. With Hale facing trial, White threatened a juror and released the juror's information online. He was subsequently arrested and convicted and has been in and out of jail for a variety of similar reasons since.

Front National Spawns Fascist New Wave

With its participation in the mass movement against neoliberalism and amid rising Islamophobic sentiment, the radical right gained substantial ground in European politics. In 2002, the Front National achieved their strongest showing ever in the polls. Sociologist Löic Wacquant had warned the Socialist Party, "So long as

---

29   Rafal Pankowski, *The Populist Radical Right in Poland* (New York: Routledge, 2010), 40.

30   Anton Shekhovtsov, "Far-Right Election Observation Monitors," in Laruelle, ed., *Eurasianism and the European Far Right*, 233–35.

the Socialists of France, and the rest of Europe, continue to ignore the growing social insecurity spawned by welfare retrenchment and economic deregulation, they will continue, stone by stone, to pave the road toward fascism."[31] Socialist Prime Minister Lionel Jospin refused to move the Socialist Party to the left, insisting instead that no true socialism exists outside of capitalist markets. In the election's first round, Le Pen defeated Jospin by 200,000 votes, winning nearly 17 percent of the electorate but falling three points below incumbent center-right politician Jacques Chirac.

The Front National's gains had been precipitated by a well-publicized split in 1999, when Vial left with Mégret. The nature of the split lies in the splinter groups created—the Mouvement National Républicain (MNR—National Republican Movement) and Terre et Peuple (Land and People). The former group would become a floundering political party based on a kind of fusion closer to neoconservatism in style but with the same radical-right politics. Linking up with the Spanish group Movimiento Social Republicano (MSR—Republican Social Movement), Mégret's MNR produced propaganda and expanded networks but failed to attain a following. As the MNR floundered, Mégret joined forces with Bouchet of Nouvelle Résistance to create Unité Radicale (UR—Radical Unity), and the Spanish MSR followed suit. UR advocated an intifada against "Zionists" in France. When a UR member attempted to assassinate President Chirac on Bastille Day, 2002, however, the group dissolved and Bouchet left the European Liberation Front, leading to its disintegration as well.[32]

Unphased, UR members moved on to form a new group called Bloc Identitaire (BI—Identity Bloc) based on the "archeofuturist" ideas of former Nouvelle Droite ideologue Guillaume Faye.[33] BI's ideology advanced the idea of confronting "the aftermath of chaos, the *post-catastrophic world*" by returning to "a pre-modern,

---

31   Löic Wacquant, quoted in Magnus E. Marsdal, "Loud Values, Muffled Interests: Third Way Social Democracy and Right-Wing Populism," in Wodak et al., eds., *Right-Wing Populism in Europe*, 49.

32   Lebourg, "Arriba Eurasia?," 134.

33   Jon Henley, "France's Neo-Nazi Breeding Ground," *Guardian*, July 19, 2002, https://www.theguardian.com/world/2002/jul/20/thefarright .france.

non-egalitarian and non-humanistic outlook" that would reevaluate the utility of "the advancements made in technology and science, particularly in biology and computer science." This feat would be accomplished by reconciling "Evola and Marinetti, Doctor Faust and the Labourers…raising traumatic problems and sending ideological electroshocks: *shocking ideas*."[34] BI also rejected Eurasianism for its call to ally with similar groups in the Middle East, insisting instead on a "Eurosiberian" movement from Dublin to Vladivostok.

Also grounded in many of Faye's ideas, Terre et Peuple has tended to focus more on the mythical core of the past and its reappropriation through modern science in a kind of post-collapse scenario. Founded in the mid-1990s as part of Vial's effort to strengthen the Front National's regionalism while enhancing its theoretical basis, Terre et Peuple bases its ideas on Barrès's ideology of *enracinement*, or rootedness, which "connotes links with the past, ties to places of origin, ties to biological or cultural forebears, and hence, ties to one's native community."[35] In order to preserve its roots, the group claims, France must fight ferociously against the inauthentic and decadent forces that seek to unravel the connection between French nationals and their land. Using the symbol of the Edelweiss, a white alpine flower, the movement of Terre et Peuple hopes for the rebirth of "community of work, combat, and faith in service to cultural rootedness," in Vial's words.[36]

Terre et Peuple includes a rotating cast of Nouvelle Droite veterans like Faye, Dominique Venner (founder of Europe-Action), and Pierre Bérard, as well as younger members. Standing against the United States and its consumerist, neoliberal globalization, Terre et Peuple also embraces neo-paganism and an emphasis on myth and history dating to the Bronze Age and Indo-Aryan ancestry. It ties French ancestry to Celtic peoples, and supports not only regional independence for the Breton and Alsatian portions of France, but also for Ireland.

Vial's notion of destiny encompasses ethnic war, which will bring about the dawning of a new cultural and political

---

34 Guillaume Faye, *Archeofuturism: European Visions of the Post-Catastrophic Age*, trans. Sergio Knipe (UK: Arktos Media, 2010), 13–15. His emphasis.

35 Flood, "The Cultural Struggle of the Extreme Right," 5:174.

36 Pierre Vial, quoted in Ibid., translated by the author.

revolutionary order. His mentor, Marc Augier, became a leading collaborator in the Vichy regime and fought with a French division of the Waffen-SS before escaping France after its liberation, and returning in the mid-1950s to a successful career as a novelist and contributor to Europe-Action. Augier and Vial's beliefs extend to the spiritual—particularly the legends of the quest for the Grail, Merlin, and a deep, pagan undercurrent that they locate within the rituals and carnivals of Christianity. The group has also proclaimed the Hyperborean origins of Indo-Europeans, and its contributors also reference Arthur Moeller van den Bruck, Jünger, Spengler, and Bardèche. This combination is described by scholar Christopher Flood as, "best described as neo-Nazi in its attachment to a völkisch, organicist conception of ethnic community based on biological and cultural descent."[37]

While Terre et Peuple represents perhaps the most traditional neo-Nazi intellectual trend in France, the work of former GRECE intellectual Robert Steuckers has done more to key into the ideas of direct action and Eurasianism. After hooking up with Dugin in Moscow in the early 1990s, Steuckers left GRECE, arguing against metapolitics and in favor of decisive action. Since the break, Steuckers has worked to "enter" Indymedia and Peoples' Global Action in order to influence social movements toward fascism. This kind of work persists today in the Duginist Green Star/New Resistance group that has grown largely through a broad social media network promulgating national revolution against the backdrop of general "anti-imperialist" ideology.

In discussion with Dugin's bizarre geopolitical theories, Steuckers has created a group called European Synergies (Synergies européennes), which identifies pan-European unity as a phenomenon of "synergies"—concurrent events developing across time and space through mutual forces and energies intertwined with spiritual and world-historical elements. Steuckers's syncretic style has drawn support from members of the left, as well as Alain Soral, a self-described "social nationalist" who abandoned the Communist Party and has since openly embraced the anti-Semitic ideas of Dugin. Steuckers is also known to collaborate with other groups in the neofascist movement, as in 2007 when

---

37   Ibid., 175.

he co-organized a colloquium on globalization with the Walloon faction of Vial's Terre et Peuple.[38]

Putin's Russia, which also supports the Front National financially, has opened space for competing schools of "raciology" other than Duginism through the White World (Belyi Mir) movement. In 2006, Guillaume Faye visited Moscow to present a paper on the Eurosiberian destiny at a White World conference. Ostensibly, the White World's Eurosiberianism differs from the Eurasianism of Dugin's synergism in that identitarianism typically views Islam not as a mystical point of interest but as a colonizing force against Europe's indigenous peoples.[39] Nevertheless, the Duginist European Synergies has also opened a branch in Russia in collaboration with White World, revealing that the distinctions between groups are actually quite insignificant.

While Faye has also spoken at American Renaissance conferences in the United States, David Duke has also become intertwined with the identitarians in Russia, calling for the White World to take on "the resolution of the Jewish question" and identifying Russia as the final frontier of white nationalism. In 2000, Duke had drawn up a pamphlet called *The ABCs of Slavic Skinheads*, which fast became an Internet mainstay of Russian fascist culture.[40] He was invited to a White World conference in 2007, also attended by Front National ideologue and former GRECE member, Emmanuel Le Roy. Furthering the trans-Atlantic crossovers, between 2004 and 2010, Russian-based Dvizheniye Protiv Nelegalnoy Immigrazii (DPNI—Movement Against Illegal Immigration) hosted American white nationalists for their marches. The US participants wore cowboy hats, almost reminiscent of the Marquis de Morès's anti-Semitic butcher boys; however, the display of US culture led some Russian groups to refuse to participate.[41]

---

38   Laruelle, "Russia's Radical Right and its Western European Connections," 94.

39   Ibid., 99.

40   Ibid., 100.

41   The leader of the DPNI, Aleksandr Belov, attempted to found a new populist radical-right party based on the model of the FN, FPÖ, and NA, but the movement failed to distance itself from its skinhead-based orientation before facing a ban (Ibid., 100).

A Bit About CasaPound

Among the most successful and innovative neofascist groups attempting to tap into street-level politics and international relations is CasaPound in Italy, which evokes the more distinctive legacy of Mussolini and the Blackshirts. Emerging in 2003 through squatter networks, rock bands, and violent media stunts, CasaPound continues to thrive on the public spectacle of public political clashes against leftist opponents over issues of patriotism, nationalism, and xenophobia. A neofascist countercultural group that takes its name from the fascist poet Ezra Pound, CasaPound utilizes spectacular protests to draw media attention to shift feelings about the commonly felt economic crisis toward a far-right agenda. They use "cultural" issues like immigration, gay rights, and social welfare to do so, because it allows them to blur some of the difference between left and right.

Explicitly calling for a return to the Fascist epoch, their ideology draws most directly from Mussolini's *Dottrina del fascismo* and Evola's writings. Wherever they become entrenched, their activists are found with blood on their hands, engaged in notoriously violent protests and random street violence. Yet by supporting gay rights, protesting austerity, and running squatted social centers, CasaPound is able to appropriate many of the hegemonic positions of the left while maintaining active alliances with the far right.[42] The similarities with the left, of course, only go so far. In fact, CasaPound has been known for initiating violence against the left while appealing to left-leaning members of the public. CasaPound opens squats, typically viewed as the terrain of the autonomist and anarchist left wing, but only for Italian nationals, prohibiting immigrants. The struggle for social services and housing, when fought by white nationalists, is also a struggle against immigrants and Muslims.[43]

---

42   See Dr. Caterina Froio and Dr. Pietro Castelli Gattinara, "Neo-Fascist Mobilization in Contemporary Italy: Ideology and Repertoire of Action of CasaPound Italia," *Journal for Deracialization* 2 (Spring 2015): 110.

43   Unaired interview between an antifascist named Enzo in Trento, Italy, by Paul Roland, KBOO, Portland, OR, February 16, 2015.

This anti-immigrant struggle, though, is not as clear-cut as the conservative line of most radical-right parties. Rather than oppose immigration and support imperialism, CasaPound insists on solidarity: "Against the infernal machine of the multi-racist society we propose the problems created by migration through: the blockage of the migratory waves; cooperation with the economic areas outside Europe thus to create their development and liberation from the yoke of the multi-nationals; support to all those extra-European independent movements so to create the conditions for a settlement of the autochthonous populations."[44]

Presented as antiracist, CasaPound's "blockage of migratory waves" is also posited as an anticapitalist response to a flattening modern world devoid of culture and tradition. This cultural ensemble of ethnopluralism comes from the same Nouvelle Droite strains of Tarchi and Benoist and the National Bolshevism of Thiriart, Mutti, and Limonov; it relies on semiotic appropriation of the left's key symbols, as well as the recuperation and reworking of other key symbols and vocabulary from Evola and Mussolini-era fascism.

Although their name references Ezra Pound, it is more about Pound's esoteric economic and political ideology than his poetry or aesthetics. During his fascist period, Pound sought to unite the antibanker concept of "social credit" and the Proudhonist ideas of market-based mutualism advocated by Silvio Gesell. While the former promised to distribute equal credit to all individual citizens, the latter proposed taking away interest-based loans while "accelerating the circulation of commodities."[45] Uniting the two would offer an economy based on merit and the producerist impetus of a national community, they claim, appealing both to more humble, rustic ideas of social credit and futurist impulses of accelerated economic advancement in urban market flows.

CasaPound runs a web-based radio station called Radio Bandiera Nera, and their organization also includes a youth group called

44   Quoted in Anna Castriota and Matthew Feldman, "'Fascism for the Third Millennium': An Overview of Language and Ideology in Italy's CasaPound Movement," in Feldman and Jackson, eds., *Doublespeak*, 236.

45   Rasmus Fleischer, "Two Fascisms in Contemporary Europe? Understanding the ideological split of the Radical Right," in Deland et al., eds., *In the Tracks of Breivik*, 61.

the Blocco Studentesco (Student's Bloc), which uses the logo of Mosley's Union Movement party, a circle with the diagonal lightning flash through it. Founder Gianluca Iannone declared, "CasaPound is based around four principles: culture, solidarity, sport, and (obviously) politics.… We try to communicate in a radical mode and renew our dream. We want to launch it and give it a new spin. It could be through music or art."[46] As of 2014, their squatter network housed some five thousand people, and it also ran fifteen bookshops, twenty bars, and eight sporting associations.

CasaPound did not grow to that size without assistance. While Lega Nord had no role in starting CasaPound or developing its ideology, it has, along with the Alleanza Nazionale, Fiamma Tricolore, and the relatively recent La Destra, given the group a kind of political umbrella to work under in exchange for a bit of street cred. According to Italian Nouvelle Droite ideologue Marco Tarchi, Lega Nord typically utilizes larger-scale populism based on emotional and affective politics: "Although the Lega [League] had always pushed to enter regular politics via parliament and the local authorities, it also proposes itself as the expression of a popular will that refuses to be expressed solely in rational forms through formal procedures, and which instead seeks channels of manifestation located beyond the institutional context that value emotions and affective ties."[47]

CasaPound's emotional and affective framework takes on a subtle subversive power through their political affiliation with Lega Nord. At the same time, their affinity with CasaPound has given Lega Nord access to a young, countercultural movement, which adds to their affective, irrational allure a sense not only of the "common man" but also of the common man who is beyond and above the politician. Even while Lega Nord rages against globalization, their coalition with the neoliberal, "post-political" leader Silvio Berlusconi undermines their credibility. Joining with CasaPound shows that their affective bonds to their imagined community are still serious in some way—potentially even revolutionary and secessionist.

CasaPound denounces violence as a method of gaining hegemony, but they accuse their victims of being the aggressors.

46   Castriota and Feldman, "'Fascism for the Third Millennium,'" 227.
47   Marco Tarchi, "Populism Italian Style," in Yves Méni and Yves Surel, eds., *Democracies and the Populist Challenge* (UK: Palgrave Macmillan), 127.

Although more than half of CasaPound's protest events involve aggressive and violent acts, a mere 16 percent of their literature is concerned with violent events, while 60 percent is taken up with accusations of violence against the other side.[48] Meanwhile, one-third of their actions are reported by the media as violent, allowing them to exploit the spectacle by promoting a kind of nationalist "self-defense."[49] This ends up justifying aggression in the name of an ambiguous political platform defined as neither right nor left, while co-opting the ideological and semiotic positions of both. Members adhere to *Turbodinamismo*, defined as "the glorification of the gratuitous, violent and inconsiderate gesture."[50] Yet according to Enzo, an antifascist organizer in Trento, it has been extremely difficult to get the police and media to report CasaPound's assaults as anything but random violence or street fighting.[51] One of CasaPound's trademarks is *Cinghiamattanza*, or "belt-fighting," which involves "a macabre dance…a physical expression of style and force…street fighting, but with an ethics of its own; constructive confusion, sweat and will…an act of love."[52]

Their impunity also has much to do with CasaPound's political ties. In 2001, Berlusconi's reconstituted government included several Alleanza Nazionale members, among them Pino Rauti's son-in-law, Gianni Alemanno. A former youth leader of the MSI, Alemanno served in the Chamber of Deputies at the beginning of the MSI's original parliamentary push in 1994 and rode the wave into the 2000s. Serving as minister of agriculture until 2006, Alemanno became perhaps the leading member of the Destra Sociale (Social Right) faction of the Alleanza Nazionale. Alemanno lost the 2006

48   Froio and Gattinara, "Neo-Fascist Mobilization in Contemporary Italy," 105; Pietro Castelli Gattinara and Caterina Froio, "Discourse and Practice of Violence in the Italian Right: Frames, Symbols, and Identity-Building in CasaPound Italia," *International Journal of Conflict and Violence* 8, no. 1 (2014): 9–10.

49   Froio and Gattinara, "Neo-Fascist Mobilization in Contemporary Italy," 103.

50   Castriota and Feldman, "'Fascism for the Third Millennium,'" 230.

51   Unaired interview between an antifascist named Enzo in Trento, Italy, by Paul Roland, KBOO, Portland, OR, February 16, 2015.

52   Castriota and Feldman, "'Fascism for the Third Millennium,'" 232.

elections for mayor of Rome, and the next year the Alleanza Nazionale merged with Berlusconi's Il Popolo della Libertà coalition. Alemanno was elected mayor of Rome in 2008.

A representative of typical "post-fascist" ideology, Alemanno explained away the problem of skinheads raising the Roman salute and chanting "Duce! Duce!" at him upon election by claiming, "It would be impossible for a fascist to be elected mayor of Rome. Rome is a city that has solid democratic roots and that respects everyone. The Romans are not mad and neither am I." Fascism, Alemanno stated, "was fundamental to modernizing Italy."[53] Alemanno wears the Celtic cross symbol on a necklace, insisting that it was worn by his friend Paolo Di Nella, a former MSI Fronte della Gioventù (Youth Front) member killed during the Years of Lead. While Alemanno's victory was that of "a pragmatic strategy of political renewal and survival inherited from Alain de Benoist and Marco Tarchi," he supports violent paramilitary Blackshirts on the side.[54] In spite of the tragic events of December 13, 2011, in which a CasaPound member named Gianluca Casseri opened fire on Senegalese street vendors killing two and injuring three, his political support for CasaPound did not wane. Instead, one of his mayoral projects was an initiative to purchase CasaPound's squatted social center in Rome with 11.8 million euros from the municipal treasury and "donate" it back to the group as a gift.[55] In 2014, Alemanno had abandoned Il Popolo della Libertà for a party called Fratelli d'Italia (Brothers of Italy), which brought the tricolor flame of the MSI back into its logo. The next year, however, he jumped ship again for the Fini-led Azione Nazionale (National Action), which remains billed as a "national-conservative" cultural association that fields candidates in elections.

---

53   John Follain, "Italy Needed Fascism, Says the New Duce," *Sunday Times*, May 11, 2008, http://www.thesundaytimes.co.uk/sto/news/world_news/article91789.ece.

54   Tamir Bar-On, "Italian Postwar Neo-Fascism," *Analysing Fascist Discourses: European Fascism in Talk and Text*, eds. Ruth Wodak and John E. Richardson (New York: Routledge, 2013), 47–49.

55   Unaired interview between an antifascist named Enzo in Trento, Italy, by Paul Roland, KBOO, Portland, OR, February 16, 2015; Castriota and Feldman, "'Fascism for the Third Millennium,'" 238.

New Coalitions, New Synthesis

Other Third Positionists have joined the fray on the continent through attempted coalitions with parties. Roberto Fiore seized the moment to organize the European Hammerskins into a fighting force. He also initiated the European National Front which included Golden Dawn, Germany's NPD, the newly-established La Falange in Spain, the recently formed Romanian Noua Dreaptă (New Right), and Poland's Narodowe Odrodzenie Polski (National Revival of Poland).[56] Perhaps the most active organization in Fiore's assemblage in building transnational alliances, Golden Dawn connected further with the National Socialist Underground in Germany, as well as the neo-Nazi group Freie Netz Süd (Free Network South), and the Fränkische Aktionsfront (Frankish Action Front). In 2005, Golden Dawn members attended the NPD's convention in Rostock, and NPD members joined Golden Dawn during anti-Turkish marches in 2006 and 2007 commemorating the 1996 Imia Crisis (a sovereignty dispute between Greece and Turkey over Aegean islands). Golden Dawn's network today extends to Madrid's MSR, the banned German FAP, and CasaPound. Much of its modern network has been facilitated through Golden Dawn's alliance with Dugin.[57]

The success of populist parties like the NPD, Golden Dawn, and the Front National relies on what Aristotle Kallis calls an increasing "zero-sum" notion of "fierce, almost existential, competition for material prosperity and cultural self-determination against perceived outsiders."[58] This attitude, also known as "Haiderization," influenced the Dutch Party for Freedom and the British National Party (BNP). The BNP formed after John Tyndall abandoned the National Front during its initial turn toward Third Positionism. Tyndall remained in the driver's seat until Nick Griffin joined the party after leaving the faltering International Third Position. After Griffin's successful struggle against Tyndall for leadership of the party in 1999, the BNP embarked on a "modernization" campaign,

---

56   Tipaldou, "The Dawning of Europe and Eurasia?," 205.

57   Ibid., 205–10.

58   Aristotle Kallis, "Breaking Taboos and 'Mainstreaming the Extreme,'" in Wodak et al., eds., *Right-Wing Populism in Europe*, 59–60.

where fascist features were publically played down through a propaganda campaign coordinated by an in-group of intellectuals.[59] Griffin's break-out article, "BNP—Freedom Party!," deployed many of the same themes used by the FPÖ, while the BNP's public economic platform of "distributism" rehashed the old policies of the National Front and British Union of Fascists advanced by A. K. Chesterton more than sixty years earlier.[60] However, Griffin did not manage the "modernization" scheme very well, as his arrest for Holocaust denial and persistent refusal to recant would indicate. After September 11, 2001, and the English equivalent of July 7, 2005—a railway bombing in London—Griffin's party would launch into more vitriolic polemics against immigrants through its journal, *Identity*.[61]

Among the most insurgent right-wing parties to emerge in the 2000s was Jobbik, which was created in 2003 to fill the void created by the ailing MIÉP party, which failed to attain strong showings in the polls. Originally formed as the Right-Wing Youth Association (Jobboldali Ifjúsági Közössség, or Jobbik) to inject life into the old right, Jobbik emerged as a political contender and soon merged with MIÉP. Jobbik's agenda advanced a revival of Magyar nationalism, and it reconstituted the anti-Semitism, xenophobia, and homophobia of the far right, as well as a historical redemption of the authoritarian conservative regime of Miklós Horthy. While the moderate right attempted to downplay the significance of Jobbik's sudden appearance (while co-opting some of its positions), scholar András Kovács claims that the left deployed "overexcited anti-fascist rhetoric, which enabled Jobbik to appear in the media as an agenda-setting political force."[62] This analysis is a double-edged sword, though, because it presumes that it is antifascist rhetoric and not its dismissal that opens the space for radical-right politics to grow.[63]

Exploiting the average Hungarian's lack of confidence in the political system, Jobbik continues today to explicitly stress a continuity between the communist period and the post-communist

---

59   John E. Richardson, "Ploughing the Same Furrow?" in Ibid., 106.

60   Ibid., 110.

61   John Solomos, "Contemporary British Racist Movements," in Ibid., 126.

62   András Kovács, "The Post-Communist Extreme Right," in Ibid., 225.

63   Let us recall that those who travelled to Spain to fight in the Spanish
       Civil War were labeled "premature antifascists."

transition: the common theme they declare is the country's "colonial status" enforced by "your kind" whose "beloved boss, Shimon Peres" wants "our kind" to respond to "the buying up of Hungary, by saying: Shalom, Shalom, just come and help yourself." Jobbik continues: "It would be nice if there were just a little bit of truth to the supposed fear that the likes of you feel, owing to the alleged anti-Semitism and fascism etc. raging here.… On the contrary, your kind visibly do not fear at all.… We shall take back our homeland from those who have taken it hostage!" Here, Jobbik expresses the sincere wish that Jews feared Hungarian anti-Semitism and fascism, because such a fear would drive them away and stop them from putting "your grubby hands on the Hungarian people's property, our factories, our industrial plants, our hospitals."[64] With strong pride in their heritage from Atilla and the Magyar people, Jobbik took an "Eastern turn" in 2010 and now advocates closer connections to Russia and Eurasia, observing the need for a "sacral alternative" to Judeo-Christian values.[65] Although Jobbik is perhaps not Third Positionist, they are united with the BNP, Forza Nuova, Golden Dawn, and the NPD in joining Russia in alliance against the European Union.

Hence, as the populist radical right drew in fascist participants by the groupful, it also spewed out new fascist groupuscules that would activate more revolutionary strategies for dismantling liberal democracy, disseminating propaganda, and fighting the left as well as immigrants. As the century continued, the economic crisis would further radicalize sectors of the right, bringing new force to assemblages that sought to enter broad-based movements usually associated with the left and steer them in the direction of ultranationalism.

---

64   Quoted in Kovács, "The Post-Communist Extreme Right," 227.
65   Quoted in Ibid., 228; See also Umut Korkut and Emel Akçali, "Deciphering Eurasianism in Hungary: Narratives, Networks, and Lifestyles," in Laruelle, ed., *Eurasianism and the European Far Right*, 181.

CHAPTER 8: AUTONOMOUS NATIONALISM AND FASCIST GEOPOLITICS

The New Brownshirts

It is 6 September 2008 in Dortmund, a city with a population of 580,000 in western Germany. On the anti-war day celebrated by trade unions (traditionally on 1 September), a large demonstration with 1,100 participants is held in the city. Today, the first 500 activists are dressed black, their faces shielded by sunglasses and baseball caps, some even masked and wearing leather gloves. A large black banner displays the slogan "Against war and capitalism" and the unlabeled symbol used by the far left's "antifascist action," two waving flags in a circle. What could be understood to be a far-left event turns out, on closer inspection, to actually be the opposite—a neo-Nazi demonstration.[1]

The phenomenon that scholar Jan Schedler describes above pertains to a recent evolution in strategy that has a specific history dating back to interwar fascism. In Europe, the financial crisis created a wave of resentment against the neoliberal rule that tacitly held power between center right and left parties throughout the

---

1   Jan Schedler, "The Devil in Disguise: Action Repertoire, Visual Performance and Collective Identity of the Autonomous Nationalists," *Nations and Nationalism* 20, no. 2 (2014): 240.

1990s and 2000s. A generation gap emerged between those who always expected to see better days ahead and those millennials facing a world of bleak prospects.[2] Out of that gap rose the left-fascist Autonomous Nationalists, who gleaned their style from leftists and also won support from some who, in previous decades, would have unquestionably moved with the left.

First emerging as an idea in the late 1980s and early 1990s, the Autonomous Nationalists began to grow in small numbers during the early antiglobalization movement at the turn of the twenty-first century. Instead of openly collaborative structures tied to traditionalism and the old style, the Autonomous Nationalists tuned in to pop music and radical aesthetics. Theirs was an upgrading of SA-style brownshirt paramilitarism to suit the new era of protest politics forged in the 1980s through the left-wing Autonomen's rejection of official politics. The initial surge toward Autonomous Nationalist organization emerged through a restructuring of the German and Czech fascist scenes, springing up in the Netherlands as well. One of the first groups, Nationaal-Socialistische Aktie (National Socialist Action), boasted that they could listen to hip-hop and punk music and join in black bloc-type actions to advance their status among the youth.[3] Unrestricted by membership and organizational obligations, Autonomous Nationalist groups promoted spontaneous direct action and mobilization techniques linked to issue-oriented protests and demonstrations rather than movement building. As a result of this strategic decision to generate autonomy, neo-Nazi demonstrations in Germany from 2008 to 2009 increased 70 percent.[4]

Explicitly calling on the youth to join their ranks, one group, Autonome Nationalisten Haltern am See, proclaimed, "We aren't simple-minded thugs with skinhead, bomber jackets and combat boots up to the knee. We are young people like you from the heart of our country. We carry pride in our hearts and hope in our eyes. We fight to ensure that the future will be better than the conditions that we have now. Germany will sparkle like fresh dew in the

---

2   Anton Pelinka, "Right Wing Populism: Concept and Typology," in Wodak et al., eds., *Right-Wing Populism in Europe*, 19.

3   Gerrit de Wit, "Autonome neo-nazi's op de linkse toer?," *Gebladerte Archief, De Favel van de illegal* 95/96 (Autumn 2008): 10.

4   Schedler, "The Devil in Disguise," 240–44.

CHAPTER 8: AUTONOMOUS NATIONALISM AND FASCIST GEOPOLITICS   219

morning."⁵ This position is indicative of the way that Autonomous Nationalists place the emphasis on social rather than political revolution. In the words of the group Autonome Nationalisten Salzgitter, "Autonomous activism is a promising new strategy of offering active political resistance. The stiff structures of parties, fellowships or associations are far too vulnerable to state repressions and attacks by the political enemy."⁶ Although some Autonomous Nationalists consider their self-proclaimed autonomism "a form of action" not "a distinct worldview," the focus on DIY organizing, stenciling, and scene building tends to constantly return to the völkisch identity of ultranationalism tied into ecology and authenticity.⁷ Autonomous Nationalist groups have even claimed to "distance ourselves clearly from chauvinistic ideas" in terms of conquest and imperialism, but on the geopolitical stage, they have played integral roles in complex nationalist struggles both for and against the EU.

Clad in black like their Autonomen predecessors and supporting causes like workers' rights and ecology, the National Autonomen join demonstrations on May Day, building barricades in the streets and hurling bottles and rocks at the police. Although the NPD did not formally recognize the Autonomous Nationalists, they did begin to co-opt their rhetoric, citing multiculturalism as "the murder of autonomous peoples," which acknowledged the way that the new rhetoric of autonomy snapped into place among the "right to difference" and "ethnopluralism."⁸ Soon, the Autonomist Nationalists would be joining the NPD in joint protests with other radical-right parties throughout *Mitteleuropa*.

From 2007 to 2008, the number of Autonomous Nationalists in Germany grew, doubling from some 220 to 440, out of a total of around five thousand violent neo-Nazis in the country—a sharp increase, but still less than 10 percent of the neo-Nazi scene. By 2011, however, police noted 160 Autonomous Nationalists in

---

5   Quoted in Schlembach, "The 'Autonomous Nationalists,'" 299.
6   Ibid.
7   Ibid., 306.
8   Robert Grimm, "The Geographic Distribution of the Extreme Right in Germany," *MYPLACE* (blog), September 25, 2012, https://myplacefp7 .wordpress.com/2012/09/25/the-geographic-distribution-of-the -extreme-right-in-germany.

Brandenburg alone—half the total number of neo-Nazis in the state.[9] The phenomenon had also spread to Ukraine, England, Romania, the Czech Republic, Sweden, and elsewhere. According to Heinz Fromm, head of the Federal Office for the Protection of the Constitution, the Autonomous Nationalists represented a "new quality" of nationalist violence.[10] In that regard, the Autonomous Nationalists' form of violence did not focus on big marches making demands on the state, but rather on violent antistate and anticapitalist protests. As opposed to the antiglobalist protests of the early 2000s, which had highlighted national sovereignty over multiculturalism, the anticapitalist adaptation more clearly called for a decentralized and autonomous overthrow of the nation-state in favor of social welfare and ecological integrity.[11]

How Autonomous Nationalist Networks Developed

The Autonomous Nationalists still in operation present another imitation, or perverse evolution, of a number of social movement forms developed through prewar, interwar, and postwar Europe. The initial attempts to wed revolutionary syndicalism and ultranationalism, which bred fascism in the 1910s, had mutated into the bizarre conflations of Maoism, anarchism, and fascist terror that characterized the "Third Position" during the Cold War, transforming once again to incorporate contradictory reactionary and autonomous tendencies. Wearing Palestinian kaffiyehs and black-bloc clothing, the Autonomous Nationalists could almost be mistaken for leftists. Yet their Palestinian solidarity has generally signified anti-Semitic sentiment masked as "anti-Zionism," or the even more padded rhetoric of nationalist differentialism developed by former FAP activist Christian Worch. Their operations tend to take the form of vandalism and "anti-antifascist" campaigns that involve targeting and harassing antifascist activists, while also transforming antifascist symbols into fascist ones.

9   Schlembach, "The 'Autonomous Nationalists,'" 297.
10   Stefan Nicola, "Analysis: Terror Threat Growing in Germany," UPI, May 19, 2009, http://www.upi.com/Analysis-Terror-threat-growing -in-Germany/19261242775186.
11   Schlembach, "The 'Autonomous Nationalists,'" 310–11.

The first major action of Autonomous Nationalists occurred on May 1, 2008, in Hamburg. The NPD gathered a march of some 1,500 neo-Nazis, one third of whom formed into organized Autonome-style blocs, breaking off from the protest to attack antifascists, bystanders, and journalists. The protest shocked authorities and the general public with the most destructive riots seen in years—and because the Autonomous Nationalists involved deliberately targeted journalists. On September 6 of that year, a mobilization drew one thousand Autonomous Nationalists to the Ruhr region, where speakers railed against "speculators and globalists," calling on "the peoples of Europe" to rise up against "war and capitalism." In addition to German speakers, there were representatives from Russia, Bulgaria, the Netherlands, France, and the Czech Republic.[12]

Throughout the next year, Autonomous Nationalist activities were observed in North Rhine-Westphalia with "increasing energy," building on the same slogans of "National Socialism Now," "Freedom, Social and National," and "Autonomous, Militant, National Resistance." The new tactic also exhibited an advanced capacity to coordinate actions between nations whose established fascist parties only contributed to sectarianism. Exposing this new capacity, on May 1, 2009, buses set out to bring Autonomous Nationalists to Hannover for a large, violent protest; the fallback plan, according to the head of the Nationaler Widerstand (National Resistance) Dortmund chapter, Dennis Giemsch, was to direct the buses to the Czech city of Brno, to a planned demonstration organized by Autonomous Nationalist groups Narodni odpor (National Resistance) and Svobodný Nacionlaisté Chebsko (National Freedom of the Cheb Region).[13]

In the Czech Republic, the Autonomous Nationalists share members and organize with the Národní/svobodný odpor (National/Free Resistance), a neo-Nazi outfit that once served as part of the broader network of the radical-right Sdružení pro Republiku–Republikánská strana Československa

12   Ibid., 297–98.
13   Von Olaf Sundermeyer, "Autonome Nationalisten: Rechte Schläger im Kapuzenpulli," *Spiegel Online*, April 27, 2009, http://www.spiegel.de/politik/deutschland/autonome-nationalisten-rechte-schlaeger-im-kapuzenpulli-a-620467.html.

(SPR-RSČ—Association for the Republic–Republican Party of Czechoslovakia), which also maintained ties with Schönhuber's Republikaner party in Germany before declaring bankruptcy in 2000. Out of the SPR-RSČ came more overtly fascist groupuscules like the Národně sociální blok (National-Social Bloc) and the Dělnická strana (DS—Workers' Party), which founded a paramilitary arm called Ochranné sbory Dělnické strany (Workers' Party Protection Corps) and a youth wing, Dělnická mládež (Workers' Youth). These formations came together for violent protests that marked the anti-Roma campaign of 2008, but the state formally barred and dissolved DS in 2010. The implementation of both party-form public organizations and smaller, elite skinhead and Autonomous Nationalist groupuscules has enabled not only an increased intellectual marketing capacity, like Nick Griffin's "modernization" attempt, but also the merging of angry citizens with violent groups to inflame anti-Roma protests into episodes of collective violence.[14] After the state repression of the Workers' Party, a new group emerged that could absorb the old leaders: the Dělnické strany sociální spravedlnosti (DSSS—Workers' Party of Social Justice), which advocates national socialism but rejects both Hitlerist Nazism and communism. This ploy keeps the state authorities at bay while heightening the same societal tensions.

When the DSSS received an infusion of DS leaders, Czech Autonomist Nationalists posted a document on their website Revolta.info denouncing the DS and DSSS for intolerance of other forms of national socialism. In the controversy that followed, however, other Autonomous Nationalists refused to join the condemnation, and DSSS propaganda has found a hub in Revolta.info and sites like it. Autonomist Nationalists may simply have had a difficult time fitting into the DSSS's hopes to avoid a government ban by appearing sincere in their parliamentary ambitions. Although the DSSS has lacked sufficient popularity or trust to gain parliamentary seats, when they have called for protests in times of ethnic unrest, the police have blocked antifascist counterprotests, effectively enabling anti-Roma violence.[15] Because of the appearance

---

14   Miroslav Mareš, *Right-Wing Extremism in the Czech Republic* (Berlin: Friedrich Ebert Stiftung, 2012), 4.

15   Ibid., 5. (It should be noted that this form of police support is not unique

and possibility of violence surrounding the DSSS's campaigns, it is not surprising that some Autonomous Nationalists have returned to the fold.

While the DSSS has not focused on Jews, its platform militates against Roma, immigrants, and people perceived as abusing social welfare. It has made alliances with the Slovak party Ľudová strana Naše Slovensko (People's Party Our Slovakia), marking a post-communist European pattern in which Czech organizations function as inspiration for the strategies and tactics of Slovakian groups. The DSSS also forged alliances with the Austrian Nationale Volkspartei (National People's Party) and the German NPD and seeks greater cross border cooperation, such as joint protests against "The Invasion of Foreign Workers" held on May Day of 2011 in the cities of Brno, Czech Republic, and Heilbronn, Germany. Polish Autonomous Nationalists were also slated to join these protests, but a falling out with their German would-be allies preempted their contribution.[16] Among the groups supporting the 2011 joint protests was CasaPound—which had a small presence in the Czech Republic—as well as networks of Freie Kameradschaft. By the end of the year, groups with names like National Action or National Resistance had sprung up throughout Europe, and neo-Nazis dressed in black bloc attire featured prominently in populist demonstrations of groups like the English Defense League.

The Impact of Autonomous Nationalists in Bulgaria

Like the skinhead movement and Freie Kameradschaft, Autonomous Nationalism has had what Schedler describes as "a liberating effect" for the neo-Nazi youth scene, in which "one could be a neo-Nazi and also use different cultural expressions."[17] A neo-Nazi could listen to and appreciate rap music while rhetorically keeping ethnic populations at a respectful distance and joining in mob violence to attack immigrants, Jews, leftists, and Roma. Most importantly, the Autonomous Nationalists represent a creeping tendency

---

to the Czech Republic.)

16   Ibid., 7.

17   Jan Schedler, "Einleitung," in Schedler and Häusler, eds., *Autonome Nationalisten*, 11.

of ultranationalists and neofascists to enter mass demonstrations and turn them toward their own ends. This tendency was also evidenced in Eastern Europe—most famously perhaps in Bulgaria, where nationwide demonstrations against electricity bill hikes led to the downfall of Boyko Borisov's government.

Although Bulgaria's radical-right party, Ataka (Attack), fielded a presidential candidate who received almost a quarter of the vote in 2006, their numbers have not broken through fourth place in parliamentary or presidential elections since. Ataka did register in 2007 with the same Identity, Tradition, Sovereignty EU parliamentary group that included the Front National, FPÖ, and Fiamma Tricolore. Nevertheless, the autonomous fascist groups have made a greater impact domestically. Since 2003, neofascist and neo-Nazi groupuscules have consolidated around annual gatherings dedicated to pro-Nazi minister of war General Hristo Lukov, who was assassinated in 1943 by communist partisans. On February 13 every year, these torchlight marches have been accompanied by open displays of racism, xenophobia, and Islamophobia.[18] Acts of vandalism and violence against LGBQTI people, Muslims, Roma, and leftists have accompanied the increase of fascist movement building, with soccer games becoming regular training grounds. "In 2009, neo-Nazi soccer clubs massively sabotaged a protest campaign against privatization in the student quarter in Sofia and in protected areas," anthropologist Mariya Radeva told me. "Since then, communist student organizers have been attacked by fascist organizations such as National Resistance."[19]

In 2013, the wave of demonstrations against electricity rates culminated on February 24 with a large procession beginning at the Ministry of Economics. That morning, some twenty neo-Nazis attacked six male and female members of the Federation of Bulgarian

18 "Lukov March and the Neo-Nazi Provocations in Bulgaria," XOPA (ХОра срещу РАсизма), stopnazi-bg.blogspot.bg, Febuary 12, 2011, http://stopnazi-bg.blogspot.com/2011/02/lukov-march-and-neo-nazi-provocations.html.

19 This information comes from an interview with anthropologist Mariya Radeva, March 9–12, 2016; also see Mariya Ivancheva, "The Bulgarian Winter of Protests," *openDemocracy*, March 15, 2013, https://www.opendemocracy.net/mariya-ivancheva/bulgarian-winter-of-protests.

Anarchists. When the procession reached Eagle's Bridge, a woman took the mobile platform, greeting Levski and CSKA soccer fans, and expressing support for those "unfairly" accused of violence. A man followed with a call, "Will we allow them to build a second mosque in Sofia?" The audience shouted back, "No!" When members of the demonstration shouted, "Racists out!" they were shouted down, and neo-Nazis then violently attacked and chased away people raising leftist slogans for universal solidarity, yelling "Go to a protest of your own!" Racists and neo-Nazis were able to control the narrative of protests at the street level. As a result, the downfall of the government in Bulgaria took a far-right-wing, nationalist turn in a situation that portended the much more infamous revolution later that year in Ukraine.[20]

Fascism and Ukrainian Independence

Perhaps nowhere has Autonomous Nationalist presence had such a profound and revolutionary impact than Ukraine, where their ability to link to and delink from populist, radical, right-wing parties has allowed them to pull leftists toward nationalism while also advancing the agenda of revolutionary nationalism in party form—largely associated with the Freedom Party, also called Svoboda. Originally launched as a paramilitary group called Varta Rukhu (Guard of the Movement), composed of some five thousand anticommunist fighters, Svoboda's forerunner, the Sotsial-natsional'na partiya Ukrayiny (SNPU—Social-National Party of Ukraine) was formed in 1991 under the leadership of Oleh Tyahnybok. It began building a power base among students and youth in the western city of Lviv. Creating "popular guard units" and calling for the elimination of Russian influence on Ukraine, the SNPU promoted the lost "national character" of the country through their "social-nationalist" platform and proposed policies.

In 2000, the SNPU made contacts in a growing nationalist alliance called EuroNat (European Nationalists), composed of the Front National, BNP, Forza Nuova, Fiamma Tricolore, the Dutch

---

20   Ibid; People against Racism (HoRa), "Neo-Nazi Terror Marked the Protests in Sofia (Bulgaria)," LibCom.org, February 26, 2013, https://libcom.org/news/neo-nazi-terror-marked-protests-sofia-bulgaria-26022013.

Nieuw Rechts (New Right), Partidul România Mare (Greater Romania Party), Srpska radikalna stranka (Serbian Radical Party), Sverigedemokraterna (Sweden Democrats), and others. That year, Le Pen participated in the sixth party convention of the SNPU, which increasingly abandoned the openness of their early paramilitarism. On February 14, 2004, the party held their ninth conference, where they disbanded the paramilitary Patriót Ukrayíni (PU—Patriot of Ukraine) organization, which quickly reformed as an auxiliary arm. Scholar Taras Kuzio writes that at this point, "the SNPU chose to emulate Jörg Haider's Austrian Freedom Party by changing its name in 2004 from the Nazi-sounding Social-National Party of Ukraine to the Freedom (Svoboda) Party."[21] The party worked to generate greater respectability, although they retained the Wolfsangel symbol as a reminder of their heritage—especially the collaborations between German military units Nachtigall and Galizien and Stepan Bandera's Ukrainska povstanska armiia (Ukrainian Insurgent Army), which committed genocide against Poles in Eastern Ukraine.[22] Their electoral gains remained meager, but the radical right in Europe was poised at a turning point: changes would come about through an economic crisis that delegitimized the ruling system and transformed the character of public discourse.

According to Ukrainian activist Dmytriy Kovalevich, "All organizations of anarchists in the 1990s were deeply internationalist—any sort of nationalism was rejected by default. So it was quite surprising (for me, at least) that, since the early 2000s, nationalism began to infiltrate the movements."[23] These infiltrators were largely Autonomous Nationalists, who adopted the styles and ideas of the left to influence the direction and ideology of their movements.

Personifications of left-right unity included the anarchist figure of Makhno and the red-and-black flag he carried, which for Ukrainians also could signify the "blood and soil" of Bandera's

---

21   Taras Kuzio, *Ukraine: Democratization, Corruption, and the New Russian Imperialism* (Santa Barbara: Praeger, 2015), 180.

22   The German head of the SS Nachtigall Battalion, Theodor Oberländer, later became the postwar minister of refugees under Konrad Adenauer.

23   Interview with Dmytriy Kovalevich, January 16, 2016.

fascist group. Since he is remembered for fighting Bolsheviks, Makhno is presented as a nationalist hero of Ukrainian independence by those who seek autonomy from Putin's Russia. So Makhno gradually became infused with the ultranationalist myth, which included a phony story about his wife sewing the nation's yellow-and-blue colors on his hat. Through this narrative, Makhno merges with the "national ancestor myth" of the Zaporozhian Sich, a Cossack territory that rejected monarchs and defended Ukraine against invading hordes from the fifteenth to the eighteenth century. Makhno, man of action, represents the defiance of Ukraine, while his anarchism takes new shape as, if not pre-nationalist, then as an outgrowth of an ancestral national spirit imbued with the culture and history of the wild Steppes.[24] When the economy failed after the shock of 2008, increasing numbers of declassed industrial workers and petit bourgeois shopkeepers joined the drift toward the ultranationalist myth.

Particularly important to the Ukrainian Autonomous Nationalists is healthy living—a rejection of decadence, TV, drunkenness, and junk food. They strongly believe that their opponents are engaged in attempts "to liquidate us as a community of blood and spirit, as the social tie of worker-warrior and anthropological type." To fight these enemies, the Autonomous Nationalists often turn to leading ideologues of Svoboda, such as Yurii Mykhal'chyshyn, whose writing appeals to the younger generation while focusing on key themes broad enough to entice people who seek power: "The social-nationalist Weltanschauung is based exclusively on positive values: Freedom. Totality. Force. Dedication. Justice. Hierarchy. Order. Authority. Discipline. Brotherhood. Faith. Sacrifice. Pride. Messianism. Faithfulness. Passionate dedication. Equality. Nonconformity. Hatred. Passion. The desire for something greater than yourself. The impossible."[25]

---

24   Denys Gorbach, "Anarchists in Makhno's Homeland: Adventures of the Red-and-Black Flag," openDemocracy, September 30, 2015, https://www .opendemocracy.net/od-russia/denys-gorbach/anarchism-in-makhno's -homeland-adventures-of-red-and-black-flag.

25   Yurii Mykhal'chyshyn, quoted in Per Anders Rudling, "The Return of the Ukrainian Far Right," in Richardson and Wodak, eds., *Analysing Fascist Discourse*, 242.

Spiritual, intellectual, and moral ideals are united with health in terms of birth and ecstasy in a kind of strange union of radical right and fascism that Mykhal'chyshyn has adapted from the theories of early Ukrainian fascist Iuryi Lypa, who claimed that "Marriage is the duty of the woman to her own gender. The duty of the state, in turn, is to assist her in this.... The 300 ovulations of every Ukrainian woman, as well as the 1,500 ejaculations of every Ukrainian man are the same national treasures as, say, energy resources, or deposits of iron, coal, or oil."[26]

Among their pantheon of saints and martyrs who have sacrificed for their ideology, the Autonomous Nationalists of Ukraine list not only Stepan Bandera and other figures of Ukrainian integral nationalism and "social nationalism" or "socio-nationalism," but also "José Antonio Primo de Rivera, and Léon Degrelle, Corneliu Codreanu and Oswald Mosley... the conceptual arsenal of the German conservative revolution (Ernst Jünger, Arthur Moeller van den Bruck, Oswald Spengler, Otto Strasser, Carl Schmitt); Italian integral corporativism (Giuseppe Bottai, Ugo Spirito, Sergio Panunzio)."[27]

Autonomous Nationalists appeared in strong numbers with anticapitalist slogans in Ukrainian black blocs first in 2009 and again in 2011. For example, a group of Autonomous Nationalists worked with Svoboda to organize a march to commemorate the establishment of the Waffen-SS Galizien that drew some seven hundred participants.[28] In Lviv, the Avtonomy Opir (Autonomous Resistance) group marched in 2011, and many mistook them for leftists, since their message was broadly anticapitalist and they appropriated leftist images. However, the group was, on closer examination, obviously ultranationalist. Two years later, the same group held a march dedicated to Makhno incorporating the usual colored road flares and black-bloc-style.

---

26   Ibid.

27   Ibid., 242–43.

28   Per Anders Rudling, "They Defended Ukraine: The 14 Waffen-Grenadier-Division der SS (Galizische Nr. 1) Revisited," *Journal of Slavic Military Studies* 25, no. 3 (2012): 231.

Ideology and Development of Ukraine's EuroMaidan

Although the momentum of Autonomous Nationalist tendencies in Western Europe seemed to be dissipating by 2013 with key organizers abandoning the trend, in Eastern Europe, the practices of wearing black, moving as a bloc, and organizing spontaneously converged with the paramilitary exercises attached to parties like Svoboda in an extremely intimidating and radical revolutionary force. In that year, the Ukrainian government led by Viktor Yanukovych made a risky move. He postponed an important agreement with the EU in an attempt to negotiate its terms. The rejection was seen by liberals as another of Yanukovych's Putin-friendly maneuvers, made against the backdrop of the country's sizeable debt for gas from Russia.

An encampment grew virtually overnight at Independence Square (Maidan Nezalezhnosti) similar to the gatherings of the Orange Revolution between 2004 and 2005 and an earlier 1990 nationalist encampment. Ostensibly made up of liberals, mainstream nationalists, and NGOs, the EuroMaidan demonstrations expressed hope for economic development and human rights that would follow greater integration with the EU. While some compared the gathering to the Occupy movement in the United States, others noted that the dressing up in historic costumes and daily prayers led by priests gave the proceedings a more Tea Partyesque atmosphere. Really, it was both.

The movement garnered funding and media support from EU-friendly foundations and advocated for both Ukrainian nationalism (vis-à-vis independence from Russia) and a closer relationship with the EU. NGO support worked through the opportunism of young activists hoping to make a living for themselves in accordance with what is perceived as a Western standard of living. Since these NGOs were fueled by NATO dollars, activists working for them brought their energy, enthusiasm, and loyalty to NATO's EU backers. Leftist commentators like Viktor Shapinov argue that oligarchs adjusting from the economic crash of 2008 had also invested their money in the EU agreement, using media and the social mobilization capacity of NGOs to unseat Yanukovich's old economic model.[29]

---

29   Viktor Shapinov, "A Class Analysis of the Ukrainian Crisis," trans.

After police attacked the demonstration, dispersing crowds with metal truncheons, protesters returned with greater resolve and increased nationalist resentment against the regime. Protests became increasingly aggressive, as barrages of rocks and bricks were followed by a tractor driven into police barricades and intense hand-to-hand combat. As the brutality of the police increased to include live ammunition, and protesters were shot down in the streets, the mood of the Maidan encampment fostered an increasingly nationalist, right-wing spirit. Leftist protesters were beaten on-site by nationalists in EuroMaidan when they attempted to raise antinationalist positions, and militant ultranationalism was afforded the opportunity to set agendas.[30] A security detail called Pravy Sektor (literally, "Right Sector" or "Right Wing") was organized by a coalition of far-right groups, including the national-revolutionary Trident (Tryzub) and the Social-National Assembly, which as can be gleaned from their name, is a largely neo-Nazi organization with close links to Svoboda.[31]

Pravy Sektor occupied the fifth floor of the Trade Union Building, which became the headquarters of the EuroMaidan movement. Composed of paramilitary fighters and former army soldiers, the defense units gutted a state assault vehicle with Molotov cocktails

---

Renfrey Clarke, *Links International Journal of Socialist Renewal*, June 13, 2014, http://links.org.au/node/3903.

30   Dmitry Kolesnik, "Euromaidan: The Play with EU Integration," CriticAtac, December 4, 2013, http://www.criticatac.ro/lefteast/euromaidan -the-play-with-eu-integration/.

31   Lesser known is that the "Trident"'s full name is the Stepan Bandera All-Ukrainian Organization "Trident." See Anton Shekhovtsov and Andreas Umland, "Ukraine's Radical Right," *Journal of Democracy* 25, no. 3 (July 2014): 59. It should be noted that Umland and Shekhovtsov have been criticized for their articles surrounding the Ukraine crisis, one of which appeared in Russian on May 21, 2014, calling EuroMaidan an "anti-authoritarian movement." See Stephen Shenfield, "Maidan: Democratic Movement or Nationalist Mobilization?," CriticAtac, July 7, 2014, http://www.criticatac.ro/lefteast/maidan-democratic-or-nationalist; also see Volodymyr Ishchenko, "По поводу клеветы Антон Шеховцова о членах редакции 'цпильного,'" Commons/Спільне, March 12, 2014, http://commons.com.ua/po-povodu-klevety-antona-shehovtsova-o-ch.

and carried out an often-vicious campaign of internecine war with state forces. EuroMaidan activists were followed, harassed, kidnapped, and beaten by police, and the trade union headquarters set ablaze. The EuroMaidan demonstrations only grew increasingly autonomous in their struggle against the entire political establishment, including even long-standing opposition parties. [32]

Civil War in Ukraine

By the end of February 2014, faced with police forces crossing over to the EuroMaidan side and the prospect of an all-out assault from its defense forces, Yanukovych fled Ukraine. New elections were held, with opposition parties gaining control of the government. In the civil war that followed Putin's seizure of the Crimea, radical-right groups joined with neo-Nazis to inflict casualties against pro-Russian demonstrators. In May, Pravy Sektor carried out a massacre in Odessa, driving Russia supporters into the trade union building and setting it on fire with Molotov cocktails. Though the incident was documented on video, it was largely ignored or denied by the mainstream media. [33]

The new Kiev government ordered Pravy Sektor to turn in their arms, leading to a shootout in Western Ukraine, and a brief, small uprising was put down. Although members of the radical right assumed positions in office under the renewed oligarchy, Svoboda received a mere half of the votes they had obtained in 2012 before EuroMaidan. The organized radical right had reached a peak during EuroMaidan, but as they lost institutional support, many of their leading members were ushered into more mainstream parties like Arseniy Yatsenyuk's Narodnyy front (Popular Front), Petro Poroshenko's Blok Petra Poroshenka "Solidarnist" ("Solidarity" Bloc), and Oleh Lyashko's Radykal'na Partiya Oleha Lyashka (Radical Party). Ukrainian scholar Volodymyr Ishchenko highlighted the contradictions in an article for the *Guardian*: "It is short-sighted and formalistic to conclude that the Ukrainian

---

32   Shenfield, "Maidan: Democratic Movement or Nationalist Mobilization?," CriticAtac, July 7, 2014, http://www.criticatac.ro/lefteast/maidan-democratic-or-nationalist.

33   Ibid.

far right is insignificant based on the lack of electoral success. The rhetoric of many politicians which could be called centralist or even liberal has moved significantly to the right, competing for the increasingly patriotic and even nationalist voters."[34] Putin's seizure of the Crimea, along with the uprising of pro-Russian separatists in the Donbass region of Eastern Ukraine, gave the radical right new energy. In a sense, the forces of the extreme right and neo-Nazism needed to steer away from parliamentarism in order to maintain their antagonistic presence as militants in favor of dictatorship by a coup d'état.

These forces shifted to control security and the military, with a new volunteer battalion from the Azov coast gaining a particular amount of attention. Released as "political prisoners" by the new government, the neo-Nazi PU became the core of the Azov Battalion, which claimed to fight the new patriotic war against Russian ultranationalist invaders. Despite the fact that members of the battalion wore the SS's Wolfsangel badge on their uniform and had swastika tattoos, the national guard incorporated them into its structure. This collusion between the new state and neo-Nazis seems to have stemmed from a more deeply rooted relationship between fascist and government forces in post-Cold War Ukraine—for instance, the leader of the Patriot of Ukraine (PU) and the Minister of the Interior (who oversees the national guard) came from the same province and had already worked together for five years in a number of shady dealings.[35]

In the meantime, Russian fascists have become split between joining separatist groups against the EuroMaidan movement and its new government, on the one hand, and demonstrating against Russian aid to separatists, on the other. Other far-right battalions include Aidar, accused of war crimes by Amnesty International, battalion OUN, the battalion of Pravy Sektor, the Svoboda

34   Volodymyr Ishchenko, "Ukraine Has Ignored the Far Right for Too Long—It Must Wake Up to the Danger," *Guardian*, November 13, 2014, https://www.theguardian.com/commentisfree/2014/nov/13/ukraine-far-right-fascism-mps.

35   Anton Shekhovtsov, "Whither Ukrainian Far Right?," *Anton Shekhovtsov's Blog*, January 30, 2015, http://anton-shekhovtsov.blogspot.com/2015/01/whither-ukrainian-far-right.html.

battalion "Sich," and more—thirty to forty battalions ranging from parafascism to neo-Nazism.[36]

Fighting on the Donbass side of the civil war were other groups of neofascists, including a group that united French, Spanish, and Serbian Duginists in combat under the banner of Unité Continentale (Continental Unity), clearly referencing Unité Radicale. On the French side, two activists formerly of Jeunesses identitaires—an early youth affiliate of Bloc Identitaire—joined Unité, one of whom had also been a member of Bouchet's old outfit, Troisième Voie. This combatant, named Guillaume Cuvelier, acted as a member of the Front National's security service in 2014. Others who came to fight on the separatist side included the Polish Falanga and an Italian organization called Millenium, which has connections with Mutti and Dugin and whose leaders showed up in Donetsk to a reception by Pavel Gubarev, head of the Narodnoye opolcheniye Donbassa (Donbass People's Militia), who hailed them as "Italian antifascist volunteers." In the words of scholar Giovanni Savino at the time, their involvement actually "indicates that the Donetsk People's Republic was becoming a playground for fascist-inspired nationalism from all over Europe."[37]

While Dugin supported the separatists with unequivocal animosity, calling for "genocide ... of the race of Ukrainian bastards," other fascists in Russia reject separatism in the Donbass.[38] The 2014 "Russian March" to express patriotic sentiment for Russia and protest involvement in the Ukrainian civil war was peopled by groups like Natsional'naya Sotsialisticheskaya Initsiativa (National-Socialist Initiative), Pamyat, Russkii ob'edinennyi natsional'nyi soiuz (Russian Joint National Alliance), Russkoe Soprotivlenive (Resistance), Bloka svobodnykh natsional-sotsialisticheskikh obshchestv (Bloc of Free National Socialist Societies), and Russkoe

---

36   Amnesty International, "Ukraine: Abuses and War Crimes by the Aidar Volunteer Battalion in the North Luhansk Region," September 8, 2014, https://www.amnesty.org/en/documents/EUR50/040/2014/en/;   David Stern, "Ukraine Crisis: Is Conflicting Fuelling Far-Right Threat?," *BBC News Magazine*, September 8, 2015, http://www.bbc.com/news/world-europe-34176602.

37   Savino, "From Evola to Dugin," 112.

38   Quoted in David Speedie, "Foreword," in Ibid., vii.

Pravozashchitnoi Ligi (Russian Right Party). Their slogans include
"Russians Against War with Ukraine," "Novorossiya Sucks—Glory
to Kievan Rus," and "Stop Feeding the Donbass." (The second slogan refers to the belief that the truly authentic ethnic Rus come
from Kiev.) A competing protest formed in favor of Novorossiya,
or a deeper connection to Ukraine, including organizations like
the Black Hundreds, Cossack groups, Green World, and Volia (the
Will party). The pro-Novorossiya group carried the standards of the
Donetsk Republic, as well as Serbian flags and the Hungarian flag
in an apparent tribute to Jobbik. On the same day, a "unity rally"
took place in central Moscow bringing together the Communist
Party leader Zyuganov and national liberal Zhirinovsky, who called
for recognition of the separatist regions.[39]

Limonov's National Bolshevik Party was not at the rally, because it had been banned in 2007. By that point, Limonov had
experienced a number of unpleasant splits starting perhaps with
Dugin in the late 1990s. In 2006, a new splinter group called
Natsional-bol'shevistskiy front (NBF—National Bolshevik Front)
emerged, led by Alexei Golubovich and tied to Dugin's network.
The NBF abandoned Limonov's Bolshevik Party due to his attempts to join with liberals in overthrowing Putin's regime, which
culminated in the formation of a party called Drugaya Rossi-
ya, or the Other Russia. More recent splinter groups include
Natsional-Bol'shevistskaya Platforma (NB-Platforma—National
Bolshevik Platform), struggling against Limonov for hegemony
while also supporting EuroMaidan, as well as the National Bolshevik Party–Ukraine, which promotes Makhnovist ideas in the
framework of pro-Russian nationalism.[40] Highlighting their traditionalist and militant ideology, the NB-Platforma group published
a piece by the Misanthropic Division of pro-Maidan fighters called
"Grandchildren of Wotan, Sons of Maidan." Calling themselves "a
racialist and social nationalist paramilitary group that has emerged

39   "'Russian March' 2014 in Moscow: For and Against Novorossiya," SOVA
      Center for Information and Analysis, November 11, 2014, http://www
      .sova-center.ru/en/xenophobia/news-releases/2014/11/d30652/.

40   Пресс-служба, "Шестве в День Рождения Нестора Махно—
      «Антикапитализм-120,»" Nazbol.info, October 24, 2008, http://www
      .nazbol.info/rubr1/index346/2817.html.

during the revolution of the Maidan," the Misanthropic Division boasts of "more than a dozen groups, including in Western Europe and North America, among them: The United States, Spain, Germany, France and Italy." They claim that Pravy Sektor is not national socialist enough and insist that they would like to "to win this war in the Donbass and clean in Kiev thereafter."[41]

---

41   Бнуки Вотана, цыны Майдана, nbplatforma.org, November 16, 2016, http://tanjoapp.com/contents/513344.

CHAPTER 9: FROM THE TEA PARTY TO OCCUPY WALL STREET

A Conservative Revolution

During the election campaign of 2008, presidential hopeful Ron Paul declared the 234th anniversary of the Boston Tea Party to be a grassroots "day of action" for his supporters to donate to his campaign. It was a surprising popular success. Most importantly, Paul had connected the patriotic 1776 Revolution against "taxation without representation" to the 2008 bailouts deployed by the federal government as an answer to the financial crisis. The conceptual link, amounting to a kind of "conservative revolution," spread to key figures in the Republican Party and libertarian corporate elite like the Koch Brothers and Dick Armey, who had emerged at the forefront of Wise Use in the 1990s. The election of Barack Obama became the catalyst for a new movement promoted by these figures called the Tea Party.

In early 2009, CNBC commentator Rick Santelli called for Tea Party events to protest the bailouts on the floor of the Chicago Board of Trade in a dramatic rant. Largely through the publicity of FOX News and the financial support from libertarian foundations FreedomWorks and Americans for Prosperity, the new Tea Party movement accumulated a widespread following virtually overnight. Grassroots networks of Patriots and conservatives converged through nationwide protests, the largest of which took place on April 15, 2009, rallying an estimated 311,460 protesters in 346 cities.[1] Though these tax day rallies ostensibly opposed the federal bailouts of big banks after the financial crisis, their deeper currents involved a strongly held racist reaction against the Obama Administration. In the weeks following Obama's election, the Southern Poverty Law Center tracked more than two hundred hate-related incidents, and over the course of the year the FBI and the Secret Service tracked some 650 threats against the president, a hundred of which were racially motivated.[2]

Spurred on by personalities like Glenn Beck, Bill O'Reilly, and Ann Coulter, the Tea Party became a container for the hatred and violence taking place in the wake of Obama's election. Such commentators encouraged wanton violence with statements like Beck's "We should thin out the herd, you know what I mean?" Journalists David Neiwert and John Amato observed that Beck wrapped "racial ignorance and blind hypocrisy in the trappings of an 'honest racial discussion' that only reinforced the hoary stereotypes of white nationalism."[3] Like Beck, Coulter similarly reproduced the most problematic elements of US society with statements such as "My only regret with Timothy McVeigh is he did not go to the New York Times Building."[4]

In attempts to maintain some aspects of respectability, reactionary talk show hosts, media players, and ideologues attempted to play down the fascist proclivities of the influx of radicals while calling the Obama Administration fascist. When James von Brunn, a Posse Comitatus believer and associate of Willis Carto, opened fire on the Holocaust Memorial Museum on June 10, 2009, Rush Limbaugh declared, "He hated both Bushes. He hated neocons. He hated John McCain. He hated Republicans. He hated Jews as well. He believed in an 'inside job' conspiracy of 9/11. This guy is a leftist, if anything. This guy's beliefs, this guy's hate, stems from influence that you find on the left." Right-wing pundit Jonah Goldberg

---

1   John Amato and David Neiwert, *Over the Cliff* (Sausalito: PoliPointPress, 2010), 128.

2   See Ibid., 62, and David Neiwert, *The Eliminationists* (Sausalito: PoliPointPress, 2009), 7.

3   Amato and Neiwert, *Over the Cliff*, 204.

4   Neiwert, *The Eliminationists*, 19.

declared, "Just as Hitler did, [von Brunn] hails socialism as the solution to the West's problems." Goldberg went on in other interviews to call Posse Comitatus mere "radical localists," denying their connection to anything remotely fascist. Similarly, Beck called von Brunn "a lone gunman nutjob," complaining about a government "witch hunt" that unfairly targeted right-wing extremists.[5] Beck refrained from mentioning his own right-left syncretism.

Libertarianism and White Nationalism

Driving its radical message into the heart of the Republican Party, the Tea Party relied on a kind of outsider legitimacy derived from the importance of marginal groups within the United States's mainstream right wing—groups like Ron Paul's libertarians. Among the most important triumphs of the right in the United States has been the appropriation and transformation of the formerly anarchist ideology of libertarianism, in no small part through the work of Paul. Throughout the 1980s and 1990s, Paul built up his radical-right credibility through publications like the *Ron Paul Political Report* and the *Ron Paul Survival Report*, which carried many racist formulations that offered an "outside the Beltway" view of Washington, DC. Since the Patriot movement rejected obvious racism while retaining racist politics, Paul's official antigovernment radicalism, apocalyptic rhetoric, and implicit racism found an appealing market. One newsletter from 1989 states, "Racial Violence Will Fill Our Cities," because "mostly black welfare recipients will feel justified in stealing from mostly white 'haves.'" Another newsletter asserted, "I think we can assume that 95 percent of the black men in [Washington, DC] are semi-criminal or entirely criminal." In 1992, he infamously characterized black politician Barbara Jordan as "the archetypal half-educated victimologist," and the same year, he stated, "Opinion polls consistently show that only about 5 percent of blacks have sensible political opinions."[6]

---

5   Amato and Neiwert, *Over the Cliff*, 103–5.

6   See Michael Brendan Dougherty, "The Story Behind Ron Paul's Racist Newsletters," *Atlantic*, December 21, 2011, http://www.theatlantic.com/politics/archive/2011/12/the-story-behind-ron-pauls-racist-newsletters/250338/.

Paul would later declare that he never read a single one of his newsletters, they were written by other people, and he was sincerely sorry: "I never read that stuff. I never—I would never—I came—I was probably aware of it 10 years after it was written.... Well, you know, we talked about [the newsletters] twice yesterday at CNN. Why don't you go back and look at what I said yesterday on CNN, and what I've said for 20-some years. It was 22 years ago. I didn't write them. I disavow them and that's it."[7] Yet in prior interviews with newspapers and journals dating back to 1996, Paul defended the newsletters' offensive content on a regular basis. Doubling down on a 1992 statement that Barbara Jordan is a "moron" and "fraud" whose "race and sex protect her from criticism," Paul also told *Roll Call* that "such opinions represented our clear philosophical difference."[8]

A deeper look into Paul's newsletters reveals repeated mention, between 1990 and 1994, of an esoteric intellectual who was a growing influence on US fascism: Jared Taylor. In 1990, Taylor launched the magazine *American Renaissance* (AmRen), which became a sounding board for racist theories dressed up in the palatable, scientific opinions of the white business class. Through his magazine and biannual conferences, also endowed by the Pioneer Fund, Taylor rose to become one of the most influential white nationalists in the world. In much the same vein as the populism of Duke and Carto, Taylor's views became an echo chamber of reverse racism and white civil rights, painting a portrait of black communities as violent and crime-ridden due to racial inferiority.

Rather than a cultural, mythical, or aesthetic form of racism, Taylor attempted to use biology and genetics to show that the impoverished condition of black communities resulted from racial inadequacies. Although Taylor accepted neo-Nazi attendees at his

---

7   Josh Hicks, "Ron Paul and the Racist Newsletters (Fact Checker Biography)," *Washington Post*, December 27, 2011, https://www.washingtonpost.com/blogs/fact-checker/post/ron-paul-and-the-racist-newsletters-fact-checker-biography/2011/12/21/gIQAKNiwBP_blog.html.

8   Judd Legum, "Fact Check: Ron Paul Personally Defended Racist Newsletters," ThinkProgress, December 27, 2011, https://thinkprogress.org/fact-check-ron-paul-personally-defended-racist-newsletters-bb1432cfb972#.vahbklhd8.

conference, often as speakers, he rejected anti-Semitism, and invited Jews to take part as well—a mixture that sometimes created volatile problems. American Renaissance conferences became a rallying point in the 1990s for fascists to vent their concerns about the mishandling of the economy and the perceived crisis of immigration. As the fascist movement increasingly adopted the term "white nationalists" to set themselves apart from specific fascism and embrace coalitions of Klansmen and Patriots, AmRen became a central hub in the new populism, drawing participants from the usual suspects organized through Carto's network to the old Council of Conservative Citizens, Patriot movement leaders, "race realists," and open fascists.

Taylor's position did not fall too far from mainstream politicians like Bill Clinton and former-hippie Newt Gingrich. Calling forward the legacy of Daniel Patrick Moynihan, whose 1965 report *The Negro Family: The Case for National Action* declared that poverty stems from the "cycle of dependency" and "tangle of pathology" derived from "depraved family structures" rather than class oppression.[9] During that period of cutting social programs, including welfare for needy families, establishment politicians called for a War on Crime that expanded the prison industry complex. Part of the highly racialized justification behind such policies was the idea that the absence of black fathers caused crime to run out of control, leading to the necessity of cutting off social funding that enabled the alleged unhealthy cycles needy families were caught in and sending their young men to prison.[10] However, Taylor's ideology veered sharply from Gingrich, Clinton, mainstream neoconservatives, and even some paleoconservatives insofar as he became an outspoken and explicit advocate for white identity and community. While much of the mainstream continued to appeal to a "middle America" of racial integration, at least in rhetoric, Taylor's writings characterized nonwhite crime as directly corresponding to race and IQ.

---

9   See William DiFazio, *Ordinary Poverty: A Little Food and Cold Storage* (Philadelphia: Temple University Press, 2006), 73.

10   See Ruth Wilson Gilmore, *Golden Gulag: Prisons, Surplus, Crisis, and Opposition in Globalizing California* (Berkeley: University of California Press, 2007), 113; Michelle Alexander, *The New Jim Crow: Mass Incarceration in the Age of Colorblindness* (New York: The New Press, 2012), 45.

The year after Taylor's book *Paved with Good Intentions: The Failure of Race Relations in Contemporary America* appeared, a blockbuster in the field of "race realism" emerged called *The Bell Curve*. Written by Richard Herrnstein and libertarian Charles Murray, the book used a pseudo-scientific theory of intellectual development to attempt to prove that white people excelled in contemporary society because of their relative intelligence. Perhaps unsurprisingly, thirteen of the "scholars" the book cited had received over four million dollars from the Pioneer Fund across the previous two decades.[11] With the publication of *The Bell Curve*, Taylor's AmRen announced, "The rules of dialogue may finally have changed."[12] Although his rhetoric largely faltered before a mainstream audience, the Tea Party helped bring it into the realm of acceptable watercooler chitchat. It gained further traction through former leftist David Horowitz's *FrontPage*, among other sites.[13] For Taylor and "race realists," racism no longer meant degrading a nonwhite person's intelligence—science had already proven Europeans' intellectual superiority. Instead, they insisted that true racism is the rejection of a person's racial identity—for instance, denying or degrading whiteness. Hence, they declared that it is not the "race realists" who are racists, but rather their detractors who are guilty of being racist against whites. Glenn Beck exemplified Taylor's brand of fake antiracism when he argued in 2009 that "[Obama] has exposed himself as a guy, over and over and over again, who has a deep-seated hatred for white people, or the white culture.… This guy is, I believe, a racist."[14]

From Radical Right to Fascism

Among the far-right politicians embracing *The Bell Curve* was Pat Buchanan, another Tea Party leader who has promoted, as received wisdom, the genetic inferiority of nonwhites. One of Buchanan's

---

11   Steven J. Rosenthal, "The Pioneer Fund: Financier of Fascist Research," *American Behavioral Scientist* 39, no. 1 (September–October 1995): 44; Charles Lane, "The Tainted Sources of the Bell Curve," *The New York Review of Books* 41, no. 20 (December 1, 1994): 14–19.

12   Zeskind, *Blood and Politics*, 398.

13   See Neiwert, *The Eliminationists*, 71.

14   Glenn Beck, quoted in Amato and Neiwert, *Over the Cliff*, 197.

paleocon cohorts who sought to help mainstream the influence of the radical right was Sam Francis, who not only glommed onto *The Bell Curve* but also became a close associate with Taylor. Like Buchanan, Francis argued against intervention in Iraq and also critiqued Clinton's neoliberal policies. Yet Francis also drew on Gramsci's thought to advocate a "culture war." According to Zeskind, "Francis believed that the dispossession of the white majority was legitimized by the widespread acceptance of concepts such as egalitarianism. This was the meaning of ideological hegemony in this context. As a result, a war of ideas had to be fought and the notion of egalitarianism itself had to be attacked."[15]

An editor at Ronald Reagan's favorite newspaper, the *Washington Times*, Francis worked under the Korean magnate and spiritual leader Sun Myung Moon of the Unification Church, which maintained controversial connections to the Reagan Administration, the Christian Right, Japanese Yakuza, and the World Anti-Communist League.[16] However, in 1994, Francis appeared at AmRen's annual conference, and one of the conservative attendees, Dinesh D'Souza, was shocked by his performance. In the *Washington Post*, he described Francis as attacking "the liberal principles of humanism and universalism for facilitating 'the war against the white race.'" D'Souza mentioned Francis's dislike of Garth Brooks's multiculturalism and his urging of "his fellow whites" to "reassert our identity and our solidarity…in explicitly racial terms through the articulation of a racial consciousness as whites."[17] The article led to Francis's firing, allowing him to move further from the religious right and venture more deeply into the white nationalist shark tank.

Francis became editor of the *Citizens Informer*, the journal of the Council of Conservative Citizens (CofCC), penning that group's statement of principles, which insist on small, decentralized government and a return to down-home, white nationalist values. With spokesperson Jared Taylor and director Paul Fromm, who previously

---

15   Zeskind, *Blood and Politics*, 328.

16   Berlet and Lyons, *Right-Wing Populism in America*, 252.

17   Dinesh D'Souza, "Racism: It's a White (and Black) Thing," *Washington Post*, September 24, 1995, https://www.washingtonpost.com/archive/opinions/1995/09/24/racism-its-a-white-and-black-thing/46284ab5-417c-4c0c-83e1-029d51655d91/?utm_term=.a9cbaf7cf192.

ran a podcast on the fascist Stormfront website, CofCC was, and remains, among the most important "respectable racist" faces of the modern fascist creep. Among the regular contributors to the *Citizens Informer* was Republican Senator Trent Lott, who told the group that they "stand for the right principles and the right philosophy."[18]

This "right philosophy" is, in fact, neo-Confederate secessionism with overtones of fascism. The CofCC has extensive connections with the League of the South, and the two groups have held joint events. Significantly, the first of their collaborations was a protest staged in opposition to the Georgia state capitol's planned removal of a statue of Populist Party leader Tom Watson. Watson had been a fiery representative of small agrarian interests in the South before increasingly supporting lynchings and racism in the early 1900s. The CofCC and the League of the South include a steady rotation of staunch racists, Holocaust deniers, and white nationalists in their gatherings.[19] Among their leading lights is one of Ron Paul's chief economic allies, Thomas J. DiLorenzo.[20]

Perhaps the most respected of the "respectable racists" attracted to Taylor's AmRen is former California State University professor Kevin B. MacDonald, who argues that Judaism manifests a "group evolutionary strategy" and is a racialized religion that seeks to dominate other ethnicities through logic, argumentation, and collectivism.[21] In his book *A People that Shall Dwell Alone*, MacDonald claims that Freud and other Jewish intellectuals are the product of "eugenics practices that have been an important aspect of Judaism."[22] Like Buchanan and other paleocons, MacDonald criticizes neoconservatism; however, where other leaders hint at

---

18   Neiwert, *The Eliminationists*, 62.

19   "Council of Conservative Citizens," Southern Poverty Law Center's website, https://www.splcenter.org/fighting-hate/extremist-files/group/council-conservative-citizens.

20   Dana Milbank, "Ron Paul's economic Rx: A Southern Secessionist," *Washington Post*, February 9, 2011, http://www.washingtonpost.com/wp-dyn/content/article/2011/02/09/AR2011020905879.html.

21   Kevin MacDonald, *A People that Shall Dwell Alone: Judaism as a Group Evolutionary Strategy, with Diaspora Peoples* (San Jose: Writers Club Press, 2002), 349.

22   Ibid., 276.

Jewish connections, MacDonald openly describes neoconservatism as a Jewish platform developed to appeal to whites but to carry out the interests of Zionism.[23] Very popular among white supremacists at AmRen, MacDonald has also edited the pseudo-academic *Occidental Quarterly*, despite his theories being roundly criticized by figures such as John Tooby, the founder of evolutionary psychology (Taylor's alleged field of specialty), and Steven Pinker. In 2009, MacDonald joined Stormfront administrator Jamie Kelso and the host of the anti-Semitic radio show *The Political Cesspool*, James Edwards, to found American Third Position (A3P), thus officially exposing himself as a fascist.

A Note on Third Positions and Third Parties

The A3P has its roots in a violent, racist California street gang called Freedom 14, which attempted to enter the political scene by organizing a political entity called the Golden State Party via Stormfront in 2008. When their chairperson, Tyler Cole, was found to have a violent criminal record, the core of the Golden State Party dissolved the organization, created the A3P, and began to network with the International Third Position and other groups. Contemporary activist group Anonymous eventually managed to hack Kelso's accounts and subsequently leaked emails that show the A3P openly contributed to and held meetings with the Ron Paul campaign.

Kelso, a longtime associate of David Duke, caught on to the Ron Paul "Revolution" in 2007. In an interview he gave to the Southern Poverty Law Center, Kelso insisted, "Let's appreciate this big (Paul) audience that's overwhelmingly white. This is our audience, this is our public. These are our people. If we can't persuade these people of the rightness of our cause, then we're finished."[24] The mission of the A3P was to enter Libertarian political campaigns and guide them toward fascism.

---

23   Kevin MacDonald, "Neoconservatism as a Jewish Movement: A Study in Ethnic Activism," *The Occidental Quarterly,* Monograph #1 (Augusta: Washington Summit Publishers, 2004).

24   Gianluca Mezzofiore, "Ron Paul, the American Third Position Party and Stormfront," *International Business Times*, February 1, 2012, http://www.ibtimes.co.uk/anonymous-ron-paul-neo-nazi-bnp-a3p-291000.

As Kelso wrote to a supporter in 2009, "My own opinion is that the White revolution has already begun, and that the good White folks like Quinn [a member of A3P] that fills these Ron Paul crowds and marching armies ARE the start of the revolution."[25] Hence, Kelso hoped to forward white nationalism in part by drawing Paul's "marching armies" toward open fascism. Speaking on his radio show, Edwards stated, "The initial basis of our own upstart organization is the racial nationalist movement. It has been in disarray for the last 20 years so there's not as large a base for us to draw on."[26]

Those twenty years (counting down since Metzger's 1989 trial, perhaps) saw efforts to build a revolutionary, national socialist political movement fail time and again, leading to renewed attempts to enter extant political organizations or to create leaderless resistance cells to commit lone-wolf actions. The A3P's strategy, then, was to develop organizational solidarity between the Libertarian Party and the white nationalist movement. By 2010, the A3P dropped their neo-Nazi sounding name for the more Euro-populist sounding American Freedom Party. The American Freedom Party is known to hold white pride rallies and to represent the CofCC in Portland, Oregon.[27] They are a radical-right political party aiming to attract the white nationalist movement, and their global connections reach deeply into the recesses of the international fascist movement.

That a fascist group could form a political party led by some of the foremost figures of the US radical right suggests that the integration between fascism and radical right is extensive and complex. That the A3P held meetings with and supported the Libertarian Party also exposes the complex mixture of shared interests, if not strategic coordination. The embrace of Holocaust deniers has been a tendency

---

25   Ibid.

26   "American Freedom Party," Southern Poverty Law Center's website, https://www.splcenter.org/fighting-hate/extremist-files/group/american -freedom-party.

27   Rose City Antifa, "Meet the Oregon Chapter of the American Freedom Party, Parts I & II," Rose City Antifa's blog, October 10, 2015, http:// rosecityantifas.weebly.com/articles/meet-the-oregon-chapter-of-the- american-freedom-party-part-one and http://rosecityantifas.weebly.com/ articles/meet-the-oregon-chapter-of-american-freedom-party-part-two.

among US right-wing libertarians since Rothbard's praise of Barnes (and the latter's Holocaust-denying articles that appeared in Koch's *Rampart Journal*) only exposes the tip of the iceberg of conspiracy theories of black helicopters, FEMA Camps, and the UN's "Agenda 21" plans to depopulate the United States of white, Christian patriots forwarded by demagogues like Alex Jones.[28] Rather than an ideology of freedom and independence, far-right libertarianism in the United States relies on the fundamental right-left syncretism of so-called anarcho-capitalism to promote a palingenetic myth of white settler life specific to US ultranationalism—a myth popular within an extremely militant sector of the extreme right with roots in the fascist Posse Comitatus movement. It is, therefore, by definition a crucial element of the modern fascist creep.

The Bedfellows of Border Militias

One of the main forces of white nationalism that appeared during the rise of the Tea Party and was supportive of Ron Paul's campaign was a group called the National Socialist Movement (NSM), which had organized around the fringes of the scene throughout the 1980s and 1990s. However, an uptick in NSM organizing during the late 2000s occurred in no small part through the efforts of a prominent young activist named J. T. Ready. At Mesa Community College in the Phoenix area, Ready had been a member of the Republican Club, but his conservative values and his aggressive, uncontained behavior drove him to further extremes. He graduated in 1996 and joined the Marines, only to be discharged that same year after two court-martials. Some years later, he formed an anti-immigrant group called Americans First—a name that alludes to the anti-interventionist group led by fascist sympathizer Charles Lindbergh during World War II.[29]

Ready's friend, the president of the Arizona State Senate, Russell Pearce, took the young, ambitious racist under his wing and

---

28   Mark Ames, "Charles Koch's Brain Shuts Down the Holocaust," NSF-WCORP, October 8, 2013, https://www.nsfwcorp.com/dispatch/shuts-down-the-holocaust.

29   "J. T. Ready," Southern Poverty Law Center's website, https://www.splcenter.org/fighting-hate/extremist-files/individual/jt-ready.

into his faith. Pearce joined a small gathering to celebrate Ready's baptism into the Church of Jesus Christ of Latter-day Saints sometime around 2003 or 2004. The two shared many closely held beliefs—particularly that the most important obstacle to the existence of the white race in Arizona is immigration. According to their personal emails, Pearce was always supportive of Ready, who advocated spreading land mines along the borderlands. And Ready backed Pearce after he mass emailed an article (without attribution, so he could take credit for it) by Frosty Wooldridge, a favorite author of David Duke, who compared Mexican immigrants to lepers. In May 2006, Ready led Americans First in a protest outside the Mexican Consulate in Phoenix, Arizona and declared, "We are advocating that the government of Mexico should be designated a 'threat nation' because they are openly subverting our laws and sovereignty."[30] Controversy struck during his campaign for Mesa City Council when he got into an armed altercation with a Latino man. It was a narrow race, but Ready was annihilated when his military record surfaced. Switching horses, Ready ran for a different seat—precinct committeeman for Mesa, Arizona—completely unopposed, and he won by a landslide of thirty-six votes.

Around this time, Ready also cofounded the Minuteman Civil Defense Corps, a volunteer group of armed citizens dedicated to preventing illegal border crossings into the United States. Senator Pearce's son, Sean, was also a member of the corps, and Ready used the group to build up his political connections while putting his ideological extremism into practice.[31] As a Republican, Ready joined and spoke at rallies alongside party chairman Randy Pullen and joined him in United for a Sovereign America meetings.

In October 2006, as Ready's political stature improved, Pearce again sparked controversy when he sent his supporters a mass email featuring a Holocaust-denying diatribe originally published in the 1990s by *National Vanguard* magazine: "Who Rules America, The Alien Grip on Our News and Entertainment Media Must Be

---

30   Ibid.

31   Stephen Lemons, "J. T. Ready's Neo-Nazi Patrols for Migrants in the Vekol Valley, and Its Discovery of a Body," *Phoenix New Times*, June 21, 2010, http://www.phoenixnewtimes.com/blogs/jt-readys-neo-nazi-patrol-for-migrants-in-the-vekol-valley-and-its-discovery-of-a-dead-body-6503453.

Broken."[32] Once the publication of William Pierce's National Alliance, the *National Vanguard* splintered off after Pierce's death. The year before Pearce's email imbroglio, the Phoenix chapter of the National Alliance had switched to a National Vanguard chapter. That National Vanguard chapter was led by a longtime neo-Nazi and Phoenix contact for the CofCC named Jerry Harbin, whose son Jeffrey was a friend of Ready's.[33] Sharing old propaganda of the ambitious new National Vanguard looked a lot like fascist movement building—or at least promotion.

At the end of the year, Ready joined Harbin and some eighty other neo-Nazis at the National Vanguard gathering, Winterfest. The evening's events began with notorious Holocaust denier Friedrich Paul Berg, whose slogan was "Nazi Gassings Never Happened." Berg started Holocaust-denying in 1983 and wrote key articles for the *Revisionist* journal and Carto's Institute for Historical Review. Next up came Verohnika Clark, holder of associate degrees in diesel mechanics and liberal arts. Speaking about the religion of Hitler, Clark put forward her opinion that Hitler believed in "positive Christianity," which embraces paganism and rejects "materialistic Bolshevism." After the speakers, MC Jesse Curnow, unit coordinator of the Arizona National Socialist Movement, introduced the folk-rock act Noble Son, exclaiming, "Few care more for our people than Noble Son." At one point, the band joined Harbin for a theatrical reading of "The Lay of Harbard," featuring Odin and Thor. The next musical act, an Irish flute performance, was disrupted by a Mexican mariachi band playing next door, and, as one Nazi commentator put it, "the hall became a little tense." The peak of National Vanguard's celebrity experienced at Winterfest 2006 was diminished less than a

32   "Arizona State Rep. Candidate Russell Pearce Distributes Article From Neo-Nazi National Alliance Website," *Intelligence Report* (online edition), Southern Poverty Law Center, January 16, 2007, https://www.splcenter.org/fighting-hate/intelligence-report/2007/arizona-state-rep-candidate-russell-pearce-distributes-article-neo-nazi-national-alliance.

33   Evelyn Schlatter, "Neo-Nazi indicted for bombs is son of movement stalwart," Southern Poverty Law Center's website, January 28, 2011, https://www.splcenter.org/hatewatch/2011/01/28/neo-nazi-indicted-bombs-son-movement-stalwart.

week after the festival, when the FBI arrested their leader, Kevin
Alfred Strom, on child pornography charges, to which he would
later plead guilty.[34]

Pearce came out publicly as Ready's führer-figure at a 2007
anti-immigrant rally. A photograph retains the emotional impact of
the event, with the two arm in arm; Ready is beaming, and Pearce
looks as proud as a father attending his son's graduation party. Indeed, Ready actually called Pearce a "father figure," and the respect
was mutual, as Pearce announced in a campaign ad for Ready his
status as a "true patriot."[35]

In the fall of that year, Ready joined the NSM for a march
in Omaha, Nebraska, giving a speech as an "Arizona Republican activist." During a raucous after-party featuring hate-rock
slam-dancing, Jerry Harbin appeared as Odin, standing between
two giant, flaming swastikas. "Kindred of mine," he declared, "fair
and beautiful children of the light. You know me. I am known to
you as all-father Odin. Lord of the wolves and of the ravens."[36]
The racist Asatru act continued amid chants of "Sieg Heil" and
"White Power!"

Soon, Ready's goateed, smiling face would adorn a profile
under the sobriquet "Viking Son" on the NSM-run social network, New Saxon. The profile boasted about his favorite band, the
teeny-bop white-pride duo, Prussian Blue, made up of fraternal
twins Lynx and Lamb Gaede, whose songs include "Sacrifice,"
written in honor of leader of the Order, Robert Mathews. Viking
Son's favorite book was Pierce's *The Turner Diaries*, and he added
a whimsical photo of himself wearing a kilt and a bulletproof vest

34   Ready would later boast of recruiting Harbin's son, Jeffrey, into the NSM—
     perhaps as a result of Harbin's disillusionment with the National Vanguard
     following Strom's conviction. In January of the next year, Jeffrey Harbin was
     pulled over by police in his pickup truck carrying twelve IEDs. Ibid.

35   Ibid.

36   These quotes are taken from a report by Susy Buchanan and David Holt-
     house, "Norse God Odin Visits Neo-Nazi Anti-Immigration Rally Af-
     ter Party in Omaha, Neb," *Intelligence Report* (online edition), Southern
     Poverty Law Center, December 1, 2007, https://www.splcenter.org/fight-
     ing-hate/intelligence-report/2007/norse-god-odin-visits-neo-nazi-anti-
     immigration-rally-after-party-omaha-neb.

at the border.[37] His posts included gems like, "The jew is the most vile parasite ever to infest this planet. All the cancer ever to exist…is far less to loathe than the evil of the average living jew."[38]

Around this time, published photographs of the NSM rally in Omaha showing Ready among the brownshirts started to make the Republican higher-ups uncomfortable—not to mention his "NSM USA" license plate. Three Arizona congressional representatives signed a letter demanding Ready's expulsion from his position in the GOP, but by that time he carried too much weight to be dismissed.

Model Legislation for the Fascist Creep

Ready stayed on until the end of his term in 2008, and the next year he was drawing attention again for pushing a protester who attempted to take a large portrait of Hitler away from him at an anti-immigrant rally. Despite his reputation, the Tea Party invited him to speak at a July 4th event. Also, in October of that year, "NSM USA" joined Jeff Hall, NSM's southwest regional director, at a rally blocking a day-laborer site in Riverside, California. In a video recorded at the event, Ready's gold Totenkopf pin seems a bit diminutive next to Hall's tattooed Totenkopf over an iron cross on the back of his skull, but Ready still talks a good game (even if his attempts at reasoned conversation were drowned out by chants of "Jews Go Home").

In response to the question of whether National Socialism is "supremacist," Ready retorts, "Isn't that what the Jews are doing when they exploit the Palestinians?"[39] When asked about Nazi

---

37   Susy Buchanan, "Jason 'J.T.' Ready Revives New Saxon, Popular White-Supremacist Social Networking Site," *Intelligence Report* (online edition), Southern Poverty Law Center's website, December 1, 2007, https://www.splcenter.org/fighting-hate/intelligence-report/2007/jason-%E2%80%9Cjt%E2%80%9D-ready-revives-new-saxon-popular-white-supremacist-social-networking-site.

38   Stephen Lemons, "Racist Daisy Chain," *Phoenix New Times*, November 22, 2007, http://www.phoenixnewtimes.com/news/racist-daisy-chain-6395220.

39   Hatecenter, "NSM Neo-Nazi Rally / CA's Jeff Hall / AZ's JT Ready, Riverside 10/24/09," YouTube, uploaded October 28, 2009, 4:30, https://www.youtube.com/watch?v=Ey7JtRzpcmA.

Germany, Ready fires back, "Nazi Germany was a great country.... Adolf Hitler was an excellent white civil rights leader."[40] Responding to the surprised reporter's further inquiries into the Holocaust, Ready replies, "That's a lie," insisting that he has been to Auschwitz and speaks fluent German.

According to the group's "25 Points of American National Socialism," "Only those of pure White blood, whatever their creed, may be members of the nation. Noncitizens may live in America only as guests and must be subject to laws for aliens. Accordingly, no Jew or homosexual may be a member of the nation." Asked about whether nonwhites fit into his vision, Ready replies, "Africa has an entire continent. Where's our continent?"[41] Whites are not genetically superior, just different, "like Chihuahuas and Rottweilers are different."[42]

In California, Ready played the role of a militant fascist street fighter, insisting that "the Northwest of the United States of America should be white."[43] Back in Arizona, Ready attempted to cultivate his image as a white guardian of the United States by joining together with Hall and other neo-Nazis and militia members, from places as far flung as Utah, for armed "border ops."[44] While ABC called them a "citizens group taking [the] border battle into [its] own hands," the *Phoenix New Times* was more descriptive: "Sorry, but a vigilante operation led by a neo-Nazi with a criminal record and a checkered past that includes being court-martialed twice and booted from the Marines—an operation that includes a heavy contingent of neo-Nazis—is, in essence, a neo-Nazi patrol."[45]

Like the larger Patriot movement, Ready's Arizona Border Guard helped camouflage the appearance of fascism, replacing the black storm trooper gear and NSM swastika flags of Riverside with

40   Ibid., 4:20.
41   Ibid., 6:09.
42   Ibid., 5:30–5:32.
43   Ibid., 6:19.
44   Lemons, "J. T. Ready's Neo-Nazi Patrols for Migrants in the Vekol Valley, and Its Discovery of a Body," *Phoenix New Times*, June 21, 2010, http://www.phoenixnewtimes.com/blogs/jt-readys-neo-nazi-patrol-for-migrants-in-the-vekol-valley-and-its-discovery-of-a-dead-body-6503453.
45   Ibid.

fatigues and US flags. The group of a dozen or so "border guards" even included one person who identified himself as an Apache tracker, regardless of Ready's remarkably low opinion of Native American peoples.[46]

Pearce, facing a lawsuit at this time, began to distance himself from Ready. Undaunted, Ready prepared to lead the NSM on a march through Phoenix in an Americans First rally. An aggressive antifascist presence and negative media made the event a public relations failure. Writing for the weekly *Phoenix New Times*, Stephen Lemons reported, "Whatever bad rep the anarchists had before Saturday—deserved or undeserved—has now been absolved." Exemplifying the bizarre convergences and divergences of the extreme right, right-wing libertarian activists actually joined the demonstration against the NSM in this case. The march was halted numerous times by the counterprotest, and it was assailed with rocks and paint bombs. In a phenomenal denouement to the event, a Nazi was hauled away in an ambulance after breaking his leg in a car accident trying to escape the rally. Adding insult to injury, the police wrote it up as the Nazis' fault. As the disheartened and disgruntled Nazis Sieg Heiled outside their wrecked car, workers came out of their shops to laugh at them. Passing cars were heard yelling things like "Karma's a bitch, ain't it!"[47]

Pearce had greater success using the apparatus of the state for white supremacist ends. He was the main sponsor of Arizona Senate Bill 1070, which turned every routine traffic stop into an immigration raid by requiring police to determine every person's immigration status. SB 1070 had been drafted with the aid of the American Legislative Exchange Council (ALEC), a special interest group cofounded by Paul Weyrich and linked to the Koch brothers. ALEC drafts pro-corporate "model legislation," which is

---

46   Earlier that year, Ready had publically insulted and humiliated a Native person, telling him, "Go dance around naked and enjoy yourself. Get back to your culture. It's a great culture that invented nothing. Stone tools. Stone age." Ibid.

47   Crudo, "Phoenix: Where Anarchists Pack Heat and Send Nazis Packing," *Fires Never Extinguished* (blog), November 7, 2009, http://fires neverextinguished.blogspot.com/2009/11/phoenix-where-anarchists-pack-heat-and.html.

then passed onto Congress, often with only very minor alterations. Their track record includes busting unions, deregulating industry, increasing the prison industrial complex, and supporting the Wise Use movement. Pearce sat on their board as he spouted false data produced in the warped machines of the Tanton Network and peddled by the CofCC.[48]

Despite tremendous public opposition, SB 1070 was passed in 2010. Parents were separated from their children on the streets of Arizona, and families torn apart. To determine whom to question over immigration status, police were encouraged to follow hunches based on color, race, and cultural signifiers like Mexican flags or bumper stickers displaying Spanish words. While the number of deportations rose by more than three thousand people in 2010, more striking was the sharp increase of noncriminal deportations— from just over one-third of the total to nearly one-half.[49]

Occupy

The large opposition to SB 1070 was joined by a number of environmental and social justice movements around the United States during 2010, including student occupations and the occupation of the capitol in Madison, Wisconsin. These movements precipitated the radical movement that took shape in public squares across the country under the name of Occupy Wall Street. When Occupy touched off in November 2011, encampments sprung up in every major city across the United States and even smaller towns in more rural areas. Like the antiglobalization protests of the 1990s and early 2000s, Occupy drew different kinds of constituents. Generally

---

48   Terry Greene Sterling, "Russell Pearce and Other Illegal-Immigration Populists Rely on Misleading, Right-Wing Reports to Scapegoat Immigrants and to Terrify Penny-Pinched Americans," *Phoenix New Times*, December 2, 2010, http://www.phoenixnewtimes.com/news/russell-pearce-and-other-illegal-immigration-populists-rely-on-misleading-right-wing-reports-to-scapegoat-immigrants-and-to-terrify-penny-pinched-americans-6446724.

49   Data from the United States Department of Homeland Security, "ICE Removals Through July 31, 2011," https://www.ice.gov/doclib/about/offices/ero/pdf/ero-removals.pdf.

appearing as an opposition to the increasing speculation and continuing stagnation following the financial crisis, Occupy encampments manifested prefigurative communities seeking to produce new spaces for everyday life and oppose the state-based organization of the economy.

Leftists extolled the principles of class struggle with the motto "We are the 99%," creating a populist framework for an anti-establishment movement, while Ron Paul supporters also showed up to protest "big government" financial bailouts and advocate for a return to the gold standard. Although some of its initial progenitors, like *AdBusters*'s Micah White, hoped to maintain a left-to-right spectrum of political participants in Occupy, the movement remained firmly in the leftist camp. Dan Sandini and other Tea Party journalists in Portland entered some encampments to both ridicule the left and try to link the Occupy movement to the Tea Party and a legacy of neo-populist resistance that transcended traditional left- and right-wing polarization. Despite being the most visible and constant attempt to press for independent right-wing goals, the populist formula also caught the attention of white supremacists who discussed what to do with Occupy over Stormfront and other message boards. The American Third Position chapter in Indiana stated their intention to enter Occupy Indianapolis, while the American Nazi Party praised Occupy's "breath of cleansing air," and Lyndon LaRouche took credit for Occupy's "leading demand" for reinstating the Glass-Steagall Act of 1933.[50] Then, on October 15, 2011, Ready and several other members of his Arizona Border Guard set a new standard by showing up to the Occupy encampment in Phoenix.

Dressed in military fatigues and brandishing semi-automatic rifles and military equipment, the "border guard" looked like part of an occupying force, to be sure. A local anarchist group called the Phoenix Class War Council wrote about the visit immediately, stating Ready and his group were there to "counter protest."[51] However,

---

50   Matthew N. Lyons, "Rightists Woo the Occupy Wall Street Movement," *Three Way Fight* (blog), November 8, 2011, http://threewayfight.blogspot .com/2011/11/rightists-woo-occupy-wall-street.html.

51   "The National Socialist Movement Scum Show Up Armed to Counter Protest #occupyphoenix," *Fires Never Extinguished* (blog), October

in an interview given to "Morpheus," an independent, libertarian journalist on the scene as a member of the Occupy demonstration, Ready claimed that the armed group of vigilantes was "exercising our second amendment rights so that everybody can have a first amendment right.... Regardless of different beliefs, the moment we give up our second amendment rights, that's when tyrants come in, that's when the big boys with guns can sweep through and take anybody's rights away."[52]

He followed that point with an immigration primer, insisting that "there are 60,000 dead in Northern Mexico from guns that our government provided from training to the Los Zetas.... We really should be working with our neighbors, not against them."[53] He continued: "'We're not Wall Street bankers, let's put it that way."[54] Striking up a friendly rapport, Morpheus told Ready that former Ron Paul aide Stewart Rhodes, the leader of the libertarian paramilitary group the Oath Keepers, was his friend.

The two then shared qualms about fiat currency, and frustrations that "they're taking away our freedom." Listening to Ready talk about the US government putting guns in the hands of drug cartels in Mexico while an Occupy Phoenix libertarian protester-journalist fawned over him is a fascinating example of the problems with the populist form that "the 99%" took on. "This is exactly what we need," declared the interviewer. The video closes with the cameraman walking through the gathering calling out, "Protect yourself against government tyranny! Get your V-Mask [Guy Fawkes mask]!" Eventually Ready's group was kicked out of the encampment.[55]

Not only was the presence of the NSM members, operating through the front group Arizona Border Guards, deeply unnerving,

---

15, 2011, http://firesneverextinguished.blogspot.com/2011/10/national
-socialist-movement-scum-show.html.

52   Morpheus, "Occupy Phoenix with AR-15s," YouTube, https://www
.youtube.com/watch?v=rjOwSIsgE8c, 0:53–1:09.

53   Ibid., 1:14–1:34.

54   Ibid., 1:59–2:01.

55   "The National Socialist Movement Scum Show Up Armed to Counter Protest #occupyphoenix," *Fires Never Extinguished* (blog), *op. cit.* October 15, 2011, http://firesneverextinguished.blogspot.com/2011/10/national
-socialist-movement-scum-show.html.

but the affinity between Ready and the libertarian protester-journalist seemed to justify and validate the NSM's presence. The open arms that many offered during the Occupy movement reflected similar vulnerabilities as the antiglobalization and antiwar movements—a degree of naivety when dealing with the threat of ideological overlap with fascism. When Third Positionists joined the encampments and talked about consumerism, advocating producerism and the need for ecological conservation, their racism, masked in respectability, was easily ignored.

When local anarchists confronted Ready and began to explain to other demonstrators the political positions of the men aligned with the NSM, the Occupiers reproached the critics for their intolerance and passion. One woman explained that she, too, believed in socialism and attempted to discuss the political integrity of socialism without nationalism to the border guards. The antifascists were informed that the national socialists were also part of the 99%, and that the anarchists' raised voices amounted to "violent" actions in a "nonviolent" protest.[56]

The impact of armed militia members at Occupy demonstrations was felt as far away as Portland, Oregon. When news spread to Occupy Portland that armed paramilitaries had appeared at a demonstration, activists largely ignorant of the context grew excited. The sentiments for many were similar to the libertarian interviewing Ready: "This is what we need." According to people I interviewed who lived on-site at the Occupy Portland encampment, the discourse of militancy encouraged the romantic sense of revolution against the police state. If there were rumors that the militarized protest was led by Nazis, Occupiers generally rejected the notion of being led by Nazis, instead hoping that the left would also create armed groups to openly patrol police violence and defend the Occupy encampments.

By the spring of 2012, as Occupy maintained its nationwide momentum, Ready had become increasingly unhinged. On May 2, an argument erupted in Ready's household. He got his gun and

---

56   "The National Socialist Movement Scum Show Up Armed to Counter Protest #occupyphoenix," *Fires Never Extinguished* (blog), October 15, 2011, http://firesneverextinguished.blogspot.com/2011/10/national-socialist-movement-scum-show.html.

shot his girlfriend Lisa Mederos, her twenty-three-year-old daughter Amber Mederos, as well as Amber's fiancée and fifteen-month-old daughter. Ready then shot and killed himself.

Pearce had publicly renounced his relationship with Ready a few years earlier. Reeling from a recall election he lost the previous November, Pearce's political fall continued. He lost his attempt at a political comeback later that year, and the SB 1070 law he so adamantly sponsored was rendered largely inoperative by legal measures rejecting aspects of the bill as unconstitutional.

The week following Ready's suicide, federal, state, and local authorities also arrested the leaders of the American Front in Melbourne, Florida. Charged with hate crimes and conspiracy, the American Front group had undergone illegal paramilitary trainings in a survivalist compound fenced off by barbed wire.[57] The American Front website boasted of having members inside Occupy encampments, and the Florida group was planning on joining an Occupy demonstration to attack a rival skinhead crew with metal poles to which they had fastened pro-Occupy slogans. Their ultimate goal was, of course, to instigate racial war, bring down the United States, and inaugurate a "new age" of nationalist supermen. For a lawyer, they found the strange character of Augustus Sol Invictus, a fascist who would later run for public office as a Libertarian candidate.

From Wall Street to Bunkerville

The crossovers that took place during Occupy—particularly those involving libertarians—were not entirely phenomena of co-optation and infiltration. Instead, they stemmed from a sense of dislocation and alienation, shared by left and right, which was taken in different directions, though sometimes intersecting. Mass movements are conducive to such intersections. Material disenfranchisement motivates the radical right and the left—both the Tea Party and Occupy amplified and organized sentiments that already exist in society. The growth of fascism depends on the extent

---

57   Bill Morlin, "Court Documents: American Front Was Planning Violence," Southern Poverty Law Center's website, May 14, 2012, https://www.splcenter.org/hatewatch/2012/05/14/court-documents-american-front-was-planning-violence.

to which fascist groups are able to absorb and encourage such sentiments toward their explicit aims by seizing the popular narrative and public discourse.

In the United States, mass movements must contend with the fact that, according to a 2011 study, whites believe that racism is more often perpetrated against them than nonwhites. Whites see antiblack racism as having decreased substantially since 1950, while viewing antiwhite racism as more prevalent than antiblack racism during the 2000s.[58] FBI statistics show that in 2013 more than two-thirds of all racially-motivated crimes were carried out against black people (13 percent of the population). Furthermore, people of color face more police violence and harsher sentencing, as the UN, Amnesty International, and other groups have pointed out.[59] But the white persecution complex persists as an explanation for the relative erosion of white privileges over decades of "colorblind" neoliberal reforms.[60]

Despite believing themselves to be the real oppressed group, fascists and radical-right activists have occasionally supported nonwhites rioting, since they see mutual antagonism against the multicultural, liberal state as beneficial to their cause. Similarly, some leftists support racist white ranchers rebelling against the Bureau of Land Management's environmental policies, seeing them as manifesting a shared rejection of the "system." This suits fascists fine. Their end goal is a kind of polarization of racialized movements that will lead to a post-collapse world where racial differences will

---

58   Michael I. Norton and Samuel R. Sommers, "Whites See Racism as a Zero-Sum Game That They Are Now Losing," *Perspectives on Psychological Science* 6, no. 3 (2011): 215–18, available at http://www.people.hbs.edu/mnorton/norton%20sommers.pdf.

59   "Deadly Force: Police Use of Lethal Force in the United States," Amnesty International USA's website, June 18, 2015, https://www.amnestyusa.org/research/reports/deadly-force-police-use-of-lethal-force-in-the-united-states; United Nations Human Rights Council, *Draft Report of the Working Group on the Universal Periodic Review: United States of America*, Geneva, May 4–15, 2015.

60   "Latest Hate Crime Statistics Report Released," FBI.gov, December 8, 2014, https://www.fbi.gov/news/stories/latest-hate-crime-statistics-report-released. This percentage declined in 2014.

result in separate communities divided along geographic and cultural lines. Since the United States is too strong of a state for a military coup, fascists recognize the importance of eroding the belief in liberal democracy on a grassroots level—particularly the idea of equality. Therefore, fascists have often supported or even initiated radical antiliberal movements.

The difference between the apocalyptic visions of the right and the ideals of the left was put on display in April 2014, when the Bundy Ranch standoff in Bunkerville, Nevada, reminded the world of a long-simmering struggle in the West between the cowboy myth and the central government. A number of former Occupy activists supported the feisty ranchers and their Patriot movement allies, viewing them as unjustly persecuted, sharing the sentiment of one sheriff who likened Cliven Bundy to Rosa Parks. When Bundy opened up to the press about his racist views, however, most of his leftist support retreated, perhaps finally realizing the extent of complexity woven into the conflict. That two neo-Nazis leaving the camp decided to murder two police officers for the sake of instigating a racist "revolution" only accelerated the US left's learning process after Occupy's high-flown hopes of uniting left and right in an antisystemic movement.[61]

Escalating Tensions

The years closely following the wave of protests in 2011 also saw an increase in homophobic and antichoice backlash, as well as rising racial, ethnic, religious, and class tensions in the North Atlantic. In terms of women's issues and patriarchy, the United States experienced a major assault against the right to choose in 2013, when the Texas state government passed a law forbidding abortion after twenty weeks. Largely due to Tea Party agitation within the Texas state government, the antiabortion bill was voted on in spite of a mass occupation of the state capitol by protesters, most of whom were women. Virtually overnight, a third of Texas's abortion clinics

---

61   Ryan Lenz and Mark Potok, "War in the West: The Bundy Ranch Standoff and the American Radical Right," Southern Poverty Law Center's website, July 9, 2014, https://www.splcenter.org/sites/default/files/d6_legacy_files/downloads/publication/war_in_the_west_report.pdf.

shut their doors. In short order, only eight clinics were left open. The Supreme Court struck down important aspects of the law, but other even more restrictive laws had been passed, such as a Mississippi law totally banning abortion. As that case from Mississippi reached the Supreme Court, during the first quarter of 2015, fifty states introduced 332 restrictive antiabortion provisions—just three less than in all of 2014.[62]

Hate groups and radical-right political parties often fixate on gender and sexuality to promote the "natality" of the nation's genetic and cultural fabric. The United Kingdom and France registered increases in reports of homophobic actions in 2014 (an astonishing 78 percent increase in France), while radical-right and neo-Nazi groups have violently attacked Pride parades in Romania and Ukraine. Between 2013 and 2014, homophobic legislation was passed in the authoritarian conservative government of the Bharatiya Janata Party in India, in Putin's Orthodox Russia, and in Uganda, under the influence of US evangelical networks like the World Congress of Families and the International House of Prayer. These groups advance the notion that the modern world is increasingly drowning in sin and that straight, white men have become an oppressed demographic.

The success of the opinion that straight whites are persecuted indicates not only an ideological victory of the radical right but also the spatial reality of racial polarization. Studies have shown that diverse neighborhoods play host to far fewer racist attitudes than segregated ones.[63] However, due to long-range racialized narratives of law and order and economic dispossession through redlining and the foreclosure crisis, de facto segregation is indeed increasingly a problem in the United States. According to the Civil Rights Project/Proyecto Derechos Civiles, racial segregation in Northeast US schools has actually increased since the civil

---

62   Lauren Holter, "All the 2015 Anti-Abortion Legislation That's Been Passed So Far (Get a Grip, Arkansas!)," *Bustle*, April 17, 2015, http://www.bustle.com/articles/76235-all-the-2015-anti-abortion-legislation-thats-been-passed-so-far-get-a-grip-arkansas.

63   Oliver Christ et al., "Contextual Effect of Positive Intergroup Contact on Outgroup Prejudice," *Proceedings of the National Academy of Sciences* 111, no. 11 (March 2014): 3996–4000.

rights movement. The rate of attendance of children of color in schools where the overwhelming majority are nonwhites has risen from 43 percent in 1968 to over 50 percent today.[64] In the South, the number increased 10 percent from 1988 to 2011. More than half of hypersegregated schools are at the poverty rate when the majority of students are people of color. That number sits closer to 2 percent at white and Asian schools.[65] Likewise, the struggle over curricula in schools across the United States taken up by the radical right has had a critical impact on the education system. The revision of Advanced Placement United States History, for instance, includes idealized images of founding fathers and documents that look favorably on slavery, Manifest Destiny, and free-market capitalism.[66]

While conservative analysts like the Brookings Institute note that, in some places in the United States, racial and ethnic enclaves are declining and neighborhoods are integrating, they selectively ignore the role of gentrification in this form of "integration," through which traditionally black neighborhoods are transformed and former residents pushed to the suburbs and exurbs.[67] The claim that racial self-segregation will occur willingly is simply not supported by evidence: while whites tend to believe others prefer to live in segregated neighborhoods, nonwhites express a greater desire to integrate. The disparity marks the uneven experiences of whites and nonwhites, and the excuse that "people simply prefer to live among

---

64   Gary Orfield, Erica Frankenberg, Jongyeon Ee, and John Kuscera, *Brown at 60: Great Progress, a Long Retreat, and an Uncertain Future*, The Civil Rights Project/Proyecto Derechos Civiles, UCLA (2014), 18, https://www.civilrightsproject.ucla.edu/research/k-12-education/integration-and-diversity/brown-at-60-great-progress-a-long-retreat-and-an-uncertain-future/Brown-at-60-051814.pdf.

65   Ibid., 15.

66   Gabriel Joffe, "History Wars Exposed: Right-Wing Influence in APUSH Curriculum Update," Political Research Associates' website, October 19, 2015, http://www.politicalresearch.org/2015/10/19/history-wars-exposed-right-wing-influence-in-apush-curriculum-update/.

67   Rajini Vaidyanathan, "Why Don't Black and White Americans Live Together?," *BBC News Magazine*, January 8, 2016, http://www.bbc.com/news/world-us-canada-35255835.

their own race" serves to increase the material and ideological basis for deepening apartheid.[68]

At the same time, displacement and gentrification in the United States were joined by harsh, racialized policing, causing the expansion of both leftist opposition movements like Black Lives Matter and reactionary ideologies of "ethno-differentialism" and pan-secessionism. The idea that whites are the real victims of racism, coupled with the spatial separation of races and increasing economic precariousness, drives a fearful resistance to social change in the name of "multiculturalism." This is a victory for the radical right, and it owes much to the rhetoric of the Nouvelle Droite and the "respectable racist" milieu in the United States, with its fusion of populist Klan and Nazi rhetorics. Reciprocally, polarization drives fascist ideology, which correlates to the dehumanization of an out-group.

CounterJihad

The economic crisis also served as the backdrop for Islamophobia, which increased quantifiably after 2008. In 2010, 48 percent of Muslims stated that they had personally experienced religious discrimination over the last year—higher than any other religious

---

68   Robert P. Jones, "Self-Segregation: Why It's So Hard for Whites to Understand Ferguson," *Atlantic*, August 21, 2014, http://www.theatlantic.com/national/archive/2014/08/self-segregation-why-its-hard-for-whites-to-understand-ferguson/378928; Sean F. Reardon, Lindsay Fox, and Joseph Townsend, "Neighborhood Income Composition by Household Race and Income, 1990–2009," *The Annals of the American Academy of Political and Social Science* 660, no. 1 (July 2015): 78–97; David Leonhardt, "Middle-Class Black Families, in Low-Income Neighborhoods," *New York Times*, June 24, 2015, http://www.nytimes.com/2015/06/25/upshot/middle-class-black-families-in-low-income-neighborhoods.html; Daniel Denvir, "It's Mostly White People Who Prefer to Live in Segregated Neighborhoods," CityLab, June 25, 2015, http://www.citylab.com/housing/2015/06/its-mostly-white-people-who-prefer-to-live-in-segregated-neighborhoods/396887; Maria Krysan, Mick P. Couper, Reynolds Farley, and Tyrone A. Forman, "Does Race Matter in Neighborhood Preferences? Results from a Video Experiment," *American Journal of Sociology* 115, no. 2 (September 2009): 527–59.

group.[69] Over the next four years, the percentage of US respondents holding favorable attitudes toward Muslims and Arabs eroded from 43 percent in 2010 to under a third in 2014 (Arabs) and from 35 percent to 27 percent (Muslims).[70] A similar decline in favorable attitudes toward Arabs, Muslims, and immigrants in general has mushroomed across Europe, where it is also joined to a narrative of national decay by the radical right and fascists. Matching this prejudice are states' security apparatuses that disproportionately focus on Muslims as potential terrorists.[71]

In Europe, populist radical right parties broke through in unlikely places, due in no small part to Islamophobic feelings cultivated by an ideological movement directed particularly against Muslim immigrants in Europe known as CounterJihad. The first Counter-Jihad summit took place in Copenhagen, Denmark, on April 13, 2007, leading to the creation of a new organization called Stop Islamisation of Europe (SIOE), which is today considered a neo-Nazi group by the EU. Supported by radical-right populist MP Geert Wilders of the Dutch Party for Freedom and codeveloped by Vlaams Belang politicians, the movement grew rapidly to include the Lega Nord in Italy. The SIOE group has parallels in the United States that have assisted its rise. One of the United States's main "experts" on Islam, Robert Spencer, who has been invited to speak at police and military training sessions, helped launch a group called Stop Islamization of America (SIOA) with Pamela Geller, spearheading the protest against the Park51 project in Manhattan, which he calls "the Ground Zero mosque." Due in great measure to such "experts" and neoconservative backers like the Center for Security Policy and the International Free Press Society, popular support of profiling in the United States and Europe is sadly high. One such expert, Walid

---

69　"Islamophobia: Understanding Anti-Muslim Sentiment in the West," Gallup, 2014, http://www.gallup.com/poll/157082/islamophobia -understanding-anti-muslim-sentiment-west.aspx.

70　"American Attitudes Toward Arabs and Muslims: 2015," Arab American Institute, December 21, 2015, http://www.aaiusa.org/american_attitudes_ toward_arabs_and_muslims_2015.

71　Naomi Braine, "Terror Network or Lone Wolf?," Political Research Associates' website, June 19, 2015, http://www.politicalresearch.org/ 2015/06/19/terror-network-or-lone-wolf/#sthash.3xjOIqSP.dpbs.

Shoebat, for instance, has appeared on CNN, Glenn Beck's shows, Pat Robertson's *The 700 Club*, and other mainstream outlets, offering a veneer of legitimacy to controversial policies.

That legitimacy was strengthened by the sudden, surprising success of right-wing populist parties in some countries. Sweden was shocked by the success of the xenophobic and ultranationalist Swedish Democrats. In England, the BNP managed to get two members elected to the European Parliament. In Austria, the Netherlands, and Denmark, right parties made impressive electoral gains. Media that had dismissed the parties now began cozying up to the new power brokers. Party membership increased, and rhetorical messaging changed from "racist" to merely "xenophobic," while political ads and propaganda gained increasing currency. The political reach of the radical right now developed in terms of "freedom of expression," whereas a decade prior, no questions would have been raised if a newspaper rejected their ads.

Shoebat's influence and animus toward Islam were such that Anders Breivik cited him more than fifteen times in his manifesto. Breivik would go on to kill eighteen people with a car bomb and then open fire on the Workers' Youth League summer camp in Norway, killing sixty-nine, on July 22, 2011. Significantly, Breivik quotes Shoebat saying, "This is why the face of Islamic fundamentalism in the West has a façade that Islam is a peaceful religion. Because they are waiting to have more Islamic immigrants, they are waiting to increase in number, waiting to increase their political power."[72] This notion of Muslims as a kind of fifth column of Arab colonization runs throughout the CounterJihad movement.

Generally seen as a religious anxiety or fear, Islamophobia takes on the character of a political crusade, with fascists either seeking to unite with Israel or destroy both Islam and Judaism as two sides of the same coin. The notion that Muslims are allies in the fight against Zionism, which held sway during the Cold War, has diminished.[73] Instead, the refugee of the Arab world is considered

---

72 Anders Behring Breivik, "Review 2: Islam—What the West Needs to Know," in *A European Declaration of Independence*, available at https://archive.org/details/2083_A_European_Declaration_of_Independence.

73 Due to this more recent split, Faye's Eurosiberian camp is opposed by Bouchet's Eurasian camp in France, with the former insisting that the

inferior to "white Europe." Furthermore, current anti-Muslim/
Islam/"Middle Eastern" ideologies have overlapped with resentment against elites during the financial crisis to generate significant
transversal relationships on the far right, tying together CounterJihad with the Euroskeptic phenomenon.[74] Indeed, the fear of Islamization has become such a crucial nexus for radical-right and fascist positions that even a country like Lithuania, which has seen a
relatively slight growth in Muslim population, plays host to fear-
mongering on the websites of groups like the Lithuanian National Front about the "cosmopolitan... extravagance" of immigration
policy, linking traditional anti-Semitic, xenophobic, and Counter-
Jihad watchwords.[75]

Ignorance Fuels Rage

While some experts on fascism argue that the fear of Islamization manifests a genuine response to social ills, others find
something far more insidious at its core. For instance, Rasmus
Fletcher looks at places where CounterJihad has emerged strongest, like Denmark, Switzerland, and the Netherlands, insisting
that radical-right parties have evolved into a "semi-formalized network...in which bloggers and politicians connect with hooligan
groups like the English Defense League. Within this network, it
is common to portray the presence of Muslims in Europe as merely a symptom of the general weakening of Western civilization,
caused by an enemy within: a conspiracy of 'cultural Marxists.' In
its fully developed form this worldview amounts to a fascist ideology, which may also motivate terrorism, as in the case of Anders

---

latter is pro-Muslim, and the latter insisting the former is pro-Israel. For
this reason, perhaps, CounterJihad has been a challenge to the radical
right and fascism as much as it has been a useful tool for aggravating
Islamophobia among the general population while providing legitimacy
to other hateful opinions of white nationalists.

74   Egdūnas Račius, "The Place of Islamophobia/Muslimophobia Among
       Radical Lithuanian Nationalists—A Neglected Priority?" in Deland, et
       al., eds., *In the Tracks of Breivik*, 146–48.

75   Ibid., 151.

Behring Breivik."[76] Herein lies a deep observation of the "fascist creep" wherein the "ideal type" that distinguishes fascism clearly from the radical right breaks down amid a hybridization process that incorporates both entities together in a shared network with a common goal or set of goals.

The numbers show that much of the problem is based on demagoguery, which stimulates anxiety by scapegoating out-groups. According to a poll taken in 2014, the average French citizen believed that nearly one in three people in their country were Muslim. The actual number was less than one in ten, and that was the highest in Europe. In Belgium, the differential was the same—they thought 29 percent, but the actual number fell closer to 6. Italians and Britons inflated numbers by 16 percent, Spaniards by 14, and Swedes by 12. US citizens missed the mark by a multiple of fourteen, by far the most considerable relative disparity.[77]

At the same time, these countries all imagined that a far smaller percentage of Christians composed their populations, developing an image of Christianity drowning in a swamp of Islamic immigrants. US citizens underestimated the number by 22 percent, Canadians by 21, Britons by 20, Swedes by 19, Belgians by 18, Spaniards by 15, and French and Italians both by 14. When asked about the percentage of the populace composed of immigrants in general, the numbers were similarly overestimated across the board. Other inflated numbers related to pregnant teens and the unemployed. The sense these fantasies produce is of a population in utter decline, a feeling of being trapped in a dark age and searching for a strong leader who will lift up the people.[78]

Due to fascists' tendency to alternately incorporate or militate against Zionism, Islamophobia has also accompanied further violence against Jews. The year that the above poll was taken, 2014, marked another year of Israeli attacks on Gaza, which created a humanitarian crisis that sent ripples of outrage throughout the

---

76   Fleischer, "Two Fascisms in Contemporary Europe?," 54.
77   Alberto Nardelli and George Arnett, "Today's Key Fact: You Are Probably Wrong About Almost Everything," *Guardian*, October 29, 2014, https://www.theguardian.com/news/datablog/2014/oct/29/todays-key-fact-you-are-probably-wrong-about-almost-everything.
78   Ibid.

world. Anti-Semites exploited this sentiment to embark on a wave of violence against Jews not seen since the early 1990s. An FBI study on religious violence showed that more than 60 percent of religious attacks were carried out against Jews, with the second-highest number being 15 percent against Muslims.[79] According to the Anti-Defamation League (ADL), anti-Semitic attacks in the United States rose by more than a fifth.[80] Among those attacks was the shooting in Overland Park, Kansas, carried out by a longtime Nazi organizer, Frazier Glenn Miller Jr., infamous for his involvement in the Greensboro Massacre and the Order. According to the *Antisemitism Worldwide 2014* annual report, the increase of anti-Semitic attacks worldwide doubled that of the United States, marking it as the second worst year in the last ten years.[81] In a study conducted across 101 countries, one-quarter of those surveyed by the ADL held anti-Semitic beliefs.[82] These statistics explain the growing fear

---

79   Joanna Markind, "Jews Are Still the Biggest Target of Religious Hate Crimes," *Forward*, December 5, 2015, http://forward.com/news/325988/jews-are-still-the-biggest-target-of-hate-crimes/.

80   "Audit: In 2014 Anti-Semitic Incidents Rose 21 Percent Across the U.S. in a 'Particularly Violent Year for Jews,'" Anti-Defamation League's website, March 30, 2015, http://www.adl.org/press-center/press-releases/anti-semitism-usa/adl-audit-in-2014-anti-semitic-inicidents.html?referrer=https://www.google.com/#.V7X-HbVriRs.

81   *Antisemitism Worldwide 2014*, ed. Dina Porat (Tel Aviv University, 2014).

82   "ADL Poll of Over 100 Countries Finds More Than One-Quarter of Those Surveyed Infected with Anti-Semitic Attitudes," Anti-Defamation League's website, May 13, 2014, http://www.adl.org/press-center/press-releases/anti-semitism-international/adl-global-100-poll.html. Furthermore, in the Netherlands, 2014 saw a 71 percent increase in anti-Semitic violence. In Germany, a report released in 2015 marked a five-year high in attacks, and the same year, sources in the United Kingdom recorded the most anti-Semitic attacks since records began. See Jack Moore, "Anti-Semitic Attacks Increase by 71% in Holland," *Newsweek.com*, April 14, 2014, http://www.newsweek.com/securing-jewish-sites-will-not-solve-rising-anti-semitism-says-top-dutch-rabbi-322258; Matthew Holehouse, "Attacks on Jews Rise to Five Year High in Germany—More Than Any Country in Europe," Telegraph.co.uk, October 1, 2015, http://www.telegraph.co.uk/news/worldnews/europe/eu/11904654/

felt by Jews in Europe, captured in a cover story for the *Atlantic* in 2015 titled "Is It Time for the Jews to Leave Europe?"[83]

At the same time, mob violence against African immigrants in Israel, along with the massive bombing campaigns against Gaza and numerous chauvinist statements by high level politicians caused experts to ponder whether the country had turned a page in its politics. During the 2014 bombardment of Gaza, Israel Prize laureate and one of the most respected scholars on fascism today, Zeev Sternhell, warned that "Israeli democracy has become increasingly eroded, until it reached a new nadir in the current war.... People here say, 'It's not so terrible, it's nothing like fascism—we have free elections and parties and a parliament.' Yet, we reached a crisis in this war, in which, without anyone asking them to do so, all kinds of university bodies are suddenly demanding that the entire academic community roll back its criticism."[84]

As Sternhell indicates, both Islamophobia and anti-Semitism can be inflated by current events in which tensions are heightened and society is polarized. Indeed, the conflict of religions and politics today bears a strong likeness to the struggle between left and right during the Years of Lead, where violence was deployed deliberately against civilians to push them toward a traditional "state of order"—to condition people to fear their own freedom. The development of the Islamic State of Iraq and Syria (ISIS) out of terrorist networks and Sunni militias, their palingenetic belief in the rebirth of a Caliphate against modern nation-states, and their celebration of sacrifice, violence, and cruelty suggested a kind of fascist cult arising in Southwest Asia.[85] On the other hand, Kurd-

---

Attacks-on-Jews-rise-to-five-year-high-in-Germany-more-than-any-country-in-Europe.html; Sanchia Berg, "Antisemitism Hit Record Level in 2014, Report Says," BBC.com, February 5, 2015, http://www.bbc.com/news/uk-31140919.

83 Jeffrey Goldberg, "Is It Time for the Jews to Leave Europe?," *Atlantic*, April 2015, http://www.theatlantic.com/magazine/archive/2015/04/is-it-time-for-the-jews-to-leave-europe/386279/.

84 Gidi Weitz, "Signs of Fascism in Israel Reached New Peak During Gaza Op, Says Renowned Scholar," Haaretz.com, August 13, 2014, http://www.haaretz.com/israel-news/.premium-1.610368.

85 Stephen Sheehi, "ISIS as a Fascist Movement," Mondo Weiss, November

ish forms of organization around libertarian municipalism, their apparent incorporation of militant feminism, and their assertion of a cosmopolitan openness to ethnic and ideological difference seemed to evoke Popular Front struggles against the rise of fascism in Spain in 1936.

It has been the struggle against ISIS and Bashar Al-Assad's regime in Syria that has caused refugees to flee in their millions, feeding the success of perhaps the most effective CounterJihad group—Patriotische Europäer gegen die Islamisierung des Abendlandes, or Pegida (Patriotic Europeans Against the Islamization of the Occident). Emerging in October 2014 for a protest with only a small group of people, Pegida's initial demonstration was not against ISIS or militant Islam at all; it was an attempt to rally a far-right counterdemonstration against a pro-Kurdish march through Dresden. More of an anti-immigration group than an anti-Islam group, Pegida increased their numbers to some 7,500 by December and 10,000 by the start of 2015. According to independent political analyst Eric Draitser, the Duginist New Resistance web ring and Green Star network mobilized to co-opt the Pegida demonstrations early on, needling organizers to move toward a pro-Russia stance on Ukraine.

The attempt by Duginists to pull the German far right toward National Bolshevism is not without its prominent allies. Jürgen Elsässer, a former Maoist, has come to popularity on the right through his magazine *Compact*, which proposes an anti-imperialist "Paris–Berlin–Moscow" axis. Bridging the divide between Pegida's rowdy protest culture and the "conformist revolution" of the far-right Alternative für Deutschland (AfD—Alternative for Germany), *Compact* boasted an interview with Dugin in 2013 in which he proclaimed that "the Eurasian idea is [...] a realistic and idealistic concept, it is not just a romantic idea, it is a technical, geopolitical, and strategic position, which all Russians who think responsibly support."[86] Connecting the electoral AfD and the informal Pegida is Elsässer's ersatz anti-imperialism—the product

---

18, 2015, http://mondoweiss.net/2015/11/isis-fascist-movement.

86   Thomas Korn and Andreas Umland, "Russland: Jürgen Elsässer, Krem-lpropagandist," *Zeit Online*, July 19, 2014, http://www.zeit.de/politik/deutschland/2014-07/juergen-elsaesser-russland-propaganda.

of a generation of elitist Islamophobia cultivated by academics and intellectuals that has only begun to spread among the populous as a result of a broader reaction to compromises between Angela Merkel's Christian Democrats and the Social Democrats. Thus, the rejection of immigration as part of the "social democratization" of the neoliberal agenda could be fused with support for purportedly anti-imperialist nations, like Syria and Iran, which did not kowtow to finance capital and the globalist elites.[87] This alliance pushes CounterJihad further away from what Rasmus Fleischer calls "mono-fascism" (or imperialist, anti-intellectual Eurocentrism) and toward a "multi-fascism" linked to antiglobalism, religious heterodoxy, and racist identitarianism.[88]

In a public statement, Draitser declared that "fascists, and fascist ideology, have infiltrated anti-imperialist circles all over social media, and in the political space in general…and anyone who challenges these lies is a 'Zionist' (irrespective of the issue or the politics) or a 'puppet' or a 'traitor' or a 'liar' or a 'najdi' or 'anti-Resistance.'" Concluding his statement, Draitser admitted, "I was not as aware of the depth of this infiltration until the refugee crisis really began last fall [of 2015]."[89] The particular form of intervention in anti-imperialist politics, which emerges from the tradition of Thiriart, Mutti, and Bouchet, is not only carried forward by established National Bolsheviks like Elsässer. Rather, it is energized by a younger generation of Duginists who advocate an ethnopluralist "multi-polar world" of nationalist apartheid on social media and in the streets, and it finds allies among some leftists who still adhere to Cold War iterations of anti-imperialism. For instance, in late 2014, an antiglobalization conference was held in Moscow under the auspices of the Duginist "Multipolar world" slogan and featuring the Italian fascist group Millenium, seperatists from the Donbass and Srpska, the Russian far-right party Rodina, the neo-Confederate group League of the South, and, among

87   Anthony Fano Fernandez, "Germany's New Far Right," *Jacobin*, February 20, 2015, https://www.jacobinmag.com/2015/02/germany-far -right-pegida.

88   Fleischer, "Two Fascisms in Contemporary Europe?," 57.

89   Eric Draitser's Facebook page, July 25, 2016, http://www.facebook.com/ EricDraitser1.

others, the left-wing coalition United National Antiwar Coalition (UNAC) and the International Action Center (IAC)—both associated with the Trotskist Workers World Party. When I caught up with UNAC head Joe Lombardo about the conference, he insisted it was an international conference of generally pro-Putin separatists and anti-imperialists. Although UNAC is not generally pro-Putin, he told me, they support Putin as anti-imperialist insofar as he stands against the hegemony of NATO.

Islamophobia's Transatlantic Impact

After the January 7, 2015, attack on the offices of the weekly cartoon periodical *Charlie Hebdo* left eleven dead and as many injured, a national outcry emerged in France that resonated throughout the world. The spirit of the mass demonstrations in Paris was largely in favor of peace, coexistence, and freedom of speech. In Dresden, Germany, a large anti-Pegida demonstration drew 35,000 people to the Frauenkirche to mourn the victims. However, Pegida was able to rally 25,000 to support their stance against the "Islamization of the West," and street-level violence against immigrants increased dramatically throughout Europe. French reactionaries seized on the opportunity to forward PATRIOT Act–style legislation through parliament, while the Front National's new leader, Marine Le Pen, declared that France should reimplement the death penalty and legalize torture. Pegida had hit its peak, however, as photos of its leader Lutz Bachmann posing as Hitler with the words "He's Back" were splashed across front pages all over Europe.

In the United States, Patriots called for an extensive antimosque day of protest for October 12. The most visible representative of this mobilization was Jon Ritzheimer in Arizona, who filled the power vacuum left after Ready's suicide. These gatherings took place in some twenty cities across the country and involved hundreds of people, among them open white nationalists and neo-Nazis. The year would end with a total of seventy-eight attacks on mosques across the United States, the highest level ever recorded.[90]

---

90   Sara Rathod, "2015 Saw a Record Number of Attacks on US Mosques," *Mother Jones*, June 20, 2016, http://www.motherjones.com/politics/2016/06/islamophobia-rise-new-report-says.

Coordinated attacks by Muslims in Paris a month later on November 13, 2015, killed 130 people, causing an increasing groundswell of anger against immigrants and fear of refugees fleeing the war in Syria. The Front National rode the wave of hatred to one of their best showings ever at the polls during the regional elections, but in the second election, the Socialist Party told its members to vote for the mainstream conservative party in order to break the "national revolutionary" wave. Following another attack—this time during a Christmas event of the Department of Public Health in San Bernardino, California—a new wave of resentment and violence came sweeping the United States. Ritzheimer's name entered headlines again, as his hateful rhetoric toward Muslims became increasingly violent shortly before the occupation of the Malheur Refuge, which seemed to fill his life with new meaning.

Ritzheimer's prominence in the Patriot movement began, not with his leadership role in the Islamophobic antimosque protests, but rather with his participation in the Bundy Ranch showdown and the Sugar Pine Mine occupation. Along with other Patriot movement stalwarts like Blaine Cooper, Ryan Payne, and the Bundy family, Ritzheimer helped form a new, mobile inner-group of the renewed national Patriot movement, growing out of the 1990s-era militia movement and infused with CounterJihad, border militias, and sovereign citizens. With a quasi-insurrectionist strategy, these activists travel from occupation to occupation attempting to spark similar events elsewhere, with hopes of culminating in a broad revolution against the federal government.

Survival of the Three Percent

The radical right and the neofascists throughout the world today generate and exist within a mixed state of fear of, and hope for, looming catastrophe. The sense of doom, the need to build bulwarks against a dreaded multicultural flood, can take many forms. In 2014, Church of the Creator adherent Craig Cobb moved to Leith, North Dakota, attempting to draw white supremacists into a landgrab that would make them the effective power brokers in town. Leaders like Tom Metzger were invited to purchase property in Leith, which brought a large contingent of antifascists to protest against the settlement. In response, the National Socialist

Movement expressed support for Cobb, but the townspeople rose
up against him. Without plumbing and at the end of his rope, Cobb
decided to take a stroll through town with his housemate carrying
large rifles. The two were arrested shortly thereafter, and Cobb's
co-defendant testified against him in court, sending him to jail.[91]
These ideas of Pioneer Little Europe (PLE) continue to be prominent among pan-secessionists around the world. PLE groups have
advocated survivalism and self-defense, called for "white mask"
protests to draw antifascists into a fight, and maintain an online
presence that can be aggressively "anti-antifascist."

In the words of one skinhead woman: "Prepare yourself for war
constantly. Don't speak if you can't defend yourself in every way.
Prepare by knowing, first of all, then work on guns and amass food
and water supplies, first aid kits, medication, clothing, blankets.
Try to become self-sufficient."[92] The insistence on "preparedness"
and "survivalism" stretches through the skinhead movement to the
Patriot movement, which has become notorious for its compounds,
redoubts, and enclaves. Perhaps the most intense group of survivalist Patriots today is the Three Percenters—also known as IIIP,
3%ers, III%ers, or Threepers—whose name is purportedly based on
the dubious claim that the first American Revolution was won by
the armed resistance of only 3 percent of the population.

Started in 2008 by a self-declared former leftist and longtime
veteran of the militia movement named Michael Brian Vanderboegh, the Three Percenters styled themselves as moderates in the
Patriot movement but pushed for violent acts against politicians
and the police. In 2010, Vanderboegh joined the Tea Party frenzy
against Obamacare, calling for his followers to throw bricks at the
windows of those politicians who voted in favor of Obama's health
care plan—a call that was answered in a number of districts across
the United States. The Three Percent movement began to grow
rapidly, despite the inevitable splits that took place once Vanderboegh gained notoriety as an "authority" after some appearances
on FOX News.[93]

---

91   See *Welcome to Leith*, directed by Michael Beach Nichols (Christopher K.
     Walker First Run Features, 2015).
92   Blee, *Inside Organized Racism*, 6.
93   "Michael Brian Vanderboegh," Southern Poverty Law Center's website,

A new leader, Christian Hyman (aka Sam Kerodin), emerged with a more clearly antipolice and antigovernment position. Hyman and his wife, Holly, initiated the Three Percenter Society and some eleven businesses in Idaho, all sporting the organization's name; they also registered fifty-seven domain names online. Part of their network included websites that published extreme Islamophobia and racism, much of it along the lines of: "Kill every last Muslim, Burn every last copy of their Satanic book. Burn every last mosque to the ground. Burn every dwelling where they have lived, And wherever you must burn, salt the ground heavily. Make no exceptions. Take no excuses."[94] The other aspect of their work has involved planning separatist compounds and schools—including one teaching "prepping" (canning, storing useful supplies, and generally preparing for a catastrophic event) as well as "sabotage, infiltration, exfiltration, assassination, demolitions and subversion," according to the couple's former associate, Kenny Lane.[95] Another Hyman project was the "Citadel" in Idaho, a compound that would horde equipment for the impending collapse of Western civilization and build a model community based on traditional values.[96] Most of these plans seemed to degenerate into rumors of money traps and led nowhere. Despite their failures and infighting, though, the Three Percenters expanded dramatically over a period of a few years, from an organization that could only bring a small presence to a march or demonstration to a network that could influence key events, like the occupation of the Malheur Refuge.

The general growth in militia groups like those that flocked to Malheur—from 202 in 2014 to 276 in 2015—undoubtedly helped

---

https://www.splcenter.org/fighting-hate/extremist-files/individual/michael-brian-vanderboegh-0.

94   See J. C. Dodge, "Who Is Courtland Grojean, And Why Should You Care?," Mason Dixon Tactical, November 11, 2016, https://masondixontactical.wordpress.com/2015/11/11/who-is-courtland-grojean-and-why-should-you-care/.

95   Wirecutter (Kenny Lane), "Methinks Thou Bullshit Too Much—The Kerodin v Lane Debacle," Knuckledraggin My Life Away (blog), January 13, 2016, http://knuckledraggin.com/2016/01/44734/.

96   Bill Morlin, "Behind the Walls," Intelligence Report (online edition), Southern Poverty Law Center's website, May 16, 2013, https://www.splcenter.org/fighting-hate/intelligence-report/2013/behind-walls.

fuel the Three Percenters' growth.[97] This increasingly antagonistic Patriot movement finds expression and articulation through a network of Internet livestreamers, "citizen journalists," and talk show hosts like Alex Jones, FBI informant Brandon Darby of right-wing libertarian hub Breitbart.com, and Pete Santilli's GuerillaMedia-Network.com. Not only did Santilli report as a fully supportive, embedded journalist within border militias, the Bundy Ranch, and the Malheur Refuge, but he also went to Baltimore to support "we the people" against the "police state" after Governor Larry Hogan activated the Maryland National Guard to put down an uprising catalyzed by the death of a young black man named Freddie Gray in police custody. This despite going on air the previous year to state, "I'm calling for the military to restore our Republic. Is it a military coup? I would say that it's probably the most orderly fashion to do this."[98] Santilli's show bills itself as the "voice of the oppressed and targeted in this country" and segues from discussions of wage theft and unions to pro-rancher attacks on the Bureau of Land Management.[99] Like his call for a national strike, Santilli's apparent support for the Baltimore riots reflected the interests of a white nationalist movement prepared to support black liberation struggles insofar as they can be construed as resisting the same liberal, multicultural "system" that white nationalist border militias and Patriots loathe. The news site, Breitbart, riffs on many of these motifs, directing much of its attention to racialized themes like the celebration of the Confederate flag and the decrying of black criminals. At one time declaring himself a Leninist who sought the destruction of the federal government, Breitbart's former chair Steve Bannon maintained the Tea Party line criticizing "state capitalism" and parasitic elites while positioning Christian values at the fore of

---

97   "Antigovernment Militia Groups Grew by More Than One-Third Last Year," Southern Poverty Law Center's website, https://www.splcenter. org/news/2016/01/04/antigovernment-militia-groups-grew-more-one-third-last-year.

98   Pete Santilli Live Stream, "Episode #597—Assassination Attempted on Intel Whistleblower James Garrow—Pete Santilli Show," YouTube, January 3, 2014, https://www.youtube.com/watch?v=54rZ8IeO_Hs.

99   See "Pete Santilli Show," YouTube, February 23, 2016, http://www .youtube.com/watch?v=2Jirh-G6sac.

productive capital and national unity, as opposed to radical Islam and undocumented citizens.[100]

Into this swamp of media-savvy organizers, pseudo-journalists, and Patriot faithful swaggered aspiring presidential candidate Donald Trump, who brought Bannon on as campaign manager and strategist during—and after—a successful presidential campaign that courted fascist and protofascist movements by insisting on the closure of mosques throughout the United States, the monitoring of Muslims, and the deportation of immigrants. Trump had made a name for himself on the right in the 1980s when he joined in the condemnation of the "Central Park Five," five black teenagers wrongfully convicted of raping a white woman in New York's Central Park. However, his racist legacy extended back into the 1970s, when, under the advice of his lawyer, Roy Cohn—a notorious anti-Semite, former Red Scare prosecutor, and John Birch Society official—he countersued the US government for charging his real estate firm with discriminatory practices.

Trump, a billionaire, inherited his company from his father, a first generation German-American who participated in a Klan riot during the 1920s. Trump maintained his father's fortune by using a variety of questionable tactics in the casino industry, helped along by Roger Stone, a former Nixon dirty trickster who has flirted with white nationalism and Holocaust denial. During the height of the Tea Party, Trump acted as a mouthpiece for the Birther movement demanding President Obama's birth certificate. After Obama's re-election, he angrily tweeted, "We should have a revolution in this country." On the campaign trail, Trump had good things to say about Putin's strongman regime in Russia and, on a trip to Scotland, commended the people of the United Kingdom for voting to leave the EU. In this regard, Trump played into the hands of the Euroskeptic radical right and their brand of anti-imperialism, despite promoting a foreign policy that would use military strength to force countries around the world into economic subordination. He fueled racial tensions again by coyly denying that he knew anything

---

100   Ronald Radosh, "Steve Bannon, Trump's Top Guy, Told Me He Was 'A Leninist' Who Wants To 'Destroy the State,'" *The Daily Beast*, August 21, 2016, http://www.thedailybeast.com/articles/2016/08/22/steve-bannon-trump-s-top-guy-told-me-he-was-a-leninist.html

about white supremacism after gaining the public support of David Duke, Jared Taylor, the Klan, and other members of the fascist movement. That same day, Trump tweeted out a Mussolini quote, "It is better to live one day as a lion than 100 years as a sheep," which was later redeployed by a militia group haphazardly formed to monitor anti-Trump protests.

Trump's insistence that he would deport eleven million migrants mimicked the platform of white nationalists across the United States known as "peaceful ethnic cleansing," and it was matched by his fellow candidate, Tea Party Republican Ted Cruz, who doubled down, insisting that he would not let any of them back across the border again. Yet, without Trump's popularity, propelled by middle-American radicals' anger over the decline of the white race and the decadent principles of multiculturalism, it is likely that Cruz's political platform would have been more moderate. It was the white nationalist platform that Trump advanced that moved the entire Republican primary race further toward ethnocentric populism. In itself, this would not have been possible without the creeping web of networks of radical-right paleoconservatives, "race realists," and neo-Nazis that had widely become recognizable under the banner of the "alternative right" or simply "alt-right." Trump drew on these networks for grassroots campaign work. Jared Taylor's American Renaissance made robocalls for Trump, campaign volunteers with Nazi tattoos were exposed on national TV, and his campaign even nominated William Johnson, leader of the American Freedom Party, to act as a delegate to the Republican National Convention.

During the convention, a pro-Trump tweet coming from a fascist Twitter account flashed onto four screens around Quicken Loans Stadium repeating the line from Trump's speech, "Tonight I'm with you, I will fight for you, and I will WIN for you!" Notable fascist Kevin MacDonald later proclaimed:

> The Alt Right is the only identifiable political perspective that provides an intellectual defense of the central themes of Trump's campaign which really come down to defending the traditional people and culture of America. Nationalism, populism, much less White interests, have been eradicated by elite consensus to the far fringes of American political discourse. But with the rise of Trump, it's inevitable that they edge toward the mainstream.

The confident dismissals of any claim for the reality of race and racial interests…will seem more and more hollow as they confront articulate, science-based arguments and the reality of racial conflict all around them. This is a great moment for the Alt Right—and for America.[101]

In the next chapter, we will dig deeper into the alt-right and its appeals to anarchism, ecology, and the revolutionary left to "make America great again." Per MacDonald's claims that the alt-right will be (and in fact has been) mainstreamed through Trumpism, this macabre mixture of men's rights activists, pan-secessionists, and neoreactionaries is the latest, most technologically adept manifestation of the fascist creep—the resentment-filled fusion of left- and right-wing themes directed toward an ultranationalist rebirth.

---

101   Kevin MacDonald, "Donald Trump in Cleveland: Nationalism, Populism, and the Rise of the Alt Right," *Occidental Observer*, July 23, 2016, http://www.theoccidentalobserver.net/2016/07/donald-trump-in-cleveland-nationalism-populism-and-the-rise-of-the-alt-right/.

CHAPTER 10: THE NEW SYNTHESIS

Pan-Secessionism

Among those who joined in Occupy, pan-secessionists had influence in places like the Pacific Northwest, where a politics of bioregional separatism melds left- and right-wing ideas. Although it can appear to be a cogent radical, leftist ideology, pan-secessionism actually attempts to convince the left to join the fascist movement through PLEs and white nationalist enclaves in order to bring down the "system." Particularly coordinated through national-anarchist groups and the constellation of groupouscules surrounding the American Right, pan-secessionism maintains a kind of home base in the blog AttacktheSystem.com. Mostly maintained by Keith Preston, the site fantasizes of a hopeful alliance of Zapatistas, Black Panthers, the American Freedom Party, and various ethno-nationalist groups. The goal is for white nationalist identitarianism to gain credibility through association with other ethnic and racial identities, underwritten by an agreement to respect one another's ethnic boundaries and spaces.

In an interview with Radio Wehrwolf, Preston calls himself a "well-traveled veteran of radical movements in the United States."[1] Preston entered radical left movements in the 1970s and moved on to libertarianism in the 1980s. After joining Love and Rage anarchist

---

1   Keith Preston, interview with Dion, Radio Wehrwolf, January 5, 2016, 4:30–4:50, http://radiowehrwolf.weebly.com/radio-archives/keith-preston.

network for their founding conference in 1989, Preston circulated a critique, accusing the group of, in his words, "[being] a bunch of crypto-commies trying to coopt anarchism for some kind of totalitarian leftism and promote a race war in the process."[2] For the rest of the 1990s, Preston floated around the militia movement "or the various Patriot groups that came out of that time period." Through this association, he states, he "became interested in the radical right in Europe and the Nouvelle Droite, and other movements of that type."[3]

While navigating the militia movement, Preston also discovered the "neosecessionism" of the Republic of Texas (constituents of which made it to the 2015 conference in Moscow with UNAC). He thinks of secessionism as "an old anarchist idea, but applied to American context, it could be something entirely different."[4] In the mid-2000s, Preston initiated a group called the American Revolutionary Vanguard and the website AttacktheSystem.com to advocate pan-secessionism as a "tactical concept." He explains his support for a fundamentally fascist syncretism in a favorable critique of the racial separatist program of Americans for Self-Determination (ASD):

> The ASD plan is remarkably similar to the ideas found in an obscure but growing form of European radicalism known as the "Third Position" whose most radical tendency is a newer school of anarchist thought known as "national-anarchism." If revolutionary anarchism is to have any sort of future (and why shouldn't it, given the intellectual bankruptcy of the traditional Left and the traditional Right?) it will probably be in some form such as that generally favored by national-anarchists, a unity of separatists and decentralists within the context of class struggle, anti-statism and anti-imperialism.[5]

---

2   Keith Preston, "Former Love and Rage leader and Defector from Anarchism to Maoism Denounces Keith Preston," *Attack the System* (blog), January 31, 2012, https://attackthesystem.com/2012/01/31/former-love -and-rage-leader-and-defector-from-anarchism-to-maoism-denounces -keith-preston/.

3   Preston, Radio Wehrwolf, 5:15–5:27.

4   Ibid., 15:30–15:45.

5   Keith Preston, "Critique of the Americans for Self-Determination Plan for Separatism and Decentralism," *Attack the System* (blog), https://

Preston's affinity with white nationalism has been on display in his talks at the National Policy Institute, where he has parroted the points of the Nouvelle Droite and Dugin, insisting that US imperialism denies the right to sovereign cultures, requiring a return to a "multi-polar world" as an antidote.[6] He writes, "The solution would be to make urban and metropolitan areas into independent city-states, free of control by regional or state governments."[7] Preston's populist antisystem ideology would remain impervious to co-optation by carving out regions for each set of people, he claims. In his interview with Radio Wehrwolf, Preston mentions the white nationalist "Northwest Republic" beloved of both the Aryan Nations and the green, bioregionalist Cascadia movement, stating that he would "really look at these kinds of movements as a means of advancing anarchism."[8]

In particular, Preston also supports the Middlebury Institute's attempts at drawing together different separatists from right and left persuasions, including the Second Vermont Republic, the sovereignty movement of Hawaii, and the infamous League of the South.[9] Led by bioregionalist Kirkpatrick Sale, the Middlebury Institute suggests significant overlap between left and right on the same terrain Dugin seeks to exploit—large-scale separatism that brings fascists greater legitimacy. While not explicitly statist, bioregionalism, itself, can pull from discordant groups.

On the website WhiteBiocentrism.com, nationalist voices come together to discuss secessionism, immigration, the National Alliance, and the New World Order. One of the more high-profile

---

attackthesystem.com/critique-of-the-americans-for-self-determination
-plan-for-separatism-and-decentralism/.

6   Keith Preston, "Keith Preston Speaks to the National Policy Institute on the Question of U. S. Imperialism," Ibid., November 3, 2015, https:// attackthesystem.com/2015/11/03/keith-preston-speaks-to-the-national -policy-institute-on-the-question-of-u-s-imperialism/.

7   Preston, "Critique of the Americans for Self-Determination Plan for Separatism and Decentralism."

8   Preston, Radio Wehrwolf, 17:10–17:20.

9   Matthew N. Lyons, "Rising Above the Herd: Keith Preston's Authoritarian Anti-Statism," *New Politics*, April 29, 2011, http://newpol.org/content/ rising-above-the-herd-keith-prestons-authoritarian-anti-statism.

posters is Kevin Alfred Strom, fresh out of jail for child pornography charges. Perhaps the most insidious pro-bioregional white nationalist in the United States today, however, is Harold Covington, who organized the United Racist Front that perpetrated the 1979 Greensboro Massacre and cocreated the UK-based neo-Nazi terrorist group Combat 18. Covington has carved out a niche for himself writing militaristic novels about "the collapse" and advocating for a Northwest Front in keeping with Richard Butler's Northwest Imperative. He claims that Cascadia (generally the Pacific Northwest) should become a liberated territory for whites only. Although Covington has burned too many bridges to be politically relevant, the continuing popularity of bioregionalism and secessionism amid the white nationalist movement has unsettling implications.

A fine example is the retreat to "ethnic enclaves," which proclaims a return to the authentic national experience on a basic tribal level, supposedly dismantling the multicultural homogenization of consumerism. In the spirit of this return of ethno-differentialism, the National-Anarchist Movement's website, National-anarchist.net, cross posts the work of former Black Liberation Army anarchist Ashanti Alston along with Afrikaner separatist Attie Schutte and the left anarchist writings of David Graeber. Relying heavily on the rhetoric of white genocide, white separatists declare that their culture is being deconstructed by "cultural Marxists" whose authoritarian tendencies are eroding the decent, hard-working Volk. Using arguments couched in the rhetoric of "culture," these separatists try to present a sympathetic history of their given ethnicity, nation, or "culture," glossing over racial violence in an effort to show that their separate nation would not only be peaceful but it would also be based on the simple, natural desires of people of the same background who prefer to live among one another.

The words of one poster on a national-anarchist site based in Shropshire, United Kingdom, illustrate to what extent such groups have absorbed the ideology of the Nouvelle Droite:

> Yes, people are not the same and they are not equal. They are differentiated and diverse, and should be free to live with those most like them. I have more respect for the Black gangbanger who would slit my throat because I am White, than I do for the "Uncle Tom" who would sell-out his own race to be

a second-rate "adopted" White.... This is not racism, it is just common sense, that all peoples should be supported in their nationalistic struggles for their own people, on their own land. I support Black Power, La Raza, Asian Autonomy, and White Identity. All cultural-ethnic groups are unique and should have their autonomy respected.[10]

Aside from claiming to support white power, just as they support black power and brown power, the national-anarchist site boasts an epigram from National Bolshevik Eduard Limonov, stating, "There's no longer any left or right. There's the system and the enemies of the system."

As with national-anarchism, pan-secessionists have also made "entryist" attempts to turn radical movements toward more syncretic left-to-right ideologies on the murky fringes of radical politics. Independence movements, whether Basque, Catalonian, or Scottish, often become key points of unity for left and right, allowing the ethnic and nationalist separatism of Preston's pan-secessionist theorizations to extend their reach. While often presented as leftist and incorporating leftist positions, popular separatist movements tend to obscure both their ultranationalist origins and their deep traditionalist trends. As a result, they provide providential breeding grounds for national-anarchism, national syndicalism, and other forms of contemporary fascism.

Michael Schmidt and Fascist Creep

One illustrative case of the confused ideology of the fascist creep is that of Michael Schmidt.[11] A South African author and journalist

---

10   "National Anarchism—'A Reply to a Leftist'—courtesy of 'Lefty' Hooligan & Archonis," NAMS-UK's website, December 30, 2011, http://namshropshire.blogspot.com/2011/12/national-anarchism-reply-to-leftist.html.

11   This section is based on a longer investigative series. For further details, see Alexander Reid Ross and Joshua Stephens, "About Schmidt," Chapters 1–5, Medium website, October 12–29, 2015, https://medium.com/@rossstephens/about-schmidt-how-a-white-nationalist-seduced-anarchists-around-the-world-chapter-1-1a6fa255b528#.1b46m7k8e.

who identifies as an Afrikaner anarchist, Schmidt focused his political work on class struggle for years, gaining a solid reputation (and publishing two widely read books through AK Press), despite increasing signs of racist, right-wing proclivities. He worked within the anarchist-communist tendency known as Platformism, which advocates for a more organized approach to revolutionary activity and "ideological unity" within anarchist groups trying to influence or build mass organizations that might usher in a new, revolutionary society. Unbeknownst to most people outside his Platformist group, however, Schmidt had promoted a division between middle-class (white) and poor (black) sections of the collective based on the understanding that black people lacked the cultural background to capably execute the rigorous intellectual demands of Platformism. In his words, black South Africans are "incapable of other than the basest service to the revolution."[12] Relegating poor, black workers to the frontlines while placing the middle-class whites on a perch of intellectual leadership transformed a political tendency constructed to ensure basic unity among all anarchist militants into one paradoxically deployed to actuate an intellectual hierarchy between blacks and whites.

In an interview, Schmidt told me, "As a white person living in Africa as a minority the bulk of which are working class (3.2-million out of 4.5-million), I taste a smack of genocide in the desire by race fanatics to destroy even cultural whiteness."[13] This open desire to protect white people from cultural genocide at the hands of the black majority was implicit in several of his articles, both mainstream and anarchist. A significant number of his articles for South African newspapers employ the idea of "black racism" or "Bantu racism" (similar to the idea of "reverse racism" or "anti-white racism" in the United States).[14] He expands

---

12   Michael Schmidt, "The Politico-Cultural Dynamics of the South African Anarchist Movement," Internal Discussion Document, July 2008, https://www.pdf-archive.com/2015/10/12/schmidt-memo/schmidt-memo.pdf.

13   Personal correspondence with the author via Facebook, June 22, 2015.

14   See for example Michael Schmidt, "Attacks on Somalis are put down to jealousy and racism," Xaajo.com, 2006, http://www.xaajo.com/newsdetails.php?subaction=showfull&id=1157987638&archive=&start_from=&ucat=2&. For an overview of many of Schmidt's articles, see Alexander Reid

the concept to state and geopolitical levels, pointing to a "de facto racist strain within the ANC [African National Congress]," comparing the black-majority party's exploits to the "expansionist mission" of Nazi Germany, and elsewhere raising the specter of white genocide at the hands of black "génocidaires" threatening both whites and lighter-skinned blacks.[15] In other articles, he has expressed subtle sympathy for Afrikaner paramilitaries and fascists like the Afrikaner Weerstandsbeweging (AWB—Afrikaner Resistance Movement).[16]

Against this looming threat of white genocide or "Boer genocide," Schmidt publicly flirted with the notion of pan-secessionism—albeit with numerous caveats. In a newspaper article in support of pan-secessionism, for instance, Schmidt criticizes "extreme" secessionist tactics in some places—for instance, Somalia and the Balkans—while favoring movements in Western European countries like Scotland and Catalonia. He then turns his pen to South Africa, questioning whether a positive secessionist movement would be possible, or if it had already "died on the vine" due to the weakness of the Cape Party and the failure of the ultranationalist,

Ross, "I fact-checked Michael Schmidt's autobiography, and it's worse than we thought," Medium website, December 25, 2015, https://medium.com/@areidross/i-fact-checked-michael-schmidt-s-autobiography-and-it-s-worse-than-we-thought-9df765516095.

15 Michael Schmidt, "The Wallpaper War: the United States a decade after 9/11," Anarkismo, June 14, 2012, http://www.anarkismo.net/article/23123; Michael Schmidt, "Reappraising the Legacy of an Icon," Anarkismo website, December 10, 2013, http://www.anarkismo.net/article/26519; Michael Schmidt, "It's Not a Phobia, the Crime Is Genocide," The Star Early Edition, April 22, 2015, http://www.pressreader.com/south-africa/the-star-early-edition/20150422/282011850899291/TextView.

16 Michael Schmidt, "'Vigilante' farmers expose Zim refugees," Independent Online, August 5, 2007, http://sbeta.iol.co.za/news/south-africa/vigilante-farmers-expose-zim-refugees-364982; Michael Schmidt, "Farmer sells land to black neighbors," The Independent on Saturday, September 29, 2007, http://www.highbeam.com/doc/1G1-169285469.html; Michael Schmidt, "Death and the Mielieboer: The Eugène Terre'Blanche Murder & Poor-White Cannon-fodder in South Africa," Anarkismo website, April 18, 2010, http://www.anarkismo.net/article/16353.

Afrikaner radical right party Vryheidsfront Plus (VF+—Freedom
Front Plus) to remain true to its stated goals.[17]

In addition to his "legitimate" mainstream and anarchist publications, I discovered that Schmidt had an account on the white
nationalist online community, Stormfront, and a secret national-
anarchist and pan-secessionist blog called Black Battlefront, as well
as at least two additional Facebook accounts under other names.
These various personae voiced explicitly fascist versions of some
of Schmidt's more obliquely framed public positions. Collectively,
they advocated a pan-secessionist, national-anarchist strategy by
which white people would enter into a separatist party like the VF+
or the Cape Party in efforts to direct it to a national syndicalist state
with a tacitly white nationalist order.[18]

When coauthor Joshua Stephens and I exposed his duplicitous
dealings, Schmidt claimed that he used Stormfront as an undercover journalist to research white nationalists, which he said could be
confirmed by his former editor. I reached the editor, Brendan Seery,
but Schmidt's claim could not be corroborated. Instead, a horrified
Seery stated that he would never have given Schmidt permission for
such a research project, viewing it as unethical. "There's absolutely
no way I would have forgotten something like that," Seery insisted.
"I repeat: this was never discussed with me. It is not something I
would have forgotten. I would like to think I am known for my
ethical behavior as a journalist and I take ethics very seriously, as
anyone who has worked under me will testify. I would never forget
someone asking to put aside ethics in favour of a story."[19]

In reality, it was not incredibly shocking that Schmidt's alibi
failed, given his long list of questionable articles and his reputation

---

17   Michael Schmidt, "The two faces of global separatism," *Daily Maverick*,
      November 16, 2016, http://www.dailymaverick.co.za/article/2014-09-22
      -the-two-faces-of-global-separatism/#.WDALDEvQeRs.

18   For more details about Schmidt's various fascist personae, see Alexander
      Reid Ross and Joshua Stephens, "About Schmidt: How a White Nationalist
      Seduced Anarchists Around the World (Chapter 3), Medium website, Oc-
      tober 16, 2015, https://medium.com/@rossstephens/about-schmidt-how
      -a-white-nationalist-seduced-anarchists-around-the-world-chapter-3
      -7d288d84b170#.cjvp0vtdz.

19   Personal correspondence with Brendan Seery, November 30, 2015.

among the people I interviewed who had spent time in the South African anarchist scene. In one article that he sent to me during our extensive interview—which was reportedly rejected by Anarkismo, a website to which he regularly contributed—he quoted Julius Evola as a mere "conservative critic of fascism." Other individuals we interviewed also revealed that Schmidt had attempted to influence his comrades through online pseudonyms and front groups touting his ideas, encouraging them to consider the merits of national-anarchism.

We discovered that Schmidt also posted under a pseudonym (his family name, Le Sueur) on Keith Preston's forums. For his part, Preston positively featured "Le Sueur" in his book *Attack the System*, including Le Sueur's lengthy critique of antifascist author Matthew Lyons.[20] *Attack the System* also dedicates four pages to Schmidt's non-pseudonymous public writings, including three pages of solid block quotes.[21] At first, when confronted, Schmidt claimed that his false identities were in fact real people involved in a constellation of secretive intelligence agencies and private security companies with dangerous motives. Eventually, he admitted ownership of these false profiles and the front groups they had created.[22] Yet he did not admit what an overwhelming burden of evidence indicated: that he used those profiles to attempt to lure other anarchists toward white nationalism while also deploying his Stormfront account to encourage white nationalists to organize in South Africa.[23]

Despite these revelations, Schmidt continues to have supporters within left-wing groups, illustrating a dangerous tendency to put on sectarian blinders as fascism creeps into radical communities. More generally, Schmidt's success in radical milieus, until the exposure of his extracurricular activities, illustrated the susceptibility of the

20   Keith Preston, *Attack the System* (London: Black House Press, 2013), 243.

21   Ibid., 116–18, 124.

22   Feyd Saif'ulisaan, "Two swallows don't make a summer—Michael Schmidt's reply to AK Press allegations," Facebook, September 27, 2015, http://www.facebook.com/AKPress/posts/10156169461510249

23   See, for instance, Schmidt's post to Stormfront as KarelianBlue on May 22, 2010 in which he states, "I suggest that, [contrary to a mere boycott,] white nationalists flood the SA during the World Cup." See also Alexander Reid Ross, "I fact-checked Michael Schmidt's autobiography."

radical left to closet authoritarians who use radical analysis as a bully pulpit. Strains of nationalism went largely unchallenged among his early supporters. There was no outcry among his comrades when he produced articles denying the fascist underpinnings of national-anarchism and expressed sympathy over the death of South African fascist Eugene Terre'Blanche and "our white farmers" in general.[24] This is not due to a generally accepted fascism or authoritarianism underlying left-wing politics, but to the stealth with which fascists continue to adapt and cultivate ideological platforms parallel to and integrated with the left. Indeed, this practice is one of the basic aspects of fascism.

Enclaves in Cyberspace

While pan-secessionism and national-anarchism seek to appear as populist movements in which white nationalism plays only a decentralized and segregated role, in reality this exact form of neopopulism has been prominent in fascist movements since Benoist's work in the 1970s and '80s, and even further back to Carto's *Right*. It can include a number of facets, including but not limited to survivalist ideas and rhetoric of "white racial enclaves"; ethnocentric syndicalism or socialism; deep ecology critiques of modern social formations; and ultranationalist constructs of family and community. These qualities can coalesce in some unusual ways, creating strange hybrids like the fusion of contemporary technological futurism and reactionary politics known as the "neoreactionary" movement.

Building on reactionary elements of the early hacker movement, the growth of Usenet, and the Singularity Institute for Artificial Intelligence, the neoreaction consolidated around the ideas of a former continental philosophy professor named Nick Land. Deploying a macabre array of futurist, surrealist, and sadomasochistic ramblings, Land's writings spiral into a kind of alternate reality of bizarre post-structuralist, philosophical ravings and hierarchical theories about the Internet, gender, and race. Once a Marxist theorist with a relatively good reputation as an interesting, if edgy, writer, Land

---

24   Michael Schmidt, "South Asian Anarchism: Paths to Praxis," Anarkismo website, July 16, 2012, http://www.anarkismo.net/article/23404; Michael Schmidt, "Death and the Mielieboer."

was a fan of avant-garde figure Georges Bataille before experiencing a schizophrenic break and falling into a world of "dark enlightenment." Not unlike Ernst Jünger's "deeper Enlightenment," this reactionary movement sees humanity and civilization with a jaundiced eye, transforming dystopian horizons into a kind of paradise of sadism. Land's writing is filled with sexually violent imagery—which he considers ecstatic—and both a deep sense of decadence and a strong desire to transcend that decadence. His work is very similar to that of Limonov.

Although Land's "dark enlightenment" was influenced by the neoreaction, the movement's overlap with fascist strategies like pan-secessionism is broader. On October 2, 2013, the *New York Times* ran a story about a Stanford University lecturer named Balaji S. Srinivasan, who advocates "Silicon Valley's ultimate exit," which "basically means build an opt-in society, ultimately outside the United States, run by technology."[25] The opt-in society would include tax shelters, 3-D printed tools, and networks of start-ups producing things that the government cannot regulate. Perhaps unsurprisingly, Srinivasan is plugged into the neoreaction through the financing of PayPal founder Peter Thiel.

A Thiel Fellowship also went to a start-up company formed by neoreactionary Curtis Yarvin, whose writings also found a spot on Thiel's business partner's published list of recommended readings.[26] Yarvin calls himself Mencius Moldbug and is relatively influential in Silicon Valley's neoreactionary underbelly. Lashing out against democracy from a platform built upon the individualist works of Evola and Thomas Carlyle, Yarvin rejects the Declaration of Independence and advocates libertarian economics. He warns of a conspiratorial node of liberal media, academia, and government bureaucracy, which he believes acts as the modern day "Cathedral" to oppress the minds of everyday people. At a popular open-source version of TED talks called the BIL conference, Yarvin upgraded his generally monarchist ideas with a call to install a CEO of

---

25   Anand Giridharadas, "Silicon Valley Roused by Secession Call," *New York Times*, October 28, 2013, http://www.nytimes.com/2013/10/29/us/silicon-valley-roused-by-secession-call.html.

26   Patri Friedman, "Beyond Folk Activism," *Cato Unbound*, April 6, 2009, http://www.cato-unbound.org/2009/04/06/patri-friedman/beyond-folk-activism.

America.[27] His fans online draw comparisons between the neo-reactionaries and their classical heroes: "What exactly is the difference between a Moldbug and a Carlyle, a Land and an Evola?" writes a blogger on the now-defunct Banner of Cosmos website. "Are they not fulfilling similar roles? Are they not serving as our teachers?"[28] Thiel's Seasteading Institute, devoted to the prospects of an ocean-borne city-state, was set to host Yarvin at its 2009 conference, but the lecture was cancelled.[29] At around that time, Thiel wrote in a blog entry for the Cato Institute's libertarian website, Cato Unbound, "I no longer believe that freedom and democracy are compatible."[30]

The Machine Intelligence Research Institute, which receives funding from Thiel, had staff member Michael Anissimov turn to neoreaction. Anissimov tried to reconcile neorection with transhumanism, a broad ideology of self-enhacement. Accelerationism hopes to exacerbate not only economic and political crises but also perceived technological and biological ones, pushing society's contradictions forward and speeding up their consequences in order to bring about an inevitable collapse. The outcome of this, for transhumanists like Anissimov, will be a kind of superman, part-flesh, part-machine, who will be able to accomplish more in terms of production and reproduction than ever imagined in human history. This greatness will supposedly transcend the prior limitations of human experience, while layering sensation on sensation to develop an ecstatic mode of daily life over and against the unlucky masses mired in their suffering. The future, for transhumanist neoreactionaries, lies in a kind of nanowar that will overcome the

---

27   Mencius Moldbug, "BIL2012—Mencius Moldbug: How to Reboot the US Government," BILtalks, October 20, 2012, https://www.youtube.com/watch?v=ZluMysK2B1E.

28   "Sophomores and Sages," BannerofCosmos.wordpress.com, May 29, 2013. (This website has since been taken down.)

29   Klint Finley, "Geeks for Monarchy: The Rise of the Neoreactionaries," Techcrunch.com, November 22, 2013, https://techcrunch.com/2013/11/22/geeks-for-monarchy/.

30   Peter Thiel, "The Education of a Libertarian," *Cato Unbound*, April 13, 2009, http://www.cato-unbound.org/2009/04/13/peter-thiel/education-libertarian.

dilemmas of the nation-bound mass man by returning to monarchic forms of sovereignty.[31]

Of course, fascists never completely agree on anything. One hacker associated with Bitcoin, Andrew Alan Escher Auernheimer, who goes by the name "weev," is a white nationalist complete with a swastika tattoo. Gaining his bona fides from hacking AT&T, Auernheimer has criticized the neoreaction and particularly Anissimov for being gay. Auernheimer insists that neoreactionaries "lack the requisite brutality necessary to carry out purges" and that their condescending elitism cannot gain the attention of the working class, which is necessary for a real revolution. For Auernheimer, Anissimov represents this softness, attributable to his sexuality and demonstrated by an online breakdown in which Anissimov twitter-stalked a journalist. "It feels weird that my life is a piece of garbage that will be sacrificed to kill a couple of internet ppl who insulted me, but idgaf," he wrote to the female journalist. "I just want to cut someone's face and see blood running down it and their crying in the meanwhile, lol."[32] That Auernheimer depicts this sort of harassment as "soft" only exhibits the depths of depredation among the neoreactionaries.

Anissimov's violent rhetoric is not unknown among neoreactionaries—particularly when members floated the idea of establishing "Phalanxes" in cities around the country. "Phalanx is a reactionary fraternity for the cultivation of masculine virtue and the development of social, moral, and martial capital. If degeneracy is the cancer that's killing the West, Phalanx is regeneracy."[33] And, despite the bizarre call for violent neoreactionary cells, it is uncertain as to whether or not anything has come of the Phalanx

---

31   Michael Anissimov, "Reconciling Transhumanism and Neoreaction," MoreRight.net, May 13, 2013, http://www.moreright.net/reconciling -transhumanismand-neoreaction. This website has been taken down, yet the essay can be found at https://jbboehr.github.io/NeoreactionaryCanon .epub/NeoreactionaryCanon.pdf.

32   Andrew "weev" Auernheimer, "The Hilarious Meltdown of Mike Anissimov," Storify.com, December 2015, https://storify.com/weev/ the-meltdown-of-mikeanissimov.

33   Nyan Sandwich, "Introducing Phalanx," MoreRight.net, October 19, 2014, http://www.moreright.net/introducing-phalanx/. (This thread has been taken down.)

idea. Regardless, Auernheimer's critiques and Anissimov's melt-down have fed a split in which the neoreactionaries' increasing cruelty may reflect the transformation of the Bay Area itself, from a more-leftist center toward a hub for Silicon Valley's libertarian ethos, hipster irony, and egoism.

Some, like Justine Tunney of Occupy Wall Street, have advanced the disturbing profile of the neoreaction by shifting from left to right. Tunney claims to have been a "founder" of Occupy Wall Street and to have established its Twitter handle. After a public struggle in 2014, she took sole control of the Twitter account, ending the posting privileges of most of the activists who had been using it. Soon after, Tunney took a job with Google and fully turned against the leftism of social movements. In March 2014, she petitioned the White House to appoint Google CEO Eric Schmidt to the new post of "CEO of America," retire all government employees, and shift all administrative authority to the tech industry (three Moldbug plans that also have broad Libertarian support).[34] Establishing herself among Silicon Valley elites, Tunney instructed her 4,334 Twitter followers to "read Mencius Moldbug" on April 27, 2014. On July 25, she offered a question: "Ever since the French Revolution, the merchant caste (aka Wall Street) has ruled the West. Why not bring back the aristocracy? (aka Techies)." Just months later, on October 18, Tunney declared, "Neoreaction is basically a memetic adaptation of conservative thought, for blue-state culture," linking of course to Moldbug's website.[35]

Other members of the tech industry cozy up to neoreaction—if not by intention, then simply by dint of their wanton disregard for

---

34   Alex Hern, "Occupy Founder Calls on Obama to Appoint Eric Schmidt 'CEO of America,'" *Guardian*, March 20, 2014, https://www.theguardian .com/technology/2014/mar/20/occupy-founder-obama-eric-schmidt -ceo-america.

35   Justine Tunney's Twitter account, April 27, 2014, https://twitter.com/ justinetunney/status/460666429897834496; the July 25, 2014, post can be found in Sam Biddle, "Why Does Google Employ a Pro-Slav-ery Lunatic," Gawker.com, July 30, 2014, http://valleywag.gawker .com/why-does-google-employ-a-pro-slavery-lunatic-1612868507; and October 18, 2014, https://twitter.com/JustineTunney/status/ 523350663892172800.

others. When former chief technology officer of Business Insider Pax Dickinson was forced out for sexist tweets, the neoreaction embraced him. Venture capitalist Tim Draper hopes that the state of California will be broken into six separate states to rid Silicon Valley of its poorer neighboring regions. Airbnb, Uber, and other tech companies continue to flout wage and FCC rules, perpetuating the tech industry's presumed superiority over local companies and federal regulations.[36] Aside from the unanalyzed racism of the "Midas List" elites, there are also basic economic realities in Silicon Valley— for instance, a study from the American Institute for Economic Research revealed that Asian and Hispanic tech workers make thousands of dollars less in annual wages than white workers, and men make thousands more than women.[37] Yet these simple facts merely underscore the reality that the neoreactionary trend, while not an explicit ideology of Silicon Valley's tech industry, can be traced to its origins and to a process galvanized by the establishment of *Reason* and think tank strongholds like the Cato Institute in the 1970s, all started by the same people as the Tea Party movement.[38]

The Hipster Who Would Be King

The ethos of egoism and the vision of city-states run like corporations headed by monarch-CEOs that underwrite much of the

---

36   Sam Biddle, "Why Does Google Employ a Pro-Slavery Lunatic"; Arthur Chu, "Occupying the Throne: Justine Tunney, Neoreactionaries, and the New 1%," Daily Beast, August 1, 2014, http://www .thedailybeast.com/articles/2014/08/01/occupying-the-throne-justine -tunney-neoreactionaries-and-the-new-1-percent.html.

37   Katie Benner, "The Color of Money in Silicon Valley," Bloomberg.com, October 9, 2014, http://www.bloomberg.com/view/articles/2014-10-09/ the-color-of-money-in-silicon-valley; Samantha Allen, "We Need to Talk About Silicon Valley's Racism," Daily Beast, August 22, 2014, http:// www.thedailybeast.com/articles/2014/08/22/we-need-to-talk-about -silicon-valley-s-racism.html.

38   Mark Ames, "Homophobia, Racism and the Kochs: The Tech-Libertarian 'Reboot' Conference is a Cesspool," *Pando*, September, 18, 2014, https://pan- do.com/2014/07/18/homophobia-racism-and-the-kochs-san-franciscos -tech-libertarian-reboot-conference-is-a-cesspool/.

dark enlightenment and the neoreaction are tied to the spatial relationships of Silicon Valley and the nearby communities that the
tech industry displaces—particularly in the Bay Area. The pattern
of gentrification there is an extreme version of a national trend
that inflames racial tensions in the United States, although it also
appears across the Atlantic. Wealthier people adopt hip, edgier
fashion, moving into urban enclaves and transforming them into
higher-class artistic districts while displacing prior working-class
inhabitants. These groups of "hipsters" often adopt pro-environment
and protectionist localism.

Around 2012, a growing trend among hipsters in Germany was
observed, which has also appeared in the United States: hipsters
were seen wearing symbols and slogans playing with the repre-
sentations of fascism, bringing the aesthetic Third Positionism of
Death in June and other neofolk groups into the twenty-first century. These "Nipsters" (Nazi-hipsters) defy the traditional image of
conservatism, with its Christian focus, sexual repression, and roots
in industrial capitalism. Instead, they reference Evola's celebration
of spiritual exploration and Jünger's ideas of the boundless forest
of the self and the power of the Anarch. The Nipster version of
"returning to one's roots" is based on a rejection of consumerism
wedded to an updated and more upscale form of völkisch culture.
Like the Autonomous Nationalists, metro Nipsters are skilled at
manipulating signifiers—skinny jeans, plug piercings, and woods-
men beards—happily ensconced in milieus typically associated
with the alternative left, like veganism, café culture, and bicycle
co-ops.[39] It is a kind of "boutique fascism" that might remind one
of Drumont's movement of petite-bourgeoise shopkeepers and declassed intellectuals longing for a greater stake in the economy and
unwilling to abandon the privileges they enjoy for the sake of social
justice, despite their consumer-conscious support of local businesses
boasting organic goods from appropriate sources.

At the forefront of the new synthesis of fascist theory and style
is a white nationalist named Richard Spencer. As a young man,

---

39   Thomas Rogers, "Heil Hipster: The Young Neo-Nazis Trying to Put a Styl-
     ish Face on Hate," *Rolling Stone*, June 23, 2014, http://www.rollingstone
     .com/culture/news/heil-hipster-the-young-neo-nazis-trying-to-put-a
     -stylish-face-on-hate-20140623.

Spencer supported Pat Buchanan and Ross Perot before turning toward the left in graduate school and studying the Frankfurt School.
When his winding ideological path took him back to the right, it
was tinged with the left's criticisms of conventional conservatives.
After abandoning his PhD studies for "a life of thought-crime,"
Spencer found himself editing Buchanan's *American Conservative*, but left after his racist treatment of a rape scandal at Duke
University. He then joined the white-nationalist *Taki's Magazine*,
founded by *American Conservative* cofounder Panagiotis (Taki) The-
odoracopulos. His reputation grew as a popular speaker at the H.
L. Mencken Club of paleoconservatives and Rothbardians. Spencer
launched AlternativeRight.com as a kind of switchboard to connect
the radical-right positions of paleoconservatism and libertarianism
to white nationalism.[40] With the financial help of paleoconservatives at the more mainstream VDARE.com, the alt-right movement
has come to define and shape the linkages between traditionalism,
neoreaction, pan-secessionism, race realism, esoteric fascism, and
the mainstream radical right—despite Spencer's often divisive behavior.[41] Spencer has gone on to found the biannual *Radix Journal*
as a sounding board for alt-right ideology, trading in repackaged
eugenics theories to rid the world of degenerates and return to a
technologically upgraded version of a simpler age.[42]

One of his articles, "Up with Anarchy!," outlines a hypothetical
scenario where the Federal Reserve crashes, armies fail, and people
split into racial tribalism in which adulteresses and homosexuals
would be publicly stoned, "great swathes of land would be fenced

40 Devin Burghart, "White Nationalists Descend on D.C. for Nation-
    al Policy Institute Conference," Institute for Research & Educa-
    tion on Human Rights' website, October 23, 2013, http://www.irehr
    .org/2013/10/23/npi-conference-2013.
41 Antifascistfront, "Crack in the Facade: How Splits in the White National-
    ist Movement Can Help Anti-Fascists," *Anti-Fascist News* (blog), Febru-
    ary 6, 2016, https://antifascistnews.net/2016/02/06/crack-in-the-facade
    -how-splits-in-the-white-nationalist-movement-can-help-anti-fascists.
42 For examples, see Richard B. Spencer, "The Eugenics Taboo," *Radix Jour-
    nal*, January 11, 2014, http://www.radixjournal.com/journal/2014/1/11/
    the-eugenics-taboo; Spencer, "The E Word (Eugenics)," Ibid., April 2,
    2012, http://www.radixjournal.com/podcast/podcast/218.

off with barbed-wire," and "bands of thieves, vagrants, and thugs would roam the countryside and godforsaken inner cities, giving rise to a new Samurai class that, though guided by a code of honor, would apprehend and execute criminals without a pretense of a trial."[43] He calls this scenario "fascism without any of the fun qualities."[44]

Against the influential firebrands of Christian fundamentalism, Spencer believes that whites must get back in touch with nature in a way that will bring them out of nihilism and toward a renaissance.[45] The natural course of humanity is to move toward self-segregation, he believes, for humanism, multiculturalism, and liberalism oppressively force different people together, creating the decadent modern world. The answer would be to create "organic states" that learn from anarchism's rejection of both Christianity and the modern, globalist nation-state while embracing "natural hierarchies."[46] Despite his fascist ideology, Spencer tends to shy away from biological racism in his speeches and podcasts, focusing more on white identitarianism, consciousness, culture, and aesthetics to make his points.

From the H. L. Mencken Club and *American Conservative*, Spencer became involved in the National Policy Institute (NPI), which was founded by the neo-Gramscian, paleoconservative Sam Francis as a means to evolve the conservative movement and achieve

---

43   Richard Spencer, "Up with Anarchy!," Ibid., April 9, 2010, http://www .radixjournal.com/altright-archive/altright-archive/main/blogs/untimely -observations/up-with-anarchy.

44   Keith Preston, interview with Richard Spencer, "Anarchy in the USA," *Vanguard Radio* (podcast), April 21, 2014, 9:00–10:00, http://www .radixjournal.com/podcast/2014/4/21/anarchy-in-the-usa?rq=keith %20preston. For more on the Christian Reconstructionist program of Rousas John Rushdoony and his son-in-law Gary North, See Max Blumenthal, *Republican Gomorrah: Inside the Movement that Shattered the Party* (New York: Nation Books, 2010), 20–21.

45   Interview with Richard Spencer, "Richard Spencer—Cuckservatives, Social Justice Warriors & the White Problem," Radio 3Fourteen, Red Ice radio network, August 15, 2015, available at http://www.radixjournal .com/blog/2015/8/1/richard-spencer-on-red-ice-radio.

46   Spencer and Preston, "Anarchy in the USA," 15:00–21:00.

a "conservative revolution" from above.[47] Under Spencer's leadership, the NPI has become a place for volatile and sometimes combative meetings between conventional radical right groups, like the Council of Conservative Citizens, and other more fascist trends. Keith Preston, Jack Donovan, and Paul Ramsey mingle with American Freedom Party cofounder Kevin MacDonald and ex-hippie Tomislav Sunic at the NPI's popular annual conference, held on the pagan holiday of Samhain and funded by Regnery.[48] The American Freedom Party's goal of creating a Haiderized radical-right party to contain the various interests and egos of the white nationalist movement has so far been fringe at best. Nevertheless, their very presence has been so toxic that, when Spencer and Sunić journeyed to Hungary to lecture at a NPI conference for European white nationalists, the Hungarian authorities (who are by no means leftists) banned the event and arrested and deported Spencer.[49] While Spencer has also been banned from the United Kingdom, it is more difficult to dismiss his *Radix Journal* podcasts, which can garner tens of thousands of full listens depending on the episode. The streams flowing from Spencer's podcasts and neoreaction blogs saturate related milieus like video game culture and men's rights activists (MRAs), turning cultural alienation into fertile ground for white supremacy.

Men's Rights

The extreme misogyny and sadism of neoreactionism is reflected in a variety of modern men's rights groups that, besides being hate

47   Devin Burghart, "White Nationalists Descend on D.C. for National Policy Institute Conference," Institute for Research & Education on Human Rights' website, October 23, 2013, http://www.irehr.org/2013/10/23/npi-conference-2013.

48   Antifascistfront, "Anti-Fascist Action: Challenging the National Policy Institute's 2015 Conference," *Anti-Fascist News* (blog), October 19, 2015, https://antifascistnews.net/2015/10/19/anti-facist-action-challenging-the-national-policy-institutes-2015-conference.

49   Hatewatch Staff, "White Nationalists Gather in Hungary, Richard Spencer Arrested," Southern Poverty Law Center's website, October 6, 2014, https://www.splcenter.org/hatewatch/2014/10/06/white-nationalists-gather-hungary-richard-spencer-arrested.

groups themselves, have numerous connections to Holocaust de-niers and other hate groups.[50] There is significant overlap between MRAs and neoreactionaries, since most MRAs live largely reclu-sive, technology-oriented lives, as became clear during the hor-rifying "GamerGate" scandal in which male video game fanatics threatened game women developers with rape and murder.

GamerGate began as a reaction to false—though typical of in-secure males—accusations that developer Zoë Quinn had dated a journalist to gain good reviews for her game. It quickly grew to en-compass allegations against fellow developer Brianna Wu and crit-ic Anita Sarkeesian, who simply had the nerve to speak out against the depiction of women in computer games. The online attacks turned to death threats, including a threat of a mass shooting at a Sarkeesian speaking event. Predictably, the radical right smelled blood, and white nationalist and men's rights ideology began to build up within the wild, psychotic flow of GamerGate. Even on-line forums notorious for their refusal of censorship, like Reddit and 4chan, began to restrict comments and users. As people began to stalk the women involved in real life, GamerGate traveled onto an even more explicit site called 8Chan, an area of the web cre-ated by a white supremacist named Frederick Brennan, who once penned an article advocating eugenics for the neo-Nazi site the Daily Stormer. On 8Chan, where child pornography used to be traded along with stolen credit card and social security numbers, and where mercenaries could be hired to dox accounts, GamerGate found its natural habitat.[51]

---

50   David Futrelle, "The Author of A Voice for Men's Martial Rape Ap-ologia is a Holocaust Denier and Hitler Fan. No, Really," *We Hunted the Mammoth* (blog), May 7, 2015, http://www.wehuntedthemammoth .com/2015/05/07/the-author-of-a-voice-for-mens-marital-rape -apologia-is-a-holocaust-denier-and-hitler-fan-no-really; Men's rights activists also have strong representation on AttacktheSystem.com, with Preston plainly mouthing the movement's respectable rhetoric: "In an institutional context, men have more disadvantages than women." See Preston, Radio Wehrwolf, 58:40–58:47.

51   Chrisella Herzog, "When the Internet Breeds Hate," *Diplomatic Courier*, March 8, 2015, http://www.diplomaticcourier.com/2015/03/08/when-the -internet-breeds-hate/.

Men's rights groups agree that modern masculinity has failed to produce self-fulfilling communities, and they see a future day of violence and brutality on the horizon unless society changes to suit their desires. Men must assert themselves one way or another to force women to recognize their subservient place in the world, they claim. Blogger David Futrelle explains, "Like doomsday preppers with well-stocked bunkers and enough ammo to kill every living thing within a 500 mile radius, they can't wait for the end of the world."[52] One MRA named Peter Nolan gave voice to the belief that the West is facing "a lawful state of war" against men in which "killing women is the only path to justice."[53] Perhaps unsurprisingly, Nolan is also a sovereign citizen who praised Anders Breivik and threatened to murder women who would mock his Facebook spin-off, known as ManBook.[54]

Nolan's behavior is not unique among MRAs who lash out against women on innumerable online Facebook groups, websites, and forums, bragging about their exploits and complaining about disrespectful behavior from women and nonwhites. At root is a deep-seated sense of entitlement to a superior place in society (and, indeed, the world) based on their sex and gender—and a sense that whites and men are oppressed by the expression of nonwhite and female identity and power. MRAs have reacted to this frustration with extreme violence, shooting and killing strangers as well as acquaintances thought to have committed a slight or to have wronged the man in question.

Before attempting to rape his ex-girlfriend after stabbing her repeatedly and beating her nearly to death, mixed martial arts fighter War Machine declared, "The oppression of MEN is worse than oppression of Jews in Nazi Germany, worse than the slavery of Blacks in early America."[55] In preparation for opening fire on a

---

52   David Futrelle, "MRA Peter Nolan: 'Killing Women Is the Only Path
      to Justice for Men Now,'" *We Hunted the Mammoth* (blog), July 6, 2015,
      http://www.wehuntedthemammoth.com/2015/07/06/mra-peter-nolan
      -killing-women-is-the-only-path-to-justice-for-men-now.

53   Ibid.

54   Ibid.

55   Aaron Sankin, "Inside the Men's Rights Movement," *The Week*, June 7, 2015,
      http://theweek.com/articles/538670/inside-mens-rights-movement.

group of people from his BMW, killing seven, mass shooter Elliot Rodger proclaimed on his YouTube account, "You will finally
see that I am in truth the superior one. The true Alpha Male."[56]
In Oregon the next year, mass shooter Chris Harper-Mercer
maintained a 4chan account from which he cautioned students at
Umpqua Community College before killing ten the next day. He
complained about being a "beta."[57] When a mall security guard
shot and killed a woman for reporting his sexual harassment,
MRAs jumped to his defense on the Internet. And when Dylann
Roof shot nine churchgoers in a black church in Charleston,
South Carolina, declaring, "You rape our women and you're taking over our country," MRA leader Dean Esmay, of the Internet
site A Voice for Men, blamed "lies about our 'rape culture,'" not
racism and misogyny.[58]

The strong presence of MRAs online is not a coincidence,
as the pathology of online rage reproduces an antisocial profile
that feeds back into itself. MRAs have also launched concerted
efforts within the science fiction community to sway the votes in
the prestigious annual Hugo Awards toward "apolitical" or right-
wing literature. In one article, the *Anarcho-Geek Review* noted
that the conservative protest was framed as an antiauthoritarian
struggle against the oppressive power of diversity forced on the
sci-fi world by "social justice warriors."[59] This voting bloc of
frustrated white reactionaries split into two factions—the Sad

56   Caitlin Dewey, "Inside the 'Manosphere' that Inspired Santa Barbara
     Shooter Elliot Rodger," *Washington Post*, May 27, 2014, https://www
     .washingtonpost.com/news/the-intersect/wp/2014/05/27/inside-the
     -manosphere-that-inspired-santa-barbara-shooter-elliot-rodger/.

57   Akira Watts, "Did Men's Rights Activist Movement Play Role in Oregon
     Shooting?," *Reverb Press*, October 2, 2015, http://reverbpress.com/news/
     us/mens-rights-activist-movement-play-role-oregon-shooting.

58   "Prominent MRA Tries to Blame Charleston Shooting on Fem-
     inism and its Alleged 'Lies About Rape Culture,'" *We Hunted the
     Mammoth* (blog), June 18, 2015, http://www.wehuntedthemammoth
     .com/2015/06/18/prominent-mra-tries-to-blame-charleston-shooting
     -on-feminism-and-its-alleged-lies-about-rape-culture.

59   D. Markotin, "Hugo Scandal 2015," *Anarcho-Geek Review*, April 10,
     2015, http://www.anarchogeekreview.com/opinion/hugo-scandal-2015.

Puppies and the Rabid Puppies. The latter faction found its leader in sci-fi writer Theodore Beale (also called Vox Day). A Christian dominionist, Beale has urged Christian leaders to "start learning from #GamerGate" in order to destroy non-Christian elements in the United States. "Now it's just a raw power struggle and we have the numbers, we have the indomitable will of the martyrs, and we have the certain knowledge of God on our side," he declared.[60] Beale's open statements against women's suffrage and favorable commentary on the practice of disfiguring unfaithful wives with acid are matched by attacks on nonwhites as "not equally homo sapiens sapiens" and homosexuality as "a birth defect."[61] Perhaps unsurprisingly, Beale also identifies as a neoreactionary.[62] Beale's Puppies lost after voters turned out in huge numbers to oppose their hate, but they still comprised an estimated one-fifth of the ballots cast. By running their campaign, the Puppies managed to bump would-be finalists like Amal El-Mohtar and Ursula Vernon. Writing for NPR, Tasha Robinson noted that they "turned the 2015 Hugos into an openly cynical referendum not about which works were best, but about whose politics and tactics were the best."[63] The next year, they lost again in a fashion that suggested their increased isolation from the majority of the sci-fi community. The struggle against the fascist creep seemed to be working.

---

60   David Futrelle, "Vox Day: Christians Need to Follow the Lead of #Gamer-Gate and the Spanish Inquisition to Defeat Seculars, Satan," *We Hunted the Mammoth* (blog), April 4, 2015, http://www.wehuntedthemammoth .com/2015/04/04/vox-day-christians-need-to-follow-the-lead-of -gamergate-and-the-spanish-inquisition-to-defeat-seculars-satan.

61   Phil Sandifer, "Guided by the Beauty of their Weapons: An Analysis of Theodore Beale and his Supporters," EruditorumPress.com, April 2015, http://www.eruditorumpress.com/blog/guided-by-the-beauty-of-their -weapons-an-analysis-of-theodore-beale-and-his-supporters/.

62   Vox Day (Beale), "Neoreactionary space," *Vox Populi* (blog), April 27, 2013, https://voxday.blogspot.com.ar/2013/04/neoreactionary-space_27.html.

63   Tasha Robinson, "How the Sad Puppies Won—By Losing," NPR.org, August 26, 2015, http://www.npr.org/2015/08/26/434644645/how-the -sad-puppies-won-by-losing.

Red Pillers

MRAs and neoreactionaries who favor accelerating the contradictions of capitalism in a tech-fueled Mad Max-style drive off a cliff
call themselves "red pillers," deriving their name from the scene in
The Matrix where Morpheus offers Neo the red pill that will awak-
en him to the reality that lies behind the ideological illusions of
contemporary society. Red pillers haunt websites like Zero Hedge,
which offers some financial analysis mixed with libertarianism,
left-wing ideology, and conspiracy theories. Red pillers also gravi-
tate toward "anarcho-capitalists" like Christopher Cantwell, whose
participation in the antipolice site CopBlock was cut short when he
insisted that all law enforcement officers should be shot on sight.
Despite his radical antistate, antipolice rhetoric, Cantwell gradually
developed a disdain for "social justice warriors" and drifted toward
"race realist" notions of white identitarianism and inequality, ending with support for Donald Trump.[64] His podcasts and appearances on white nationalist, crossover talk shows like Red Ice Radio
garner thousands of listens and feature the standard plenitude of
alt-right, MRA, and fascist figures and memes.

   With its reactionary motifs tailored to a self-identified
avant-garde, the neoreactionary return to counterrevolutionary
forms of social organizing, anti-egalitarian ideas of "human biodiversity" (HBD) and, of course, misogyny bear the essential traits of
the Nouvelle Droite. Those who listen to Land's ravings see them
as a kind of cyberpunk futurism with striking similarities to Guillaume Faye's archeofuturism. They endorse an active nihilism that
could bring about a brave new technological world. Neoreactionaries state that races and genders are unequally based on genetic
differences observable in IQ test results, and they extoll ideas of
HBD, which asserts that particular racial traits like intelligence or
speed are inherent to the genetic evolution of humans in accordance
with their particular environmental surrounds. It follows that the
migration of people from native habitats displaces traditional values
and blends together ancestral qualities that are better maintained in

---

64   Christopher Cantwell, "Radical Agenda EP094—The Libertarian Case
      for Trump," YouTube, January 24, 2016, https://www.youtube.com/
      watch?v=W3SQqgaJ7fg.

place. That HBD theory comes from Steve Sailer—a white nationalist columnist with a penchant for secessionism and no training in biology or genetics—does not seem to dissuade neoreactionaries from the notion that they sit at the apogee of science and human achievement. In fact, HBD mashes together different ideas on eugenics in order to explain the biological crafting of humanity in a manner that agrees with fascist ideology and that reinforces their own idea of themselves as "great men."[65]

Among the more influential neoreactionary commentators, video blogger Paul "RamZPaul" Ramsey boasts a nerdy bravado that strikes a chord with the sense of downtrodden pride of "Aryans" over the Internet and at American Renaissance conferences. His influence on the larger neoreactionary scene stems from an emerging technological savvy that matches podcasts and video blogs with an often demented humor that has extended its audience beyond white nationalism while still informing more rigorously defined fascist groups. One such disturbing podcast calls itself *The Daily Shoah*, a sort of white supremacist version of alternative media based on Comedy Central's *The Daily Show*. *The Daily Shoah* is hosted by a website called The Right Stuff, which anonymous sources tell me is web-mastered by none other than Auernheimer, who now considers himself "post-neoreactionary." Hosts Seventh Son and Mike Enoch use racial slurs, both traditional and new, when referring to other ethnicities or nationalities, like the term "dindus" applied to black people. Although they are certainly fascists, *The Daily Shoah* has significant cultural influence through social media, as was displayed when the term "cuckservative," a play on "cuckold" and "conservative" that they worked hard to promote as an attack on moderate Republicans, began "trending" in social media.[66]

---

65   Steve Sailer, "Yeah, Yeah, Diversity Is Strength. It's Also Secession," VDARE.com, May 31, 2002, https://www.vdare.com/articles/yeah-yeah -diversity-is-strength-its-also-secession; for an interesting discussion on this modern form of eugenics and its coding, see Shane Burley, "Fascism Against Time: Nationalism, Media Blindness, and the Cult of Augustus Sol Invictus," Gods and Radicals, a Site of Beautiful Resistance, March 24, 2016, https://godsandradicals.org/2016/03/24/fascism-against-time -nationalism-media-blindness-and-the-cult-of-augustus-sol-invictus/.

66   Antifascistfront, "#Cuckservative: How the 'Alt Right' Took off their Masks

Like many neoreactionaries, Ramsey's philosophy tends to converge with the New Atheists led by Sam Harris, who insists that free
will does not exist. If humanity functions almost like a "quantum
computer," in Harris's view, it makes choices only out of biochemical
response systems rather than self-determination.[67] Harris and other New Atheists like Bill Maher and Richard Dawkins have drawn
significant criticism for their disdain for Muslims, coming to a head
when one of their supporters murdered three Muslims out of pure
hatred for their religion.[68] Maher, Harris, and Dawkins have also
drawn public ire for sexist behavior, a criticism they tend to glibly di-
minish as "politically correct."[69] Maher's own former television show,
Politically Incorrect, and his current show, *Real Time*, have played on
this populist trope to promote his quasi-libertarian "neither left nor

and Revealed their White Hoods," *Anti-Fascist News* (blog), August 16,
2015, https://antifascistnews.net/2015/08/16/cuckservative-how-the-alt
-right-took-off-their-masks-and-revealed-their-white-hoods.

67   Sam Harris, *Free Will* (New York: Free Press, 2012), 29–30.

68   Nathan Lean, "Dawkins, Harris, Hitchens: New Atheists flirt with Islamophobia," Salon, March 30, 2013, http://www.salon.com/2013/03/30/
dawkins_harris_hitchens_new_atheists_flirt_with_islamophobia; Michelle Boorstein, "Chapel Hill Killings Shine Light on Particular Tensions Between Islam and Atheism," *Washington Post*, February 11, 2015,
https://www.washingtonpost.com/news/local/wp/2015/02/11/chapel
-hill-killings-shine-light-on-particular-tensions-between-islam-and
-atheism; Elizabeth Bruenig, "The Chapel Hill Murders Should Be a
Wake-Up Call for Atheists," *New Republic*, February 11, 2015, https://
newrepublic.com/article/121036/chapel-hill-muslim-murders-show
-atheism-has-violent-extremists-too.

69   Katha Pollitt, "Atheists Show Their Sexist Side," *Nation*, September 24,
2014, https://www.thenation.com/article/atheists-show-their-sexist
-side; Marcie Bianco, "Brazen Sexism Is Pushing People Out of
America's Atheism Movement," Quartz, February 12, 2016, http://
qz.com/613270/brazen-sexism-is-pushing-women-out-of-americas
-atheism-movement; Amanda Marcotte, "Atheism's Shocking Woman Problem: What's Behind the Misogyny of Richard Dawkins and
Sam Harris?," AlterNet, October 3, 2014, http://www.salon.com/
2014/10/03/new_atheisms_troubling_misogyny_the_pompous_sexism
_of_richard_dawkins_and_sam_harris_partner/.

right" attitude.[70] Islamophobia, sexism, and a sort of biological deter-
minism serve as important points for neoreactionaries like Ramsey,
whose belief in organic hierarchies and natural order constitute an
anti-Enlightenment rejection of liberty—something that distorts the
blunt biological reasons for success, failure, and class.

Just as trends started by *The Daily Shoah* have gone on to common use in the Twittersphere among libertarians and the mainstream radical right, trends started by New Atheists wend their
way through the culture. In 2012, the British New Atheist Maajid
Nawaz coined a term called "Regressive Left" to describe what he
considered a form of cultural relativism that prevented liberals from
condemning nonwhites and Muslims. The term found its way to a
Real Time discussion between Maher and Dawkins in October of
that year, and it was tweeted out by Dawkins in December—the
same month that it garnered significant play in a book by Nawaz
and Harris called *Islam and the Future of Tolerance*. Since then, #Re-
gressiveleft has been promoted by prominent MRA Sargon of Ak-
kad and other popular bloggers of the alt-right who follow New
Atheists closely. Writing for *BuzzFeed*, Joseph Bernstein observed
that the meme's lifespan "reveals the wiring by which the kind of
cable news-appropriate Western values-traditionalism practiced by
Bill Maher and Sam Harris can flow through the substations of the
alt-right internet—Twitter, Reddit, YouTube, 4chan—to emerge
overnight as a power source for cutting-edge internet rhetorical
warfare. In other words, it's a sign that the sentiments behind the
alt-right may not be as far out of the American mainstream as some
of us would like to think."[71]

Collective Violence and Disenfranchisement IRL

That these clusters of alt-right antagonism and provocation extend
beyond the small circles of Internet podcasts and blogs was revealed
on the evening of November 23, 2015, when excitable keyboard

70   Dann Halem, "Is Bill Maher a Libertarian?," Salon, August 1, 2001,
      http://www.salon.com/2001/08/01/maher_4/.

71   Joseph Bernstein, "The Rise of the #RegressiveLeft Hashtag," *BuzzFeed*,
      March 15, 2016, https://www.buzzfeed.com/josephbernstein/the-rise-of
      -the-regressiveleft-hashtag.

fascists who frequented racist forums on 4chan and promoted racism on YouTube gunned down five Black Lives Matter protesters keeping a peaceful vigil in Minneapolis. It is significant that, in their private lives as well as on 4chan, the shooters used slurs like "dindus," popular among fans of *The Daily Shoah*, and while fleeing the crime, they yelled "Race War" and "Trump 2016."[72] Like GamerGate and the Phalanx, the event exposed the way that the credible difference between Live Action Role Playing, trolling, and real-life behavior is relative and often nonexistent. At the same time the interface of screen and social media tends to reenforce the sense of alienation whereby harm cannot be measured or understood. Self-victimization and egoist notions of will replace embodied individuals with real needs.

This sort of dehumanization is a critical aspect of the ongoing and one-sided social war against women, sexual diversity, and nonwhites. At the basis of the politics of hate is an underlying anxiety, a fear that privileges are being lost and that personal safety is in danger. A belief that the world is ending and that some out-group is causing the cataclysm is joined by the desire to deepen the crisis in order to get things over with and come out on top in the "new age" that follows. This meeting of neoreaction and traditional white nationalism is perhaps the most dangerous convergence that looms on the horizon. It combines a number of divergent trends in a dynamic and flexible ideological sphere that encourages anti-left, misogynist, and racist violence, and maintains a powerful network of adherents, from Silicon Valley billionaires to the hipster fascists riding the coat tails of Spencer's National Policy Institute. Yet these clusters must have a seedbed to take root, and that soil is being prepared by a creeping sense of despair and hopelessness.

The alarming convergence of misogyny, racism, pan-secessionism, and tech is, as I have been trying to indicate, a possibly "organic" confluence of alienated people tethered to a fictional world

---

72   According to reports at the time, the gunmen left the scene in a truck yelling "RAHOWA," or "Racial Holy War." Tom Cleary, "Shooting at Protests in Minneapolis: 5 Fast Facts you Need to Know," Heavy.com, November 24, 2015, http://heavy.com/news/2015/11/minneapolis-jamar-clark-4th-police-precinct-protests-shooting-shots-fired-white-supremacists-victims-suspects-injuries-photos-video-black-lives-matter.

removed from real consequences and human interaction. People like Spencer and Preston tend to identify a Nietzschean discourse of nihilism as the reason, claiming that the world is in a stage of decline and only active nihilism can lead to a rebirth. What Preston identifies as his "anarchism" (hardly worthy of the word) returns to the Stirnerist concept of the ego, which is then transported through Nietzsche into an elitist construct drawing from social Darwinist tropes in which the strong excel and the weak fall into a kind of "slave morality."[73] Although he agrees with members of the left that nonwhite identitarianism can empower marginalized groups to overcome de facto white male privilege in society, Preston insists that part of the "slave morality" appears in the refusal to acknowledge a white identity among identitarian platforms.[74]

Preston's condemnation of an antiracist platform as prejudiced against whites is reminiscent of Benoist's similar critiques and can be found elsewhere among radical groups. Preston sees the backlash against nonwhite identitarianism as a cause of the rise in white identity politics, which he views as auspicious for his own kind of organizing.[75] Indeed, white identitarians see struggles for black liberation as incitements to further entrench their appeal to "pro-white"

---

73   A sampling of Keith Preston's views on the "slave morality" of modern life and anarchists can be found at a number of sites. See Keith Preston, "Marginalia: On radical thinking Keith Preston on Balkanization and the State of Exception," *Attack the System* (blog), March 13, 2012, https://attackthesystem.com/2012/03/13/marginalia-on-radical-thinking-keith-preston-on-balkanization-and-the-state-of-exception; also see "Politically Correct Universities and Slave Morality," Ibid., September 18, 2010, https://attackthesystem.com/2010/09/18/politically-correct-universities-and-slave-morality; "The Pressure Project #133: Attack the System! A Talk with Pan-Anarchist Keith Preston," *The Pressure Project* (podcast), May 6, 2016, https://www.youtube.com/watch?v=iKIzhZ0AI_k; Legionscatz, "The Slave Morality of Social Justice—Part One," *Attack the System* (blog), February 24, 2013, https://attackthesystem.com/2013/02/24/the-slave-morality-of-social-justice-part-one/.

74   For a leftist defense of black identity, for instance, see Chris Crass, *Towards Collective Liberation* (Oakland: PM Press, 2013). For Preston's spin, see Radio Wehrwolf, 55:00–56:00.

75   Ibid., 1:03:00–1:10:06.

attitudes in counter-universalist claims (for instance, #AllLives-Matter or assertions of "free speech" against hate speech laws). The fascist attempt to seize the narrative of antiracist movements and direct it toward white identitarianism (e.g., "Black Lives Matter is racist against whites!") is meant to increase popular disillusionment with antiracist movements in general.[76] The frustration of the left over an apparent impasse regarding "identity politics," including attacks on "political correctness" and the inability to stop austerity when socialists are in power, increases pessimism and anxiety, leading to an observable trend toward nihilism both in mainstream society and counterculture. The sense that the struggle against racism is failing, along with the women's and other oppressed movements, is matched by a feeling that it is those movements themselves that are responsible, rather than external forces. This is a feeling the right clearly endorses, attempting to offer another way through a sense of authenticity and loyalty to one's folk.

"The New Nihilism"

If Stirner can influence both the left and rightists like Barrès, Mussolini, and Jünger, it is not surprising that sometimes "post-left" anarchist theorists—who harbor deep suspicions about easy left pieties and how alleged radicals become little more than capitalism's loyal opposition—can wind up drawing from both left and right sources. One of the foremost writers of the post-left, Hakim Bey (Peter Lamborn Wilson), for instance, distorts the history of the irredentist protofascist state of Fiume to present it as a kind of utopian haven for desperados and freethinkers.[77] This historical revision of a totalitarian, imperial regime avoids the underlying intent of reclaiming disputed parts of Croatia for Italy, which, as we saw in Chapter 1, even the Italian government rejected as imperialist.[78] D'Annunzio's

---

76   This paradigm is used by alt-right activists like libertarian Christopher Cantwell. Libertarian Realist, "Uncucking with Cantwell," YouTube, November 22, 2015, 5:00–9:00, https://www.youtube.com/watch?v=DsVCDdD3xmI.

77   Hakim Bey, "The Temporary Autonomous Zone," chap. 25 in *Crypto Anarchy, Cyberstates, and Pirate Utopias*, ed. Peter Ludlow (Cambridge, MA: MIT Press, 2001), 426.

78   See Barbara Spackman, "D'Annunzio and the Antidemocratic Fantasy,"

Charter of Carnaro was written by the national syndicalist Alceste De Ambris, and it would go on to influence Mussolini's government.[79] After returning from his adventures, D'Annunzio endorsed the National Fascist Party. That the early phase of fascism included everyone from anarchists to occultists does less to provide a backdrop of romance to the imperial state of Fiume than it does to expose the deep-seated contradictions from within the left and, apparently, post-left.[80]

Writing about the societal shift toward nihilism in a more sobering tone, Wilson expresses concern over the fact that, given their ideological similarities, "it seems impossible to distinguish here between the action of post-leftist anarcho-nihilists and the action of post-rightist neo-traditionalist reactionaries." They seem instead to be both responses, or perhaps iterations, of an existential and material disenfranchisement. He continues, "The post-left can now appreciate Traditionalism as a reaction against modernity just as the neo-traditionalists can appreciate Situationism. But this doesn't mean that post-anarchist anarchists are identical with post-fascist fascists!" Noting the partially complimentary relationship, Wilson draws a direct comparison to "the situation in *fin-de-siècle* France that gave rise to the strange alliance between anarchists and monarchists; for example, the *Cerce* [sic] *Proudhon*." While not rejecting such an alliance, Wilson declares, "Of course, as we know, the problem with the Traditionalists is that they were never traditional enough… they should have realized that the *real* tradition is the 'primordial anarchy' of the Stone Age, tribalism, hunting/gathering, animism—what I call the Neanderthal Liberation Front." Although he calls the Nouvelle Droite "evil," Wilson notes his affinity with certain Nouvelle Droite positions, identifying his own form of anarchism with a tongue-in-cheek "Paleolithic reaction."[81]

chap. 4 in *Fascist Virilities: Rhetoric, Ideology, and Social Fantasy in Italy* (Minneapolis: University of Minnesota Press, 1996), 77–100; Nunzio Pernicone, *Carlo Tresca: Portrait of a Rebel* (Oakland: AK Press, 2010), 256.

79   Sternhell, *The Birth of Fascist Ideology*, 187–88.

80   See also Payne, *A History of Fascism*, 92; Roger Griffin, *Modernism and Fascism* (New York: Palgrave MacMillan, 2007), 213–14; Griffin, *The Nature of Fascism*, 68.

81   Peter Lamborn Wilson, "The New Nihilism," *Anvil Review* 5 (2014):

Post-left nihilism and primitivist yearnings present an intellectual movement both reactionary and against "the system" in ways that can crossover with fascism—particularly through the Nietzschean narratives of the master morality and the active nihilism of the superman, both of which entail the denunciation of humanism and democracy and the rejection of equality. This is not necessarily to single out such anarchist subcultures: as we have seen, there are no subcultural or countercultural movements that do not feel the encroachment of fascism, from black metal and Asatru to skinheads and antiglobalization activist movements. To resist fascism and reclaim ideological territory, movements must sharply define and defend boundaries against racism, misogyny, and other forms of oppression. Still, when someone on the open-source Anarchy101.org website raised the question "Is there a connection between nihilist, post-left anarchy or antipolitics and reactionary or fascist politics?," the two answers that came back were vague and facile ("all ideas are interconnected in some way or another").[82]

Blood and Soil, CTD

In a certain sense, post-left nihilism simply bears resemblances to fascism, as Wilson points out. However, when it, or any other anarchist or leftist position, begins to fetishize a mythical core of an ethnic, racial, national, or "tribal" group, we're entering dangerous territory. This convergence is particularly palpable regarding many ecological claims, which can easily begin to echo fascist values of blood and soil. Perforce, the post-left often melds with a reactionary "deep green" ideology that hopes to bring about the collapse of civilization, recognizing that millions will have to die in the process, in order to save the world. Here, the left's deconstruction of nationalism as a homogenizing and multicultural narrative, through which "equality" is seen as little more than equal-opportunity oppression,

25–26, available at https://theanarchistlibrary.org/library/peter-lamborn-wilson-the-new-nihilism.

82   "Anarchy101 Q&A," Anarchy101.org, August 5, 2016, http://anarchy101.org/7877/connection-nihilist-politics-reactionary-fascist-politics?show=7877#q7877.

can creep toward a discourse of ultranationalist "authenticity" by honoring the paganism of Europe's past or learning about ancestral survival techniques in preparation for the coming collapse.

These attacks on multiculturalism, liberalism, and modernity, joined to the quest for the authentic, can land in highly reactionary places. Evoking a time-honored ultranationalist turn of phrase, "deep green" ideologue and former neoconservative Derrick Jensen states, "That's how you get to own land—by living there and entering into that predator-prey relationship for generation after generation, and having your blood mix with the soil and the soil mix with your blood."[83] This sense of ownership returns more to the authenticity discourse of nineteenth-century völkisch ultranationalism—e.g., *la terre et les morts* and *Blut und Boden*—than to existing indigenous notions of the human relationship to land.

In Jensen's work, this sense of ownership also lends itself to deeply opportunistic efforts to exploit nativism—for instance, in an interview where he declares, "I'm all for closing the border to Mexico (and everywhere else, for that matter, all the way down to closing bioregional borders), so long as we close it not only to people but to resources as well."[84] With this sort of walled-off bioregionalism in mind, Jensen's eco-radical group Deep Green Resistance (DGR), formed with Lierre Keith, makes explicit its belief in the decadence of both consumerism and the left, asserting the need to expedite the collapse of civilization desperately required to reconnect humanity to earth.[85]

Given its authenticity discourse, it is not surprising that DGR is supported by McNallen's Asatru Folk Assembly, which sees DGR's call to action as compatible to, if different from, their own call to

---

83   Derrick Jensen, "Delusions," track 2, CD 2, in *Now This War Has Two Sides*, spoken word record (Oakland: PM Press, 2008), 1:48–1:58.

84   "Deep Green Resistance: An Interview with Derrick Jensen and Rachel Ivey," Derrick Jensen's website, June 7, 2013, http://www.derrickjensen .org/2013/06/deep-green-resistance-interview-rachel-ivey.

85   See John Sanbonmatsu, "John Sanbonmatsu Replies to Derrick Jensen," *Upping the Anti*, http://uppingtheanti.org/news/article/response-to-derrick-jensens-letter-from-john-sanbonmatsu; Michelle Renée Matsons and Alexander Reid Ross, "Against Deep Green Resistance," in "Justice," *Perspectives on Anarchist Theory* 28 (Spring 2015): 101–18.

connect the modern world to its "spiritual" roots.[86] Going even further, in January 2016, amid the much-publicized cases of migrant
sexual harassment in Germany, McNallen accompanied his racialist constructions of spiritual practice with a Facebook comment,
"Where are the Freikorps when we need them?" To bring about
the spiritual rebirth of white people through violent suppression of
cosmopolitanism and modern spiritual distortions, McNallen states
that European streets must be defended against "the abuse of an
invading throng that will forever end the German nation as we have
known it."[87] Sure enough, a group had formed in Finland just a few
months prior called Soldiers of Odin, actively patrolling and intimidating migrants and Muslims in Europe. The group rapidly spread
to the US and Australia where it adapted to the anti-government
flavor.[88] Aside from McNallen's apparent support for such an entity,
his group also joins DGR in their rejection of non-binary gender
roles for reasons that range from spiritual to biological reduction-
ism.[89] While it would be easy to dismiss such groups as marginal
and largely polemical, DGR thrives somewhat ironically on online
platforms and on social media, where its soft, populist memes have
attracted, as of writing, more than a hundred thousand "likes" on
its public Facebook page.

A similarly instructive connection between eco-radical ideology and fascism appeared in 2014, made explicit when antifascists
discovered the Tumblr account of Nathan "Exile" Block, a former

---

86   "Stephen McNallen and Racialist Asatru Part 3: In His Own Words,"
      Circle Ansuz (blog), September 2, 2013, https://circleansuz.wordpress
      .com/2013/09/02/stephen-mcnallen-part-3.

87   For an interesting article about this, from an antiracist heathen perspec-
      tive, see Josh W., "Dear Steve McNallen," HeathenTalk.com, January 14,
      2016, http://heathentalk.com/2016/01/14/dearstevemcnallen.

88   Jason Wilson, "Fear and Loathing in the Streets: the Soldiers of Odin
      and the rise of anti-refugee vigilantes," *Guardian*, October 27, 2016,
      https://www.theguardian.com/commentisfree/2016/oct/28/fear-and
      -loathing-on-the-streets-the-soldiers-of-odin-and-the-rise-of-anti
      -refugee-vigilantes.

89   Jason Mankey, "Paganism Has Some Dead Ends," *Patheos*, August
      22, 2016, http://patheos.com/blogs/panmankey/2016/08/paganism
      -has-some-dead-ends.

political prisoner of the Earth Liberation Front (ELF, not to be confused with the European Liberation Front). Titled *Loyalty Is Mightier than Fire*, Block's blog features quotations from Jünger, Evola, Spengler, Savitri Devi, and Chilean Nazi Miguel Serrano, alongside pictures of swastikas, the Austrofascist symbol of the Kruckenkreuz, and the occult black sun image. This esoteric fascist constellation of symbols blended with the activists' experiences of Block's racist sentiment to form a picture of a kind of deep green national-anarchism.[90]

According to one person I interviewed who knew Block in Olympia, Washington, during the late-1990s, before his activities with the ELF led to his incarceration as a political prisoner of the radical environmental movement, Block "always had a fondness for the extremes of industrial and metal [music] that struck me as hella sketch. He also had a particular brand of anarcho-primitivism that, in hindsight seemed open to being swayed by right-wing tendencies."[91] The presence of Block's blog and the reaction against it deepened the divide between antifascists and the black metal scene, which is peopled by both Block's defenders as well as antifascists. Demonstrations held in 2014 against Death in June and other crypto-fascist bands contributed to a growing movement. When fascist demonstrators in Olympia came out in defense of police who shot two youths in the back for shoplifting in late May 2015, a large antifascist contingent met them in the streets, with some also turning their ire on a black metal bar called Cryptatropa that was viewed as complicit in the area's disturbing political murkiness.[92] That September, a fascist skinhead named Jascha Manny attempted to organize a rally and some one hundred

---

90   Valdinoci, "Former ELF/Green Scare Prisoner 'Exile' Now a Fascist," NY-CAntifa, August 5, 2014, https://nycantifa.wordpress.com/2014/08/05/exile-is-a-fascist/.

91   Interview with anonymous, February 8, 2016.

92   Others claimed that the bar was not connected to white nationalists at all. See OPP HQ, "Nazis in Olympia, WA Learn the Hard Way that Black Lives Matter," *One Peoples Project* (blog), May 31, 2015, http://onepeoplesproject.com/index.php/archive/86 -archive/1572-nazis-in-olympia-learn-the-hard-way-that-black-lives -matter.

antifascists held a countermarch, with no sign of the fascists them-selves.[93] On December 6, as a tribute to Robert Mathews of the Order, Hammerskins planned to march in Seattle, drawing five hundred antifascists from Portland and Olympia in a counter-demonstration. Again, the fascists failed to show up.[94]

White Indigeneity

There is a growing sense on the left that one must use caution when approaching the awkward alliances built on the basis of anti-civilization leanings, egoism, and a desire for a reconnection to the authentic spirit (ancestral or not). For example, the Cascadian bio-regional conference, Cascadia Rising, scheduled for April 20, 2014, at Portland State University, faced difficulty when people realized that a panel on bioregionalism featured Vince Reinhart of Attack-theSystem.com. Organized by members of Occupy Portland, Earth First!, social ecologists, and leftists inspired by the recent events in Ukraine, the panel was set to discuss indigenous sovereignty, solidarity, and food security. When local antifascist group Rose City Antifa cautioned the organizers against the panel, it sparked a broader discussion about the political alignment of ecology and its problematic past.

The panel was cancelled. About two weeks earlier, Reinhart had appeared on the podcast of local white nationalist Jack Don-ovan to discuss indigenous tribalism and the necessity for white people in the United States to create tribal social structures in order to return to their authentic being:

> I don't think that there's one cohesive tribal identity with white people. I'm of the opinion that a tribe makes the race, and not necessarily vice-versa.... So I think it would just be the process

---

93   "About 100 demonstrate against Nazis, police in downtown Olympia," *Olympian*, September 5, 2015, http://www.theolympian.com/news/local/article34227510.html.

94   Charlette LeFevre, "Neo Nazi Counter Protest Draws Hundreds to Capitol Hill," Seattlepi.com reader's blog, December 6, 2015, http://blog.seattlepi.com/capitolhill/2015/12/06/neo-nazi-counter-protest-draws-hundreds-to-capitol-hill/.

of building your tribal identity from the ground up where you're developing that unique culture, that story of who you are, and it probably starts with your kinship network—especially, moving forward, if what we expect to happen happens which is, you know, the nation-states start to fail us *all* increasingly, and we start to rely on one another.[95]

Reinhart urges Donovan and other white people to forge a racial consciousness by returning to their native traditions and "tribal identity," which will enable them to survive impending collapse. Bound together through an eschatological frame, the kinship community forms a tribe, a nation, and then ultimately a race, which entails a unique biological and spiritual phenomenon. This revolutionary conflation of race and national identity constructed through tribal claims can clearly be located in fascist ideology as white nationalism.[96]

Called *Start the World*, Donovan's podcast is centered around himself. A queer powerlifter, Donovan rejects the labels "homosexual" and "gay" but reserves the right to hurl the invective "fag" at those he deems weak. He conceives of himself as an "Androphile"—a man's man who is not only a good man but also good at being a man. For Donovan, who is also a contributing editor to AttacktheSystem.com and has been a guest on *Heathen Harvest* podcast, men have become emasculated by contemporary society and need to return to primitive lifeways by reconnecting with their

---

95   "Start the World Podcast—Episode #2—Vince Reinhart," *Start the World* (podcast), April 2, 2014, 18:30–21:00, http://www.jack-donovan.com/axis/2014/04/start-the-world-podcast-episode-2-vince-rinehart.

96   When the Bundys occupied the Malheur National Wildlife Refuge, Reinhart expressed sympathy with their message on his own blog, stating, "If we oppose rightwing protests to the oppressive system we live under, then we are allying ourselves with the left wing of the financial-military-industrial-complex known as the US government." With no feeling for the ire of the Northern Paiute, whose lands the Bundys had occupied, Reinhart finds any dissent from reactionary antigovernmental positions to be supportive of the government. See Vince Reinhart, "LaVoy Finicum's Message to Native Americans," *Lingit Latseen* (blog), January 28, 2016, https://lingitlatseen.com/2016/01/28/lavoy-finicums-message-to-native-americans.

ancestral heritage. Donovan is currently a member of the white nationalist group Wolves of Vinland, which advocates the same tribal ideology while also indulging in what they consider the sacred rites—animal sacrifice and other practices—of their versions of bioregionalism and ecology.

Alongside ecological struggles and bioregionalism, Wolves of Vinland maintain an autonomous, hard-driving ethos not unlike a motorcycle gang. With three hundred members, a tract of land near Lynchburg, Virginia, and chapters in Wyoming and Colorado, they are a secretive and somewhat intimidating presence. According to an anonymous source, the Wolves of Vinland purportedly spend a long time recruiting their members, with a year of observation, and their recruits are subjected to grueling trials, forced to sprint for miles without reprieve or exception. Their particular insistence, along with Donovan's powerlifter network, is on an elitist, warrior mentality tied to the spirituality of Julius Evola, and they ridicule all forms of perceived weakness and disability. Yet their public rhetoric is also in sync with certain leftist ideas of decentralized villages off-the-grid barter economies, and locally grown food.[97]

Donovan's acceptance of some forms of queerness—when it is expressed through new tribalism and male warrior culture—marks a division within fascism. Though his stance often fits well in certain Nipster milieus, his appearance at Richard Spencer's trendy fascist National Policy Institute in 2015 led some, like League of the South president Michael Hill, to boycott the event. At the same time, his publisher, Greg Johnson at Counter-Currents, has caused some controversy by widening fascism's scope in other ways. Johnson is critical of making Holocaust denial a fascist centerpiece, which has led to some bitter divisions among white nationalists. Holocaust denial, like hate rock, has long been one of the defining features of modern fascism and a baseline of the white nationalist movement. This has been true ever since Francis Parker Yockey's *Imperium*. However, some associate it with the baggage of stodgy intellectuals who have damaged the reputation of fascism and created a hardcore, cultish

---

97   Eric Wallace, "Eco Punks: The Wolves of Vinland Badasses Dare You to Re-Wild Yourself," *Blue Ridge Outdoors*, May 5, 2015, http://www .blueridgeoutdoors.com/go-outside/eco-punks-the-wolves-of-vinland -badasses-dare-you-to-re-wild-yourself/.

following without a mass, popular base. While they still deny the Holocaust, publishers like Counter-Currents seek to shake off the cobwebs of the twentieth century. These trends have enabled fascists to play down their ugly past and unpopular ideas while presenting themselves instead as an alternative to both right and left—traditional, small, local, tech-savvy but also downhome and agrarian, rustic but also metro hipster, diverse but with respectable borders, intellectual but organic—the natural, elite synthesis.

Violence and State Legitimacy

As I have indicated throughout this work, fascism has never gone unopposed. Whether it was the anarchist, communist, and liberal attempt at an Arditti del Popolo in Italy or the RKB and Reichsbanner in Germany, the left Autonomists in Italy and Germany having it out with fascists in the streets or antiracist skinheads attempting to extract themselves from the fascist creep while fending off police, fascist groups, and Wise Use Patriots, antifascism has played an important role in the development of left-wing movements. Nevertheless, it is worthwhile contemplating the complexities of different movements and their modern manifestations.

The Autonomen-inspired antifa networks that grew out of brave opposition to emergent fascism during the 1980s and 1990s prize secrecy and often try to remain clear of the mainstream media. By contrast, the Anti-Racist Action quasi-mass movement and affiliated groups that emerged in the United States during the same time often sought to publicize their actions to the media, attempting to expose fascists while gaining positive coverage for antifascism. During the mid-1990s, ARA also branched out into abortion clinic defense, and a number of its members joined the Love and Rage Revolutionary Anarchist Federation, which also advanced causes like queer liberation. Although Love and Rage dissolved in 1998, the ARA network continued to promote actions across the United States, including public demonstrations at fascists' apartment buildings and places of business, and countermarches and event disruptions against the mobilizations of groups like the Klan, the Confederate Hammerskins, and the Church of the Creator.

The first group in the United States to effect a synthesis of ARA and European antifa strategies was Rose City Antifa (RCA), which emerged in the 2000s to oppose the skinhead group Volks-front in Portland, Oregon. Working to both oppose fascists in the streets and garner information on their meeting and event locations in order to raise a public outcry and shut them down, RCA inject-ed a fresh model into the US antifascist community. With the rise of militia groups after the election of Obama, alternate formations sprung up elsewhere with similarly interesting qualities. In Phoenix, Arizona, as stated earlier, the Phoenix Class War Council called for anti-Americans First countermarches to oppose J. T. Ready's fascist demonstrations. These protests drew on what was then a thriving anarchist network stretching from Flagstaff to Tucson, which also participated in demonstrations in solidarity with indigenous peo-ples and migrants against Sheriff Joe Arpaio, the Border Patrol, and SB 1070. The anti-Americans First countermarches included some anarchists "open-carrying" guns, a recent turn in antifascist action in the United States.

An Anarchist Black Cross chapter in Florida had created a Tactical Defense Caucus to train activists under pressure from far-right groups in self-defense during the 1990s. Other groups like the John Brown Gun Club in Northeast Kansas and the Denver Armed Resistance Committee also organized to provide self-defense train-ings for activists engaged in community organizing efforts threat-ened by the right. Such self-defense trainings enable antifascists and antiracists to feel more comfortable around one another and more empowered in carrying out the roles of community organiza-tion often compromised by right-wing terror.

In the aftermath of Hurricane Katrina, armed confrontations between white militias patrolling the predominantly black neigh-borhood of Algiers and anarchists working to rebuild the commu-nity showed many the dangerous prospects of a world in which the state's control over violence has deteriorated. Community defense became integral to the maintenance of an active presence of soli-darity with the local community. Without it, not only would the Common Ground Collective that worked to reconstruct the neigh-borhood have failed to get off the ground, but also white militias would have continued to patrol, harass, and even murder the local black population.[98]

---

98   scott crow, *Black Flags and Windmills* (Oakland: PM Press, 2012).

During rising racial tensions after the murder of Trayvon Martin on February 26, 2012, and the string of ensuing police killings of innocent black and brown men in the following years, the Rural Organizing Project (ROP) received numerous threats, many aimed at speaker Walidah Imarisha, who conducted an annual tour of rural towns called "Why Aren't There More Black People in Oregon?" In response, a security team of people of color assembled to guarantee the safety of Imarisha and other ROP organizers. The security team reestablished confidence in the mission of the ROP and the speaking tour, ensuring that information on the deep roots of racism in Oregon could reach people who need it.

As the Black Lives Matter movement rose up after the slaying of Mike Brown in August 2014, black demonstrators conducted an "open carry" march in a predominantly black neighborhood of Dallas to display their willingness to defend their neighborhood from white supremacists.[99] With the antimosque movement that followed closely thereafter, armed right-wing protesters, many of them obvious fascists, came out in force. In one tense, armed standoff in April of 2016, the New Black Panther Party turned up in Dallas to defend a Nation of Islam mosque from the so-called Bureau of American Islamic Relations, whose members donned skeleton masks and carried semi-automatic weapons.[100] Later that year, a "White Lives Matter" demonstration converged outside of the NAACP offices in Houston, Texas, brandishing assault rifles and Confederate flags in a clear act of intimidation.

The increasingly militant direction of right-wing protests and demonstrations against immigrants, Muslims, and LGBTQI people has led to an ensuing focus on self-defense by antiracists. At one counterdemonstration in Anaheim, California, against a

---

99   Aaron Lake Smith, "The Revolutionary Gun Clubs Patrolling the Black Neighborhoods of Dallas," VICE.com, January 5, 2015, http://www.vice.com/read/huey-does-dallas-0000552-v22n1.

100   "Armed Stand-Off at Texas Mosque: Racial Tensions Erupt in Dallas as Gun Toting Anti-Muslim Protesters Clad in Skeleton Masks Clash with the New Black Panther Party Outside a Nation of Islam Mosque," *Daily Mail Online*, April 3, 2016, http://www.dailymail.co.uk/news/article-3521831/Racial-tensions-erupt-Dallas-opposing-armed-groups-clash-outside-Nation-Islam-mosque.html.

Klan march on February 29, 2016, three anti-Klan protesters were stabbed. Another counterdemonstration in Sacramento against a joint manifestation by skinhead groups and the Duginist Traditionalist Worker Party saw seven antifascists stabbed. Thus far, public armed standoffs and slashings have not led to murder, but they do suggest a very real crisis of legitimacy for the state, whereby forces of the right and left decide to take violence into their own hands. While the right's fixation on armed protest emerged as a paranoid response to the perceived threat of government disarmament of the citizenry, the left's more recent move to armed self-defense has apparently come about through the experience of actual threats not only from the right but also from the police.

As the FBI admitted, the Klan and other white supremacist organizations have worked to infiltrate law enforcement for decades, with relatively little preventative action. Numerous instances of collaboration and even integration between white supremacist organizations and the justice system have been reported—for instance, the FBI has revealed connections between police, the Klan, and the National Alliance, and more recently a state appointed defense attorney for police charged with unlawfully arresting a black man in Baltimore was discovered to have long-standing economic ties with the National Alliance.[101] The real extent of white nationalist infiltration and general presence in US law enforcement is unknowable, but it is clearly deeper than most find comfortable.

Nevertheless, it is important to note that the much-glorified antifascist street presence addresses only a small part of the problem. The increasingly international transversality and connectivity of the fascist movement, in particular its Duginist networks, both online and in real life, have proven difficult for leftists to confront. Whereas ARA has always been able to cut off a fascist by starting a phone call campaign, shutting down a webpage, a Facebook group, or a podcast often requires some adaptation. Yet antifascist groups like the One People's Project persist in closing fascists' PayPal accounts, getting

---

101   See Kristian Williams, *Our Enemies in Blue* (Oakland: AK Press, 2015), 165–66; Tom Jackman, "Baltimore Terminates Contract with Government Lawyer Accused of Past Neo-Nazi Ties," *Washington Post*, August 19, 2016, http://washingtonpost.com/news/true-crime/wp/2016/08/19/baltimore-fires-city-government-lawyer-with-seeming-neo-nazi-ties.

them blocked from podcast sites, and humiliating them publicly. The latter is often not as difficult as it seems, although it requires time behind the keyboard to dig up important details. Fascist presence on Facebook is often tantamount to Live Action Role Playing, with "organizers" based in Florida attempting to set up events all the way across the United States and failing to bring out any supporters. Still they have effectively stalked leftists, women, journalists, and others. For modern life, much of which is felt as "lived online," harassment can translate to the same anxiety as if it were "real life."[102]

To a serious extent, however, the Trump campaign and subsequent election brought fascists into the public, first through a reckoning with issues of online harassment and campus organizing, in particular, and then through the explosion of racial violence and harassment. Trump's appointees in the transition period leading up to his presidency evinced his loyalties—Tanton network politicians Kris Kolbach and Jeff Sessions, Tea Party leaders like Mike Pompeo, CounterJihad figures like Mike Flynn, as well as Christian Reconstructionists Mike Pence and Ken Blackwell, who is a fellow at the anti-LGBQTI hate group, the Family Research Council—all under the chief strategist, Breitbart's Steve Bannon, who David Duke commended for "basically creating the ideological aspects of where we're going."[103]

Attempts at International Fascism

Although awareness about fascist intrigues and networks is increasing, efforts to unite radical-right populist parties and neofascist groups and groupuscules unfortunately seem to be gaining ground as well. In 2009, Dugin provided a theoretical backdrop for such new syntheses by calling for an end to "classical political theories," including liberalism, communism, and fascism. He offered a "fourth

---

102   Rose City Antifa, "Online Fascists Attempt Action on Portland Streets," Rose City Antifa's blog, July 26, 2016, http://rosecityantifas.weebly.com/articles/online-fascists-attempt-action-on-portland-streets.

103   Ben Sales, "David Duke Leads Chorus of Racists and Neo-Nazis Cheering Steve Bannon Pick," Forward.com, November 15, 2016, http://forward.com/news/breaking-news/354488/david-duke-leads-chorus-of-racists-and-neo-nazis-cheering-steve-bannon-pick.

political theory"—a "crusade" against the "enemy" that distorts tradition and a pursuit of a rebirth of the archaic and futuristic at once.[104] This purportedly nonfascist ideological space provides ample room for the denial of "fascism" while reproducing its ideology under other names. After courting the left under an anti-imperialist front in the fall of 2015, the Rodina party in Russia called a conference to create the World National-Conservative Movement (WNCM).

Bringing some fifty-eight parties, groups, and private individuals together in September 2015 to condemn "the erosion of nations [and] massive migration" brought about by "liberalism, multiculturalism, and tolerance," the WNCM presented a new stage in the quest for a "Fascist International." Austria's FPÖ was going to show up, but dropped out, leaving the usual suspects of Golden Dawn, Jobbik, and the British National Party, as well as the Polish Falanga, Forza Nuova, and the National Democratic Party of Germany, among others. On their list of agreements, the WNCM include "joint camps for military and athletic instruction."[105] Among individuals and organizations who signed up after the conference, Jean-Marie Le Pen is named as honorary chairman, with the American Freedom Party, the Council of Conservative Citizens, American Renaissance, Autonomous Nationalists of Serbia, New Resistance, and Generation Identity appearing alongside Global South fascist groups like Venezuela's Movimiento Patriota (Patriot Movement), the Philippine National Front, Syria's Social Nationalist Party, Chile's Acción Identitaria (Identitarian Action), and South Africa's Front Nasionaal (Front National).[106] Some fascists, like Alain Soral, who contributed an introduction to Dugin's *Fourth Political Theory*, seek to work not only with anti-imperialists but even members of the non-white community in

104 Alexander Dugin, *The Fourth Political Theory* (London: Arktos, 2012).
105 See Anton Shekhovtskov, "Russian Politicians Building an International Extreme Right Alliance," *Interpreter*, September 15, 2015, http://www.interpretermag.com/russian-politicians-building-an-international-extreme-right-alliance/.
106 This list comes from Nordic Resistance Movement's news site Nord-Front, "Nyy gränsöverskridande nationalkonservativ rörelse har bildats," Nordfront.se, December 29, 2015, https://www.nordfront.se/ny-gransoverskridande-nationalkonservativ-rorelse-har-bildats.smr.

Europe who assert that Marxism and the Enlightenment, like feminism and homosexuality, are colonial impositions on a decolonial movement—represented by anti-Semitic comedian Dieudonné, for instance—that cannot be either right or left.[107]

Perhaps the most pressing question ahead is whether—and, if so, how—the white nationalist movement will attempt to integrate into the different factions of the radical right. Given the strategy of Trumpism, the WNCM has some chance of joining with the more successful blocs of radical-right parties that manage to tone down the rhetoric of xenophobia, anti-Semitism, and racism. It is impossible to ignore the complex webs that weave neofascist groupuscules together with radical right parties in broader formations that make for dynamic political movements. There are also new groups emerging that might compete for the Fascist International, such as the new incarnation of the European Social Movement, based in Italy with an ideological platform of corporatism, Eurasianism, and the "natural hierarchy" of "family-cooperatives-foundations-trade unions."[108]

Similarly, in the United States, an explicit radical-right party like the American Freedom Party will not be able to gain traction against the Republican Party, but the latter has been able to recuperate members of the alt-right by "stealing their luggage." Bannon, for instance, declared Breitbart "the platform for the alt-right," which was only true insofar as Breitbart became a nexus through which members of the alt-right could interface with the radical right and conservative movement on common ground.[109] With

107 See Houria Bouteldja, "Beyond You: With You, Against You: Dieudonné through the prism of the white Left, or conceptualizing a domestic internationalism," trans: Samer, Parti Indigenus de la République, March 1, 2014, http://indigenes-republique.fr/dieudonne-through-the-prism-of-the-white-left-or-conceptualizing-a-domestic-internationalism/; Houria Bouteldja, "Gay universalism, homoracialism and «marriage for all,»" trans. Karen Wirsig, Decolonial Translation Group, February 12, 2013, http://www.decolonialtranslation.com/english/gay-universalism-homoracialism-and-marriage-for-all.html.

108 Savino, "From Evola to Dugin," 116.

109 Sarah Posner, "How Donald Trump's New Campaign Chief Created an Online Haven for White Nationalists," MotherJones.com, August 22, 2016, http://www.motherjones.com/politics/2016/08/stephen-bannon

gay blogger Milo Yiannopoulos asserting a pro-alt-right position, however, much of the movement revolted, insisting that Milo's homosexuality and Jewish ancestry ruled him out. Despite Milo's loathing of feminists, Muslims, and the left—despite sending his fans on a Twitter "raid" against *Ghostbusters* star Leslie Jones—a black woman—he will never be alt-right enough. Thus, Breitbart established not so much "the platform" as a kind of porous populist membrane known as the "alt-light" through which fascism could creep in and out of mainstream discourse. In a sense, the white nationalist movement had been given a perfect medium.

The Trump campaign showed the Republicans' ability to adapt and draw in the extremes from paleoconservatives to radical-rightists and open neofascists. When armed groups appear at mosques in the United States to decry Muslims and refugees, they are only presenting a radical material version of the ideology mouthed by leaders like Donald Trump, with his thinly veiled calls to kill Muslims using bullets dipped in pig's blood and other such horrifying hate speech. When similar groups, clad in black and aping leftist styles, scream "Go home!" at migrants in Europe or commandeer environmental protests for nationalist causes, they are only providing a less polite expression of the talking points crafted by the Nouvelle Droite and fascist political demagogues like Christian Bouchet and Alain Soral who enter and leave radical-right parties at will.

Indeed, following the election of Trump, traditional groups that like to maintain a viable distance from fascism, like the League of the South, unraveled their vague disguise: "Once the globalist-progressive coalition of Jews, minorities, and anti-white whites stops reeling in confusion from the results of yesterday's election, we can expect them to start striking back with trickery and violence.... Now, more than ever, we need tight organization and numbers to help drive a stake through Dracula's heart and keep him from rising once again to menace our people and civilization," the League's president Michael Hill declared. "No mercy should be shown to the enemies of our God, our Folk, and our civilization. None would be afforded us."[110] In a similar vein, conspiracy theorist

-donald-trump-alt-right-breitbart-news.

110   Brian Tashman, "League of the South Hails Trump, Wants 'No Mercy'

Alex Jones began to rant about Jews involved in a criminal conspiracy against the US, further opening a line that he had begun just weeks prior when he began to lash out against a "Jewish mafia" ruining the country.[111]

The emboldening of anti-Semitism after Trump's victory exposed how vital it is to recognize the mainstreaming of fascist counterculture and its "respectable" ideological analogues. The overlap of these two sectors has created what is, in my view, protofascist conditions in the United States straddling stages one and two of Paxton's delineation of fascist evolution ("a movement-building base dedicated to creating a 'new order'" and "a process of 'rooting in the political system'") while beginning to move into stage three by seizing power through a kind of "creeping coup" for which Trump has presented the perfect, perhaps disposable, populist figurehead. Throughout Europe, radical-right populist parties are determined to join Trump in an alliance with Putin against the EU and the remnants of the multicultural state in exchange for more hardline platforms influenced by fascists. The outbreak of violence following Trump's election serves as a warning to all the people of Europe, however: go down this road, and there may be no turning back.

Towards Jews, Minorities and Anti-White Whites," RightWingWatch.org, November 10, 2016, http://www.rightwingwatch.org/post/league-of-the -south-hails-trump-wants-no-mercy-towards-jews-minorities-and-anti -white-whites.

111   JTA, "'Jewish Mafia' Controls the U.S., Says Alex Jones, Prominent Trump Supporter, Radio Host," Haaretz.com, October 27, 2016, http:// www.haaretz.com/world-news/u-s-election-2016/1.749440.

CONCLUSION: SWORDS INTO PLOWSHARES

In writing this book, the conclusions I came to were not at all what I had expected to discover. I have attempted to shed light on lesser-known currents within the fascist movement, how they intertwine, and how they are distinguished from the radical-right populist parties gaining stature in the modern world. Generally speaking, fascist groups exist today in many forms, shapes, and sizes. There are national-anarchists and autonomous nationalists, pan-secessionists and neoreactionaries, all with somewhat distinct philosophies but important agreement on numerous issues. Overlaid onto an ideological mapping of the left and post-left, a number of key similarities appear. Reflecting back on the numerous tendencies—the neo-Gramscian Nouvelle Droite, Evolian "universal individualism," Third Positionist "political soldiers," Strasserist integral nationalism, völkisch ecology, esoteric spiritualism, and nihilism—it is not difficult to observe where, when, how, and why this overlapping has occurred.

The era of neoliberal deregulation has recently met a more powerful populist opposition than it has ever seen. The radical left and right appear to have different approaches; however the early failure of socialist political parties to fulfill their promises of defeating austerity has encouraged the successes of a movement that fuses the radical left and right in attempts to overthrow the neoliberal structures into which socialism has inserted itself. Populism appeals to people's desires and frustrations, usually calling for unity against some horrifying opponent. The radical right uses rhetorical hyperbole to turn migrants and Muslims into that opponent.

Vague promises delivered with an aggressive fixation on collapse, panic, anxiety, and despair are all that demagogues have to offer. It is only by instilling fear that the far right has any real hope of gaining power. In order to make appropriate decisions about their futures, people must be informed. Through a careful understanding of reality, people can make their own decisions in life and foster the imagination necessary to help build the future. It is fascism and the radical right's distortion of truth that poses the greatest threat to the world—not immigration or "Islamization." Combatting fascism requires the bravery and courage of facts. Knowledge pierces prejudice. Education around politics, immigration, Islam, and Judaism—to name only a few hot points—remains crucial.

Although it has some roots in totalitarian political ideals that emerged from the Enlightenment, fascism, and particularly the neoreaction, relies more strongly on the anti-Enlightenment tradition. More specifically, it depends on the instrumental failures and hypocrisies in the practice of Enlightenment ideas of liberty and equality.[1] That the US Constitution affirmed freedom and equality while hypocritically maintaining genocidal war and slavery against Native and African peoples only exposes even more the contradictions between Enlightenment notions of equality and the forms of political domination that would ultimately contribute to the development of fascism. Still, wholesale rejections of the ideas of democracy and equality themselves will never prove sufficiently resistant to reactionary tendencies. We must instead return to the words and deeds of such organizers as Lucy Parsons, who pronounced the goal of removing "all bars of prejudice and superstition" from "universal truth" to forward the "development of self-thinking individuals."[2]

The rejection of goals like Parsons's is a capitulation to the pressures of angst, alienation, and despair that turn modern society toward self-destruction. As Adorno presciently observed, the fascist's theoretical system is "like a highly developed credit system:

1   See Zeev Sternhell, *The Anti-Enlightenment Tradition*, trans. David Maisel (New Haven: Yale University Press, 2010).

2   Lucy Parsons, *Freedom, Equality & Solidarity: Writings & Speeches, 1878–1937* (Chicago: Charles H. Kerr, 2004), 31.

one concept borrows from the other."[3] At its core, fascism's conceptual palingenesis has no grounding in history or reality; its ultranationalist pretensions are the product of inflated egos that mask something even more banal than mediocrity. In the end, the germination of fascism requires mass glorification of absurdity and the championing of meaningless cruelty. Only by reasoning through its oppressive contradictions and opposing it in spirit, will, and deed can it be overcome.

Fascism is fidelity to inequality and brutality. Their reflexive leap from belief in inequality and oppression to "national revolution" against foreigners and internal foes pits fascists against the idea of collective liberation for all people, despite their claims to working-class values of ethnocentric "solidarity." Theirs is a solidarity of cruelty, of the belligerent against the defenseless, masked as spiritual truth for lack of rigorous understanding of fact.

If Hitler demanded that the Nazi Party make the people of Germany into his sword, it is our task to break the "sword" of that "national revolution," turning its shards into plowshares by growing supportive communities that can sustain and defend themselves against fascism. Humanity's struggle with the dilemma of contemporary nihilism (the dilemma of no dilemma, in a way) is long-standing and will not be overcome by political or spiritual promises of a solution. Pessimism in the era of climate change can only destroy the formulation of clear strategies for the survival of humanity. Ideas only exist insofar as they can be set into practice. Authoritarianism and its affective cycles of violence and revenge against those deemed "unequal" or "weak" can only be halted through the ethic of cooperation and mutual aid. Hope is the only way forward.

---

3   Theodor W. Adorno, *Negative Dialectics*, trans. E. B. Ashton, 2nd ed. (New York: Bloomsbury Academic, 1981), 76.

WORKS CITED

"About 100 demonstrate against Nazis, police in downtown Olympia." *Olympian*, September 5, 2015. http://www.theolympian.com/news/local/article34227510.html.

Adler, Franklin Hugh. *Italian Industrialists from Liberalism to Fascism: The Political Development of the Industrial Bourgeoisie, 1906–1934.* Cambridge: Cambridge University Press, 1995.

Adorno, Theodor W. *Negative Dialectics.* Translated by E. B. Ashton. New York: Bloomsbury Academic, 1981.

Adorno, Theodor et al. *The Authoritarian Personality.* New York: Harper, 1950.

Agamben, Giorgio. *Homo Sacer: Sovereign Power and Bare Life.* Translated by Daniel Heller-Roazen. Stanford: Stanford University Press, 1998.

———. *State of Exception.* New York: Verso, 2008.

Ahmed, Sara. "Affective Economies." *Social Text* 22, no. 2. Summer 2004: 117–39.

Aladag, Züli, Florian Cossen, and Christian Schwochow. *NSU: German History X.* Television mini-series. Munich, Germany: Das Erste, 2016.

Alexander, Michelle. *The New Jim Crow: Mass Incarceration in the Age of Colorblindness.* New York: The New Press, 2012.

Allen, Samantha. "We Need to Talk About Silicon Valley's Racism." Daily Beast, August 22, 2014. http://www. thedailybeast.com/articles/2014/08/22/we-need-to-talk-about-silicon-valley-s-racism.html.

Amato, John and David Neiwert, *Over the Cliff* (Sausalito: PoliPoint-Press, 2010)

Ames, Mark. "Charles Koch's Brain Shuts Down the Holocaust." NSFWCORP, October 8, 2013. https://www.nsfwcorp.com/dispatch/shuts-down-the-holocaust.

———. "Homophobia, Racism and the Kochs: The Tech-Libertarian 'Reboot' Conference is a Cesspool." *Pando*, September, 18, 2014. https://pando.com/2014/07/18/homophobia-racism-and-the-kochs-san-franciscos-tech-libertarian-reboot-conference-is-a-cesspool/.

Amnesty International. "Deadly Force: Police Use of Lethal Force in the United States." Amnesty International USA website, June 18, 2015. https://www.amnestyusa.org/research/reports/deadly-force-police-use-of-lethal-force-in-the-united-states.

———. "Ukraine: Abuses and War Crimes by the Aidar Volunteer Battalion in the North Luhansk Region." Amnesty International website. September 8, 2014. https://www.amnesty.org/en/documents/EUR50/040/2014/en/

Anarchy 101. "Anarchy101 Q&A." Anarchy101.org, August 5, 2016. http://anarchy101.org/7877/connection-nihilist-politics-reactionary-fascist-politics?show=7877#q7877.

Angella, Michele. *La nuova destra: oltre il neofascismo fino alle "nuove sintesi."* Florence: Fersu, 2000.

Anissimov, Michael. "Reconciling Transhumanism and Neoreaction." MoreRight.net. May 13, 2013. http://www.moreright.net/reconciling-transhumanismand-neoreaction. This website has been taken down, yet the essay can be found at https://jbboehr.github.io/NeoreactionaryCanon.epub/NeoreactionaryCanon.pdf.

Anti-Defamation League. "ADL Poll of Over 100 Countries Finds More Than One-Quarter of Those Surveyed Infected with Anti-Semitic Attitudes." Anti-Defamation League website, May 13, 2014. http://www.adl.org/press-center/press-releases/anti-semitism-international/adl-global-100-poll.html.

———. "Audit: In 2014 Anti-Semitic Incidents Rose 21 Percent Across the U.S. in a 'Particularly Violent Year for Jews.'" Anti-Defamation League website, March 30, 2015. http://www.adl.org/press-center/press-releases/anti-semitism-usa/adl-audit-in-2014-anti-semitic-inicidents.html?referrer=https://www.google.com/#.V7X-HbVriRs.

————. "Funders of the Anti-Immigrant Movement." Anti-Defamation League website, January 27, 2014. http://www.adl.org/civil-rights/immigration/c/funders-of-the-anti-immigrant.html.

Antifascistfront. "#Cuckservative: How the 'Alt Right' Took off their Masks and Revealed their White Hoods." *Anti-Fascist News* (blog), August 16, 2015. https://antifascistnews.net/2015/08/16/cuckservative-how-the-alt-right-took-off-their-masks-and-revealed-their-white-hoods.

————. "Anti-Fascist Action: Challenging the National Policy Institute's 2015 Conference." *Anti-Fascist News* (blog), October 19, 2015. https://antifascistnews.net/2015/10/19/anti-facist-action-challenging-the-national-policy-institutes-2015-conference.

————. "Crack in the Facade: How Splits in the White Nationalist Movement Can Help Anti-Fascists." *Anti-Fascist News* (blog), February 6, 2016. https://antifascistnews.net/2016/02/06/crack-in-the-facade-how-splits-in-the-white-nationalist-movement-can-help-anti-fascists.

Arab American Institute. "American Attitudes Toward Arabs and Muslims: 2015." Arab American Institute, December 21, 2015. http://www.aaiusa.org/american_attitudes_toward_arabs_and_muslims_2015.

Archer, Jules. *The Plot to Seize the White House.* New York: Skyhorse Publishing, 2015.

Arm the Spirit. "Interview with a Member of Anti-Racist Action." *Arm the Spirit* 16 (Fall 1993).

Arnett, George, and Alberto Nardelli "Today's Key Fact: You Are Probably Wrong About Almost Everything." *Guardian*, October 29, 2014. https://www.theguardian.com/news/datablog/2014/oct/29/todays-key-fact-you-are-probably-wrong-about-almost-everything.

Art, David. *The Politics of the Nazi Past in Germany and Austria.* Cambridge: Cambridge University Press, 2006.

Atkins, Stephen E. *Encyclopedia of Modern Worldwide Extremists and Extremist Groups.* Westport, CT: Greenwood Publishing Group, 2004.

————. *Encyclopedia of Right-Wing Extremism in Modern American History.* Santa Barbara: ABC-CLIO, 2011.

————. *Holocaust Denial as an International Movement.* Westport: Praeger, 2009.

Auernheimer, Andrew "weev." "The Hilarious Meltdown of Mike Anissimov." Storify.com, December 2015. https://storify.com/weev/the-meltdown-of-mikeanissimov.

Aust, Stefan, and Dirk Laabs. *Heimatschutz: Der Staat und die Morderie des NSU.* Munich: Pantheon Publishing, 2014.

Bale, Jeffrey M. "The 'Black' Terrorist International: Neo-Fascist Paramilitary Networks and the 'Strategy of Tension' in Italy, 1968–1974." PhD diss., University of California–Berkeley, 1994.

———. "Fascism and Neo-Fascism: Ideology and 'Groupuscularity.'" In *Fascism Past and Present, West and East: An International Debate on Concepts and Cases in the Comparative Study of the Extreme Right*, edited by Griffin, Roger, Werner Loh, and Andreas Umland. Stuttgart: ibidem Press, 2006.

———. "'National Revolutionary' Groupuscules." In *Fascism: Critical Concepts in Political Science*, edited by Roger Griffin and Matthew Feldman, vol. 5. New York: Routledge, 2004.

———. "Right-Wing Terrorists and the Extraparliamentary Left in Post-World War 2 Europe: Collusion or Manipulation?" *Lobster Magazine*, no. 18 (October 1989): 14. Available at 8bitmode.com/rogerdog/lobster/lobster18.pdf.

Balkani. "Russian Writer Shooting at Sarajevo." YouTube, March 9, 2010. https://www.youtube.com/watch?v=tH_v6aL1D84.

Banham, Mark. "US White Supremacist Website Stormfront Says Donald Trump is Boosting its Popularity." *International Business Times*, December 28, 2015. http://www.ibtimes.co.uk/us-white-supremacist-website-stormfront-says-donald-trump-boosting-its-popularity-1535119.

Banner of Cosmos. "Sophomores and Sages." BannerofCosmos.wordpress.com, May 29, 2013. (This website has since been taken down.)

Bar-On, Tamir. "A Critical Response to Roger Griffin's 'Fascism's New Faces.'" In *Fascism Past and Present, West and East: An International Debate on Concepts and Cases in the Comparative Study of the Extreme Right*, edited by Roger Griffin, Werner Loh, and Andreas Umland. Stuttgart: Ibidem Press, 2006.

———. "Intellectual Right-Wing Extremism." In *The Extreme Right in Europe: Current Trends and Perspectives*, edited by Uwe Backes and Patrick Moreau. Oakville: Vandenboeck & Ruprecht, 2011.

———. "Italian Postwar Neo-Fascism." In *Analysing Fascist Discourses: European Fascism in Talk and Text*, edited by Ruth Wodak and John E. Richardson. New York: Routledge, 2013.

———. *Where Have All the Fascists Gone?* New York: Routledge, 2007.

Battistelli, Pier Paulo, and Piero Crociani. *Italian Blackshirt, 1935–1945*. Long Island City: Osprey Publishing, 2010.

Beirich, Heidi. "Hate Across Waters." In *Right-Wing Populism in Europe*, edited by Ruth Wodak, Majid Khosravinik, and Brigitte Mral. London: Bloomsbury, 2013.

Bellant, Russ. *Old Nazis, the New Right, and the Republican Party*. Boston: South End Press, 1991.

Benner, Katie. "The Color of Money in Silicon Valley." Bloomberg. com, October 9, 2014. http://www.bloomberg.com/view/articles/ 2014-10-09/the-color-of-money-in-silicon-valley.

Benoist, Alain de. "Regenerating History." In *Fascism*, edited by Roger Griffin. Oxford: Oxford University Press, 1995.

Berg, Sanchia. "Antisemitism Hit Record Level in 2014, Report Says." BBC.com, February 5, 2015. http://www.bbc.com/news/uk-31140919.

Berghaus, Günter. *Futurism and Politics: Between Anarchist Rebellion and Fascist Reaction, 1909–1944*. Providence: Berghahn Books, 1996.

Berlet, Chip, and Matthew Lyons. *Right-Wing Populism in America: Too Close for Comfort*. New York: The Guilford Press, 2000.

Bernstein, Joseph. "The Rise of the #RegressiveLeft Hashtag." BuzzFeed, March 15, 2016. https://www.buzzfeed.com/josephbernstein/the -rise-of-the-regressiveleft-hashtag.

Bey, Hakim. "The Temporary Autonomous Zone." In *Crypto Anarchy, Cyberstates, and Pirate Utopias*, edited by Peter Ludlow. Cambridge, MA: MIT Press, 2001.

Bianco, Marcie. "Brazen Sexism Is Pushing People Out of America's Atheism Movement." *Quartz*, February 12, 2016. http:// qz.com/613270/brazen-sexism-is-pushing-women-out-of -americas-atheism-movement.

Biddle, Sam. "Why Does Google Employ a Pro-Slavery Lunatic." Gawker.com, July 30, 2014. http://valleywag.gawker.com/why -does-google-employ-a-pro-slavery-lunatic-1612868507.

Biehl, Janet and Peter Staudenmaier, *Ecofascism: Lessons from the German Experience*. Oakland: AK Press, 1995.

Bild. "Die Karte der Schande." *Bild*, February 22, 2016. http://
www.bild.de/news/inland/fluechtlingskrise-in-deutschland/die
-karte-der-schande-44653590.bild.html.

Blee, Kathleen. *Inside Organized Racism: Women in the Hate Movement.*
Berkeley: University of California Press, 2002.

Blumenthal, Max. *Republican Gomorrah: Inside the Movement that
Shattered the Party.* New York: Nation Books, 2010.

Bobbio, Norberto. *Left and Right: The Significance of a Political Distinction.* Translated by Allan Cameron. Chicago: University of Chicago Press, 1996.

Bohlen, Celestine. "Russia's Stubborn Strains of Anti-Semitism."
New York Times, March 2, 1999. https://partners.nytimes.com/
library/world/europe/030299russia-fascism.html.

Boorstein, Michelle. "Chapel Hill Killings Shine Light on Particular
Tensions Between Islam and Atheism." *Washington Post*, February 11, 2015. https://www.washingtonpost.com/news/local/
wp/2015/02/11/chapel-hill-killings-shine-light-on-particular
-tensions-between-islam-and-atheism.

Braine, Naomi. "Terror Network or Lone Wolf?" Political Research Associates, June 19, 2015. http://www.politicalresearch
.org/2015/06/19/terror-network-or-lone-wolf/#sthash
.3xjOIqSP.dpbs.

Breivik, Anders Behring. "Review 2: Islam—What the West Needs
to Know." In *A European Declaration of Independence.* Available
at https://archive.org/details/2083_A_European_Declaration_
of_Independence.

Bruenig, Elizabeth. "The Chapel Hill Murders Should Be a Wake-
Up Call for Atheists." *New Republic*, February 11, 2015. https://
newrepublic.com/article/121036/chapel-hill-muslim-murders
-show-atheism-has-violent-extremists-too.

Buchanan, Susy. "Jason 'J. T.' Ready Revives New Saxon, Popular
White-Supremacist Social Networking Site." *Intelligence Report*
(online edition), Southern Poverty Law Center website, December 1,
2007. https://www.splcenter.org/fighting-hate/intelligence-report
/2007/jason-%E2%80%9Cjt%E2%80%9D-ready-revives
-new-saxon-popular-white-supremacist-social-networking-site.

Buchanan, Susy, and David Holthouse. "Norse God Odin Visits
Neo-Nazi Anti-Immigration Rally After Party in Omaha,
Neb." *Intelligence Report* (online edition), Southern Poverty

Law Center, December 1, 2007. https://www.splcenter.org/
fighting-hate/intelligence-report/2007/norse-god-odin-visits
-neo-nazi-anti-immigration-rally-after-party-omaha-neb.

Bull, Anna Cento. "Self-Narratives of the *anni di piombo*: Testimonies
of the Political Exiles." In *Imagining Terrorism: The Rhetoric and
Representation of Political Violence in Italy 1969–2009,* edited by
Pierpaolo Antonello and Alan O'Leary. London: Modern Humanities Research Association and Maney Publishing, 2009.

Bunzl, John. "Who the Hell is Jörg Haider." In *The Haider Phenomenon
in Austria,* edited by Ruth Wodak and Anton Pelinka. London:
Transaction Publishers, 2002.

Burghart, Devin. "White Nationalists Descend on D.C. for National
Policy Institute Conference." Institute for Research & Education
on Human Rights website, October 23, 2013. http://www.irehr
.org/2013/10/23/npi-conference-2013.

Burley, Shane. "Fascism Against Time: Nationalism, Media Blindness,
and the Cult of Augustus Sol Invictus." Gods and Radicals, a Site of
Beautiful Resistance, March 24, 2016. https://godsandradicals.org/
2016/03/24/fascism-against-time-nationalism-media-blindness
-and-the-cult-of-augustus-sol-invictus/.

Burrin, Philippe. *La Derive Fasciste: Doriot, Déat, Bergery (1933–1945).*
Paris: Le Seuil, 1986.

Camus, Jean-Yves. "A Long-Lasting Friendship: Alexander Dugin
and the French Radical Right." In *Eurasianism and the European Far Right: Reshaping the Europe-Russia Relationship,* edited by
Marlene Laruelle. Boulder: Lexington Books, 2015.

Cannistraro, Philip V. "Mussolini, Sacco–Vanzetti, and the Anarchists: The Transatlantic Context." *The Review of Italian American Studies,* edited by Frank M. Sorrentino and Jerome Krase.
Lanham, MD: Lexington Books, 2000.

Cantwell, Christopher. "Radical Agenda EP094—The Libertarian
Case for Trump." YouTube, January 24, 2016. https://www
.youtube.com/watch?v=W3SQqgaJ7fg.

Cantwell, Christopher, and Libertarian Realist. "Uncucking with
Cantwell." YouTube, November 22, 2015. https://www.youtube
.com/watch?v=DsVCDdD3xmI.

Carioti, Antonio. "From the Ghetto to the Palazzo Chigi: The Ascent
of National Alliance." In *Fascism: Critical Concepts in Political Science,* edited by Roger Griffin and Matthew Feldman, vol. 5. New

York: Routledge, 2004.

Castriota, Anna, and Matthew Feldman. "'Fascism for the Third Millennium': An Overview of Language and Ideology in Italy's CasaPound Movement." In *Doublespeak: The Rhetoric of the Far Right Since 1945*, edited by Matthew Feldman and Paul Jackson. Stuttgart: ibidem-Verlag, 2014.

Cavanagh, James. "Piss Poor Poet Found in the Dustbin of History." Who Makes the Nazis, March 3, 2011. http://www.whomakesthenazis .com/2011/03/piss-poor-poet-found-in-dustbin-of.html.

Chrisafis, Angelique. "French Elections: Front National Makes No Gains in Final Round." *Guardian*, December 14, 2015. https:// www.theguardian.com/world/2015/dec/13/front-national-fails -to-win-control-of-target-regions-amid-tactical-voting.

Christ, Oliver et al. "Contextual Effect of Positive Intergroup Contact on Outgroup Prejudice." *Proceedings of the National Academy of Sciences* 111, no. 11 (March 2014).

Christie, Stuart. *General Franco Made Me a "Terrorist": The Christie File: Part 2, 1964–1967*. Hastings: ChristieBooks, 2003.

Christie, Stuart. *Stefano Delle Chiaie: Portrait of a Black Terrorist*. London: Anarchy/Refract, 1984.

Chu, Arthur. "Occupying the Throne: Justine Tunney, Neoreactionaries, and the New 1%." Daily Beast, August 1, 2014. http://www .thedailybeast.com/articles/2014/08/01/occupying-the-throne -justine-tunney-neoreactionaries-and-the-new-1-percent.html.

Circle Ansuz. "Stephen McNallen and Racialist Asatru Part 3: In His Own Words." *Circle Ansuz* (blog), September 2, 2013. https:// circleansuz.wordpress.com/2013/09/02/stephen-mcnallen-part-3.

Cleary, Tom. "Shooting at Protests in Minneapolis: 5 Fast Facts you Need to Know." Heavy.com, November 24, 2015. http://heavy.com/ news/2015/11/minneapolis-jamar-clark-4th-police-precinct -protests-shooting-shots-fired-white-supremacists-victims -suspects-injuries-photos-video-black-lives-matter.

Coogan, Kevin. *Dreamer of the Day: Francis Parker Yockey & the Post-war Fascist International*. New York: Autonomedia, 1999.

Copsey, Nigel, and John E. Richardson. *Cultures of Post-War British Fascism*. New York: Routledge, 2015.

Crass, Chris. *Towards Collective Liberation: Anti-Racist Organizing, Feminist Praxis, and Movement Building Strategy*. Oakland: PM Press, 2013.

crow, scott. *Black Flags and Windmills: Hope, Anarchy, and the Common Ground Collective.* Oakland: PM Press, 2012.

Crudo. "Phoenix: Where Anarchists Pack Heat and Send Nazis Packing." *Fires Never Extinguished* (blog), November 7, 2009. http://firesneverextinguished.blogspot.com/2009/11/phoenix-where-anarchists-pack-heat-and.html.

D'Souza, Dinesh. "Racism: It's a White (and Black) Thing." *Washington Post*, September 24, 1995. https://www.washingtonpost.com/archive/opinions/1995/09/24/racism-its-a-white-and-black-thing/46284ab5-417c-4c0c-83e1-029d51655d91/?utm_term=.a9cbaf7cf192.

Dailymail.com Reporter. "Armed Stand-Off at Texas Mosque: Racial Tensions Erupt in Dallas as Gun Toting Anti-Muslim Protesters Clad in Skeleton Masks Clash with the New Black Panther Party Outside a Nation of Islam Mosque." *Daily Mail Online*, April 3, 2016. http://www.dailymail.co.uk/news/article-3521831/Racial-tensions-erupt-Dallas-opposing-armed-groups-clash-outside-Nation-Islam-mosque.html.

Dakin, Edwin. "Henry Ford, Man or Superman?" *Nation*, March 26, 1921.

Davies, Peter. *The National Front in France: Ideology, Discourse and Power.* New York: Routledge, 2001.

De Grand, Alexander J. *Italian Fascism: Its Origins and Development.* Lincoln: University of Nebraska Press, 2000.

Dees, Maurice, and Steve Fiffer. *Hate on Trial.* New York: Villard Books, 1993.

Degras, J. "Comintern Debates over the Dangers Posed by Fascism." In *Fascism: Critical Concepts in Political Science*, edited by Roger Griffin and Matthew Feldman, vol. 2. New York: Routledge, 2004.

Deland, Mats, Michael Minkenberg, and Christin Mays, eds. *In the Tracks of Breivik: Far Right Networks in Northern and Eastern Europe.* Berlin: LIT Verlag, 2014.

Denvir, Daniel. "It's Mostly White People Who Prefer to Live in Segregated Neighborhoods." *CityLab*, June 25, 2015. http://www.citylab.com/housing/2015/06/its-mostly-white-people-who-prefer-to-live-in-segregated-neighborhoods/396887.

Dewey, Caitlin. "Inside the 'Manosphere' that Inspired Santa Barbara Shooter Elliot Rodger." *Washington Post*, May 27, 2014. https://www.washingtonpost.com/news/the-intersect/wp/2014/05/27/

inside-the-manosphere-that-inspired-santa-barbara-shooter
-elliot-rodger/.

DiFazio, William. *Ordinary Poverty: A Little Food and Cold Storage.*
Philadelphia: Temple University Press, 2006.

Diggins, John Patrick. *Mussolini and Fascism: The View from America.*
Princeton: Princeton University Press, 2015.

Dinneen, Joseph F. "An American Führer Organizes an Army." *American* 74, no. 2. (1937).

Dobratz, Betty A., and Stephanie L. Shanks-Meile. *The White Separatist Movement in the United States: "White Power! White Pride!"*
Baltimore: Johns Hopkins University Press, 2000.

Dodge, J. C. "Who Is Courtland Grojean, And Why Should You
Care?" Mason Dixon Tactical, November 11, 2016. https://
masondixontactical.wordpress.com/2015/11/11/who-is
-courtland-grojean-and-why-should-you-care/.

Dolgoff, Anatole. *Left of the Left: My Memories of Sam Dolgoff.* Chico:
AK Press, 2016.

Donovan, Jack. "Start the World Podcast—Episode #2—Vince Reinhart." *Start the World* (podcast), April 2, 2014. http://www.
jack-donovan.com/axis/2014/04/start-the-world-podcast-episode
-2-vince-rinehart.

Dougherty, Michael Brendan. "The Story Behind Ron Paul's Racist
Newsletters." *Atlantic*, December 21, 2011. http://www.theatlantic
.com/politics/archive/2011/12/the-story-behind-ron-pauls-racist
-newsletters/250338/.

Drake, Richard. *The Revolutionary Mystique and Terrorism in Contemporary Italy.* Bloomington: Indian University Press, 1989.

———. *Apostles and Agitators: Italy's Marxist Revolutionary Tradition.*
Cambridge, MA: Harvard University Press, 2009.

Draitser, Eric. Facebook post, July 25, 2016. http://www.facebook
.com/EricDraitser1.

Drumont, Édouard. *La fin d'un monde: etude psychologique et social.* Edited by Albert Savine. Paris, 1889.

Дугин, Александрп. «Настоящий посмодерн»!, Арктогея, http://
arcto.ru/article/922.

Dugin, Alexander. "Fascism—Borderless and Red" [1997]. Translated by Andreas Umland. May 30, 2009. https://www.linkedin
.com/pulse/syrizas-moscow-connection-fascism-borderless
-red-dugin-umland.

———. *The Fourth Political Theory.* London: Arktos, 2012.

Dunbar-Ortiz, Roxanne. *An Indigenous Peoples' History of the United States.* Boston: Beacon Press, 2014.

Dunlop, John B. *The Moscow Bombings of September 1999: Examinations of Russian Terrorist Attacks at the Onset of Vladimir Putin's Rule.* Stuttgart: Ibidem, 2012.

Eatwell, Roger. *Fascism: A History.* New York: Viking Books, 1996.

———. "Towards a New Model of Generic Fascism." In *Fascism: Critical Concepts in Political Science,* edited by Roger Griffin and Matthew Feldman, vol. 1. New York: Routledge, 2004.

Ebenstein, Alan. *Hayek's Journey: The Mind of Friedrich Hayek.* New York: Palgrave MacMillan, 2003.

Eco, Umberto. "Ur-Fascism." *New York Review of Books,* June 22, 1995. http://www.nybooks.com/articles/1995/06/22/ur-fascism.

Ehrenreich, Barbara. "What Happened to the White Working Class?" *Nation,* December 1, 2015. https://www.thenation.com/article/what-happened-to-the-white-working-class/.

Evans, Richard J. "The Conspiracists." *London Review of Books* 36, no. 9 (May 8, 2014): 3–9.

Evola, Julius. "Cose a posto e parole chiare." *La Torre,* April 1, 1930.

———. *Doctrine of Awakening.* Translated by H. E. Musson. Rochester, VT: Inner Traditions, 1995.

———. "Il mito Marcuse." In *Gli uomini e le rovine.* Rome: Volpe, 1967, 263–69.

———. *Men Among the Ruins.* Translated by Guido Stucco, edited by Michael Moynihan. Rochester, VT: Inner Traditions, 2007.

Faye, Guillaume. *Archeofuturism: European Visions of the Post-Catastrophic Age.* Translated by Sergio Knipe. London: Arktos Media, 2010.

Federal Bureau of Investigation. "Latest Hate Crime Statistics Report Released." FBI.gov, December 8, 2014, https://www.fbi.gov/news/stories/latest-hate-crime-statistics-report-released.

Feldman, Matthew, and Paul Jackson. Introduction to *Doublespeak: The Rhetoric of the Far Right Since 1945,* edited by Matthew Feldman and Paul Jackson. Stuttgart: ibidem-Verlag, 2014.

Felice, Renzo. *Mussolini,* vol. 1. Turin: Einaudi, 1965.

Fernandez, Anthony Fano. "Germany's New Far Right." *Jacobin,* February 20, 2015. https://www.jacobinmag.com/2015/02/germany-far-right-pegida.

Findlay, L. M. Introduction to *The Communist Manifesto*, by Karl Marx. Peterborough, ON: Broadview Press, 2004.

Finley, Klint. "Geeks for Monarchy: The Rise of the Neoreactionaries." Techcrunch.com, November 22, 2013. https://techcrunch.com/2013/11/22/geeks-for-monarchy/.

Fleischer, Rasmus. "Two Fascisms in Contemporary Europe? Understanding the ideological split of the Radical Right." In *In the Tracks of Breivik: Far Right Networks in Northern and Eastern Europe*, edited by Mats Deland, Michael Minkenberg, and Christin Mays. Berlin: LIT Verlag, 2014.

Flood, Christopher. "The Cultural Struggle of the Extreme Right." In *Fascism: Critical Concepts in Political Science*, edited by Roger Griffin and Matthew Feldman, vol. 5. New York: Routledge, 2004.

Flynn, Kevin, and Gary Gerhardt. *The Silent Brotherhood: Inside America's Racist Underground*. New York: Free Press, 1989.

Follain, John. "Italy Needed Fascism, Says the New Duce." *Sunday Times*, May 11, 2008. http://www.thesundaytimes.co.uk/sto/news/world_news/article91789.ece.

Forbes, Robert. *Misery and Purity: A History and Personal Interpretation of Death In June*. Amersham: Jara Press, 1995.

Foner, Eric, and John A. Garraty. *The Reader's Companion to American History*. Boston: Houghton Mifflin, 1991.

Foucault, Michel. Preface to *A Thousand Plateaus* by Gilles Deleuze and Felix Guattari. Minneapolis: University of Minnesota Press, 1983.

Freund, Michael. *Georges Sorel, Der revolutionäre Konservatismus*. Frankfurt: Klostermann, 1932.

Friedman, Patri. "Beyond Folk Activism." *Cato Unbound*, April 6, 2009. http://www.cato-unbound.org/2009/04/06/patri-friedman/beyond-folk-activism.

Froio, Caterina, and Pietro Castelli Gattinara. "Neo-Fascist Mobilization in Contemporary Italy: Ideology and Repertoire of Action of CasaPound Italia." *Journal for Deracialization*, no. 2 (Spring 2015).

———. "Discourse and Practice of Violence in the Italian Right: Frames, Symbols, and Identity-Building in CasaPound Italia." *International Journal of Conflict and Violence* 8, no. 1 (2014).

Fromm, Erich. *Escape from Freedom*. New York: Henry Holt and Company, 1969.

Futrelle, David. "The Author of A Voice for Men's Martial Rape Apologia is a Holocaust Denier and Hitler Fan. No, Really." *We Hunted the Mammoth* (blog), May 7, 2015. http://www.wehuntedthemammoth .com/2015/05/07/the-author-of-a-voice-for-mens-marital-rape -apologia-is-a-holocaust-denier-and-hitler-fan-no-really.

———. "MRA Peter Nolan: 'Killing Women Is the Only Path to Justice for Men Now.'" *We Hunted the Mammoth* (blog), July 6, 2015. http://www.wehuntedthemammoth.com/2015/07/06/mra-peter -nolan-killing-women-is-the-only-path-to-justice-for-men-now.

———. "Prominent MRA Tries to Blame Charleston Shooting on Feminism and its Alleged 'Lies About Rape Culture.'" *We Hunted the Mammoth* (blog), June 18, 2015. http://www.wehuntedthemammoth .com/2015/06/18/prominent-mra-tries-to-blame-charleston -shooting-on-feminism-and-its-alleged-lies-about-rape-culture.

———. "Vox Day: Christians Need to Follow the Lead of #GamerGate and the Spanish Inquisition to Defeat Seculars, Satan." *We Hunted the Mammoth* (blog), April 4, 2015. http://www .wehuntedthemammoth.com/2015/04/04/vox-day-christians -need-to-follow-the-lead-of-gamergate-and-the-spanish -inquisition-to-defeat-seculars-satan.

Fysh, Peter and Jim Wolfreys. *The Politics of Racism in France*. New York: Palgrave-MacMillan, 2003.

Gallup. "Islamophobia: Understanding Anti-Muslim Sentiment in the West." Gallup, 2014. http://www.gallup.com/poll/157082/ islamophobia-understanding-anti-muslim-sentiment-west.aspx.

Gardell, Mattias. *Gods of the Blood: The Pagan Revival and White Separatism*. Durham, NC: Duke University Press, 2003.

Gärtner, Reinhold. "The FPÖ, Foreigners, and Racism." In *The Haider Phenomenon in Austria,* edited by Ruth Wodak and Anton Pelinka. London: Transaction Publishers, 2002.

Gentile, Emilio. *Contro Cesare: cristianesimo e totalitarismo nell'epoca dei fascismi*. Milan: Giangiacomo Feltrinelli Editore, 2010.

———. "Fascism in Power: The Totalitarian Experiment." In *Fascism: Critical Concepts in Political Science*, edited by Roger Griffin and Matthew Feldman, vol. 4. New York: Routledge, 2004.

———. "The Sacralization of Politics." In *Fascism: Critical Concepts in Political Science*, edited by Roger Griffin and Matthew Feldman, vol. 3. New York: Routledge, 2004.

Gilbert, Doug. "U.S. Hard Right Being Bolstered by the Mainstream."

Political Research Associates website, December 23, 2015. http://www.politicalresearch.org/2015/12/23/u-s-hard-right -being-bolstered-by-the-mainstream/.

Gilmore, Ruth Wilson. *Golden Gulag: Prisons, Surplus, Crisis, and Opposition in Globalizing California.* Berkeley: University of California Press, 2007.

Gingrich, Andre. "A Man for All Seasons." In *The Haider Phenomenon in Austria,* edited by Ruth Wodak and Anton Pelinka. London: Transaction Publishers, 2002.

Giordano, Benito. "The Politics of the Northern League and Italy's Changing Attitude Towards Europe." In *The EU and Territorial Politics within Member States: Conflict or Co-Operation,* edited by Angela K. Bourne. Boston: Brill, 2004.

Giridharadas, Anand. "Silicon Valley Roused by Secession Call." *New York Times,* October 28, 2013. http://www.nytimes.com /2013/10/29/us/silicon-valley-roused-by-secession-call.html.

Goi, Leonardo. "Lega Nord's last temptation: anti-politics in the time of Grillo." openDemocracy, March 28, 2013. https://www .opendemocracy.net/leonardo-goi/lega-nords-last-temptation -anti-politics-in-time-of-grillo.

Goodrick-Clarke, Nicholas. *Black Sun.* New York: New York University Press, 2002.

———. *Hitler's Priestess.* New York: New York University, 1998.

Goldberg, Jeffrey. "Is It Time for the Jews to Leave Europe?" *Atlantic,* April 2015. http://www.theatlantic.com/magazine/archive /2015/04/is-it-time-for-the-jews-to-leave-europe/386279/.

Gorbach, Denys. "Anarchists in Makhno's Homeland: Adventures of the Red-and-Black Flag." openDemocracy, September 30, 2015. https:// www.opendemocracy.net/od-russia/denys-gorbach/anarchism -in-makhno's-homeland-adventures-of-red-and-black-flag.

Gordon, Harold J. *Hitler and the Beer Hall Putsch.* Princeton: Princeton University Press, 1972.

Graham, Robert. *We Do Not Fear Anarchy—We Invoke It: The First International and the Origins of the Anarchist Movement.* Oakland: AK Press, 2015.

Grant, Madison. *The Passing of the Great Race: Or, the Racial Basis of European History.* New York: Charles Scribner's Sons, 1922.

Gregor, A. James. *The Ideology of Fascism: The Rationale of Totalitarianism.* New York: Free Press, 1969.

Griffin, Roger, ed. *Fascism.* Oxford: Oxford University Press, 1995.

———. ed. *International Fascism: Theories, Causes, and the New Consensus.* New York City: Oxford University Press, 1998.

———. *Modernism and Fascism.* New York: Palgrave MacMillan, 2007.

———. *The Nature of Fascism.* New York: Routledge, 1994.

———. "Revolts Against the Modern World: The Blend of Literary and Historical Fantasy in the Italian New Right." *Literature and History* 11, no.1 (Spring 1985).

———. Preface to *Rethinking Fascism and Dictatorship in Europe*, edited by António Costa Pinto and Aristotle Kallis. London: Palgrave MacMillan, 2014.

Griffin, Roger, and Matthew Feldman, eds. *Fascism: Critical Concepts in Political Science*, vol. 1–5. New York: Routledge, 2004.

Griffin, Roger, Werner Loh, and Andreas Umland, eds. *Fascism Past and Present, West and East: An International Debate on Concepts and Cases in the Comparative Study of the Extreme Right.* Stuttgart: ibidem Press, 2006.

Grimm, Robert. "The Geographic Distribution of the Extreme Right in Germany." *MYPLACE* (blog), September 25, 2012. https://myplacefp7.wordpress.com/2012/09/25/the-geographic-distribution-of-the-extreme-right-in-germany.

Guérin, Daniel. *Fascism and Big Business.* New York: Pathfinder, 1974

Hagedorn, Hermann. *Roosevelt in the Bad Lands.* Oyster Bay, NY: Roosevelt Memorial Association, 1921.

Halem, Dann. "Is Bill Maher a Libertarian?" *Salon*, August 1, 2001. http://www.salon.com/2001/08/01/maher_4/.

Hamerquist, Don, and J. Sakai. *Confronting Fascism: Discussion Documents for a Militant Movement.* Montreal/Chicago: Kersplebedeb, Chicago Anti-Racist Action, 2002.

Hamm, Mark S. *American Skinheads: The Criminology and Control of Hate Crime.* Westport, CT: Greenwood Publishing Group, 1993.

Hannig, Nicolai, and Massimiliano Livi. "Nach der Revolte: 1968 als Ausgangspunkt eines bewegten Jahrzehnts in Italien und Deutschland." In *Die 1970er Jahre als schwares Jahrzehnt: Politisierung und Mobilisierung swischen christlicher Demokratie und extremer Rechter,* edited by Massimiliano Livi, Daniel Schmidt, and Michael Sturm. New York: Campus Verlag, 2010.

Hatonn, Gyeorgos Ceres. *No Thornless Roses.* Las Vegas: Phoenix

Source Publishers, 1993.

Hatecenter. "NSM Neo-Nazi Rally / CA's Jeff Hall / AZ's JT Ready, Riverside 10/24/09." YouTube, uploaded October 28, 2009. https://www.youtube.com/watch?v=Ey7JtRzpcmA.

Hatewatch Staff. "White Nationalists Gather in Hungary, Richard Spencer Arrested." Southern Poverty Law Center website, October 6, 2014. https://www.splcenter.org/hatewatch/2014/10/06/white-nationalists-gather-hungary-richard-spencer-arrested.

Helvarg, David. *The War Against the Greens: The "Wise Use" Movement, the New Right, and the Browning of America*. Boulder: Johnson Books, 2004.

Henley, Jon. "France's Neo-Nazi Breeding Ground." *Guardian*, July 19, 2002, https://www.theguardian.com/world/2002/jul/20/thefarright.france.

Hern, Alex. "Occupy Founder Calls on Obama to Appoint Eric Schmidt 'CEO of America.'" *Guardian*, March 20, 2014. https://www.theguardian.com/technology/2014/mar/20/occupy-founder-obama-eric-schmidt-ceo-america.

Herzog, Chrisella. "When the Internet Breeds Hate." *Diplomatic Courier*, March 8, 2015. http://www.diplomaticcourier.com/2015/03/08/when-the-internet-breeds-hate/.

Hett, Benjamin Carter. *Burning the Reichstag: An Investigation into the Third Reich's Enduring Mystery*. Oxford: Oxford University Press, 2014.

Hibbing, John R., Kevin Smith, and John R. Alford. "Differences in negativity bias underlie variations in political ideology." *Behavioral and Brain Sciences* 37 (2014): 297–350.

Hicks, Josh. "Ron Paul and the Racist Newsletters (Fact Checker Biography)." *Washington Post*, December 27, 2011. https://www.washingtonpost.com/blogs/fact-checker/post/ron-paul-and-the-racist-newsletters-fact-checker-biography/2011/12/21/gIQAKNiwBP_blog.html.

Hockenos, Paul. *Free to Hate: The Rise of the Right in Post-Communist Eastern Europe*. New York: Routledge, 1994.

Holehouse, Matthew. "Attacks on Jews Rise to Five Year High in Germany—More Than Any Country in Europe." Telegraph.co.uk, October 1, 2015. http://www.telegraph.co.uk/news/worldnews/europe/eu/11904654/Attacks-on-Jews-rise-to-five-year-high-in-Germany-more-than-any-country-in-Europe.html.

Holter, Lauren. "All the 2015 Anti-Abortion Legislation That's Been Passed So Far (Get a Grip, Arkansas!)." *Bustle*, April 17, 2015. http://www.bustle.com/articles/76235-all-the-2015-anti-abortion-legislation-thats-been-passed-so-far-get-a-grip-arkansas.

Iordachi, Constantin. "Hybrid Totalitarian Experiments in Romania." In *Rethinking Fascism and Dictatorship in Europe*, edited by António Costa Pinto and Aristotle Kallis. London: Palgrave Mac-Millan, 2014.

Ishchenko, Volodymyr. "По поводу клеветы Антон Шеховцова о членах редакции 'цпильного.'" Commons/Спільне, March 12, 2014. http://commons.com.ua/po-povodu-klevety-antona-shehovtsova-o-ch.

———. "Ukraine Has Ignored the Far Right for Too Long—It Must Wake Up to the Danger." *Guardian*, November 13, 2014. https://www.theguardian.com/commentisfree/2014/nov/13/ukraine-far-right-fascism-mps.

Ivancheva, Mariya. "The Bulgarian Winter of Protests." openDemocracy, March 15, 2013. https://www.opendemocracy.net/mariya-ivancheva/bulgarian-winter-of-protests.

Jäckel, Eberhard, and Axel Kuhn, eds. *Hitler: Sämtliche Aufzeichnungen, 1905–1924*. Stuttgart: Deutsche Verlags-Anstalt, 1980.

Jackman, Tom. "Baltimore Terminates Contract with Government Lawyer Accused of Past Neo-Nazi Ties." *Washington Post*, August 19, 2016. http://washingtonpost.com/news/true-crime/wp/2016/08/19/baltimore-fires-city-government-lawyer-with-seeming-neo-nazi-ties.

Jensen, Derrick. "Delusions." In *Now This War Has Two Sides*, spoken word record. Track 2, CD 2. Oakland: PM Press, 2008.

Joffe, Gabriel. "History Wars Exposed: Right-Wing Influence in APUSH Curriculum Update." Political Research Associates website, October 19, 2015. http://www.politicalresearch.org/2015/10/19/history-wars-exposed-right-wing-influence-in-apush-curriculum-update/.

Jones, Robert P. "Self-Segregation: Why It's So Hard for Whites to Understand Ferguson." *Atlantic*, August 21, 2014. http://www.theatlantic.com/national/archive/2014/08/self-segregation-why-its-hard-for-whites-to-understand-ferguson/378928.

Jünger, Ernst. *Das abenteuerliche Herz. Erste Fassung: Aufzeichnungen bei Tag und Nacht*, in *Sämtliche Werke*, Band 9. Stuttgart:

Klett-Cotta, 1979.

Kallis, Aristotle. "Breaking Taboos and 'Mainstreaming the Extreme.'" In *The Haider Phenomenon in Austria*, edited by Ruth Wodak and Anton Pelinka. London: Transaction Publishers, 2002.

Kalman, Samuel. *The Extreme Right in Interwar France: The Faisceau and the Croix de Feu*. New York: Routledge, 2008.

Kaplan, Jeffrey, and Leonard Weinberg. *The Emergence of a Euro-American Radical Right*. New Brunswick, NJ: Rutgers University Press, 1998.

Karsai, László. "The Radical Right in Hungary." In *The Radical Right in Central and Eastern Europe Since 1989*, edited by Sabrina P. Ramet. University Park, PA: Penn State Press, 1999.

Katsiaficas, George. *The Subversion of Politics: European Autonomous Social Movements And The Decolonization Of Everyday Life*. Oakland: AK Press, 2006.

Kershaw, Ian. *Hitler, 1889–1936: Hubris*. New York: W.W. Norton & Company, 1999.

Kolesnik, Dmitry. "Euromaidan: The Play with EU Integration." CriticAtac, December 4, 2013. http://www.criticatac.ro/lefteast/euromaidan-the-play-with-eu-integration/.

Konan, Aude. "Black Dragons: The Black Punk Gang Who Fought Racism and Skinheads in 1980s France." okayafrica, August 10, 2016, http://www.okayafrica.com/featured/black-punk-black-dragons-france/.

Korkut, Umut, and Emel Akçali. "Deciphering Eurasianism in Hungary: Narratives, Networks, and Lifestyles." In *Eurasianism and the European Far Right: Reshaping the Europe-Russia Relationship*, edited by Marlene Laruelle. Boulder: Lexington Books, 2015.

Korn, Thomas, and Andreas Umland. "Russland: Jürgen Elsässer, Kremlpropagandist." *Zeit Online*, July 19, 2014. http://www.zeit.de/politik/deutschland/2014-07/juergen-elsaesser-russland-propaganda.

Kovács, András. "The Post-Communist Extreme Right." In *Right-Wing Populism in Europe*, edited by Ruth Wodak, Majid Khosravinik, and Brigitte Mral. London: Bloomsbury, 2013.

Krebs, Pierre. "The Metapolitical Rebirth of Europe." In *Fascism*, edited by Roger Griffin. Oxford: Oxford University Press, 1995.

Krysan, Maria, Mick P. Couper, Reynolds Farley, and Tyrone A. Forman. "Does Race Matter in Neighborhood Preferences? Results from a Video Experiment." *American Journal of Sociology* 115, no. 2 (September 2009).

Kuhn, Gabriel, ed. *All Power to the Councils: A Documentary History of the German Revolution, 1918–1920.* Oakland: PM Press, 2012.

Kuzio, Taras. *Ukraine: Democratization, Corruption, and the New Russian Imperialism.* Santa Barbara: Praeger, 2015.

Langer, Elinor. *A Hundred Little Hitlers: The Death of a Black Man, the Trial of a White Racist, and the Rise of the Neo-Nazi Movement in America.* New York: Picador, 2003.

Lanza, Luciano. *Secrets and Bombs: Piazza Fontana 1969.* Translated by Paul Sharkey. Hastings: ChristieBooks, 2002.

Laruelle, Marlene. "Dangerous Liaisons: Eurasianism, the European Far Right, and Putin's Russia." In *Eurasianism and the European Far Right: Reshaping the Europe-Russia Relationship*, edited by Marlene Laruelle. Boulder: Lexington Books, 2015.

———. ed. *Eurasianism and the European Far Right: Reshaping the Europe-Russia Relationship.* Boulder: Lexington Books, 2015.

———. "Russia's Radical Right and its Western European Connections: Ideological Borrowings and Personal Interactions." In *In the Tracks of Breivik: Far Right Networks in Northern and Eastern Europe*, edited by Mats Deland, Michael Minkenberg, and Christin Mays. Berlin: LIT Verlag, 2014.

Lean, Nathan. "Dawkins, Harris, Hitchens: New Atheists flirt with Islamophobia." Salon, March 30, 2013. http://www.salon.com/2013/03/30/dawkins_harris_hitchens_new_atheists_flirt_with_islamophobia.

Lebourg, Nicolas. "Arriba Eurasia?" In *Eurasianism and the European Far Right: Reshaping the Europe-Russia Relationship*, edited by Marlene Laruelle. Boulder: Lexington Books, 2015.

Lee, Martha Frances. *Earth First! Environmental Apocalypse.* Syracuse, NY: Syracuse University Press, 1995.

Lee, Martin A. *The Beast Reawakens: Fascism's Resurgence from Hitler's Spymasters to Today's Neo-Nazi Groups and Right-Wing Extremists.* New York: Routledge, 2000.

———. "An Overview of Far Right Politics in Europe." *Intelligence Report* (online edition), Southern Poverty Law Center, August 28, 2001. https://www.splcenter.org/fighting-hate/intelligence-report/2001/overview-far-right-politics-europe.

LeFevre, Charlotte. "Neo Nazi Counter Protest Draws Hundreds to

Capitol Hill." Seattlepi.com reader's blog, December 6, 2015. http://blog.seattlepi.com/capitolhill/2015/12/06/neo-nazi-counter-protest-draws-hundreds-to-capitol-hill/.

"Lefty" Hooligan & Archonis. "National Anarchism—'A Reply to a Leftist'—courtesy of 'Lefty' Hooligan & Archonis." NAMS-UK website, December 30, 2011. http://namshropshire.blogspot.com/2011/12/national-anarchism-reply-to-leftist.html.

Legionscatz. "The Slave Morality of Social Justice—Part One." *Attack the System* (blog), February 24, 2013. https://attackthesystem.com/2013/02/24/the-slave-morality-of-social-justice-part-one/.

Legum, Judd. "Fact Check: Ron Paul Personally Defended Racist Newsletters." *ThinkProgress*, December 27, 2011. https://thinkprogress.org/fact-check-ron-paul-personally-defended-racist-newsletters-bb1432cfb972#.vahbklhd8.

Lenz, Ryan and Mark Potok. "War in the West: The Bundy Ranch Standoff and the American Radical Right." Southern Poverty Law Center website, July 9, 2014. https://www.splcenter.org/sites/default/files/d6_legacy_files/downloads/publication/war_in_the_west_report.pdf.

Lichtblau, Eric. "Crimes Against Muslim Americans and Mosques Rise Sharply." *New York Times*, December 17, 2015. http://www.nytimes.com/2015/12/18/us/politics/crimes-against-muslim-americans-and-mosques-rise-sharply.html.

Lemons, Stephen. "Racist Daisy Chain." *Phoenix New Times*, November 22, 2007. http://www.phoenixnewtimes.com/news/racist-daisy-chain-6395220.

Lemons, Stephen. "J. T. Ready's Neo-Nazi Patrols for Migrants in the Vekol Valley, and Its Discovery of a Body." *Phoenix New Times*, June 21, 2010. http://www.phoenixnewtimes.com/blogs/jt-readys-neo-nazi-patrol-for-migrants-in-the-vekol-valley-and-its-discovery-of-a-dead-body-6503453.

Leonhardt, David. "Middle-Class Black Families, in Low-Income Neighborhoods." *New York Times*, June 24, 2015. http://www.nytimes.com/2015/06/25/upshot/middle-class-black-families-in-low-income-neighborhoods.html.

Lepsius, M. Rainer. "The Model of Charismatic Leadership." In *Charisma and Fascism*, edited by António Costa Pinto, Roger Eatwell, and Stein Ugelvik Larsen. New York: Routledge, 2007.

Lipstadt, Deborah E. *Denying the Holocaust: The Growing Assault on*

Truth and Memory. New York: The Free Press, 1993.

Loose, Gerhard. *Ernst Jünger*. New York: Twayne Publishers, 1974.

Love, Nancy S. "Playing with Hate: White Power Music and the Undoing of Democracy." In *Doing Democracy: Activist Art and Cultural Politics*, edited by Nancy S. Love and Mark Mattern. Albany: SUNY Press, 2013.

Lyons, Matthew N. "Rightists Woo the Occupy Wall Street Movement." *Three Way Fight* (blog), November 8, 2011. http://threewayfight .blogspot.com/2011/11/rightists-woo-occupy-wall-street.html.

MacDonald, Kevin. "Donald Trump in Cleveland: Nationalism, Populism, and the Rise of the Alt Right." *Occidental Observer*, July 23, 2016. http://www.theoccidentalobserver.net/2016/07/donald -trump-in-cleveland-nationalism-populism-and-the-rise-of-the -alt-right/.

———. "Neoconservatism as a Jewish Movement: A Study in Ethnic Activism." *The Occidental Quarterly*, Monograph #1. Augusta, GA: Washington Summit Publishers, 2004.

———. *A People that Shall Dwell Alone: Judaism as a Group Evolutionary Strategy, with Diaspora Peoples*. San Jose: Writers Club Press, 2002.

Macklin, Graham D. "Co-opting the Counter Culture: Troy Southgate and the National Revolutionary Faction." *Patterns of Prejudice* 39, no. 3. September 2005.

Magasich-Airola, Jorge. *Los que dijeron "No": historia del movimiento de los marinos antigolpistas de 1973*, vol. 1. Santiago: LOM, 2008.

Mahler, Horst. "Look Back on Terror." In *The German Issue*, edited by Sylvère Lotringer. Los Angeles: Semiotext(e), 2009.

Manoschek, Walter. "FPÖ, ÖVP, and Austria's Nazi Past." In *The Haider Phenomenon in Austria*, edited by Ruth Wodak and Anton Pelinka. London: Transaction Publishers, 2002.

Marable, Manning. *Black Leadership*. New York: Columbia University Press, 1998.

Marcus, Jonathan. *The National Front and French Politics: The Resistible Rise of Jean-Marie Le Pen*. New York: New York University Press, 1995.

Mark, Michelle. "Anti-Muslim Hate Crimes Have Spiked After Every Major Terrorist Attack: After Paris, Muslims Speak Out Against Islamophobia." *International Business Times*, November 18, 2015. http://www.ibtimes.com/anti-muslim-hate-crimes-have-spiked

-after-every-major-terrorist-attack-after-paris-2190150.

Marcotte, Amanda. "Atheism's Shocking Woman Problem: What's Behind the Misogyny of Richard Dawkins and Sam Harris?" Salon, October 3, 2014. http://www.salon.com/2014/10/03/new_atheisms_troubling_misogyny_the_pompous_sexism_of_richard_dawkins_and_sam_harris_partner/.

Mareš, Miroslav. Right-Wing Extremism in the Czech Republic. Berlin: Friedrich Ebert Stiftung, 2012.

Markind, Joanna. "Jews Are Still the Biggest Target of Religious Hate Crimes." Forward, December 5, 2015. http://forward.com/news/325988/jews-are-still-the-biggest-target-of-hate-crimes/.

Markotin, D. "Hugo Scandal 2015." Anarcho-Geek Review, April 10, 2015. http://www.anarchogeekreview.com/opinion/hugo-scandal-2015.

Markovits, Andrei S. "Austrian Exceptionalism." In The Haider Phenomenon in Austria, edited by Ruth Wodak and Anton Pelinka. London: Transaction Publishers, 2002.

Marsdal, Magnus E. "Loud Values, Muffled Interests: Third Way Social Democracy and Right-Wing Populism." In Right-Wing Populism in Europe, edited by Ruth Wodak, Majid Khosravinik, and Brigitte Mral. London: Bloomsbury, 2013.

Mathyl, Markus. "The National-Bolshevik Party and Arctogaia." In Fascism: Critical Concepts in Political Science, edited by Roger Griffin and Matthew Feldman, vol. 5. New York: Routledge, 2004.

Matsons, Michelle Renée, and Alexander Reid Ross. "Against Deep Green Resistance." Perspectives on Anarchist Theory 28 (Spring 2015).

Maurras, Charles. L'Action française et la religion catholique. Paris, 1913.

McDougall, Walter A. France's Rhineland Policy, 1914–1924: The Last Bid for a Balance of Power in Europe. Princeton: Princeton University Press, 2015.

McGowan, Lee. The Radical Right in Germany: 1870 to the Present. New York: Routledge, 2014.

Metzger, Tom. "Tom Metzger Interviews Underground Musician, Boyd Rice." YouTube, April 8, 2011. https://www.youtube.com/watch?v=tO6L3hrMdi0.

Mezzofiore, Gianluca. "Ron Paul, the American Third Position Party and Stormfront." International Business Times, February 1, 2012. http://www.ibtimes.co.uk/anonymous-ron-paul-neo-nazi-bnp

-a3p-291000.

Michael, George. *Theology of Hate: A History of the World Church of the Creator.* Gainesville: University Press of Florida, 2008.

———. *Willis Carto and the American Far Right.* Gainesville: University Press of Florida, 2008.

Michas, Takis. *Unholy Alliance.* College Station, TX: Texas A&M University Press, 2002.

Milbank, Dana. "Ron Paul's economic Rx: A Southern Secessionist." *Washington Post*, February 9, 2011. http://www.washingtonpost.com/wp-dyn/content/article/2011/02/09/AR2011020905879.html.

Midwest Unrest. "Death in June: A Nazi band?" Libcom.org, November 19, 2006. https://libcom.org/library/death-in-june-a-nazi-band.

Misanthropic Division. "Grandchildren of Wotan, sons of Maidan." nbplatforma.org, November 16, 2016. http://tanjoapp.com/contents/513344.

Mitchell, Otis C. *Hitler's Stormtroopers and the Attack on the German Republic, 1919–1933.* Jefferson, NC: McFarland & Company, 2008.

Mohler, Armin. *The Conservative Revolution in Deutschland.* In *Fascism*, edited by Roger Griffin. Oxford: Oxford University Press, 1995.

Moldbug, Mencius. "BIL2012—Mencius Moldbug: How to Reboot the US Government." *BILtalks*, October 20, 2012, https://www.youtube.com/watch?v=ZluMysK2B1E.

Moore, Jack. "Anti-Semitic Attacks Increase by 71% in Holland." Newsweek.com, April 14, 2014. http://www.newsweek.com/securing-jewish-sites-will-not-solve-rising-anti-semitism-says-top-dutch-rabbi-322258.

Morlin, Bill. "Behind the Walls." *Intelligence Report* (online edition), Southern Poverty Law Center website, May 16, 2013. https://www.splcenter.org/fighting-hate/intelligence-report/2013/behind-walls.

———. "Court Documents: American Front Was Planning Violence." Southern Poverty Law Center website, May 14, 2012. https://www.splcenter.org/hatewatch/2012/05/14/court-documents-american-front-was-planning-violence.

Morpheus. "Occupy Phoenix with AR-15's." YouTube, https://www.youtube.com/watch?v=rjOwSIsgE8c.

Morris, Errol, dir. *Mr. Death: The Rise and Fall of Fred A. Leuchter, Jr.* Lions Gate Films, 1999.

Mosse, George L. *The Fascist Revolution*. Madison: University of Wisconsin Press, 1999.

Moynihan, Michael, and Didrik Søderlind, *Lords of Chaos: The Bloody Rise of the Satanic Metal Underground*. Port Townsend, WA: Feral House, 2003.

Mudde, Cas. *Populist Radical Right Parties in Europe*. Cambridge: Cambridge University Press, 2007.

Mussolini, Benito. *Opera Omnia*, 35 vols. Florence: La Fenice, 1951–1963.

———. "Tutti vi dicono che sono anarchico. Nulla di più falso." In *Avanguardia Socialista*, April 2, 1904.

Neaman, Elliot. "Ernst Jünger's Millennium." In *Fascism: Critical Concepts in Political Science*, edited by Roger Griffin and Matthew Feldman, vol. 3. New York: Routledge, 2004.

Neiwert, David. *The Eliminationists*. Sausalito: PoliPointPress, 2009.

———. *In God's Country: The Patriot Movement and the Pacific Northwest*. Washington: Washington State University, 1999.

Neumann, Franz. *Behemoth: The Structure and Practice of National Socialism, 1933–1945*. Chicago: Ivan R Dee, 2009.

Nichols, Michael Beach, and Christopher K. Walker, dirs. *Welcome to Leith*. First Run Features, 2015.

Nicola, Stefan. "Analysis: Terror Threat Growing in Germany." UPI, May 19, 2009. http://www.upi.com/Analysis-Terror-threat-growing-in-Germany/19261242775186.

Nietzsche, Friedrich. *Beyond Good and Evil: A Prelude to a Philosophy of the Future*. Translated by Judith Norman, edited by Rolf-Peter Horstmann and Judith Norman. Cambridge: Cambridge University Press, 2002.

———. *On the Genealogy of Morality and Other Writings*. Translated by Carol Diethe, edited by Keith Ansell-Pearson. Cambridge: Cambridge University Press, 2007.

———. *Writings from the Late Notebooks*. Translated by Kate Sturge, edited by Rudiger Bittner. Cambridge: Cambridge University Press, 2003.

Nolte, Ernst. *The Three Faces of Fascism: Action Francaise, Italian Fascism, National Socialism*. Translated by Leila Vennewitz. New York: Holt, Rinehart and Winston, 1966.

NordFront. "Nyy gränsöverskridande nationalkonservativ rörelse har bildats." Nordfront.se, December 29, 2015. https://www.nordfront

.se/ny-gransoverskridande-nationalkonservativ-rorelse-har -bildats.smr.

Norton, Michael I., and Samuel R. Sommers. "Whites See Racism as a Zero-Sum Game That They Are Now Losing." *Perspectives on Psychological Science* 6, no. 3(2011): 215–18. Available at http:// www.people.hbs.edu/mnorton/norton%20sommers.pdf.

O'Brien, Paul. *Mussolini in the First World War: The Journalist, the Soldier, the Fascist.* New York: Bloomsbury, 2005.

O'Donnell, Guillermo. "Tensions in the Bureaucratic-Authoritarian State and the Question of Democracy." In *The New Authoritarianism in Latin America,* edited by David Collier et al. Princeton, NJ: Princeton University Press, 1979.

One People's Project. "Nazis in Olympia, WA Learn the Hard Way that Black Lives Matter." *One Peoples Project* (blog), May 31, 2015. http://onepeoplesproject.com/index.php/archive/86-archive /1572-nazis-in-olympia-learn-the-hard-way-that-black-lives -matter.

Orfield, Gary, Erica Frankenberg, Jongyeon Ee, and John Kuscera. *Brown at 60: Great Progress, a Long Retreat, and an Uncertain Future.* The Civil Rights Project/Proyecto Derechos Civiles, UCLA (2014). 18. https://www.civilrightsproject.ucla.edu/research/k-12-education/integration-and-diversity/brown-at-60 -great-progress-a-long-retreat-and-an-uncertain-future/ Brown-at-60-051814.pdf.

Origoni, Guillaume. "Pino Rauti: une figure de l'extrême droite italienne." *Fragments sur les Temps Présents,* May 31, 2013. Available at https://tempspresents.com/2013/05/31/pino-rauti-extreme-droite -italienne-guillaume-origoni/.

Pakieser, Andrea. *I Belong Only to Myself: The Life and Writings of Leda Rafanelli.* Oakland: AK Press, 2014.

Pankowski, Rafal. *The Populist Radical Right in Poland.* New York: Routledge, 2010.

Parland, Thomas. *The Extreme Nationalist Threat in Russia: The Growing Influence of Western Rightist Ideas.* New York: Routledge, 2005.

Parsons, Lucy. *Freedom, Equality & Solidarity: Writings & Speeches, 1878–1937.* Chicago: Charles H. Kerr, 2004.

Passmore, Kevin. *Fascism: A Very Short Introduction.* Oxford: Oxford University Press, 2002.

Patel, Kiran Klaus. *Soldiers of Labor: Labor Service in Nazi Germany and New Deal America, 1933–1945.* Translated by Thomas Dunlap. Cambridge: Cambridge University Press, 2005.

Paxton, Robert O. *Anatomy of Fascism.* New York: Vintage Books, 2005.

———. "The Five Stages of Fascism." In *Fascism: Critical Concepts in Political Science*, edited by Roger Griffin and Matthew Feldman, vol. 1. New York: Routledge, 2004.

Payne, John. "Rothbard's Time on the Left." *Journal of Libertarian Studies* 19, no.1 (Winter 2005).

Payne, Stanley G. *Fascism in Spain: 1923–1977.* Madison: University of Wisconsin Press, 1999.

———. *A History of Fascism, 1914–1945.* Madison: University of Wisconsin Press, 1995.

Anton Pelinka. "Right Wing Populism: Concept and Typology." In *Right-Wing Populism in Europe,* edited by Ruth Wodak, Majid Khosravinik, and Brigitte Mral. London: Bloomsbury, 2013.

Pelt, Mogens. "The 'Fourth of August' Regime in Greece." In *Rethinking Fascism and Dictatorship in Europe*, edited by António Costa Pinto and Aristotle Kallis. London: Palgrave MacMillan, 2014.

People against Racism (HoRa). "Neo-Nazi Terror Marked the Protests in Sofia (Bulgaria)." LibCom.org, February 26, 2013. https://libcom.org/news/neo-nazi-terror-marked-protests-sofia-bulgaria-26022013.

Pernicone, Nunzio. *Carlo Tresca: Portrait of a Rebel.* Oakland: AK Press, 2010.

———. *Italian Anarchism, 1864–1892.* Princeton: Princeton University Press, 1993.

Phoenix Class War Council. "The National Socialist Movement Scum Show Up Armed to Counter Protest #occupyphoenix." *Fires Never Extinguished* (blog), October 15, 2011. http://firesneverextinguished.blogspot.com/2011/10/national-socialist-movement-scum-show.html.

Pick, Hella. *Guilty Victims: Austria from the Holocaust to Haider.* New York: I.B. Tauris, 2000.

Pilkington, Hilary, Elena Omel'chenko, and Al'bina Garifzianova, eds. *Russia's Skinheads: Exploring and Rethinking Subcultural Lives.* New York: Routledge, 2010.

Pinto, António Costa, and Aristotle Kallis, eds. *Rethinking Fascism and Dictatorship in Europe.* London: Palgrave MacMillan, 2014.

Pipes, Richard. *The Degaev Affair: Terror and treason in tsarist Russia*. New Haven: Yale University Press, 2003.

Popper, Karl. *The Open Society and Its Enemies*, vol. 1, *The Spell of Plato*. London: George Routledge & Sons, Ltd., 1947.

Pollitt, Katha. "Atheists Show Their Sexist Side." *Nation*, September 24, 2014. https://www.thenation.com/article/atheists-show-their -sexist-side.

Porat, Dina, ed. *Antisemitism Worldwide 2014*. Tel Aviv University, 2014.

Potok, Mark. "The Year of Hate and Extremism." *Intelligence Report* (online edition), Southern Poverty Law Center website, February 17, 2016. https://www.splcenter.org/fighting-hate/intelligence -report/2015/year-hate-and-extremism-0.

Пресс-служба. "Шестве в День Рождения Нестора Махно— «Антикапитализм-120,»" Nazbol.info, October 24, 2008, http://www.nazbol.info/rubr1/index346/2817.html.

Preston, Keith. *Attack the System*. London: Black House Press, 2013.

———. "Critique of the Americans for Self-Determination Plan for Separatism and Decentralism." *Attack the System* (blog). https://attackthesystem.com/critique-of-the-americans-for-self -determination-plan-for-separatism-and-decentralism/.

———. "Former Love and Rage leader and Defector from Anarchism to Maoism Denounces Keith Preston." *Attack the System* (blog), January 31, 2012. https://attackthesystem.com/2012/01/31/ former-love-and-rage-leader-and-defector-from-anarchism-to -maoism-denounces-keith-preston/.

———. interview with Richard Spencer. "Anarchy in the USA." *Vanguard Radio* (podcast), April 21, 2014. http://www.radixjournal .com/podcast/2014/4/21/anarchy-in-the-usa?rq=keith%20preston.

———. interview with Dion. Radio Wehrwolf. January 5, 2016. http://radiowehrwolf.weebly.com/radio-archives/keith-preston.

———. "Keith Preston Speaks to the National Policy Institute on the Question of U. S. Imperialism." *Attack the System* (blog), November 3, 2015. https://attackthesystem.com/2015/11/03/keith-preston -speaks-to-the-national-policy-institute-on-the-question-of-u-s -imperialism/.

———. "Marginalia: On radical thinking Keith Preston on Balkanization and the State of Exception." *Attack the System* (blog), March 13, 2012. https://attackthesystem.com/2012/03/13/marginalia

-on-radical-thinking-keith-preston-on-balkanization
-and-the-state-of-exception.

———. "Politically Correct Universities and Slave Morality." *Attack the System* (blog), September 18, 2010, https://attackthesystem .com/2010/09/18/politically-correct-universities-and-slave -morality.

Preston, Paul. *The Politics of Revenge: Fascism and the Military in 20th Century Spain.* New York: Routledge, 2005.

Pribylovsky, Vladimir. "The Attitude of National Patriots Towards Vladimir Putin in the Aftermath of March 26, 2000." Panorama. ru, 2000. http://www.panorama.ru/works/patr/bp/10eng.html.

Pulzer, Peter G. J. *Jews and the German State: The Political History of a Minority, 1848–1933.* Detroit: Wayne State University, 2003.

Radosh, Ronald. "Steve Bannon, Trump's Top Guy, Told Me He Was 'A Leninist' Who Wants To 'Destroy the State.'" Daily Beast, August 21, 2016. http://www.thedailybeast.com/articles/2016/08/22/steve -bannon-trump-s-top-guy-told-me-he-was-a-leninist.html.

Rathod, Sara. "2015 Saw a Record Number of Attacks on US Mosques." *Mother Jones*, June 20, 2016. http://www.motherjones .com/politics/2016/06/islamophobia-rise-new-report-says.

Reardon, Sean F., Lindsay Fox, and Joseph Townsend. "Neighborhood Income Composition by Household Race and Income, 1990–2009." *The Annals of the American Academy of Political and Social Science* 660, no. 1 (July 2015).

Reich, Wilhelm. *The Mass Psychology of Fascism.* New York: Farrar, Straus and Giroux, 1970.

Reinhart, Vince. "LaVoy Finicum's Message to Native Americans." *Lingit Latseen* (blog), January 28, 2016, https://lingitlatseen .com/2016/01/28/lavoy-finicums-message-to-native-americans.

Renton, David. *Fascism: Theory and Practice.* London: Pluto Press, 1999.

———. *When We Touched the Sky: The Anti-Nazi League, 1977–1981.* Cheltenham, UK: New Clarion Press, 2006.

Richardson, John E. "Ploughing the Same Furrow?" In *Right-Wing Populism in Europe,* edited by Ruth Wodak, Majid Khosravinik, and Brigitte Mral. London: Bloomsbury, 2013.

Ritzer, George. "Siege Mentality." *Scorpion*, no. 18 (circa 1996).

Rizga, Kristina. "The Chilling Rise of Islamophobia in Our Schools." *Mother Jones,* January 26, 2016. http://www.motherjones.com/

politics/2016/01/bullying-islamophobia-in-american-schools.

Roberts, David D. *The Syndicalist Tradition and Italian Fascism.* Manchester: Manchester University Press, 1979.

Robinson, Tasha. "How the Sad Puppies Won—By Losing." NPR.org, August 26, 2015. http://www.npr.org/2015/08/26/434644645/how-the-sad-puppies-won-by-losing.

Rogers, Thomas. "Heil Hipster: The Young Neo-Nazis Trying to Put a Stylish Face on Hate." *Rolling Stone*, June 23, 2014. http://www.rollingstone.com/culture/news/heil-hipster-the-young-neo-nazis-trying-to-put-a-stylish-face-on-hate-20140623.

Roosevelt, Theodore. *Letter to Charles Davenport.* New York, January 3, 1913.

———. *Letters*, vol. 1. Cambridge, MA: Harvard University Press, 1951.

Rose City Antifa. "Online Fascists Attempt Action on Portland Streets." *Rose City Antifa* (blog), July 26, 2016. http://rosecityantifas.weebly.com/articles/online-fascists-attempt-action-on-portland-streets.

———. "Meet the Oregon Chapter of the American Freedom Party, Parts I & II." *Rose City Antifa* (blog), October 10, 2015. http://rosecityantifas.weebly.com/articles/meet-the-oregon-chapter-of-the-american-freedom-party-part-one and http://rosecityantifas.weebly.com/articles/meet-the-oregon-chapter-of-american-freedom-party-part-two.

Ross, Alexander Reid, and Joshua Stephens. "About Schmidt." Chapters 1–5, Medium, October 12–29, 2015. https://medium.com/@rossstephens/about-schmidt-how-a-white-nationalist-seduced-anarchists-around-the-world-chapter-1-1a6fa255b528#.1b46m7k8e.

Rothbard, Murray N. "Harry Elmer Barnes, RIP." *Left & Right* 4, no. 1 (1968), 3. Available at lewrockwell.com/1970/01/murray-n-rothbard/remembering-harry-elmer-barnes/.

Rudling, Per Anders. "The Return of the Ukrainian Far Right." In *Analysing Fascist Discourses: European Fascism in Talk and Text*, edited by Ruth Wodak and John E. Richardson. New York: Routledge, 2013.

———. "They Defended Ukraine: The 14 Waffen-Granadier-Division der SS (Galizische Nr. 1) Revisited." *Journal of Slavic Military Studies* 25, no. 3 (2012).

Sailer, Steve. "Yeah, Yeah, Diversity Is Strength. It's Also Secession."

VDARE.com, May 31, 2002. https://www.vdare.com/articles/
    yeah-yeah-diversity-is-strength-its-also-secession.
Salleti, Achille. "Limonov, la biografia avventurosa di un opposito-
    re di Putin." *Il Fatto Quotidiano*, January 22, 2014. http://www
    .ilfattoquotidiano.it/2013/01/22/limonov-biografia-avventurosa
    -di-oppositore-di-putin/477223.
Sanbonmatsu, John. "John Sanbonmatsu Replies to Derrick Jensen."
    Upping the Anti. http://uppingtheanti.org/news/article/response
    -to-derrick-jensens-letter-from-john-sanbonmatsu.
Sandifer, Phil. "Guided by the Beauty of their Weapons: An Analysis
    of Theodore Beale and his Supporters." EruditorumPress.com,
    April 2015. http://www.eruditorumpress.com/blog/guided-by
    -the-beauty-of-their-weapons-an-analysis-of-theodore-beale
    -and-his-supporters/.
Sandwich, Nyan. "Introducing Phalanx." MoreRight.net, October
    19, 2014. http://www.moreright.net/introducing-phalanx/.
    (This thread has been taken down.)
Sankin, Aaron. "Inside the Men's Rights Movement." *The Week*, June
    7, 2015. http://theweek.com/articles/538670/inside-mens-rights
    -movement.
Santilli, Pete. "Episode #597—Assassination Attempted on Intel Whis-
    tleblower James Garrow." Pete Santilli Show. YouTube, January 3,
    2014. https://www.youtube.com/watch?v=54rZ8IeO_Hs.
———. "Episode #1119—The Guerrilla Media Network 24/7 Live
    Stream & Chat." YouTube, February 23, 2016. https://www
    .youtube.com/watch?v=2Jirh-G6sac.
Savino, Giovanni. "From Evola to Dugin: The Neo-Eurasianist Con-
    nection in Italy." In *Eurasianism and the European Far Right: Re-
    shaping the Europe-Russia Relationship*, edited by Marlene Laru-
    elle. Boulder: Lexington Books, 2015.
Schedler, Jan. "The Devil in Disguise: Action Repertoire, Visual Per-
    formance and Collective Identity of the Autonomous National-
    ists." *Nations and Nationalism* 20, no. 2 (2014).
———. "'Modernisierte Antimoderne': Entwicklung des organisierten
    Neonazismus 1990–2010." In *Autonome Nationalisten: Neonazis-
    mus in Bewegung*, edited by Jan Schedler and Alexander Häusler.
    Weisbaden: VS Verlag, 2011.
Schellenberg, Britta. "Developments within Germany's Radical Right:
    Discourses, Attitudes and Actors." In *Right-Wing Populism in*

Europe, edited by Ruth Wodak, Majid Khosravinik, and Brigitte Mral. London: Bloomsbury, 2013.

Schlatter, Evelyn. "Neo-Nazi indicted for bombs is son of movement stalwart." Southern Poverty Law Center website, January 28, 2011. https://www.splcenter.org/hatewatch/2011/01/28/neo-nazi-indicted-bombs-son-movement-stalwart.

Schlembach, Raphael. "The 'Autonomous Nationalists': New Developments and Contradictions in the German Neo-Nazi Movement." *Interface: A Journal for and about Social Movements* 5, no. 2 (November 2013).

Schmidt, Michael. *The New Reich: Violent Extremism in Unified Germany and Beyond.* London: Hutchinson, 1993.

Schumacher, Elizabeth. "Report: Five Times More Attacks on Refugee Homes in Germany in 2015." *Deutsche Welle,* January 29, 2016. http://www.dw.com/en/report-five-times-more-attacks-on-refugee-homes-in-germany-in-2015/a-19011109.

Scorpion. "Illiberal Rock." *Scorpion,* no. 8 (Spring 1985).

Senato della Repubblica. *Commissione parlamentare d'inchiesta sul terrorismo in Italia e sulle cause della mancata individuazione dei responsibili delle stragi: Il terrorismo, le stragi ed il contesto storico-político—Proposta di relazione* (Rome: 1995).

———. *Commissione parlamentare d'inchiesta sul terrorismo in Italia e sulle cause della mancata individuazione dei reponsabili delle stragi: Stragi e terrorismo in Italia dal dopoguerra al 1974—Relazione del Gruppo Democratici di Sinistra l'Ulivio* (Rome: 2000).

Shapinov, Viktor. "A Class Analysis of the Ukrainian Crisis." translated by Renfrey Clarke. *Links International Journal of Socialist Renewal,* June 13, 2014, http://links.org.au/node/3903.

Sharp, Clifford. "How Strong Is Hitler?" *Readers' Digest* 23, no. 137 (1933).

Sheehi, Stephen. "ISIS as a Fascist Movement." *Mondo Weiss,* November 18, 2015, http://mondoweiss.net/2015/11/isis-fascist-movement.

Shekhovtsov, Anton. "Alexander Dugin and the West European New Right, 1989–1994." In *Eurasianism and the European Far Right: Reshaping the Europe-Russia Relationship,* edited by Marlene Laruelle. Boulder: Lexington Books, 2015.

———. "Far-Right Election Observation Monitors." In *Eurasianism and the European Far Right: Reshaping the Europe-Russia Relationship,* edited by Marlene Laruelle. Boulder: Lexington Books,

2015.

———. "The Palingenetic Thrust of Russian Neo-Eurasianism: Ideas of Rebirth in Alexandr Dugin's Worldview." *Totalitarian Movements and Political Religions* 9, no. 4 (2008).

———. "Russian Politicians Building an International Extreme Right Alliance." *Interpreter*, September 15, 2015. http://www.interpret-ermag.com/russian-politicians-building-an-international-extreme-right-alliance/.

———. "Vladimir Zhirinovsky's Contacts with the European Far Right in the Yeltsin era." *Anton Shekhovtsov's Blog*, October 28, 2014. http://anton-shekhovtsov.blogspot.com/2014/10/vladimir-zhirinovskys-contacts-with.html.

———. "Whither Ukrainian Far Right?" *Anton Shekhovtsov's Blog*, January 30, 2015. http://anton-shekhovtsov.blogspot.com/2015/01/whither-ukrainian-far-right.html.

Shekhovtsov, Anton, and Andreas Umland. "Ukraine's Radical Right." *Journal of Democracy* 25, no. 3 (July 2014)

Shenfield, Stephen. "Maidan: Democratic Movement or Nationalist Mobilization?" CriticAtac, July 7, 2014. http://www.criticatac .ro/lefteast/maidan-democratic-or-nationalist.

———. *Russian Fascism: Traditions, Tendencies, Movements.* London: ME Sharpe, 2001.

Shirer, William L. *The Rise and Fall of the Third Reich.* New York: Simon and Schuster, 2011.

Smith, Aaron Lake. "The Revolutionary Gun Clubs Patrolling the Black Neighborhoods of Dallas." VICE.com, January 5, 2015. http://www.vice.com/read/huey-does-dallas-0000552-v22n1.

Solomos, John. "Contemporary British Racist Movements." In *Right-Wing Populism in Europe*, edited by Ruth Wodak, Majid Khosravinik, and Brigitte Mral. London: Bloomsbury, 2013.

Sorel, George. *From Georges Sorel: Essays in Socialism and Philosophy*, edited by John L. Stanley. Translated by John and Charlotte Stanley. Oxford: Oxford University Press, 1987.

———. "Quelques pretentions juives (fin)." *L'Indépendance* 3 (June 1, 1912).

Soucy, Robert. *French Fascism: The First Wave, 1924–1933.* New Haven: Yale University Press, 1986.

———. *French Fascism: The Second Wave, 1933–1939.* New Haven: Yale University Press, 1997.

Southgate, Troy. "The Case for National-Anarchist Entryism." National-Anarchist.net, September 18, 2010. http://www.national-anarchist.net/2010/09/case-for-national-anarchist-entryism-by.html.

SOVA staff. "'Russian March' 2014 in Moscow: For and Against Novorossiya." SOVA Center for Information and Analysis, November 11, 2014. http://www.sova-center.ru/en/xenophobia/news-releases/2014/11/d30652/.

Spackman, Barbara. "D'Annunzio and the Antidemocratic Fantasy." In *Fascist Virilities: Rhetoric, Ideology, and Social Fantasy in Italy*. Minneapolis: University of Minnesota Press, 1996.

Spencer, Richard. "The E Word (Eugenics)." *Radix Journal*, April 2, 2012, http://www.radixjournal.com/podcast/podcast/218.

———. "The Eugenics Taboo." *Radix Journal*, January 11, 2014. http://www.radixjournal.com/journal/2014/1/11/the-eugenics-taboo.

———. "Richard Spencer—Cuckservatives, Social Justice Warriors & the White Problem." Radio 3Fourteen, Red Ice radio network, August 15, 2015. http://www.radixjournal.com/blog/2015/8/1/richard-spencer-on-red-ice-radio.

———. "Up with Anarchy!" *Radix Journal*, April 9, 2010. http://www.radixjournal.com/altright-archive/altright-archive/main/blogs/untimely-observations/up-with-anarchy.

Southern Poverty Law Center. "Arizona State Rep. Candidate Russell Pearce Distributes Article From Neo-Nazi National Alliance Website." *Intelligence Report* (online edition), Southern Poverty Law Center, January 16, 2007. https://www.splcenter.org/fighting-hate/intelligence-report/2007/arizona-state-rep-candidate-russell-pearce-distributes-article-neo-nazi-national-alliance.

———. "American Freedom Party." Southern Poverty Law Center website, https://www.splcenter.org/fighting-hate/extremist-files/group/american-freedom-party.

———. "Antigovernment Militia Groups Grew by More Than One-Third Last Year." Southern Poverty Law Center website. https://www.splcenter.org/news/2016/01/04/antigovernment-militia-groups-grew-more-one-third-last-year.

———. "Council of Conservative Citizens." Southern Poverty Law Center website. https://www.splcenter.org/fighting-hate/extremist-files/group/council-conservative-citizens.

———. "John Tanton." Southern Poverty Law Center website. https://

www.splcenter.org/fighting-hate/extremist-files/individual/
john-tanton.

———. "J. T. Ready." Southern Poverty Law Center website. https://
www.splcenter.org/fighting-hate/extremist-files/individual/jt
-ready.

———. "Michael Brian Vanderboegh." Southern Poverty Law Center
website. https://www.splcenter.org/fighting-hate/extremist-files/
individual/michael-brian-vanderboegh-0.

Spotts, Frederic and Theodor Wieser. *Italy: A Difficult Democracy; A
Survey of Italian Politics.* Cambridge: Cambridge University
Press, 1986.

Stachura, Peter. *Gregor Strasser and the Rise of Nazism.* New York:
Routledge, 2015.

Staudenmaier, Peter. "Antisemitic Intellectuals in Fascist Italy." In
Comparative Studies for a Global Perspective, vol. 4, *Intellectual An-
tisemitism from a Global Perspective.* Würzburg: Königshausen &
Neumann, 2016.

Steinmetz, George. "Fordism and the (Im)Moral Economy of Right-
Wing Violence in Contemporary Germany." In *Research on Democracy and Society, Volume 2: Political Culture and Political Structure; Theoretical and Empirical Studies,* edited by Frederick D.
Weil and Mary Gautier. Greenwich, CT: JAI Press, Inc., 1994.

Sterling, Terry Greene. "Russell Pearce and Other Illegal-Immigration
Populists Rely on Misleading, Right-Wing Reports to Scapegoat
Immigrants and to Terrify Penny-Pinched Americans." *Phoenix
New Times*, December 2, 2010. http://www.phoenixnewtimes.
com/news/russell-pearce-and-other-illegal-immigration-popu-
lists-rely-on-misleading-right-wing-reports-to-scapegoat-immi-
grants-and-to-terrify-penny-pinched-americans-6446724.

Stern, David. "Ukraine Crisis: Is Conflicting Fuelling Far-Right
Threat?" BBC News Magazine, September 8, 2015. http://www.
bbc.com/news/world-europe-34176602.

Sternhell, Zeev. *The Anti-Enlightenment Tradition.* Translated by David Maisel. New Haven: Yale University Press, 2010.

———. *The Birth of Fascist Ideology: From Cultural Rebellion to Political
Revolution.* Princeton: Princeton University Press, 1994.

———. "Fascist Ideology." In *Fascism: Critical Concepts in Political Science*, edited by Roger Griffin and Matthew Feldman, vol. 1. New
York: Routledge, 2004.

Steuckers, Robert. "Answers to the questions of Pavel Pulaev about my modest biography, my experiences in the French New Right Circus, etc." *Le blog de Robert Steuckers*, February 2014. http://robertsteuckers.blogspot.com/2014/02/answers-to-questions-of-pavel-tulaev.html.

Stiles, Cindy. *Tangents*, 1997. Available at http://www.boydrice.com/interviews/tangents.html.

Stirner, Max. *The Ego and Its Own*. Translated by David Leopold. Cambridge: Cambridge University Press, 1995.

Sundermeyer, Von Olaf. "Autonome Nationalisten: Rechte Schläger im Kapuzenpulli." *Spiegel Online*, April 27, 2009. http://www.spiegel.de/politik/deutschland/autonome-nationalisten-rechte-schlaeger-im-kapuzenpulli-a-620467.html.

Surkis, Judith. *Sexing the Citizen: Morality and Masculinity in France, 1870–1920*. Ithaca, NY: Cornell University Press, 2006.

SystemicCapital.com. "Deep Green Resistance, an interview with Derrick Jensen and Rachel Ivey." derrickjensen.org, June 7, 2013. http://www.derrickjensen.org/2013/06/deep-green-resistance-interview-rachel-ivey.

Tabachnick, Rachel. "The John Birch Society's Anti-Civil Rights Campaign of the 1960s, and its Relevance Today." Political Research Associates website, January 21, 2014. http://www.politicalresearch.org/2014/01/21/the-john-birch-societys-anti-civil-rights-campaign-of-the-1960s-and-its-relevance-today/#sthash.2CfgLij8.dpbs.

Tarchi, Marco. "Between Festival and Revolution." In *International Fascism: Theories, Causes, and the New Consensus*, edited by Roger Griffin. New York City: Oxford University Press, 1998.

———. *Dal MSI ad An: organizzazione e strategie*. Bologna: Società editrice il Mulino, 1997.

———. *La rivoluzione impossibile: dai Campi Hobbit alla nuova destra*. Florence: Vallecchi, 2010.

———. "Populism Italian Style." In *Democracies and the Populist Challenge*, edited by Yves Méni and Yves Surel. London: Palgrave Macmillan, 2001.

Tauber, Kurt. *Beyond Eagle and Swastika: German Nationalism Since 1945*, vol. 1. Middletown, CT: Wesleyan University Press, 1967.

Thalheimer, August. "On Fascism." In *Marxists in Face of Fascism*, edited by David Beetham. Manchester: Manchester University

Press, 1983.

The Pressure Project. "The Pressure Project #133: Attack the System! A Talk with Pan-Anarchist Keith Preston." *The Pressure Project* (podcast), May 6, 2016. https://www.youtube.com/watch?v=iKIzhZ0AI_k.

Thiel, Peter. "The Education of a Libertarian." *Cato Unbound*, April 13, 2009. http://www.cato-unbound.org/2009/04/13/peter-thiel/education-libertarian.

Theweleit, Klaus. *Male Fantasies*, vol. 1, *Women, Floods, Bodies, History*. Translated by Stephen Conway. Minneapolis: University of Minnesota, 1987.

Thomas, Dana Lloyd. *Julius Evola e la tentazione razzista*. Brindisi: Giordano, 2006.

Thorpe, Julie. *Pan-Germanism and the Austrofascist State*. New York: Manchester University Press, 2011.

Times Wire Services. "Extremist Admits Gang's Racial Attack." *Los Angeles Times*, June 30, 1987. http://articles.latimes.com/1987-07-30/news/mn-409_1_supremacist-gang.

Tipaldou, Sofia. "The Dawning of Europe and Eurasia?" In *Eurasianism and the European Far Right: Reshaping the Europe-Russia Relationship*, edited by Marlene Laruelle. Boulder: Lexington Books, 2015.

Trollinger, William Vance. *God's Empire: William Bell Riley and Midwestern Fundamentalism*. Madison: University of Wisconsin Press, 1990.

Vacher de Lapouge, Georges. *L'Aryen son Role Social*. Paris, 1899.

Valdinoci. "Former ELF/Green Scare Prisoner 'Exile' Now a Fascist." NYCAntifa, August 5, 2014. https://nycantifa.wordpress.com/2014/08/05/exile-is-a-fascist/.

Uecchione, Marc-Aurèle. "ANTIFA—Chasseurs de skins." Resistance Films, 2008. http://www.youtube.com/watch?v=EfDbTgb6uyc

Umland, Andreas. "Classification, Julius Evola and the Nature of Dugin's Ideology." In *Fascism Past and Present, West and East: An International Debate on Concepts and Cases in the Comparative Study of the Extreme Right*, edited by Roger Griffin, Werner Loh, and Andreas Umland. Stuttgart: Ibidem Press, 2006.

United Nations Human Rights Council. *Draft Report of the Working Group on the Universal Periodic Review: United States of America*. Geneva, May 4–15, 2015.

United States Department of Homeland Security. "ICE Removals Through July 31, 2011." https://www.ice.gov/doclib/about/offices /ero/pdf/ero-removals.pdf.

US Congress. *The Industrial Reorganization Act: Hearings, Ninety-third Congress, First Session, on S 1167, Part 9*. Washington, DC: US Government Printing Office, 1974.

US Senate, *The Militia Movement in the United States*, edited by Arlen Specter. Washington, DC: US Government Printing Office, 1997.

Vaidyanathan, Rajini. "Why Don't Black and White Americans Live Together?" *BBC News Magazine*, January 8, 2016. http://www .bbc.com/news/world-us-canada-35255835.

Vidal-Naquet, Pierre. *Torture: Cancer of Democracy*. London: Penguin Books, 1963.

Vox Day (Theodore Robert Beale). "Neoreactionary space." *Vox Populi* (blog), April 27, 2013. https://voxday.blogspot.com.ar/2013/04/ neoreactionary-space_27.html.

W., Josh. "Dear Steve McNallen." HeathenTalk.com, January 14, 2016. http://heathentalk.com/2016/01/14/dearstevemcnallen.

Wallace, Eric. "Eco Punks: The Wolves of Vinland Badasses Dare You to Re-Wild Yourself." *Blue Ridge Outdoors*, May 5, 2015. http:// www.blueridgeoutdoors.com/go-outside/eco-punks-the-wolves -of-vinland-badasses-dare-you-to-re-wild-yourself/.

Wasserman, Janek. *Black Vienna: The Radical Right in the Red City, 1918–1938*. Ithaca: Cornell University Press, 2014.

Watts, Akira. "Did Men's Rights Activist Movement Play Role in Oregon Shooting?" Reverb Press, October 2, 2015. http://reverbpress .com/news/us/mens-rights-activist-movement-play-role-oregon -shooting.

Weber, Eugen. *Varieties of Fascism*. Malabar, FL: Robert E. Krieger Publishing Company, 1985.

Wiederer, Ralf. "Mapping the Right-Wing Extremist Movement on the Internet—Structural Patterns 2006–2011." In *In the Tracks of Breivik: Far Right Networks in Northern and Eastern Europe*, edited by Mats Deland, Michael Minkenberg, and Christin Mays. Berlin: LIT Verlag, 2014.

Weitz, Gidi. "Signs of Fascism in Israel Reached New Peak During Gaza Op, Says Renowned Scholar." Haaretz.com, August 13, 2014. http://www.haaretz.com/israel-news/.premium-1.610368.

Weyembergh, Maurice. *Charles Maurras et la Révolution française*. Belgium: Vrin, 1992.

Wheaton, Elizabeth. *Codename Greenkil: The 1979 Greensboro Killings*. Athens: University of Georgia Press, 2009.

Whitaker, Stephen B. *The Anarchist-Individualist Origins of Italian Fascism*. Bern: Peter Lang 2002.

Wik, Reynold M. *Henry Ford and Grass-Roots America*. Ann Arbor: University of Michigan Press, 1973.

Williams, Kristian. *Our Enemies in Blue: Police and Power in America*. Oakland: AK Press, 2015.

Wilson, Peter Lamborn. "The New Nihilism." *Anvil Review*, no. 5 (2014): 25–26. Available at https://theanarchistlibrary.org/library/peter-lamborn-wilson-the-new-nihilism.

Winock, Michel. *Nationalism, Anti-Semitism, and Fascism in France*. Translated by Jane Marie Todd. Stanford: Stanford University Press, 1998.

Wirecutter (Kenny Lane). "Methinks Thou Bullshit Too Much—The Kerodin v Lane Debacle." *Knuckledraggin My Life Away* (blog), January 13, 2016. http://knuckledraggin.com/2016/01/44734/.

Wheller, Edward Jewitt, ed. "Maurice Barrès: The New French Immortal." *Index of Current Literature* XLII (January–June, 1907).

White, Bill. "Anti-Globalist Resistance Beyond Right and Left." In *Fascism: Critical Concepts in Political Science*, edited by Roger Griffin and Matthew Feldman, vol. 5. New York: Routledge, 2004.

Wit, Gerrit de. "Autonome neo-nazi's op de linkse toer?" *Gebladerte Archief, De Favel van de illegal*, no. 95/96 (Autumn 2008).

Wodak, Ruth. "Discourse and Politics." In *Right-Wing Populism in Europe*, edited by Ruth Wodak, Majid Khosravinik, and Brigitte Mral. London: Bloomsbury, 2013.

Wodak, Ruth, and Anton Pelinka, eds. *The Haider Phenomenon in Austria*, edited by Ruth Wodak and Anton Pelinka. London: Transaction Publishers, 2002.

Wohl, Robert. *The Generation of 1914*. Cambridge, MA: Harvard University Press, 1979.

Wolin, Richard. *The Seduction of Unreason: The Intellectual Romance with Fascism from Nietzsche to Postmodernism*. Princeton: Princeton University Press, 2009.

Wood, Ian S. *Crimes of Loyalty: A History of the UDA*. Edinburgh:

University of Edinburgh, 2006.

Worch, Christian. "SvD-Gespräch mit Christian Worch über 'Die Rechte,' nationalen Sozialismus und Israel." *Sache des Volkes* (blog), November 3, 2014. https://sachedesvolkes.wordpress.com/2014/11/03/sdv-gesprach-mit-christian-worch-uber-die-rechte-nationalen-sozialismus-und-israel/.

Wright, Paul. "Neo-Nazi lone-wolf attacks in Europe are more deadly than Isis-inspired terrorist plots." *International Business Times*, March 1, 2016. http://www.ibtimes.co.uk/neo-nazi-lone-wolf-attacks-europe-are-more-deadly-isis-terrorist-plots-1546885.

Xenos, Nicholas. *Cloaked in Virtue: Unveiling Leo Strauss and the Rhetoric of American Foreign Policy.* New York: Routledge, 2008.

XOPA. "Lukov March and the Neo-Nazi Provocations in Bulgaria." ХОРА (ХОра срещу РАсизма), stopnazi-bg.blogspot.bg, February 12, 2011. http://stopnazi-bg.blogspot.com/2011/02/lukov-march-and-neo-nazi-provocations.html.

Yeadon, Glen. *The Nazi Hydra in America: Suppressed History of a Century.* San Diego: Progressive Press, 2008.

Yockey, Francis Parker. *Imperium: The Philosophy of History and Politics.* Sausalito: Noontide Press, 1969.

Zeskind, Leonard. *Blood and Politics: The History of the White Nationalist Movement from the Margins to the Mainstream.* New York: Farrar, Straus & Giroux, 2009.

INDEX